"I highly recommend *Our Presidents Rock!* for any teacher, pa
concerned adult who wishes to instill in their children a love of Ai
appreciation for our country's leaders, including how they got t!
Juliette Turner makes history come a.
—Newt Gingrich, former Speaker of the U.S. House of Representatives

"*Our Presidents Rock!* is a fun read about our nation's presidents that brings history to life,
highlighting some of our former leaders' talents, hobbies, and other uncommon facts. A great
book for young Americans and those young at heart, *Our Presidents Rock!* will leave its readers
more knowledgeable not only about history of the presidency, but more informed about the
monumental individuals who lived and worked at the White House."
—Karl Rove, former Deputy Chief of Staff and Senior Advisor to
President George W. Bush; author, *Courage and Consequence*;
Fox News Contributor; *Wall Street Journal* Columnist

"If you don't know where you've been, how can you know where you're going? *Our
Presidents Rock!*, by Juliette Turner, offers an important contribution to the understanding
of our past by making the fascinating history of the American presidency accessible and
enjoyable for young readers."
—Donald Rumsfeld, former U.S. Secretary of Defense

Our Presidents Rock, chock full of little-known facts and fascinating nuggets,
engages readers of all ages.
-First Lady of Texas Anita Perry

"Juliette Turner not only shares here the incredibly fascinating stories of America's presidents;
in so doing, she shines a light on one of the bedrock strengths the makes our country so strong
and enduring—the willingness of our leaders to transition governmental power peacefully
through the ballot box and never through the use of force."
—Jack Quinn, former White House Counsel under President Clinton

"The lives of our U.S. presidents, from their childhoods to their adulthoods, are filled with
strife, challenges, passion, and drama. Juliette's book has them jumping off the page with their
struggles and their triumphs. It's a must read!"
—Governor Sarah Palin

"Juliette Turner is dedicated to helping her generation understand our country's history and founding
principles in a way no other young person in this nation is doing. Juliette has a way of reaching the
"Twitter generation" with a fun, concise style that emphasizes the past's relevance to today!"
—Jenny Beth Martin, co-founder of Tea Party Patriots

OUR
Presidents
ROCK!

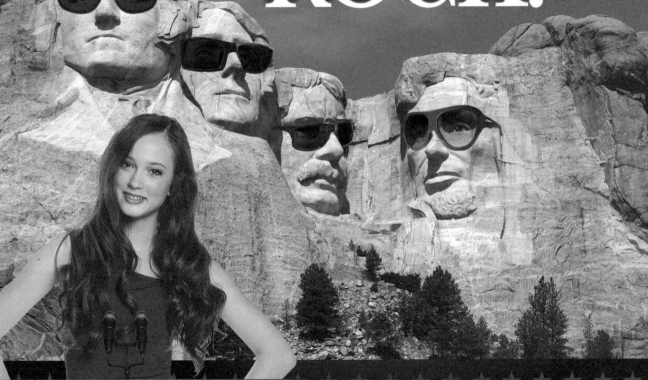

JULIETTE TURNER

**National Youth Director of
Constituting America**

Illustrations by Brian Oesch | Design by Matthew Van Zomeren

ZONDERkidz

ZONDERKIDZ

Our Presidents Rock!
Copyright © 2014 by Juliette Turner

Requests for information should be addressed to:
Zonderkidz, 3900 Sparks Dr. SE, Grand Rapids, Michigan 49546

ISBN 978-0-310-73095-8

Library of Congress Cataloging-in-Publication Data

Turner, Juliette.
    Our presidents rock! / Juliette Turner, National Youth Director of Constituting America.
       p. cm.
    Includes bibliographical references.
    Audience: Ages 8 and up.
    ISBN 978-0-310-73095-8 (softcover)
    1. Presidents--United States--Biography--Juvenile literature. I. Title.
E176.1.T87 2014
973.09'9--dc23
  [B]
                                              2014015511

All Scripture quotations, unless otherwise indicated, are taken from The Holy Bible, *New International Version®, NIV®.* Copyright © 1973, 1978, 1984, 2011 by Biblica, Inc.® Used by permission. All rights reserved worldwide.

Editors: Kim Childress and Jacque Alberta
Editorial Assistance: Alyssa Helm
Cover design: Deborah Washburn
Cover photography: Larry Travis Photography
Makeup artistry: Ro Vielma
Illustrations: Brian Oesch
Interior design: Matthew Van Zomeren

Printed in China

14 15 16 17 18 19 20 21 22 /DSC/ 29 28 27 26 25 24 23 22 21 20 19 18 17 16 15 14 13 12 11 10 9 8 7 6 5 4 3 2 1

*For my mother, who inspires
me to love, respect, and protect
our wonderful country.*

*In memory of my grandfather,
Turner Maurice Gauntt, Jr.,
a born leader and protector
of America's Republic.*

CONTENTS

THE PRESIDENTS:

BUILDING THE FIRST WHITE HOUSE

WASHINGTON D.C. 1798
MODERN WASHINGTON
is served by the
PENNSYLVANIA RAILROAD

ACKNOWLEDGMENTS

In the same way that it requires a talented campaign team to win the presidency, it takes a group of dedicated and passionate people to publish a book.

First, there is the motivator. Every presidential hopeful will talk about the one individual who really inspired them to run for office. For me, my motivator is my mother. Not only does she teach me to love my country and do my best to protect it, but she instills in me the incentive to see each project and goal to its completion.

Then there are the campaign managers. These are the absolutely vital individuals without whom the campaign would fail and fall to pieces. My "campaign managers" for my book were my dutiful editors, Kim Childress, Alyssa Helm, and Jacque Alberta, who struggled to persuade me that a five hundred page book was not the best choice to make.

A campaign likewise cannot succeed without the financial manager, and this title belongs to my book agent, Rick Hersh.

A presidential candidate would not be able to survive without his or her speech writers. In the same way, an author cannot survive without his or her fact checkers. A big thanks goes to Tony Williams and Peter Roff, who selflessly agreed to read through pages of information and pick through the facts to find any inconsistencies.

Finally, there is no campaign without volunteers—the spirited, determined, and extremely important individuals who dedicate themselves to the team no matter what the cost. Cathy Gillespie and Amanda Hughes have dedicated themselves to this project without any consideration of the demands of their own lives. I thank you.

For us, winning is not the declaration of victory on a stressful November night. Victory for us lies in knowing that, through this book, children will learn about our nation's presidents and become inspired to learn about, love, and protect America.

FOREWORD

The office of the President of the United States is exceptional, but not for the reasons most people think, especially in today's culture. The office of the President of the United States is exceptional because it requires the person holding the position to act in a manner of restraint.

The office of the president is one branch, the executive branch, in the three branches of our self-governing Republic, set forth in the United States Constitution. The legislative branch has 535 representatives from the states. The judicial branch has 9 Supreme Court Justices. The executive branch has just one person, the president. Our Founding Fathers purposely separated the powers into the legislative, executive, and judicial branches with each branch relying on, and being held accountable to, the other branches. Why? Because they knew the person holding the presidency, being singular in the executive branch, would be most susceptible to the temptation of power.

Human nature is such that when someone experiences power, they usually want more and more. History books are filled with examples of men who became corrupted by power: kings, dictators, and tyrants such as Julius Caesar, Napoleon, Hitler, and Stalin. While the person holding the office of the President of the United States should always be ethical, righteous and principled, just in case he is not, our founders ensured he would be checked. Predominantly, however, the presidents of the United States have been honorable and stellar.

One of the most remarkable aspects of the presidents has been the peaceful transfer of power from one president to the other. When President George Washington walked into the Senate chamber and peacefully transferred his presidential powers to John Adams, the rest of the world was in awe. Never before had such a remarkable feat been accomplished. Even more astounding was when President John Adams transferred his presidential powers to Thomas Jefferson, because John Adams and Thomas Jefferson were of differing political parties and political views. The peaceful transfer of opposing powers, respecting the people's vote, was a new and astonishing thing. Previously, in other countries across the globe, a transfer of power from one faction to a contradicting faction had always resulted in bloodshed. Our Constitution, and the presidents themselves, had restrained their power. American dignity had prevailed and prevails today.

Thus, the office of the President of the United States of America requires a man, or woman, of great integrity. Amazingly, the majority of men who have, thus far, held the office of the president have done honor to the executive branch. The forty-four Presidents of the United States have respected the will of the people, though inevitably there have been checks from the legislative and judicial branches upon their aspirations.

The presidents' personalities are intriguing and their characters, shaped by their trials and tribulations, varied. It is important to understand the wise and unwise decisions previous presidents have made and why. It is important to know how these decisions have affected and shaped American history. It is important to read about the Presidents of the United States because it makes you an educated and informed voter, and, finally, it is important to understand the childhoods and humanity of each president, because it will inspire you. You, too, could one day be the president of the United States of America.

Juliette has filled the pages of this book with fascinating stories, details, and aspects of the presidents' lives. Their actions and legacies will enthrall you. Never has learning about the history of the presidents been so fun and worthwhile. The presidents pop off the pages in ways that only a kid writing to another kid can do. Enjoy *Our Presidents Rock!* and be educated and encouraged! When you've finished it, check out *Our Constitution Rocks!* and be one of the smartest kids on your block!

Janine Turner
Juliette's Mom
Founder & Co-Chair of Constituting America

INTRODUCTION

You can become the president of the United States. I'm serious—you can become the president one day. It would take a brutal campaign schedule, some pretty generous donors, a lot of support, and—most importantly—resiliency and determination. However, it doesn't matter if you are rich or poor, black or white, come from a traditional family or a single-parent family, live in the city or the country, never attend college or are a world-renowned lawyer.

The president truly personifies the American Dream. Throughout our country's history, men from all walks of life have started from the bottom and risen to the most powerful office in our government. Regardless of their differing backgrounds, all these men had two things in common: love of their country and a huge dose of determination. Often having to brush off the dirt after demoralizing defeats time and time again, these individuals refused to let one loss or more prevent them from attaining their dreams.

George Washington and Thomas Jefferson were raised by single mothers; Andrew Jackson never had true schooling; Abraham Lincoln not only lived in a log cabin, he lived in a three-sided shed in Kentucky for one year; Andrew Johnson was so poor that he was considered "white trash"; Ulysses S. Grant was unable to hold a job or even grow a hardy crop; Franklin Roosevelt was confined to a wheelchair; Harry Truman's small convenience store went under; John F. Kennedy overcame terrible sickness before and during his presidency; Ronald Reagan was raised by an alcoholic father; and Barack Obama was raised primarily by his grandparents—these are just a few of our presidents' struggles.

As American citizens, we look to the president as a man who is without fault or blemish. But in reality, our presidents were and will always be people just like us, who struggle with their unique challenges, whether big or small, multiple or few. Regardless of their hardships, these individuals overcame in order to serve and protect their country.

HOW TO READ THIS BOOK

Since I am a teenager like you, I know it's important to get information quickly. We live in the age of Facebook, Twitter, and Vines, where information must be concise, coherent, and quick to read. So why should a book on the presidents be any different? In every chapter, I've broken down the information into these sections:

The Bottom Line

A two-sentence overview of the president's accomplishments during his time in office.

What Were They Thinking?

A quick explanation of the viewpoints of every president, from his views on debt and foreign relations to his views on social issues and war.

Why Should I Care?

Why should we care about a president no one even talks about anymore? Every chapter in this book contains "Why Should I Care?," which will tell you why it is necessary to learn about and understand the policies of that president in particular.

Breakin' it Down

An overview of each president's life, including his growing-up years, his family, and his political or military career prior to becoming president.

Presidency

Information about his actual time in office—from his policies to his landmark accomplishments to important events that affected his presidency.

What Has He Done for Me Lately?

Ever wonder how some presidents affect your life today? Well, every chapter has a quick overview of how the president's accomplishments shaped our country and influence our lives today.

Quick Facts

Lots of fun tidbits, including:

Presidential Times

Our Presidents Rock's official newspaper including breaking news, on-the-site reporting, and historical events occurring during each presidency.

FAST STATS

★ Quick information about the man himself.

LIBERTY Language

Easy-to-understand definitions of terms that are used in the chapter.

ELECTION RESULTS!

Everything you want to know about each election at a glance. From what states each president won in the election, to the votes he got and who he ran against.

FUN FACTS!

Interesting things you might not have known about each president.

BTW: Some necessary and fascinating facts you just couldn't do without.

THOUGHTS ON THE CONSTITUTION

The president's thoughts on what the Constitution meant to him, along with a quick explanation from me on why his words are important.

CONGRESSIONAL CORNER

The important legislation passed during each president's time in office.

PLATFORM SPEECH

Important lines from a speech the president gave that shows his feelings on an issue or event.

PRESIDENTIAL Personality

★ Information on how each president carried himself in office and in his personal life.

WHO IS THE PRESIDENT?

Explaining the Presidency

We all know the president—but what is his job? Why do we pay so much attention to his actions and his decisions?

In 1787, our Founding Fathers created the U.S. Constitution, which establishes our republican form of government. Our government has three branches: the legislative (Congress), the executive (the president), and the judicial (the Supreme Court and federal courts). Because our founders believed that "men are not angels," they separated our government into three branches in order to create a "balance of power." This balance ensures that the president is always checked by Congress and the Supreme Court. He can never obtain too much power and overthrow our government.

Because of the 22nd amendment, the president can only serve two terms, or eight years. The president may seem to have a lot of authority and control these days, but the Constitution explicitly enumerates—specifically lists—all the powers of the president. The president's primary function is to execute the laws passed by Congress (hence the name, executive branch), however he (or she) also has the power to veto these bills. The president, as the figurehead of America's government, represents the compassion, power, and ability of the American people not only here in America but across the globe.

In Article II, Section 2, the Constitution explains the powers of the president:

1. The President shall be Commander in Chief of the Army and Navy of the United States, and of the Militia of the several States, when called into the actual Service of the United States; he may require the Opinion, in writing, of the principal Officer in each of the executive Departments, upon any Subject relating to the Duties of their respective Offices, and he shall have Power to grant Reprieves and Pardons for Offences against the United States, except in Cases of Impeachment.

2. He shall have Power, by and with the Advice and Consent of the Senate, to make Treaties, provided two thirds of the Senators present concur; and he shall nominate, and by and with the Advice and Consent of the Senate, shall appoint Ambassadors, other public Ministers and Consuls, Judges of the Supreme Court, and all other Officers of the United States, whose Appointments are not herein otherwise provided for, and which shall be established by Law: but the Congress may by Law vest the Appointment of such inferior Officers, as they think proper, in the President alone, in the Courts of Law, or in the Heads of Departments.

3. The President shall have Power to fill up all Vacancies that may happen during the Recess of the Senate, by granting Commissions which shall expire at the End of their next Session.

To learn more about the presidential office and its powers, pick up a copy of *Our Constitution Rocks!*

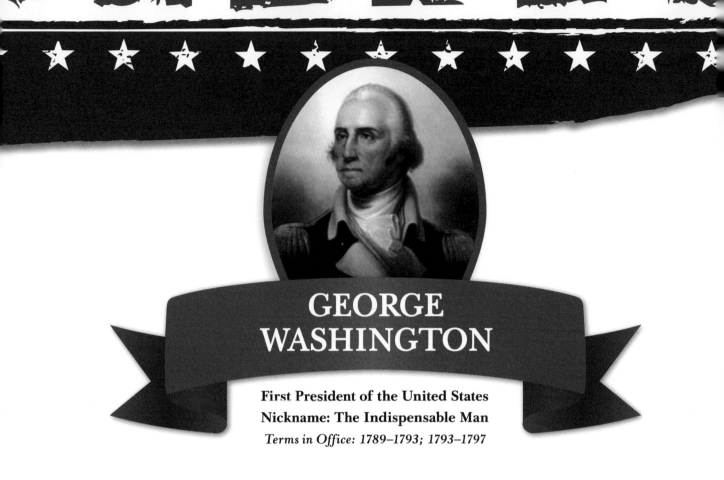

GEORGE WASHINGTON

First President of the United States
Nickname: The Indispensable Man
Terms in Office: 1789–1793; 1793–1797

The Bottom Line

During his presidency, George Washington set the precedents for all future presidents. In his first term, Washington preserved the country by maintaining peace between the United States and Great Britain—which was a big deal coming out of the Revolutionary War. During his second term, Washington established that national legislation holds authority over state legislation (meaning all state legislation and all citizens must abide by federal laws). He did so by suppressing the Whiskey Rebellion in 1794.

FAST STATS

★ Born February 22, 1732, in Westmoreland County, Virginia
★ Parents: Augustine and Mary Ball Washington
★ Died December 14, 1799, in Mount Vernon, Virginia; age 67
★ Age upon Start of First Term: 57; Age upon Conclusion of First Term: 61
★ Age upon Start of Second Term: 61; Age upon Conclusion of Second Term: 65
★ Religious Affiliation: Episcopalian
★ Political Party: Independent
★ Height: 6 feet 2 inches
★ Vice President: John Adams

What Was He Thinking?

George Washington believed that morality and honesty should always be the guiding forces for anyone holding the office of the presidency. He believed in the Constitution and a government with a system of checks and balances. He considered himself a man free of party limitations, believing that establishing political parties would ultimately

 BTW: Washington is the first and only president elected without the help of a political party.

ruin America's republican form of government. He thought political parties would influence the decisions made by the president, congressmen, and every government official, undermining the system of checks and balances established by the Constitution.

Why Should I Care?

George Washington is the father of our country. As general of the Continental Army, he led the fight that achieved the country's independence. As chair of the Constitutional Convention, he helped give the country its government. As our first president, he guided the nation safely through its most vulnerable years and established the precedents that still shape the presidency today. He was an international celebrity and a national hero, even in his own day. He had to define the Constitution, and transform the executive branch from the paper and ink of the Constitution into an actual, functioning, and governing office.

Breakin' It Down

Early Life

George Washington's father, Augustine, was a tobacco farmer, a justice of the peace, and sheriff for Westmoreland County, Virginia. Mary, George's mother, was Augustine's second wife. George had six siblings, plus two stepbrothers and one stepsister.

George's father died when he was eleven years old. His mother, who never remarried, raised him and his nine siblings by herself, and it was his oldest stepbrother, Lawrence, who mentored young George. They grew very close. George was mainly homeschooled by tutors, but he also educated himself by reading books from the family library. His interest in mathematics helped him in his first job as a land surveyor.

His brother Lawrence died in 1752, leaving the Mount Vernon estate to George. George loved to farm his property and experiment with agriculture and crop rotation. He once experimented with a tobacco crop,

Republican vs. republican

★★★★★★★★★★★★★★★★★★★★★★★★

A capital letter can make all the difference. In America, we have two major political parties: the Republicans and the Democrats. However, "republican" and "democratic" (with lowercase letters) refer to certain types of government: a republic where the people rule the government through the people they elect to a congress—the type of government we have in America—and a democracy where the people directly rule their government, for example, where everyone would vote on legislation.

POLITICAL PARTIES

★★★★★★★★★★★★★★★★★★★★★★★★

Federalist: A major political party in the early years of the United States that favored a strong, centralized national government, the adoption of the U.S. Constitution, and unification of the states into one united country. Alexander Hamilton is considered the founder of the party.

Anti-Federalist: Another major political party in the early years of the United States that favored state sovereignty and a small to nonexistent federal government. Anti-Federalists opposed the adoption of the United States Constitution because they believed it took too much power away from the states.

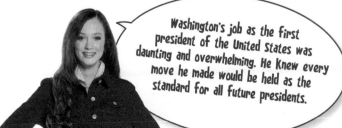

Washington's job as the first president of the United States was daunting and overwhelming. He knew every move he made would be held as the standard for all future presidents.

MARTHA WASHINGTON

but it didn't work so well financially. Washington blamed the British for his financial difficulty with tobacco because he believed the British were underselling American goods.

BTW: Martha Washington remains the only first lady to have never lived in the White House.

First Couple

George Washington married Martha Dandridge Custis on January 5, 1759. Both were twenty-seven at the time, and Martha—the wealthiest widow in Virginia—brought two children to the marriage: John and Martha (nicknamed Patsy). George and Martha never had children together. Whenever separated, they constantly wrote to one another, addressing each other as "My Dearest" or "My Love." During the war, Martha sometimes accompanied her husband to the battlefield, most notably at Valley Forge, where she mended clothes, nursed the ill and injured, and helped keep spirits up.

BTW: During Washington's first four years in office, he visited each of the states, because he believed that the American people should get to know who was running the government.

Previous Political Career

- 1758: Elected to the Virginia House of Burgesses: Washington served for fifteen years (1759–1774).
- 1774: Representative from Virginia in the First Continental Congress.
- 1775: Representative from Virginia at the Second Continental Congress.
- 1775: Appointed Commander of the American Continental Army. Washington was unanimously appointed by representatives of the Second Continental Congress—he served as commander for the entire Revolutionary War.

> I hold the maxim no less applicable to public than to private affairs, that honesty is always the best policy.

> George Washington spoke these words in Congress in 1775 when he was appointed as commander in chief. He held honesty as one of the highest virtues—though the familiar story about him and the cherry tree is actually a myth.

Presidency

The Neutrality Proclamation

During Washington's first term, the British were plundering American merchant ships, kidnapping sailors, and attempting to persuade the sailors to become British citizens. War cries ran rampant throughout the country, and the people wanted to go to war against Britain again. However, Washington knew that their young country could not sustain another war so early in its existence.

At the same time France, America's old ally, declared war on Great Britain, causing half of America to support Britain (led mainly by Alexander Hamilton) and half of the

BTW: When he came to Philadelphia to preside over the Constitutional Convention, many thousands of people came to greet him and cheer him on as he rode through the streets.

America declares independence: July 4, 1776

Washington crosses the Delaware, December 25, 1776

The Battle of Trenton, December 26, 1776

Articles of Confederation is ratified, March 1, 1781

Battle of Yorktown, October 19, 1781

Treaty of Paris: The final treaty was signed on September 3, 1783

Revolutionary War: April 19, 1775–September 3, 1783

| 1775 | 1776 | 1777 | 1778 | 1779 | 1780 | 1781 | 1782 | 1783 | 1784 | 1785 | 1786 |

BTW: George Washington, in his prime, weighed 175 pounds, stood at 6'2", and wore size thirteen shoe.

country to support France (led mainly by Thomas Jefferson). Washington realized allying with one country would outrage the other—a lose-lose situation for America. So Washington issued the Neutrality Proclamation of 1793, which stated that the United States would not interfere with British or French affairs. This not only prevented America from entering a war, but saved America from collapsing from foreign attacks and domestic arguments.

The Whiskey Rebellion

The tax on whiskey that Washington signed during his first term sparked outrage among the farmers (who were most affected by this tax), causing them to rebel against the federal government's authority to enforce such a tax on the states. When rebels began to march to the capital from Pennsylvania, Washington put an end to the movement.

He organized the militias of New Jersey, Maryland, and Virginia—15,000 troops combined—and accompanied them the entire way to meet the rebels. The rebels dispersed, but the federal troops captured 120 men. Twenty were tried in court, but only two were convicted of treason, and Washington pardoned them both. Although he pardoned the rebels, he set the standard throughout the entire country: legislation and laws passed by the national government held supremacy, or were superior, to legislation passed by the states.

Foreign Policy

In addition to Washington's Neutrality Proclamation, many foreign policy advances occurred during his time in office. Most important, Washington set the precedent that the president and executive branch could control the negotiations of treaties without consulting Congress first.

But Washington knew that once the treaty was on paper, it had to be approved by two-thirds of the Senate.

Virginia House of Burgesses: An assembly of elected representatives in the state of Virginia that met from 1619 to 1776. The House dissolved at the start of the American Revolution and was replaced with the Virginia House of Delegates.

Burgess: A term used only in British forms of government, burgess refers to an elected or appointed official of a municipality (city, town, or other district) or the representative of a town or suburb.

BTW: Eight presidents were born in Virginia: Washington, Jefferson, Madison, Monroe, Harrison, Tyler, Taylor, and Wilson.

FUN FACT!

Washington remains the only president to be inaugurated in two different cities: New York for his first term and Pennsylvania for his second term. He is also the only president who never resided in Washington, D.C.

At the end of his first term, Washington was ready to retire but the political factions at the time were so high, and the spirit of party politics so dangerous, Washington decided to stick around for a second term to help preserve the country.

The Constitution is signed by the Continental Congress, September 17, 1787

The Residence Act of 1790, District of Columbia becomes the capital of the United States.

Vermont becomes a state, 1791

Bill of Rights is ratified in 1791

Kentucky becomes a state, 1792

• Neutrality Proclamation of 1793

Construction on the
• White House begins, 1793

Whiskey Rebellion of 1794

Tennessee becomes a state, 1796

First Term in Office | **Second Term in Office**

1787 | 1788 | 1789 | 1790 | 1791 | 1792 | 1793 | 1794 | 1795 | 1796 | 1797 | 1798

French and Indian War

In 1753, at the age of twenty-one, Major George Washington was sent on a mission to confront French forces in the Ohio region. He was to deliver a message from the governor demanding that the French leave the region and stop their interference with trade. Although his trip was not successful and the French did not surrender, Washington was promoted to lieutenant colonel. In the spring of 1754, he was charged with removing the French from the Ohio region.

Washington is most remembered for his surrender at Fort Necessity—a battle that contributed to the start of the French and Indian War. Fighting was made difficult because of heavy rainfall and flooding of the marshy ground. Both sides suffered casualties, but the British lost more soldiers than the French and Indians.

During his time in the British army, he gained valuable military, political, and leadership skills. He was a tough and courageous soldier and faced many difficult situations, including disasters and retreats. However, this did not translate into a high-ranking position, and Washington retired from the military in 1758.

The Revolutionary War

Without Washington, it is very unlikely that the Revolutionary War, the war for American independence, could have been won. His determination, military strategies, and leadership held the straggling army together for nearly seven years.

Although Washington suffered many defeats, his leadership and rally cries led the men to victory, like during the Battle of Trenton on December 26, 1776, after the crossing of the Delaware River on Christmas Day. During it all, Washington held on to his humble spirit, staying alongside his men in Valley Forge and weathering the frigid conditions with little more provisions than the lowliest foot soldier.

At the end of the war, on December 29, 1783, Washington handed over his commission and his sword to Congress. He gave up all his military power to the astonishment of many, including King George III of England.

After the war, Washington's career was far from over. He reentered the political spotlight as president of the Constitutional Convention, where, after much pleading from Alexander Hamilton and James Madison, he served as president of the convention and presided over the formation of America's founding document, the Constitution. Washington's leadership at the convention legitimized the Constitution in the eyes of all Americans—if George Washington was for it, who could be against it?

FUN FACTS!

When Washington handed over his commission, he surrendered all of his military power, becoming an ordinary American citizen. This was not routine for military leaders of the time. Usually, they became "power hungry" while serving in the military and eventually became dictators or rulers of the country. Washington set a new precedent by surrendering his power, giving it back to the people.

BTW: History credits George Washington as one of the key people responsible for winning the Revolutionary War and establishing American independence. Many argue that without him the war would not have been won—at least not by the U.S.

BTW: Washington believed in being a "citizen soldier," a citizen who answered to Congress first, and a military leader second.

Washington frequently felt like he was fighting for a lost cause, once writing that he feared his country was on the "verge of ruin." But he refused to give up and kept on fighting.

BTW: During the Battle of Monongahela, two horses were shot out from under Washington, and four musket balls ripped through his overcoat.

ELECTION RESULTS!

Election of 1789

		Electoral Votes
1st	George Washington	69
2nd	John Adams	34
3rd	John Jay	9
4th	Other	26

■ Washington Won ■ Territories

Washington was elected unanimously by the sixty-nine electors in the Electoral College. Yet he only carried ten of the thirteen states. How so? North Carolina and Rhode Island had yet to sign the Constitution, so they did not take part in the election. New York could not decide who to vote for.

BTW: George Washington had to borrow $600 to travel from Virginia to New York after being elected president. He had refused pay for his services during the war, so he had significant financial troubles on the farm he had left behind while serving his country.

ELECTORAL COLLEGE
★★★★★★★★★★★★★★

Our Founding Fathers established the Electoral College as a system for electing the president. Each state gets one elector for each congressman, its number of U.S. representatives, plus its two senators. Our Founders wanted to prevent states with large populations from dominating the elections. And the electors' identities are kept secret until the last possible day, because our Founders wanted to ensure the electors wouldn't be bribed or corrupted to vote a certain way. Our Constitution leaves it up to the states to decide how they will appoint their electors. Each method is different depending on the state.

Election of 1793

		Electoral Votes
1st	George Washington	132
2nd	John Adams	77
3rd	George Clinton	50
4th	Other	5

■ Washington Won ■ Territories

Washington was once again unanimously voted president for a second term—which he did not desire—obtaining all of the 132 electoral votes from the now fifteen American states. The only additional electoral votes were due to those voting for the vice president — back then, the second-place winner became the vice president.

The Electoral College was established by Article II, Section 1, Clause 2 of the Constitution. You can read more about it in Our Constitution Rocks.

Legislation: Legislation refers to any act or bill passed by Congress or being considered and debated by Congress.

Supremacy: When certain legislation, or laws, have "supremacy" over other legislation, it means that the "supreme legislation" must be obeyed. In our country, the ultimate supreme legislation is the Constitution, and it must be obeyed and is superior over all other legislation passed in America.

CONGRESSIONAL CORNER
★★★★★★★★★★★★★★★★★★★★★★★★★

Major acts passed under Congress during President Washington's terms in office:

1. **Judiciary Act of 1789** established the nation's federal judiciary system.

2. The **first tax law**—a tariff on imported goods—was passed.

3. A charter for the **First Bank of the United States** was approved, which Washington signed into law in February 1791.

4. The **Whiskey Tax** set a tax on the sale and production of whiskey.

5. The **Residence Act of 1790** established the District of Columbia as the new capital of the United States.

6. The **Naturalization Act of 1795** required an individual to live in the U.S. for five years before becoming a U.S. citizen.

★★★★★★★★★★★★★★★★★★★★★★★★★

PRESIDENTIAL Personality

★ Although Washington was known for his quick temper, he worked his whole life to combat it. People commented on his "dignified reserve," which some mistakenly took to be a snobbish attitude. This aura of strength and dignity is partly why people looked to Washington as a leader who could reason with fairness and make level-headed decisions.

Post-Presidency

Washington adamantly refused to run for a third term, though he was most likely guaranteed to win. He awed the world by peacefully handing over his power to his elected successor, John Adams, and retiring to private life.

George finally obtained his dream: farming and living on his beloved plantation, Mount Vernon, with his wife, Martha, and their grandchildren. However, his joy was short-lived. Two years after his presidency, Washington was taking a horseback ride around his property in mid-December when it suddenly started to sleet. He returned home drenched and cold, but he was unable to immediately change into drier clothes because of unexpected company. The next day, a sore throat left him nearly unable to breathe.

THOUGHTS ON THE CONSTITUTION

The basis of our political systems is the right of the people to make and alter their Constitutions of Government. But the Constitution which at any time exists, till changed by an explicit and authentic act of the whole people, is sacredly obligatory upon all.

Here, Washington is saying that the foundation of our republican form of government lies within the power of the people to change their governing document through the amendment process in the Constitution.

BTW: Washington is one of several war-hero presidents. Others are Andrew Jackson, William Harrison, Zachary Taylor, Ulysses Grant, and Dwight Eisenhower.

26

Tariff: A tariff is a tax placed on imported and exported goods—in other words, a tax on traded goods.

For the next two days, three doctors attempted to save America's Indispensable Man through bleeding—a common practice of the day—until he begged them to stop. Soon after, he passed away, leaving behind a young country he had fought his entire life to build and preserve.

What Has He Done For Me Lately?

Washington truly was the Indispensable Man. First, he was influential as commander in chief of the Continental Army during the Revolutionary War. His leadership, determination, bravery, and example helped the colonies win independence from Great Britain.

Second, Washington's well-known reliability caused the colonies to place more trust in the Constitution during the Constitutional Convention.

Third, his humility and sensibility allowed him to hold the office of the president without overstepping his constitutional limitations, and his actions set precedents for all future American presidents. In essence, we have Washington to thank for America.

Other Treaties Negotiated by Washington

- **The Treaty of San Lorenzo:** Opened the Mississippi for U.S. citizens all the way down to New Orleans. Negotiated by Charles Pinckney.
- **Algerian Treaty:** Freed American sailors who had been taken hostage by Barbary pirates. Negotiated with the country of Algiers.
- **The Jay Treaty (with Britain):** Successfully moved British soldiers off the Great Lakes and the Ohio frontier and settled for the British to pay for the damage they caused by plundering American ships.

BTW: On his deathbed, Washington uttered his last words, "'Tis well."

FUN FACT!

Twice during Washington's terms in office, he cheated death. The first time came in May of 1790 when he fell perilously ill with pneumonia. Yet within a week, he was back in public, celebrating Rhode Island's ratification of the Constitution. The second time occurred when he underwent the dangerous removal of a growth on his leg.

PLATFORM SPEECH

[Party factions] are likely, in the course of time and things, to become potent engines, by which cunning, ambitious, and unprincipled men will be enabled to subvert the power of the people, and to usurp for themselves the reins of government.

Keep in mind, anesthesia was not around back then.

Washington believed the party system would be the demise of the country and the destruction of our liberties.

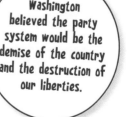

Presidential Times

Written by Juliette Turner

NOW KNOWN AS MR. PRESIDENT

April 30, 1789—Despite the urging of John Adams and pressure from the American people over his new title, George Washington decided against such lofty titles as "Your Highness" or "His Majesty."

Instead, in the humble spirit that has befallen him, George Washington has decided in his new role to be called simply, "Mr. President."

THE FIRST PRESIDENT TAKES OFFICE

April 30, 1789—Today the Chancellor of New York, Robert Livingston, administered Washington's oath of office. Upon taking office, President Washington was heard to say, "I walk upon untrodden ground."

Ever humble, in his subsequent address, Washington remarked, "The magnitude and difficulty of the trust to which the voice of my country called me, being sufficient to awaken in the wisest and most experienced of her citizens a distrustful scrutiny into his qualifications, could not but overwhelm with despondence one who (inheriting inferior endowments from nature and unpracticed in the duties of civil administration) ought to be peculiarly conscious of his own deficiencies."

A HOUSE FOR THE PRESIDENT

October 13, 1792—Washington is residing on Cherry Street, but plans to build a house for the current president and all future presidents are under way. Designed by Irish-born James Hoban, construction is set to begin next year. He plans a magnificent building built with white-painted Aquia Creek sandstone in the Neoclassical style. The house will be located on Pennsylvania Avenue in Washington D.C.

DECLARATION OF INDEPENDENCE, JULY 4th, 1776.

A BOLD MOVE: A NATIONAL BANK OF THE UNITED STATES

February 25, 1791—The Revolutionary War leaves behind a great debt. Some states are left bankrupt. In a bold suggestion, Alexander Hamilton, the Secretary of the Treasury, wants to form a national bank that will unite the states financially under one bank and create one unified currency. His idea is that a national bank will pay off the Revolutionary War debt through income received from taxes.

"The United States debt, foreign and domestic, was the price of liberty," he said. This national bank will also have the ability to tax, borrow, and loan money to American businesses to encourage the start of new enterprises.

Opponents Thomas Jefferson and James Madison are against the formation of such a bank, arguing against keeping all the money in one place. Most people assumed a plan like this would never be accepted, but in a surprise move, Washington went ahead with the plan and

Universal Images Group / Getty Images

signed the bill. The First Bank of the United States will soon become a reality.

THE CANDLELIGHT BARGAIN, OR THE COMPROMISE OF 1790

June 20, 1790—In an unprecedented move, Thomas Jefferson, Secretary of State, scheduled a dinner in New York and invited fellow politicians James Madison and Alexander Hamilton, Secretary of Treasury, to discuss the raging issue of the First Bank. During this dinner, a deal was struck. Hamilton managed to convince Jefferson and Madison to agree to the proposition of the national bank. However, this agreement was dependent on the terms that the national capital would be moved further south to a plot of land taken from Maryland and Virginia: the District of Columbia. This proposal greatly pleased the two proud southerners, and Jefferson and Madison agreed to support the bank.

INTRODUCTION OF THE MULE

December 15, 1785—Washington was recently presented with a donkey named "Royal Gift" by the King of Spain. Washington is planning to send this donkey through the southern states, where he plans for it to sire the first American mules.

"The name of American, which belongs to you in your national capacity, must always exalt the just pride of patriotism more than any appellation derived from local discriminations."

George Washington

A PRESIDENT WITH SORE GUMS?

August 27, 1793—It is no secret that President Washington has struggled with poor dental hygiene his whole life, from losing his first tooth at age twenty-one to his first year of his presidency, when only one lower left premolar remained.

This struggle is about to end. Washington has recently received dentures. Despite rumors that these dentures would be made of wood, the teeth are made either of ivory, human teeth, hippopotamus teeth, or—most shockingly—lead. Yet this inconvenience is not without its own dose of pain. Washington has complained of pain and has occasionally drunk laudanum, an opiate alcohol drink that serves as a pain killer for his aching gums.

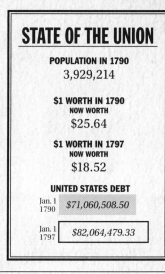

STATE OF THE UNION

POPULATION IN 1790
3,929,214

$1 WORTH IN 1790
NOW WORTH
$25.64

$1 WORTH IN 1797
NOW WORTH
$18.52

UNITED STATES DEBT

Jan. 1 1790	$71,060,508.50
Jan. 1 1797	$82,064,479.33

BTW: Adams and Jefferson were the only two presidents to sign the Declaration of Independence.

JOHN ADAMS

Second President of the United States
Nickname: Atlas of Independence
Term in Office: 1797–1801

The Bottom Line

Although Adams called for political unity among Americans, his term was still filled with party division. Many Americans urged him to declare war against France after the XYZ Affair and the naval Quasi War. Realizing war would destroy the young America, however, Adams chose to go against popular opinion and choose neutrality. Though this decision cost him reelection, his foresight preserved the young country.

FAST STATS

★ Born October 30, 1735, in Braintree, Massachusetts
★ Parents: John and Susanna Boylston Adams
★ Died July 4, 1826, in Quincy, Massachusetts; age 90
★ Age upon Start of Term: 61; Age upon Conclusion of Term: 65
★ Religious Affiliation: Unitarian
★ Political Party: Federalist
★ Height: 5 feet 7 inches
★ Vice President: Thomas Jefferson

What Was He Thinking?

Adams adamantly believed in the checks and balances of government and the limited powers of the executive branch. Adams believed the government should reflect the desires of the people to best represent them. Additionally, he believed a strong central government was necessary for solidifying the young nation and uniting the states. Adams also consistently warned against the dangers of debt and the perils of fiscal irresponsibility.

BTW: Washington almost never consulted Adams during his presidency, and the men rarely saw each other except at government social functions.

Why Should I Care?

Because Adams cared so much for the survival of America, he absolutely refused to be swayed by the passionate emotions of a country that wanted to go to war with France. Like Washington, Adams believed that the developing country would not be able to hold together if she were to go to war—especially with a major European superpower like France. Adams successfully negotiated a peace treaty with the French but not in time to encourage his reelection for a second term.

Breakin' It Down
Early Life

John's father was a church deacon, a farmer, served on local government boards, and at one time served as local tax collector. John had two younger brothers, Peter and Elihu, who both served in the Revolutionary War.

John grew up attending school at a local schoolhouse. However, he frequently skipped class to hunt and fish in the surrounding woods or, in winter, to go skating on the frozen ponds. Once, attempting to get out of going to school, he explained to his father that he wished to be a farmer, so education was unnecessary. His father made him stay in school, and John proceeded to attend Harvard University at age fifteen, where he studied languages, rhetoric, and logic, joined a literary club, and constantly practiced his public speaking, which he found he really enjoyed.

After leaving college, John decided to become a teacher at a school in Worchester, Massachusetts, while he decided his path for life. Soon law became the apparent job choice for John, and he traveled to Boston regularly to argue cases on everything from criminal to menial property disputes.

BTW: Adams's last words were "Jefferson lives." although in reality Jefferson had passed a few hours before.

FUN FACT!

Adams was the leader, the orchestrator, and the organizer behind the founding of America. He was never afraid to speak his mind—whether in the Continental Congresses, as the vice president, or as president—but Adams was rarely recognized for his accomplishments.

LIBERTY Language

Articles of Confederation: Before the Constitution, America was governed by the Articles of Confederation. This document only loosely bound the states together, resulting in much disunity and bickering among the states. As a result, delegates from every state (except Rhode Island) gathered to write a new document, which resulted in our Constitution.

FUN FACT!

While a lawyer, Adams represented the British soldiers who fired on Bostonians, marking the Boston Massacre of 1770, because he believed in upholding the law. Of the seven men, only two were convicted of manslaughter and suffered the terrible punishment of a branding on the wrist.

There are two ways to conquer and enslave a country. One is by the sword. The other is by debt.

JOHN ADAMS

Tennessee joins the Union, June 1, 1796

Edward Jenner introduces the smallpox vaccination, 1796

Catherine the Great of Russia dies, 1796

The French general Napoleon Bonaparte conquers Rome and Egypt, 1798

The Mississippi Territory is organized, April 7, 1798

The Rosetta Stone is discovered in Egypt, 1799

Napoleon becomes First Consul of France, 1799

13th president Millard Fillmore is born, January 7, 1800

William Herschel discovers infrared rays, 1800

The Indiana Territory is added, 1800

Alessandro Volta produces electricity, 1800

Term in Office

1796 1797 1798 1799 1800 1801

Adams read Latin and Greek, and preferred the company of his books to social activities like playing cards and dancing. He often carried poetry in his pocket, telling his son, "You will never be alone in the world with a poet in your pocket."

Adams wrote an essay called "Thoughts on Government," where he explained his plan for government—three branches: legislative, executive, and judicial. I wonder where I've seen that before?

BTW: In a letter to her husband during the creation of the Declaration of Independence, Abigail wrote "I desire you remember the ladies and be more generous and favorable to them than your ancestor... Remember all men would be tyrants if they could."

ABIGAIL ADAMS

[The office of the vice presidency is] the most insignificant office that the invention of man contrived or his imagination conceived.

First Couple

John Adams married Abigail Smith on October 25, 1764, and they remained together for fifty-four years until Abigail died in 1818. She was eleven years younger than John, but he often wrote to his wife, stating, "I could do nothing without you." They had five children, four of whom lived into adulthood: Abigail—called Nabby—John Quincy, Charles, and Thomas Boylston.

BTW: Nabby suffered from breast cancer and survived a mastectomy without anesthesia.

Previous Political Career

- 1774: Representative of Massachusetts at the First Continental Congress.
- 1775: Member of the Second Continental Congress. Adams soon became a leader in the group of Congress members who pushed to declare independence.
- 1776: Member of the committee in charge of writing the Declaration of Independence with Thomas Jefferson, Benjamin Franklin, Robert Livingston, and Roger Sherman.
- 1777: Adams was sent to France to help negotiate a treaty with the French to elicit funds and military assistance vital to winning the Revolutionary War.
- 1779: Member of the new Massachusetts state legislature. He helped compose the state constitution, creating a bicameral state legislature.
- 1781: Adams helped negotiate the Treaty of Paris, which brought an end to the Revolutionary War.
- 1781: Ambassador to the Netherlands.
- 1785: Adams became the first U.S. ambassador to England.
- 1788: The nation's first presidential election landed Adams in second place.

POLITICAL PARTIES

★★★★★★★★★★★★★★★★★★★★★★★★★★★

The first political parties began to form under the presidency of George Washington, but not until the election of 1796 was an election based around candidates of specific parties.

The Democratic-Republicans: the members of the Democratic-Republicans believed in small government and state sovereignty. Thomas Jefferson and James Madison formed the party in 1792 over fears that the Federalists' dream of a strong central government would lead to government corruption and favoring the northern states over those in the south.

 BTW: Talk about revolutionary sacrifice. Abigail once melted some of her pewter spoons in her cooking kettle to make bullets for her brother-in-law, Elihu.

ELECTION RESULTS!

Election of 1796

		Electoral Votes
1st	John Adams	71
2nd	Thomas Jefferson	68
3rd	Adams' VP Thomas Pinckney	59
4th	Jefferson's VP Aaron Burr	30
5th	Other	48

The first election based on the party system, the election of 1796, marked the engagement of newspapers in the campaigning process. The press, much like today but more scathing, chose sides in the election and were loyal to either Adams or Jefferson. However, with Washington's endorsement, Adams was able to pull off a slim majority, winning by only three electoral votes and only a few hundred popular votes.

■ John Adams — Federalist Won

■ Thomas Jefferson — Democratic-Republican Won

■ Territories

LIBERTY Language

Bicameral legislature: A legislative body having two branches or chambers.

Presidency

Adams assumed the office of the presidency on March 4, 1797, amid extreme political tensions. At first, he decided to keep all of Washington's cabinet. Soon, however, he found that to be a great mistake: the cabinet was loyal to Alexander Hamilton, a man who despised Adams and had worked behind the scenes in the three previous elections to try to prevent Adams from obtaining the presidency. Despite quarrels and hard feelings among his inner circle, Adams realized there were bigger problems at hand, notably one with ex-ally France.

Quasi War

Between 1798 and 1800, an informal war between the United States and France—known as the Quasi War—ensued, during which the French seized three hundred American ships. Instead of calling for an official war, which he believed would spell doom for the young country, Adams sent three envoys to France to negotiate a peace treaty. However, they found the minister would only be available to see them if they paid a hefty fee, which the envoys refused to pay.

Adams asked Congress for money to enlarge the army and create a small naval fleet in case France declared war. Congress demanded to see the record of the affair, which Adams begrudgingly turned over only after replacing the names of the envoys to France with the letters X, Y, and Z (thus the name, the XYZ Affair).

BTW: Adams almost did not run for reelection. Right before the campaign, he received news of his son Charles's death. Charles had succumbed to the effects of alcoholism.

CONGRESSIONAL CORNER
★★★★★★★★★★★★★★★★★★★★★★★★

Alien and Sedition Acts: President Adams approved these acts with the hope that they would stop French influence in American affairs and prevent America from being torn apart by divisive politics. This legislation, passed in 1798, included four acts: the Naturalization Act, which extended the waiting period for immigrants to receive citizenship and also extended the prohibition on a new immigrant's right to vote from five years to fourteen years; the Alien Act and the Alien Enemies Act, which gave the president the power to deport or jail foreign citizens during wartime; and the Sedition Act, which made it illegal to criticize the government.

★★★★★★★★★★★★★★★★★★★★★★★★

 BTW: The Adamses were staunch opponents of slavery and never owned a slave.

After the Twelfth Amendment was passed, the president and vice president had to belong to the same political party. You can read more about that in *Our Constitution Rocks!*

FUN FACT!

The Adams presidency marked the only time in history where the president and the vice president came from different parties, which created some problems. The solution came in 1804 through the ratification of the Twelfth Amendment.

FUN FACT!

Adams verbally presented his State of the Union address to Congress, as Washington had done before him. Thomas Jefferson suspended this practice and instead submitted a written report. An oral State of the Union was not given again until Woodrow Wilson's presidency in 1913.

Alien and Sedition Acts

On the domestic front, Adams and Congress passed the controversial Alien and Sedition Acts. These acts, among other things, prohibited speech that opposed the president and his views. As a result, twenty-five people were arrested—including two newspaper editors—of whom only ten were convicted.

Adams agreed to these acts because of the scathing debates about the disagreements with France, which were tearing the country in two. Adams's vice president, Thomas Jefferson, declared these acts unconstitutional and worked in secret with James Madison to author the Kentucky and Virginia Resolutions, respectively, which explained their views on how states could abolish federal laws they viewed as unconstitutional or infringed upon states' rights. These laws were either repealed or allowed to expire by 1802.

POLITICAL Rivalry

Jefferson, a friend of the French, turned bitter toward Adams over his dealings with the French during the Quasi War. He spoke behind Adams's back to his fellow Democratic-Republicans, stating Adams's mind had been "eaten to a honeycomb with ambition, yet weak, confused, uninformed, and ignorant." This was harsh criticism toward a man he had once considered his closest friend and ally.

PRESIDENTIAL Personality

★ Adams had an explosive personality, especially when debating independence. He referred to his personality as "tranquil, except when any instance of madness, deceit, hypocrisy, ingratitude, treachery, or perfidy has suddenly struck me. Then I have always been irascible [meaning hot-tempered] enough."

THOUGHTS ON THE CONSTITUTION

[The Constitution was] the result of good heads prompted by good hearts, as an experiment better adapted to the genius, character, situation, and relations of this nation and country than any which had ever been proposed or suggested ... I have repeatedly laid myself under the most serious obligations to support the Constitution.

Although he was in England while the Constitution was being drafted, Adams believed in the strength and brilliance of the nation's founding document. He strove to abide by it during his presidency and to stay within its limitations.

BTW: Adams was the first president to have negotiated a major peace agreement with a foreign power before becoming president: the Treaty of Paris.

34

The election of 1800 was one of personal attacks and vicious campaigning. Hamilton even went so far as to write a fifty-page editorial, where he accused Adams of humiliating the nation. Adams ended up losing his reelection bid to his former vice president, Thomas Jefferson, by eight electoral votes, making him the first of ten future presidents who would lose their reelection bids.

Post-Presidency

Adams retired with his wife to his farm in Braintree (now called Quincy), where he continued to write and read. During his service as vice president and president, he and Jefferson allowed politics to harden their close friendship. However, in 1812, at the request of fellow Declaration of Independence signer Benjamin Rush, the two men reconciled. On July 15, 1813, Adams wrote the first of 158 letters that would pass between the two patriots. The style of the letters represented their different personalities: Jefferson's were restrained and organized while Adams's were opinionated, witty, and impulsive.

John Adams lived to the age of ninety, dying almost a year after seeing his son inaugurated as the sixth president. He died on the fiftieth anniversary of the signing of the Declaration of Independence, July 4, 1826, the same day Thomas Jefferson died.

What Has He Done for Me Lately?

John Adams guided America through nearly every aspect of her founding. He chose Thomas Jefferson to write the Declaration of Independence and selected George Washington to lead the Continental Army. He negotiated the vital treaty with France that helped us win the Revolutionary War, and he secured a loan from the Netherlands that saved our young nation from economic collapse. He set the bar as the nation's first vice president, and he helped secure her new sea legs as the nation's second president. He kept us out of a war that would have ruined the fledging country and, like Washington, prevented the country from falling victim to party division.

Most important, independence had no greater advocate than Adams. Without Adams and his brilliant mind, who knows what America would look like today?

PLATFORM SPEECH

[N]o freeman should be subject to any tax to which he had not given his own consent.

But a Constitution of Government once changed from Freedom, can never be restored. Liberty, once lost, is lost forever.

Liberty cannot be preserved without a general knowledge among the people...

Adams believed that the government should not be able to order Americans to pay taxes without their consent.

Adams believed that an intelligent American population was the key to preserving America's government.

JOHN ADAMS

Written by Juliette Turner

IS THIS WAR?

SECRETARY OF THE NAVY

May 1, 1789—Amid concerns about the safety of American merchant ships at sea during the Quasi War with the French, Adams asked Congress to approve the funding for the creation of a new naval fleet and the position of Secretary of the Navy.

XYZ AFFAIR

July 11, 1797—In his efforts to try to subdue the high tensions with France, Adams sent Elbridge Gerry (Massachusetts politician), John Marshall (Virginia Federalist), and Charles Pinckney (former Minister to France) to negotiate a treaty with the French.

The Minister of France refused to meet with the men and instead sent three aides, who would only grant them a meeting with the minister in return for a $250,000 fee, a loan of $10 million for France, and an apology from Adams. The three men rightfully disagreed and returned to America to a disappointed president and a fuming Congress.

NAVAL FLEET ESTABLISHED

September 30, 1800—It feels like the country is at war, but the administration will not call it that. After the French successfully seized three hundred American ships at sea, Congress agreed to create a naval fleet. Congress expressed their belief that this will enhance America's ability to fight and protect this newfound nation.

PRESIDENTIAL PALACE CONSTRUCTION COMPLETED

November 1, 1800—Today the Adamses moved into the nation's first permanent presidential house. It is the largest personal residence of the day, but conditions might not be up to presidential par.

Only about half of the thirty-six rooms are plastered and the plastered walls are still wet. Closet doors have not been hung, servant bells have not been assembled, and the only decoration is a full-length portrait of George Washington by Gilbert Stuart. Adams may have to write down directions to his new home, because the Capital is so isolated that the carriage taking Abigail Adams to the new White House succeeded in getting lost in the woods on the way.

Adams reportedly considers the new seat of the Capital as a muddy, malarial swamp in the middle of nowhere, but he still considers the White House home.

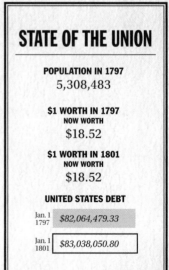

STATE OF THE UNION

POPULATION IN 1797
5,308,483

$1 WORTH IN 1797
NOW WORTH
$18.52

$1 WORTH IN 1801
NOW WORTH
$18.52

UNITED STATES DEBT

Jan. 1 1797	$82,064,479.33
Jan. 1 1801	$83,038,050.80

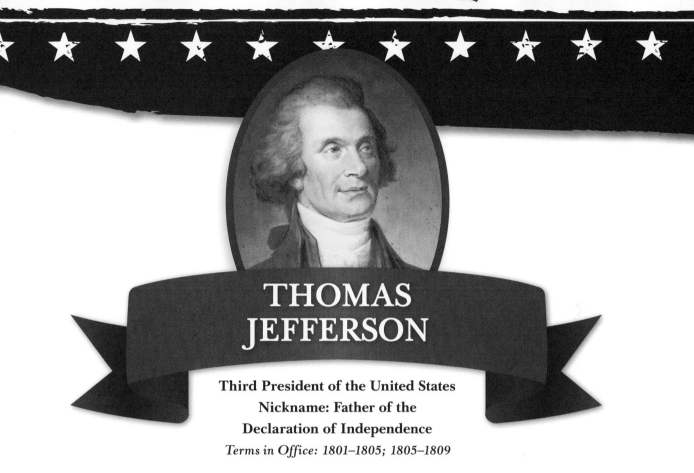

THOMAS JEFFERSON

Third President of the United States
Nickname: Father of the
Declaration of Independence
Terms in Office: 1801–1805; 1805–1809

The Bottom Line

During Thomas Jefferson's first term, America won her first official foreign war as a new nation against the Barbary pirates, America's land quantity doubled as a result of the Louisiana Purchase, and Jefferson initiated the Lewis and Clark Expedition. During his second term, the Embargo Acts were passed, causing unexpected financial misfortune in the country.

FAST STATS

★ Born April 13, 1743, in Shadwell, Virginia
★ Parents: Peter and Jane Randolph Jefferson
★ Died July 4, 1826, in Charlottesville, Virginia; age 83
★ Age upon Start of First Term: 57; Age upon Conclusion of First Term: 61
★ Age upon Start of Second Term: 61; Age upon Conclusion of Second Term: 65
★ Religious Affiliation: Christian
★ Political Party: Democratic-Republican
★ Height: 6 feet 2 inches
★ Vice Presidents: Aaron Burr (1801–1805) and George Clinton (1805–1809)

What Was He Thinking?

Jefferson believed that government's sole role was to protect the inalienable rights of every individual to life, liberty, and the pursuit of happiness. He considered the key to freedom as delicately balancing the will of the majority and the rights of the minority. He opposed a strong central government in favor of state sovereignty, and he opposed high federal taxes, believing they would weaken the power of the states. In regard to constitutional beliefs, he thought a limited government adhering strictly to constitutional guidelines to be the best form of government. Jefferson believed strongly in religious freedom and considered himself a devout Christian. Economically, Jefferson wanted the main U.S. currency to be the dollar, which he thought should be based on the decimal system.

Why Should I Care?

Although the Louisiana Purchase and the Louis and Clark Expedition remain two of the most well-known hallmarks of the Jefferson administration, Jefferson also left a legacy through the small things he did in office. Jefferson wanted to bring the presidency down to the level the people could relate to, one of humility and normalcy instead of distant formality.

Breakin' It Down

Early Life

Thomas was born in a small, one-and-a-half story farmhouse in Virginia. Thomas's father worked as a farmer and surveyor, but he also became a judge and a leader of the Albemarle County Militia. Of his nine siblings, Thomas was the oldest son and third oldest child.

Tragedy struck the happy family in 1757, when Thomas was fourteen. His father unexpectedly died of illness. His mother never remarried, making young Thomas the father figure of the household. Although he never formally attended schooling in his youth, Thomas was tutored in Latin, Greek, classical texts, modern literature, geography, and science. When he was not diligently studying, Thomas would ride on horseback or practice playing his beloved violin. In 1760, at the age of seventeen, he entered the College of William and Mary.

After graduating college, Jefferson turned to law in 1767 and then to farming. In 1769, he began constructing his own home, Monticello, on the 1,053 acres of land he had inherited from his father. Jefferson ignored the old tradition of building by a river, because he wanted his house to be on the top of a hill. He also built it out of brick, which was rare among the wooden houses of the day.

> The God who gave us life, gave us liberty at the same time.

First Couple

On January 1, 1772, Thomas married twenty-four-year-old Martha Wayles Skelton, a wealthy Virginia widow whose land nearly doubled

Congress establishes the United States Military Academy at West Point, 1802

Jefferson's inauguration, March 4, 1801

Marbury v. Madison, February 20, 1803

Ohio becomes a state, March 1, 1803

Louisiana Purchase, October 20, 1803

Lewis and Clark Expedition begins, May 14, 1804

Aaron Burr kills Alexander Hamilton in a duel, 1804

First Term in Office

| 1800 | 1801 | 1802 | 1803 | 1804 |

BTW: Jefferson was the first president to be inaugurated in Washington, D.C. The Capitol building was not yet finished, so Jefferson's swearing in took place in the only completed room in the Capitol: the Senate Chamber.

BTW: Thomas claimed to have taught himself Spanish by reading *Don Quixote* with the assistance of a Spanish vocabulary dictionary.

FUN FACT!

Jefferson often greeted diplomats while still wearing his robe and slippers. British Minister Anthony Merry claimed Jefferson greeted him in "usual morning attire, [his] pantaloons, coat, and underclothes indicative of utter slovenliness and indifference to appearances."

CONGRESSIONAL CORNER
★★★★★★★★★★★★★★★★★★★★★★★★

1. **District of Columbia Organic Act of 1801: This act, passed in 1801, officially put the District of Columbia under the control of the U.S. Congress.**

2. **Cumberland Road: This legislation, passed in 1806 and creating the Cumberland Road, marked the first time an improved highway was built by the federal government.**

3. **Act Prohibiting Importation of Slaves: This act, passed in 1807, prohibited the importation of slaves to America. Jefferson had also introduced a measure at the Continental Congress in 1784 to ban slavery in all territories west of the Appalachian Mountains. Although he helped to pass the bill in 1807, he never supported any other such emancipation legislation during his term in office.**

4. **Embargo Act of 1807: This act limited trade between the U.S. and Britain and France as a result of the European nations' attacks on American merchant ships. It was intended to punish France and Britain, but it backfired and hurt American merchants.**

★★★★★★★★★★★★★★★★★★★★★★★★

Jefferson's estate. They both loved music, which brought them together. Jefferson presented Martha with a piano during their courtship, and they were often found performing musical duets, Thomas on his violin and Martha on the harpsichord or organ. Together they had six children, only two of whom would live into adulthood. When Martha died on September 6, 1782, Jefferson remained in seclusion for three months, frequently heard sobbing uncontrollably during the night. Jefferson's sister recounted, "He fainted and remained so long insensible that they feared he would never revive." He often broke down when he had to speak. Friends and Jefferson's daughter Patsy were worried about Jefferson's stability of mind. However, answering the call from his country, he rose to the occasion and fulfilled his obligations.

Previous Political Career

- 1768: At age twenty-five, Jefferson was elected to the Virginia House of Burgesses. He championed the rights of the middle-class, self-made men over the wealthy landowners. He served from 1769 to 1774.
- 1774: Member of the First Continental Congress
- 1775: Member of the Second Continental Congress.
- 1776: Authored the Declaration of Independence, writing the document in seventeen days, stating that its purpose was to "place before mankind the common sense of the subject, in terms so plain and firm as to command their assent."

Battle of Trafalgar in the Napoleonic War between French and British, October 21, 1805

Monroe-Pinkney Treaty, December 31, 1806

Slave trade ban, January 1, 1808

Beethoven's Fifth and Sixth Symphonies are performed, 1808

Michigan Territory is added, January 11, 1805

Burr conspiracy, November 27, 1806

Robert Fulton successfully takes the first steamboat, *Clermont*, from New York City to Albany, 1807

7th president Andrew Johnson is born, December 29, 1808

16th president Abraham Lincoln is born, February 12, 1809

Second Term in Office

1805 | 1806 | 1807 | 1808 | 1809

BTW: Jefferson was the first president to shake hands with diplomatic guests. Adams and Washington had continued the previous practice of bowing in greeting.

ELECTION RESULTS!

	Election of 1800	Electoral Votes
1st	Thomas Jefferson	73
2nd	Aaron Burr	73
3rd	John Adams	65
4th	Charles C. Pinckney	64
5th	John Jay	1

■ Thomas Jefferson — Democratic-Republican Won
■ John Adams — Federalist Won
■ Territories

In 1800, Jefferson ran as a presidential candidate opposing incumbent president John Adams. Although there was no way to distinguish electoral votes between those running for vice president and those running for president, Aaron Burr and Charles Pinckney ran as vice presidential candidates. All would have gone smoothly except for Aaron Burr's refusal to accept the position of vice president when he and Jefferson obtained the same number of votes. Because of the tie, the election was placed into the hands of the House of Representatives, who voted thirty-six times in six days without successfully nominating a new president. Alexander Hamilton — who, although he hated Jefferson, despised Burr even more — persuaded the states of Maryland and Vermont to vote for Jefferson, giving him the necessary ten states to win the presidency.

Jefferson won in a landslide. His popularity escalated alongside the rising American prosperity of the day. As Charles Pinckney would prove, it's hard to defeat such a well-liked and successful president. After all, America had just won her first official foreign war and recently doubled in size. If Jefferson had run for a third term in 1808, he most likely would have won, but he instead followed Washington's precedent of only serving two terms.

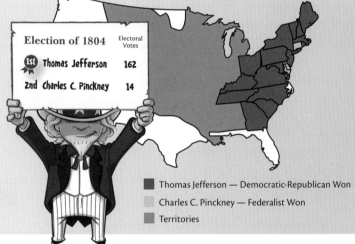

	Election of 1804	Electoral Votes
1st	Thomas Jefferson	162
2nd	Charles C. Pinckney	14

■ Thomas Jefferson — Democratic-Republican Won
■ Charles C. Pinckney — Federalist Won
■ Territories

BTW: Jefferson was known for having terrible posture and no sense of style, often dressing in whatever suited him, even if it clashed with his flaming red hair.

- 1776: Drafted Virginia's first constitution for their post-colonial government. He proposed a plan to guarantee public education for all children regardless of economic status, but the plan was rejected.
- 1779: Governor of Virginia.
- 1785: Appointed as minister to France.
- 1789: Served as George Washington's secretary of state. He often disagreed with Secretary of the Treasury Alexander Hamilton, most notably over Hamilton's idea for a national bank and his proposal for all state debts to be taken over by the national government. Jefferson was opposed to the debt accumulation because the southern states, like Virginia, had already paid off their debts and did not want to have to contribute to paying off the northern debts.
- 1797: Jefferson was elected vice president under John Adams. During Adams's presidency, Jefferson was absent for over a year because of his refusal to accept the Alien and Sedition Acts. He worked on writing a *Manual of Parliamentary Practice*, which became the rule book for the legislative branch.

BTW: When Jefferson was president, his daughter gave birth to a child she named James after Secretary of State James Madison. James was the first child to be born in the White House.

Presidency

Jefferson strove to stick to constitutional guidelines, but he set several precedents, which inevitably expanded our government's interpretation of the Constitution. The first of these precedents affected the ruling ability and power of the judicial branch. In the Supreme Court case *Marbury v. Madison*, Chief Justice John Marshall ruled that a certain piece of legislation passed by Congress, which allowed for someone to sue the federal government, was unconstitutional. So, what is the big deal? This judicial decision set the standard for the Supreme Court to be able to determine if legislation passed by Congress is constitutional or not.

FUN FACT!

When John Adams chose Jefferson to write the Declaration of Independence, Jefferson was hesitant. Adams said, "Reason first: you are a Virginian, and a Virginian ought to be at the head of this business. Reason second: I am obnoxious, suspected, and unpopular; you are very much otherwise. Reason third: you can write ten times better than I." Jefferson consented with, "I will do as well as I can."

Louisiana Purchase

Then Jefferson and the Senate approved a treaty with France that allowed the purchase of the Louisiana Territory in 1803. Jefferson had thought a constitutional amendment would be necessary for the Senate to approve the purchase, but the Senate voted 26 to 5 in favor of the land purchase. Meanwhile, Jefferson worked hard to pay off the national debt and at the same time cut domestic taxes—including Washington's Whiskey Tax. He managed to balance the federal budget, doing so by eliminating several federal offices and limiting the army to three thousand five hundred men.

Embargo Act

His second term of office did not see the same peace and prosperity as his first term. Great Britain and France had once again erupted into war, dragging American traders into the turmoil. Jefferson responded to both countries by enforcing the Embargo Act of 1807. This act intended to harm Great Britain and France by cutting off their imports and exports to and from the U.S.

Separation of Church and State

★★

Thomas Jefferson's letter to the Danbury Baptist Association is often misinterpreted as Jefferson's endorsement of separation of church and state. Jefferson wrote, "I contemplate with sovereign reverence that act of the whole American people which declared that their legislature should 'make no law respecting an establishment of religion, or prohibiting the free exercise thereof,' thus building a wall of separation between Church and State."

This quotation has been misused and misinterpreted by the U.S. Supreme Court and many Americans as a justification for prohibiting religious activities in state schools (such as school prayers). In reality, Jefferson wrote this only in regard to the national Congress—not the states or any state body. Jefferson was strongly against the national Congress establishing any religion, but he believed the states could act as they chose. Jefferson rightly saw the Bill of Rights and the First Amendment as a restriction on the national Congress, not on the state or local governments; after all, states had their own established religions at the time.

BTW: A rarity for any president. Jefferson wrote his own first inaugural address. In fact, he did so in less than three weeks.

BTW: Jefferson was in Europe during the signing and creation of the Constitution. He approved but wanted to add the Bill of Rights.

This backfired on American traders, leading to more than a 50 percent drop in national income and an increase in smuggling rates. However, it did lead to the creation of more textile mills and factories on American soil to make up for the lack of European goods. Jefferson remained popular with the citizens because he continually strove to represent the people's rights and will in the government. Jefferson decided in 1809 to continue Washington's example of only serving two terms, although he was almost guaranteed to win a third term in office if he ran.

Post-Presidency

After his presidency, Jefferson returned to his beloved home, Monticello, where he began the early workings of his ideas for a non-religious-based college in Virginia. In 1819, his dream became a reality when he opened the doors to the school he designed, planned, and organized himself. The first classes were held in 1825. He ordered that acceptance to the school be based on merit rather than wealth, representing his lifelong philosophy. This school is known today as the University of Virginia, and it still carries on the Jefferson legacy by upholding his ideals.

He often invited students to dine with him at Monticello; he once hosted student Edgar Allen Poe, who would go on to become a world-renowned poet. However, not only students were welcome at the president's home. He hosted many guests, many of whom often stayed overnight or even for several days. Most likely his favorite guests were his thirteen beloved grandchildren.

Near the end of his life, he picked up correspondence with his old friend—and enemy— John Adams. He died on the same day as Adams, July 4, 1826.

BTW: Jefferson's last words were. "Is it the Fourth?"

What Has He Done for Me Lately?

Jefferson was the last man who signed the Declaration of Independence to become president. He dedicated his entire life to his cherished country, helping her in every stage, from her birth through his authorship of the Declaration of Independence to her biggest land expansion through the Louisiana Purchase. Finally, Jefferson also helped move the presidency away from a place of formality and ceremonial tradition to an office of simplicity to the American people.

PLATFORM SPEECHES

Let us restore to social intercourse that harmony and affection without which liberty and even life itself are but dreary things.

If there be any among us who would wish to dissolve this Union or to change its republican form, let them stand undisturbed as monuments of the safety with which error or opinion may be tolerated, where reason is left free to combat it.

THOUGHTS ON THE CONSTITUTION

[B]y our Constitution I shall find resources of wisdom, of virtue, and of zeal on which to rely under all difficulties."

During Adams's presidency, America had experienced extreme political tension. In his first State of the Union address, Jefferson realized that without political harmony and compromise, liberty and democracy were of little use.

THOMAS JEFFERSON

42

Presidential Times

Written by Juliette Turner

THE PRESIDENT GETS A TICKET

June 15, 1804—The Twelfth Amendment passed by Congress last year has been ratified by the states, amending the election process. Going forth, presidential candidates will choose their running mates from the same political party, and the two nominees will form a "ticket," which voters will choose from, instead of having the runner-up become the vice president. This change is intended to create more peaceful relations between the two leaders of the country.

AMERICA WINS HER FIRST OFFICIAL FOREIGN WAR

June 12, 1805—The U.S. is victorious and the pirates have lost their booty. The Barbary pirates have, for a long time, been demanding tributes for any vessels passing their territory. They required it of any ship passing into the Mediterranean Sea. But Jefferson refused to pay the tribute.

To make matters worse, the pirates seized the *USS Philadelphia* and her crew. Jefferson declared war on the pirates, making him the first president to send troops to foreign soil. This led to a series of small naval battles, and now the U.S. has come out on top.

MARBURY V. MADISON

March 1, 1803—It seems that some of John Adams's judicial appointments (those Adams appointed to serve either in federal or Supreme Court) were not delivered. This mail mess-up "coincidentally" corresponds with Jefferson's arrival into office. It is speculated that Jefferson had something to do with it.

Upon his arrival into office, Jefferson saw this as his chance to ensure that Democratic-Republicans gained control of all three branches of government, and instructed his secretary of state, James Madison, not to deliver the letters. William Marbury, a nominee who did not receive his appointment, has appealed to the Supreme Court and has sued the federal government, unleashing a multitude of questions.

Congress has decided to pass a bill allowing Marbury to sue the federal government for withholding his appointment. The case recently reached the Supreme Court, where Chief Justice John Marshall ruled that the law passed by Congress allowing Marbury to sue the federal government is unconstitutional. This landmark decision has set the standard for judicial review. The court can now review bills passed by Congress and determine their constitutionality.

Marbury has yet to receive his appointment and the Jefferson administration has not been officially chastised—although Marshall did criticize Jefferson and Madison for their back dealings.

SLAVE IMPORTATION PROHIBITED

January 1, 1808—The slave trade has been protected for twenty years by Article 1, Section 9 of the Constitution, but now President Jefferson has called for the criminalization of slavery, calling it a "violation of human rights," and has passed the Act Prohibiting Importation of Slaves, which does not allow any new slaves to be imported from foreign contries. Could this spell the end of the slave trade?

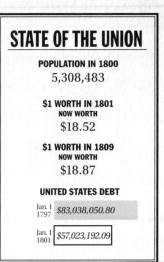

STATE OF THE UNION

POPULATION IN 1800
5,308,483

$1 WORTH IN 1801
NOW WORTH
$18.52

$1 WORTH IN 1809
NOW WORTH
$18.87

UNITED STATES DEBT

Jan. 1 1797	$83,038,050.80
Jan. 1 1801	$57,023,192.09

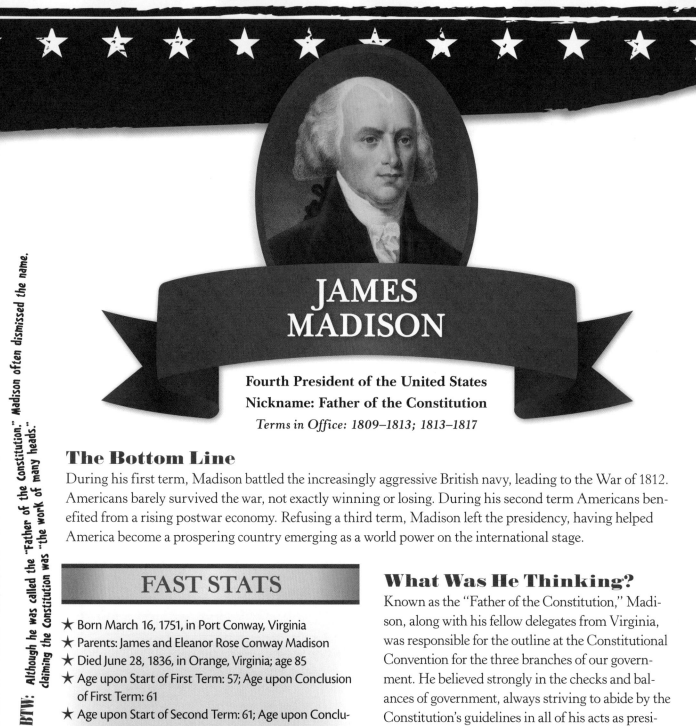

JAMES MADISON

Fourth President of the United States

Nickname: Father of the Constitution

Terms in Office: 1809–1813; 1813–1817

The Bottom Line

During his first term, Madison battled the increasingly aggressive British navy, leading to the War of 1812. Americans barely survived the war, not exactly winning or losing. During his second term Americans benefited from a rising postwar economy. Refusing a third term, Madison left the presidency, having helped America become a prospering country emerging as a world power on the international stage.

FAST STATS

★ Born March 16, 1751, in Port Conway, Virginia

★ Parents: James and Eleanor Rose Conway Madison

★ Died June 28, 1836, in Orange, Virginia; age 85

★ Age upon Start of First Term: 57; Age upon Conclusion of First Term: 61

★ Age upon Start of Second Term: 61; Age upon Conclusion of Second Term: 65

★ Religious Affiliation: Episcopalian

★ Political Party: Democratic-Republican

★ Height: 5 feet 4 inches

★ Vice Presidents: George Clinton (1809-1812) and Elbridge Gerry (1813–1814)

What Was He Thinking?

Known as the "Father of the Constitution," Madison, along with his fellow delegates from Virginia, was responsible for the outline at the Constitutional Convention for the three branches of our government. He believed strongly in the checks and balances of government, always striving to abide by the Constitution's guidelines in all of his acts as president. He wanted a small federal government with the emphasis on state sovereignty. Economically, although Madison was against Hamilton's federal bank, he ended up supporting the charter for the Second Bank during his presidency.

BTW: Although he was called the "Father of the Constitution," Madison often dismissed the name, claiming the Constitution was "the work of many heads."

 BTW: Lifelong friends Thomas Jefferson and James Madison constantly met to discuss political opinions, most of the time over a game of chess. Together they founded one of America's first political parties: the Democratic-Republicans.

Why Should I Care?

The War of 1812, sometimes referred to as "Mr. Madison's War," remains the hallmark of James Madison's presidency. Besides leading America through the war, Madison also cautiously dealt with domestic issues that arose during that time. He was careful to restrain presidential powers, setting a standard for all future presidents to never assume more powers than what are explicitly granted in the Constitution, during times of war. The first man to hold the position of president during a war on American soil, Madison succeeded in holding together the American Republic, despite the lure of martial law and possible wartime powers.

Martial law: Law established by a leader during wartime that suspends normal, peacetime laws and restraints, allowing the leader to do more—such as search people's houses without a warrant. However, in America all laws must abide by the Constitution, regardless of war or peace.

> The federal and state governments are in fact but different agents and trustees of the people, constituted with different powers, and designed for different purposes.

Breakin' It Down

Early Life

The Madison family owned a five-thousand-acre estate called Montpelier. James and Eleanor had twelve children. James's father was a tobacco farmer, also serving as colonel for the Virginia Militia.

James, nicknamed "Little Jemmy," was quite short, causing someone to once refer to him as "no bigger than half a piece of soap." However, he made up for his small stature with his brilliant and quick mind.

James's early schooling consisted of at-home tutors, and he entered the College of New Jersey, now known as Princeton, as a sophomore at age eighteen. James studied history, government, and law. He graduated in two years, but his disciplined and strenuous studying caused his health to decline significantly.

PRESIDENTIAL Personality

★ Madison was known for his skilled oratory and composed debating skills, although his voice was sometimes inaudible. Not very outgoing or sociable, Madison was once described as "mean looking," although the commenter later remarked he was quite affable in reality. The effervescent Dolley Madison, however, made up for whatever social skills Madison lacked.

> I can consciously say that I do not know in the world a man of purer integrity, more dispassionate, disinterested and devoted to republicanism; nor could I in the whole scope of America and Europe point out an abler head.

Thomas Jefferson said these words about James Madison.

First Couple

James Madison and Dolley Payne Todd were introduced by their mutual friend Aaron Burr. Although James was almost twenty years older than Dolley, they married on September 15, 1794. Dolley had one son from her previous marriage named John, who remained James's only child; James and Dolley had no children together.

DOLLEY MADISON

> BTW: The first wedding at the White House occurred during Madison's presidency.

ELECTION RESULTS!

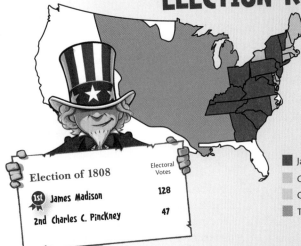

With the prosperity and stability America was experiencing as Thomas Jefferson left office, it was easy for James Madison, his fellow Democratic-Republican, to win the presidency. Attempting to gain ground in the election, the Federalist candidate, Charles Cotesworth Pinckney, focused on the failed Embargo Acts passed by Jefferson. However, Jefferson's popularity and his support of Madison made Madison an unbeatable candidate. Pinckney, who ran as John Adams's vice president in the 1800 presidential election and for president himself in 1804, suffered his third and final election defeat.

■ James Madison — Democratic-Republican Won
■ Charles C. Pinckney — Federalist Won
■ George Clinton — Independent Republican Won
■ Territories

Election of 1808

		Electoral Votes
1st	James Madison	128
2nd	Charles C. Pinckney	47

Madison won reelection in 1812 against Dewitt Clinton. Because the British continued to seize American merchant ships despite Madison's attempts at negotiations, the "War Hawks" arose during the election and called for Madison to seek war and revenge. Clinton rose as Madison's opponent, yet he came from Madison's own party. The Federalists, who were unable to decide on a candidate, rallied behind Clinton instead.

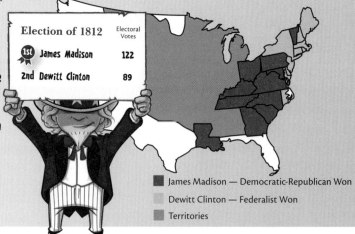

Election of 1812

		Electoral Votes
1st	James Madison	122
2nd	Dewitt Clinton	89

■ James Madison — Democratic-Republican Won
■ Dewitt Clinton — Federalist Won
■ Territories

Previous Political Career

- 1776: Member of the Virginia House of Delegates, where he helped draft the state constitution.
- 1779: Member of the Continental Congress, making him the youngest delegate at the age of twenty-nine.
- 1784: Member of the Virginia state legislature.
- 1787: Madison joins the Constitutional Convention. Before the Convention, Madison composes his ideal governmental plan: an elected chief executive possessing the veto power over legislation; a federal judiciary in a separate branch of government; and a two-chambered legislative branch.
- 1789: Member of the first U.S. House of Representatives representing Virginia.
- 1801-1809: Secretary of state under President Thomas Jefferson

FUN FACT!

Although Madison retired from the House of Representatives in 1797, he remained politically active by writing the "Virginia Resolution."

BTW: Madison always demanded a constitutional debate before every decision he made as president.

The Mexican War of Independence begins, 1810

West Florida is annexed from Spain, October 27, 1810

An 8.3 magnitude earthquake hits Madrid, Missouri, February 2, 1812

Louisiana joins the Union, April 30, 1812

Congress declares war on Great Britain to start the War of 1812

First Term in Office

| 1808 | 1809 | 1810 | 1811 | 1812 |

Presidency

Madison's presidency began with high spirits and celebration. The Madisons hosted the First Inaugural Ball at Long's Hotel in Washington, D.C. However, these good sentiments did not last for long. The Embargo Act expired upon Jefferson's leave of office, opening trade once again between American merchants and Great Britain and France. Hostilities occurred, this time worse than before, with the British forcing American sailors to defect to the British army and claiming the U.S. was weak and divided.

War of 1812

Finally, Americans had had enough, and Congress declared war on Great Britain in June 1812. The war lasted for nearly three years and, although America did not officially "win" or "lose" the war, they proved they could survive a a war as a nation. This sentiment of survival and American perseverance gave the people a new sense of pride and patriotism. This wave of nationalism helped Madison win a second term.

Madison's second term did not experience the same dilemma of foreign affairs as did his first term, letting him focus more on the domestic issues of the day.

Money Issues

To help pay off the debts accumulated because of the war, Madison was forced to raise taxes to an all-time high—a tax level that would not be seen again until the Civil War. Madison also supported the charter for the Second National Bank, quite a shocker after his adamant opposition to Hamilton's First National Bank. During the war with Britain, Madison realized that the bank was necessary to keep the country running and financially safe. Madison's bank would control federal finances like the first bank. This charter would last for twenty years.

Finally, Madison promoted the need for nationwide roadway and canal improvements that he felt would unify the country. Madison retired after his second term, leaving the United States a rising world power.

Post-Presidency

Madison returned to Virginia at the conclusion of his second term. In 1826, after the death of his good friend and colleague Thomas Jefferson, Madison became the second headmaster of the University of Virginia, which he had helped Jefferson establish. He attended the Virginia Convention of 1829, where Virginians met to revise their state constitution. He spoke of the expansion of voting rights as well as placing limitations

> Every word of the Constitution decides the question between power and liberty.

JAMES MADISON

BTW: Before the British could burn the White House during the War of 1812, Dolly Madison rescued many valuables from the White House, including Gilbert Stuart's full length portrait of George Washington.

The White House is set on fire during the War of 1812, August 24, 1814

Francis Scott Key writes the "Star Spangled Banner," September 1814

The Senate unanimously ratifies the Treaty of Ghent to end the War of 1812, December 24, 1814

Congress passes the charter for the Second Bank of the United States, April 10, 1816

George Stephenson builds the first steam locomotive, 1814

Indiana joins the Union, December 11, 1816

Congress passes the Tariff of 1816, April 27, 1816

The Alabama Territory organized, March 3, 1817

Second Term in Office

1813   1814   1815   1816   1817

BTW: Historians agree that Madison may have been a hypochondriac as a young man, often claiming illness when in reality he produced very few real symptoms.

CONGRESSIONAL CORNER

★★★★★★★★★★★★★★★★★★★★★★★★★

1. **Declaration of War of 1812:** signed by Congress on June 17, 1812 following Madison's "war message," officially declared war on Great Britain and began the War of 1812.

2. **Treaty of Ghent:** this treaty, signed by the Senate on December 24, 1814, unanimously ratified the Treaty of Ghent and ended the War of 1812.

3. **The Tariff of 1816:** this tariff, also known as the Dallas Tariff, was approved by Congress on April 27, 1816, and was the first tax intended to protect U.S. industry rather than raise federal revenue—taxing imported goods to entice consumers to buy cheaper American made products instead of products from overseas.

4. **Charter for the Second Bank of the United States:** this charter, signed in 1816, established the Second Bank of the United States, which remained for twenty years.

★★★★★★★★★★★★★★★★★★★★★★★★★

on slavery for the state. Yet neither of these ideas was included in the constitution. He also denounced the theory of nullification, which was discussed at the convention.

Near the end of his life, a lengthy illness left Madison bedridden for almost a year. Rheumatism made his writing illegible, so he dictated his concluding thoughts on politics and government to Dolley. Madison was the last of the Founding Fathers to pass away. If he had lived for one more year, he would have witnessed the fiftieth anniversary of the framing of the Constitution.

What Has He Done for Me Lately?

James Madison's contribution to the Constitutional Convention not only laid the roadmap for the formation of the Constitution, but also helped preserve it for posterity. Today the Constitution still not only preserves our everyday liberties but ensures our republican form of government, preventing any one man or woman from gaining too much power. Madison held the rare accomplishment of helping to form the office of the president and establishing its limitations and powers, then later becoming the president himself. Madison probably knew the Constitution by heart, which would have contributed to his ability to rule the country fairly and justly. He was the first president to govern during a war on American soil, and as such he set the standard for wartime presidents. Instead of increasing presidential powers through enforcing martial law, he abided in every way by the Constitution, preserving the checks and balances limitations.

THOUGHTS ON THE CONSTITUTION

[My intentions are] to support the Constitution, which is the cement of the Union, as well in its limitations as in its authorities; to respect the rights and authorities reserved to the States and to the people as equally incorporated with and essential to the success of the general system.

Madison wanted to protect and abide by the Constitution during his presidency. He knew that working within its limitations would ensure success and safety for the entire system of government. He spoke these words at his first State of the Union address.

PLATFORM SPEECH

[I]t has been the true glory of the United States to cultivate peace by observing justice.

Madison said this in his first State of the Union address. He wanted to preserve the peace and prosperity enjoyed by the country under his predecessor, Thomas Jefferson.

JAMES MADISON

48

Presidential Times

Written by Juliette Turner

WAR OF 1812: TAKING ITS TOLL

TRADE DEAL PROPOSED

May 7, 1810—Madison has proposed a deal to reopen trade with France or Great Britain, but not both. Madison inserted a clause into the agreement that states that whichever country first agrees to respect American neutrality will have trading rights. The United States will close trade with the country that does not respond first.

American trade has been suffering since former President Jefferson's second term, when Americans were prohibited from trading with France and Great Britain.

CONGRESS DECLARES WAR

June 19, 1812—Yesterday Congress approved Madison's war declaration against Britain. This comes after a long fight over trade. American citizens have expressed worry over the low number of militia soldiers and lack of financing, but Madison believes war is the only option and is confident of America's strength.

USS CONSTITUTION, "OLD IRONSIDES"

August 30, 1812—Americans are enjoying a boost in morale as news comes from the coast of Nova Scotia of the undefeatable *USS Constitution*.

During a naval battle against the British, the British ship *Guerriere* fired on the *USS Constitution*. However, the thickened hull, an American invention, prevented the cannons from penetrating the ship. The cannons bounced off, causing sailors and bystanders to yell that the ship must have been made out of iron, although she is actually built of all-American timber.

Thus, the nickname "Old Ironsides" was born. The *USS Constitution*, as many may remember, was used against the Barbary pirates under Jefferson's term. The boat is serving her country well as a beacon of patriotism.

CHRISTMAS GIFT: THE WAR IS OVER

December 25, 1814—Madison received a great Christmas gift, as the War of 1812 concluded yesterday with the signing of the Treaty of Ghent. Lasting nearly three years, this war with Great Britain cost 20,000 American lives, most of whom died from the diseases that spread rampantly throughout the army camps.

The Treaty of Ghent comes right after the recent major American victory on Lake Champlain. This treaty declares neither the U.S. nor Great Britain as winner or loser and has not resolved any of the issues that instigated the war in the first place.

All land gained from the war will be given back to the previous owner, and the British have agreed to remove troops from America's Great Lakes and Ohio Territory.

Celebrations have erupted across the nation, and citizens are expressing their relief to have simply survived the war. National patriotism is at an all-time high. America has survived her first war, and the people are glad.

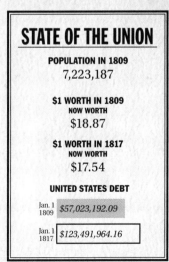

STATE OF THE UNION

POPULATION IN 1809
7,223,187

$1 WORTH IN 1809
NOW WORTH
$18.87

$1 WORTH IN 1817
NOW WORTH
$17.54

UNITED STATES DEBT

Jan. 1 1809	$57,023,192.09
Jan. 1 1817	$123,491,964.16

BTW: In 1797, Monroe and Alexander Hamilton challenged each other to a duel, but it was postponed ... indefinitely.

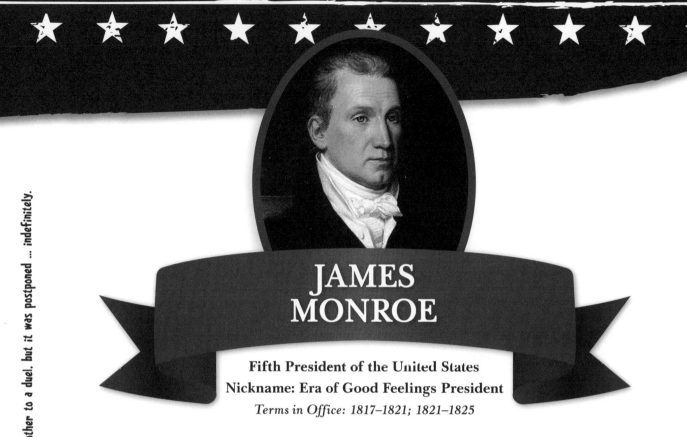

JAMES MONROE

Fifth President of the United States
Nickname: Era of Good Feelings President
Terms in Office: 1817–1821; 1821–1825

The Bottom Line

During James Monroe's first term, America prospered through the "Era of Good Feelings" and political divisiveness came to a new calm. During his second term, America domestically and economically suffered after the Panic of 1819, but prospered internationally through Monroe's issuance of the Monroe Doctrine.

FAST STATS

★ Born April 28, 1758, in Westmorland County, Virginia
★ Parents: Spence and Elizabeth Jones Monroe
★ Died July 4, 1831, in New York City, New York; age 73
★ Age upon Start of First Term: 58; Age upon Conclusion of First Term: 62
★ Age upon Start of Second Term: 62; Age upon Conclusion of Second Term: 66
★ Religious Affiliation: Episcopalian
★ Political Party: Democratic-Republican
★ Height: 6 feet
★ Vice President: Daniel D. Tompkins

BTW: Liberia's capital city is named Monrovia in honor of Monroe's work to help the slaves.

What Was He Thinking?

Monroe followed the Democratic-Republican belief that the main power lay in the hands of state governments, not the federal government. He strongly believed in the separation of the three branches of government. He believed slavery to be morally wrong and helped organize a colony in West Africa where free slaves could settle. Monroe worked hard to balance the budget, which he believed was vital to a functioning government, and he even had a nine million dollar surplus the year before he left office.

Why Should I Care?

During Monroe's time in office, America prospered through the lack of political divide when the Federalist Party collapsed upon Monroe's election. However, Monroe's greatest legacy lies in his efforts in foreign policy. Along with the annexation of the Florida Territory and the Oregon Territory, Monroe's greatest foreign policy achievement was his declaration of the Monroe Doctrine, which changed the way American foreign policy operated. It made America the protector of the entire Western Hemisphere and guardian of the rights of young colonies in South and Central America, protecting them from European invaders. As a result, America became a world power against the weakening European countries.

LIBERTY Language

Annexation: The incorporation of a territory or section of land into an existing country from another country as the result of a land sale.

LIBERTY Language

Plenipotentiary: A diplomat to foreign countries who is given the ability to make decisions in the name of their mother country.

PRESIDENTIAL Personality

★ James Monroe was known to his friends as a kindhearted and courteous man with a warm personality. However, he was also willing to bravely fight in the name of his country, both on the battlefield and in politics. Shy as a young boy, Monroe overcame his shyness to become one of America's most successful presidents. During his political career, his contemporaries noted that Monroe was sensitive to criticism—something he got a lot of as president—but Monroe never lashed out at any of his critics.

Breakin' It Down

Early Life

James's father was a carpenter and farmer of a six-hundred-acre farm in Virginia, where James grew up. James was the oldest of five children.

He was homeschooled until age eleven, when he entered the Campbelltown Academy. James excelled in mathematics and Latin, although he most enjoyed horseback riding and hunting after school.

In 1774, both of James's parents died, leaving him an orphan. His uncle, Joseph Jones, assumed the role of guardian for the five Monroe children, even helping James enroll in the College of William and Mary. But James's stay there was short-lived. In 1776, he quit college to join the Third Virginia Regiment of the Continental Army. Young James became a lieutenant, leading valiant charges against the British army. A charge on the Hessian cannons during the Battle of Trenton nearly cost him his life; James would likely have bled to death from a ruptured artery if not for the doctor who accompanied the regiment and attended him immediately.

James continued serving in the army, weathering the winter at Valley Forge. George Washington helped James attain the position of lieutenant colonel; however, his regiment was not organized before the war ended. Then James turned to a political career.

First Couple

James Monroe married Elizabeth Kortright in 1786. Elizabeth came from a Tory family, but she married a man with a passionate, revolutionary spirit. They had three children together—Eliza, James, and Maria. Elizabeth may have suffered from

It is known that we derive [our blessings] from the excellence of our institutions. Ought we not, then, to adopt every measure which may be necessary to perpetuate them?

JAMES MONROE

CONGRESSIONAL CORNER

1. **Rush-Bagot Treaty:** Ratified by the Senate on April 16, 1818, this treaty resulted from the War of 1812. It limited the number of armaments allowed on the Great Lakes and Lake Champlain.

2. **Treaty of 1818 with Great Britain:** Approved by Congress on October 20, 1818, this treaty established the 49th parallel as the boundary between the U.S. and Canada.

3. **Adams-Onis Treaty:** Through this treaty, approved by the Senate on February 22, 1819, Spain ceded Florida to the U.S.

4. **Missouri Compromise of March 6, 1820:** This legislation addressed the issue of slavery in regard to when and how to add free and slave states to the Union. The Compromise set a dividing line on the southern border of Missouri: all states north would be accepted as free states and all states south had the option to allow slavery in their state. The Compromise temporarily settled the question of slavery.

5. **Land Act of 1820:** This act ended the federal government's ability to buy public domain land on credit; they had to pay up front.

ELIZABETH MONROE

epileptic seizures later in life, as four years before her death she reportedly fell into a fireplace, burning herself severely. Upon her death, James stated he could not live long without her, and he died ten months later.

Previous Political Career

- 1782: Member of the Virginia State Legislature.
- 1783: Member of the Confederation Congress (the Congress formed under the Articles of Confederation).
- 1788: Lost election bid for the U.S. House of Representatives to James Madison.
- 1790: Appointed to the U.S. Senate, where he served for four years before resigning his seat to become minister to France.
- 1799: Virginia's twelfth governor.
- 1803: Minister plenipotentiary to France. He helped negotiate the Louisiana Purchase with Robert Livingston.
- 1809: Appointed James Madison's Secretary of State.
- 1814: Appointed James Madison's Secretary of War, while still serving as Secretary of State, to help stategize against the British invasion of Washington D.C.

Presidency

One New England reporter described Monroe's first term in office as the "Era of Good Feelings." The election of 1816 brought with it the Federalist Party's demise, ending the decades-long political divisiveness that had scourged the country.

His first term in office was filled with successes in foreign policy. The Atlantic ports were fortified to ward off any impending attacks, showing foreign countries that America was becoming a stronger and more powerful country. John Quincy Adams, Monroe's secretary of state, helped negotiate many treaties, including the Adams-Onis Treaty with Spain in 1819 that negotiated the purchase of Spanish Florida for five million dollars. As a result, America's landmass spanned the entire Atlantic coastline. Adams also negotiated with Britain to sell the Oregon Territory, which expanded America to the Pacific Ocean.

BTW: Monroe's inauguration was the first to be held outdoors.

With the Flag Act, Congress establishes the modern-day American flag, April 4, 1818

Mississippi becomes a state, December 10, 1817

Illinois becomes a state, December 3, 1818

Alabama becomes a state, December 14, 1819

Maine becomes a state, March 15, 1820

First Term in Office

| 1816 | 1817 | 1818 | 1819 | 1820 |

BTW: Monroe preferred to be called "Colonel Monroe" his whole life, even during his presidency.

ELECTION RESULTS!

Monroe's opponent was Federalist Rufus King, who was a former signer of the Constitution, U.S. Senator from New York, and previous vice presidential candidate. Monroe won all but three states in the Electoral College. King's defeat led to the collapse of the Federalist Party.

- James Monroe — Democratic-Republican Won
- Rufus King — Federalist Won
- Territories

Election of 1816 — Electoral Votes

1st	James Monroe	183
2nd	Rufus King	34

Monroe ran for reelection with no actual opponent, making him the only president besides George Washington to run unopposed. Although John Quincy Adams received a single electoral vote, he didn't actually run for president. William Plumer of New Hampshire voted for Adams to ensure George Washington remained the only president elected unanimously.

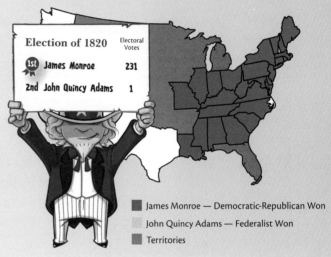

Election of 1820 — Electoral Votes

1st	James Monroe	231
2nd	John Quincy Adams	1

- James Monroe — Democratic-Republican Won
- John Quincy Adams — Federalist Won
- Territories

Panic of 1819

Monroe's domestic policy did not fare as well. The Panic of 1819 spread through the country as a result of mortgage foreclosures, the dollar's inflation, and the recall of bank loans. This caused a financial downturn for many citizens and brought national improvement projects to a halt. However, Monroe won reelection in 1820 in the largest landslide since George Washington, because he ran unopposed.

Slavery

Monroe called slavery the most "menacing issue" in the country at the time. He supported returning illegally captured slaves to their home continent in Africa. In his seventh annual address to Congress in 1823, Monroe expressed his delight in America's exemption from the slave trade, stating, "[T]here is good reason to believe that our flag is now seldom, if at all, disgraced by that traffic [slave trade]."

18th president Ulysses S. Grant is born, April 27, 1822

Brazil gains independence from Portugal, September 7, 1822

Missouri becomes a state, August 10, 1821

19th president Rutherford B. Hayes is born, October 4, 1822

Mexico becomes a republic, October 4, 1824

Simon de Bolivar liberates Peru and becomes president, December 9, 1824

Second Term in Office

| 1821 | 1822 | 1823 | 1824 | 1825 |

BTW: Monroe was the first president to ride on a steamboat.

 BTW: Monroe held the dual positions of Secretary of State and Secretary of War, the only person to hold those two titles simultaneously, helping prevent America from suffering defeat during the War of 1812.

Monroe Doctrine

Monroe also continued to focus on foreign policy. In 1823, he announced his landmark diplomacy plan: the Monroe Doctrine. The doctrine established four things: (1) the U.S. would not interfere in European conflicts; (2) the U.S. would not affect the existing colonies in the Western Hemisphere; (3) the Western Hemisphere was, in essence, "closed" to any European colony shopping; and (4) any attempt by Europe to establish colonies in the Western Hemisphere would be considered an act of war on the U.S.

Post-Presidency

Monroe considered running for governor of Virginia again in 1825, but he decided to stay in retirement. However, he found his banking accounts quite unbalanced; he was $75,000 in debt. Despite his pleas for financial assistance, Congress refused to reimburse him for his trips to Europe on behalf of the United States. He later received a congressional loan of $30,000. Tragedy struck in 1830 when his wife, Elizabeth, died. Monroe sold Ash Lawn and moved in with his daughter in New York City, where he began writing his memoirs and *The Political Writings of James Monroe*, yet he didn't get to finish his writings. He died on July 4, five years to the day after the death of Thomas Jefferson and John Adams.

What Has He Done for Me Lately?

Monroe's success was in foreign policy. Before his presidency, Monroe secured the Louisiana Purchase from France. During his presidency, he expanded America to the Pacific Ocean through the addition of the Oregon Territory and expanded America on the Atlantic side through the annexation of the Florida Territory.

The Monroe Doctrine has affected how American presidents carry out foreign policy measures. Since Monroe introduced the doctrine, many presidents have used the document as the reasoning for engaging in seventy different U.S. military conflicts, ranging from Polk's war with Mexico to Kennedy's invasion of Cuba during the Cold War. The precedents in foreign policy that Monroe set in place are still active today.

PLATFORM SPEECH

Discord does not belong to our system. Union is recommended as well by the free and benign principles of our Government, extending its blessing to every individual, as by the other eminent advantages attending it.

Monroe believed that only through unity and harmony could America reach her greatest prosperity. Monroe spoke these words at his 1817 State of the Union address.

THOUGHTS ON THE CONSTITUTION

Such, then, is the happy Government under which we live—a Government adequate to every purpose for which the social compact is formed; a Government elective in all its branches, under which every citizen may by his merit obtain the highest trust recognized by the Constitution; which contains within it no cause of discord, none to put at variance one portion of the community with another; a Government which protects every citizen in the full enjoyment of his rights, and is able to protect the nation against injustice from foreign powers.

JAMES MONROE

Written by Juliette Turner

MONROE DOCTRINE

December 3, 1823—Yesterday, the Monroe administration delivered a landmark doctrine to the U.S. Congress. This "Monroe Doctrine," the administration said, was formed in an attempt to prevent major European powers from picking on smaller and less powerful South American countries and dragging America into the mess. Secretary of State John Quincy Adams had a large hand in drafting the Monroe Doctrine. The doctrine came shortly after the announcement of the unification of the European "Holy Alliance" (Prussia, Russia, and Austria), France, and Great Britain to help Spain reclaim its South American colonies. Adams released a statement saying that he believed America should do everything short of war to prevent the European countries from reestablishing their hold on the colonies.

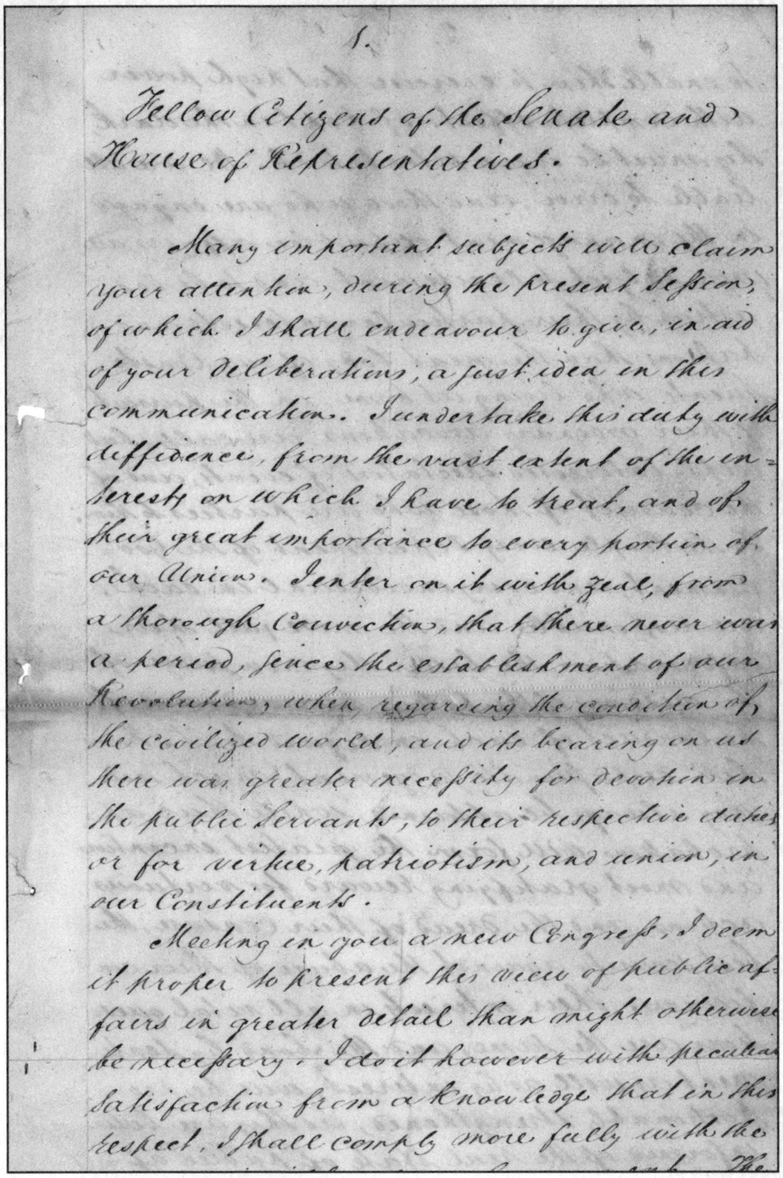

1.

Fellow Citizens of the Senate and House of Representatives.

Many important subjects will claim your attention, during the present Session, of which I shall endeavour to give, in aid of your deliberations, a just idea in this communication. I undertake this duty with diffidence, from the vast extent of the interests on which I have to treat, and of their great importance to every portion of our Union. I enter on it with zeal, from a thorough conviction, that there never was a period, since the establishment of our Revolution, when regarding the condition of the civilized world, and its bearing on us there was greater necessity for devotion in the public servants, to their respective duties or for virtue, patriotism, and union, in our Constituents.

Meeting in you a new Congress, I deem it proper to present this view of public affairs in greater detail than might otherwise be necessary. I do it however with peculiar satisfaction from a knowledge that in this respect, I shall comply more fully with the

Courtesy of the National Archives

STATE OF THE UNION

POPULATION IN 1820
9,638,453

$1 WORTH IN 1817
NOW WORTH
$17.54

$1 WORTH IN 1825
NOW WORTH
$23.81

UNITED STATES DEBT

Jan. 1 1817	*$123,491,965.16*
Jan. 1 1825	*$83,788,432.71*

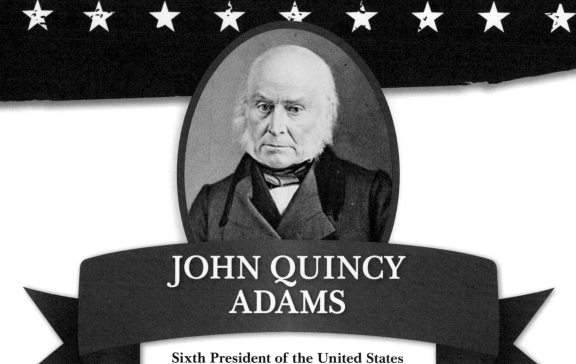

JOHN QUINCY ADAMS

Sixth President of the United States
Nickname: Old Man Eloquent
Term in Office: 1825–1829

The Bottom Line

During John Quincy Adams's term in office, he struggled with push back from a partisan Congress (led by bitter political rival Andrew Jackson), which voted down many of his ideas for reform. However, he did manage to pass multiple national improvement measures, including constructing a canal and improving the Cumberland Road. He attempted to pass other measures to promote the sciences and a national academy, but the one-sided Congress refused to pass them.

FAST STATS

★ Born July 11, 1767, in Braintree, Massachusetts
★ Parents: John and Abigail Adams
★ Died February 23, 1848, in Washington, D.C.; age 80
★ Age upon Start of Term: 57; Age upon Conclusion of Term: 61
★ Religious Affiliation: Unitarian
★ Political Party: Democratic-Republican
★ Height: 5 feet 7 inches
★ Vice President: John C. Calhoun

What Was He Thinking?

Known to be stubborn and rebellious like his father, previous president John Adams, John Quincy Adams never strayed from his beliefs, even if it meant taking unpopular positions. He cared more about preserving the freedoms of the American people and the Constitution than the views of the partisan bureaucrats. Unlike his predecessor James Monroe, Adams believed the federal government should improve roads and initiate other national improvement projects, even if this meant raising taxes slightly. Throughout his life, he was an outspoken opponent to slavery, believing that the trade directly opposed the freedoms of the Declaration of Independence and the Constitution.

Why Should I Care?

John Quincy Adams worked hard to preserve the integrity of the presidency during a time when patronage appointments in the government were highly expected. Although he accomplished comparatively little during his presidency, he did everything within the bounds of the limited presidential powers described in the Constitution. While in office, he attempted to promote the sciences and national education, though the Congress led by his bitter, previous presidential opponent, Andrew Jackson, thwarted his attempts.

Breakin' It Down

Early Life

John Quincy Adams acquired his passion for his country from his father, who was constantly away from home in service to his country, whether it was as a member of the Continental Congress or as president of the United States. Named after his great-grandfather who died two days before his birth, John Quincy Adams had five siblings.

John Quincy attended the local school until the schoolhouse closed when the headmaster left to fight in the Revolution. He kept a journal starting at age eleven and constantly read on his own to increase his knowledge, reading the Bible an hour every morning. As a young teen, he accompanied his father to Paris when he was appointed to help solicit help from the French for the Revolutionary War. Then after his father's new diplomatic appointment as ambassador to the Netherlands, John Quincy moved there with his father.

While there, John Quincy studied first at the Amsterdam Latin Academy, and then transferred to the University of Leyden, although he was only thirteen years old. John Quincy enjoyed fencing, music, art, and studied dance and classic literature.

His life drastically changed when Francis Dana, the newly appointed American minister to Russia, requested that John Quincy accompany him to Russia to serve as his secretary and French translator. John Quincy spent fourteen months in St. Petersburg.

At age eighteen, John Quincy returned to America, having learned many new languages, including French, Latin, Dutch, Greek, Russian, Italian, German, and Spanish. He enrolled in Harvard, yet failed

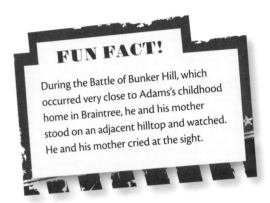

FUN FACT!

During the Battle of Bunker Hill, which occurred very close to Adams's childhood home in Braintree, he and his mother stood on an adjacent hilltop and watched. He and his mother cried at the sight.

Throughout his whole life, John Quincy would rise as early as four a.m. to begin his day by reading the Bible, sometimes in different languages so he could compare translations.

First passenger railroad in England begins, 1825

The Erie Canal opens, October 26, 1825

Joseph-Nicéphore Niépce takes the first photograph, 1826

The Baltimore and Ohio Railroad, the first major railroad in the United States, is chartered, 1827

Ludwig van Beethoven dies, 1827

Leo Tolstoy is born, 1828

The Smithsonian Institute is founded by British scientist James Smithson, who donated $500,000 for its initial founding fund, 1829

Term in Office

1824 · 1825 · 1826 · 1827 · 1828 · 1829

Whig Party: **Established during the presidency of Andrew Jackson in opposition to his policies, the Whig Party was formed primarily by prominent politician, House member, and former presidential candidate Henry Clay. The Whig Party supported businesses and corporations, a market-centered economy, and a strong central government.**

CONGRESSIONAL CORNER
★★★★★★★★★★★★★★★★★★★★★★★

1. **Treaty of St. Louis and Treaty of Washington:** These treaties, ratified in 1825 and 1826, forcibly relocated or negotiated land from the Shawnee Indians and Creek National Indians.

2. **Tariff of 1828:** This tariff, passed on May 24, 1828, raised tariff rates to help American businesses from being overrun by imported goods.

3. **Treaty with Central America of 1825:** This treaty opened trade between Central America and the United States.

★★★★★★★★★★★★★★★★★★★★★★★

his oral examination and was rejected. However, after extensive extra tutoring from his uncle, he was admitted. He joined the Phi Beta Kappa Society and graduated Harvard second of fifty-one in his class and first in speaking skills.

After graduating college, he became a lawyer, yet he did not enjoy the trade. Instead, he wrote a series of editorials for New England newspapers defending President Washington—the "Letters of Publicola," which he wrote under the pseudonym "Publicola," "Marcellus," "Columbus," and "Barneveld." These editorials were seen by President Washington and led to John Quincy Adams's appointment to his first political position.

First Couple

John Quincy Adams married Louisa Catherine Johnson in July 1797 in London, England, in the Tower of London. Together they had four children, three of whom lived into adulthood: George Washington, Jon II, and Charles Francis. Louisa was born in Europe, when her father, Joshua Johnson, was American consul to Great Britain. This makes her the only first lady to have been born outside the United States. Louisa spoke French fluently, kept a journal for many years, and wrote many essays, poems, and plays, although none were ever pub-

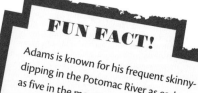

LOUISA ADAMS

lished. In 1828, Adams almost considered not running for reelection at the news of his son's death. After a night of gambling and drinking on a party boat, George Washington Adams fell overboard and drowned. His body was found on a beach about a month later.

Previous Political Career

- 1794: Appointed by President George Washington as minister to the Netherlands. Adams almost declined because he doubted he was qualified enough for the position.
- 1796: Appointed Minister to Portugal.
- 1797: Appointed Minister to Prussia under his father's presidency.
- 1799: Helped negotiate the Prussia-American Treaty of 1799, which opened the first commerce relation and peace treaty between Prussia and America.

FUN FACT!

Adams is known for his frequent skinny-dipping in the Potomac River as early as five in the morning. Once, a female reporter seeking an exclusive interview with the president refused to give Adams his clothes until he agreed.

 BTW: Adams was the first president to be photographed.

- 1802: Elected to the Massachusetts Senate.
- 1803: Appointed to the U.S. Senate.
- 1809: James Madison appointed him minister to Russia.
- 1814: Traveled to Berlin to negotiate the Treaty of Ghent, which ended the War of 1812.
- 1815: Appointed minister to Great Britain.
- 1817: Returned to the U.S. to serve as Monroe's secretary of state and drafted the Monroe Doctrine.

Presidency

John Quincy Adams's presidency was thwarted by congressional gridlock and partisan opposition. Party politics prevented him from accomplishing many of his goals for his presidency. Andrew Jackson, bitter over his loss in the election, held enough sway in Congress to block many of Adams's proposed bills and legislation. However, Adams was able to accomplish a few things, notably increasing national improvement projects and economic reform. He proposed a bill that organized federal workers to extend the Cumberland Road into Ohio and also funded the construction of a canal that connected the Chesapeake Bay and Ohio River.

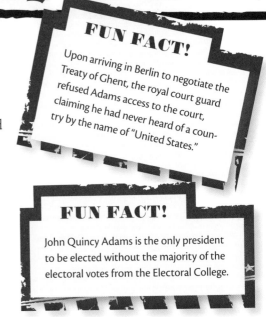

FUN FACT!

Upon arriving in Berlin to negotiate the Treaty of Ghent, the royal court guard refused Adams access to the court, claiming he had never heard of a country by the name of "United States."

FUN FACT!

John Quincy Adams is the only president to be elected without the majority of the electoral votes from the Electoral College.

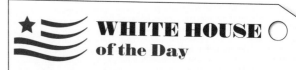

WHITE HOUSE of the Day

During Adams's presidency, cows, horses, and sheep grazed near the White House; security there was nearly nonexistent and anyone could walk in unannounced.

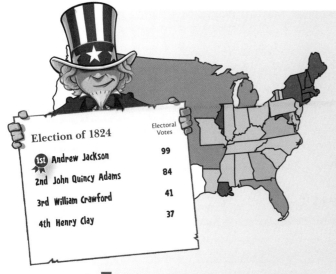

Election of 1824

		Electoral Votes
1st	Andrew Jackson	99
2nd	John Quincy Adams	84
3rd	William Crawford	41
4th	Henry Clay	37

- ■ John Quincy Adams — Democratic-Republican Won
- ■ Andrew Jackson — Democratic-Republican Won
- ■ William Crawford — Democratic-Republican Won
- ■ Henry Clay — Democratic-Republican Won
- ■ Territories

ELECTION RESULTS!

John Quincy Adams didn't win the presidency ... at first. Andrew Jackson won the most popular votes and the most electoral votes, but he failed to reach the required 131 majority because five candidates ran in the election. Thus, as the Constitution directs, the election was handed to the U.S. House of Representatives. Henry Clay, one of the candidates who came in second to last and was knocked from the running, placed his support behind Adams. This was significant because of Clay's influential status as Speaker of the House. As a result, Adams won the election on the first ballot. Yet he made the major mistake of then appointing Clay as secretary of state, causing Andrew Jackson to claim the election was the result of a "corrupt bargain." Jackson, in Congress during Adams's entire presidency, pushed to block all legislation suggested by Adams.

Bad Luck for Reelection

On the economic front, Adams helped pass the Tariff of 1828; however, the tariff led to an increase in consumer prices. This hurt Adams's reelection bid that year. The election of 1828 is known as one of the cruelest campaigns in presidential history, with insults as low as degrading the integrity of the candidates' families and wives. John Quincy Adams lost the election to rival Andrew Jackson. Because of the ill feelings between the two men, Adams refused to stay for Jackson's inauguration. John Adams (the second president) and John Quincy Adams remain the only two presidents to not attend their successors' inaugurations.

Post-Presidency

John Quincy Adams was far from finished serving his country when he left the presidency in 1829. The following year, he ran for a position in the U.S. House of Representatives as a member of the newly formed Whig Party and won, making him the only president to be elected to the House of Representatives after holding the office of the president.

He won reelection eight times, serving for approximately seventeen years. He worked to lower tariff rates and supported the Bank of the United States, becoming outraged over Jackson's attempts to create smaller state banks instead of a national, uniform banking system.

However, even more important was his attack on slavery. He believed slavery ran in direct opposition to the nation's founding principles. He helped to repeal a "gag rule" that prevented Congress members from addressing the question of slavery. The bill was repealed in 1844 in a 108 to 80 vote. His work against slavery extended outside Congress as well. In 1841, he argued before the Supreme Court in the Amistad court ruling on behalf of the slaves who were illegally captured by Spanish traders and ended up on American soil after the slaves mutinied on the ship.

John Quincy Adams died from a stroke he suffered during his House speech against the annexation of Texas in 1848. He believed the Mexican War and annexing Texas were attempts by the Democrats to extend slavery. Upon his stroke, he was taken to the Speaker's chamber nearby and died two days later. John Quincy Adams served his beloved country in every way throughout his entire life, sacrificing much for it.

What Has He Done for Me Lately?

From the start of his career as a diplomat to the end of his career as an influential congressman, John Quincy Adams helped America strive, prosper, and grow. His work as a diplomat helped end the War of 1812 (Treaty of Ghent), his work as secretary of state enlarged America and established her as a world power (Adams-Onis Treaty: addition of Florida; Treaty of 1818 with Great Britain: expansion of the Northwest; Monroe Doctrine: America's role as protector), and his work as a congressman helped to further the abolitionist movement beginning at the time. John Quincy Adams can be thanked for his work in every aspect of American history—from the abolition of slavery to America's foreign policy.

Congressional gridlock: Gridlock occurs in Congress when opposing parties cannot compromise on an issue and so the issue is never addressed.

> Partisanship is dangerous and detrimental. During Adams's time in office, Congress voted down many of his ideas—not because they disagreed with what he was proposing, but because they refused to agree with a man from a different political party. As a result, many of Adams's beneficial proposals were ignored.

BTW: In November of 1846, Adams suffered a stroke. Yet he was back in Congress, as active as ever, within three months.

BTW: Adams owned a pet alligator, which he kept at the White House during his presidency.

Written by Juliette Turner

Superstock

GRANITE RAILWAY OPENED IN MASSACHUSETTS

October 10, 1826—A railway has opened in Quincy, Massachusetts. Named the Granite Railway, this three-mile track will provide a way to carry granite from Quincy to a dock in Milton. From there, boats will carry the stone to Charlestown for construction of the Bunker Hill Monument.

Businessman and state legislator Thomas Handasyd Perkins organized the financing of the new Granite Railway Company, and was designated its president. The railroad was designed and built by railway pioneer Gridley Bryant. He has modified what has already been developed in the industry, but modified it to allow for heavier loads.

The railway will support wagons that will be pulled by horses.

CONSTRUCTION ON THE BALTIMORE AND OHIO RAILROAD BEGINS

July 4, 1828—Today, one of the most patriotic days of the year, the owners of the Baltimore and Ohio Railroad held their groundbreaking ceremony. The last surviving signer of the Declaration of Independence, Charles Carroll, laid the first stone, beginning construction. The Baltimore and Ohio Railroad will be America's first major railroad. With its headquarters in Baltimore, Maryland, the track will span 5,658 miles.

NEW YORK FREES ITS SLAVES

July 4, 1827—Slavery has been legally abolished in the State of New York and all slaves are now free.

The first movement toward the abolition of slavery came in 1781, after the Revolution. In 1790, one in three blacks in New York was free, and steps toward abolition accumulated. In 1799, the legislature passed a law for gradual abolition, which stated that children of slaves born after July 4 of that year to be legally free. But they had to serve an extended period of indentured servitude: to the age of 28 for males and to the age of 25 for females.

In 1817, a bill was passed that became effective today that frees all slaves born before July 4, 1799. The African-American community has been celebrating their emancipation with a long parade through New York City.

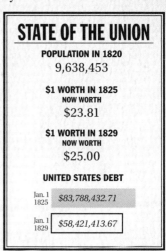

STATE OF THE UNION

POPULATION IN 1820
9,638,453

$1 WORTH IN 1825
NOW WORTH
$23.81

$1 WORTH IN 1829
NOW WORTH
$25.00

UNITED STATES DEBT

Jan. 1 1825	$83,788,432.71
Jan. 1 1829	$58,421,413.67

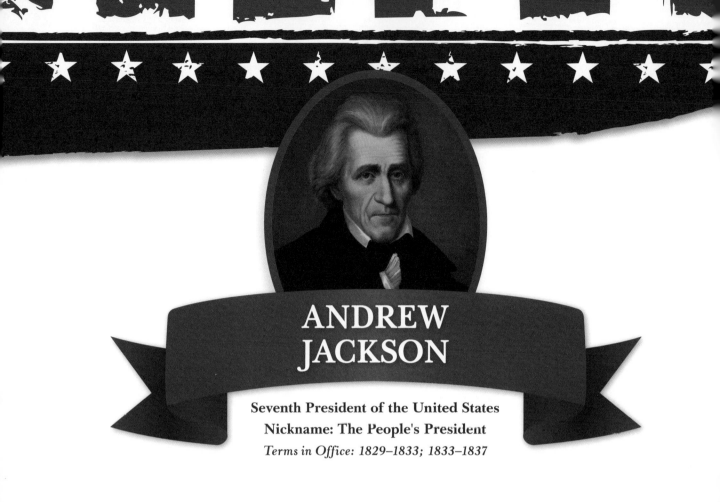

ANDREW JACKSON

Seventh President of the United States
Nickname: The People's President
Terms in Office: 1829–1833; 1833–1837

The Bottom Line

Andrew Jackson was America's first president from the Democrat party. During his first term, he forcibly relocated thousands of Native Americans. During his second term, he enacted policies that profoundly affected America politically and economically. He protected the country by preventing South Carolina from seceding during the Nullification Crisis of 1832. He defunded the Bank of the United States, leaving the nation without a central bank to monitor the nation's money.

FAST STATS

★ Born March 15, 1767, in Waxhaw, South Carolina
★ Parents: Andrew and Elizabeth Hutchinson Jackson
★ Died June 8, 1845, in Nashville, Tennessee; age 78
★ Age upon Start of First Term: 61; Age upon End of First Term: 65
★ Age upon Start of Second Term: 65; Age upon End of Second Term: 69
★ Religious Affiliation: Presbyterian
★ Political Party: Democrat
★ Height Chart: 6 feet 1 inch
★ Vice President: John C. Calhoun

What Was He Thinking?

Andrew Jackson believed state governments held more power and importance than the federal government, but during his presidency, he determined that state governments cannot overrule federal laws. Jackson opposed nullification because he believed it undermined the federal government's authority and endangered the unity of the nation. He also believed presidential elections should be based on the popular vote (the people's vote) instead of the Electoral College.

Why Should I Care?

During his presidency, Andrew Jackson permanently shaped America in two ways. The first was during the Nullification Crisis of 1832. Jackson clarified that states were sovereign, but to a point—they could not pick and choose which federal laws they would enforce. Jackson established that all states must abide by all federal laws. By using force, Jackson also kept the country intact. The second change occurred with the Indian Removal Act. By forcing thousands of Native Americans to relocate onto desolate new lands west of the Mississippi River, Jackson not only permanently changed the lives of many Americans, but he also altered the groundwork of the nation for all eternity.

LIBERTY Language

Nullification: the idea that a state can disregard federal laws if the state disagrees with the law.

Breakin' It Down

Early Life

Andrew Jackson was a first-generation American. His parents and two older brothers migrated to America in 1765. Three weeks before Jackson was born, his father died in a logging accident at age twenty-nine. His mother raised her three sons by herself, striving to instill good values in them and encouraging them "to expend their lives, if it should become necessary in defending and supporting the natural rights of man."

> While Jackson was a prisoner of war, a British officer demanded he shine his shoes, and Jackson refused. The soldier responded by striking Jackson across the forehead with a sword, leaving a lifelong scar.

Jackson had no formal education. He attended a frontier schoolhouse, which only held school when convenient, where he only learned the basics of reading and writing. Nevertheless, he was a talented speaker and became known as a great orator. In 1776, the town called on him to read aloud a new document sent from Philadelphia—the Declaration of Independence.

Jackson joined the Continental Army at age thirteen. He was the last president who fought in the Revolutionary War, and he was held as a prisoner of war.

Shortly after being released from captivity at the age of fourteen, Jackson became an orphan. As his mother was on her way to help care for sick and injured American soldiers, she died of cholera and was buried in an unmarked grave. Jackson received a small inheritance, but he gambled it away on horse racing, card games, and cockfighting. He became a teacher to support himself, studying law at the same time. Later he became an attorney, and he quickly realized he wanted to play a larger part in society.

First Couple

Andrew Jackson married Rachel Donelson Robard in 1791. However, her previous husband, an extremely abusive man, had never officially filed for divorce, although she believed the divorce had been filed. Hearing about her marriage to Jackson, her husband filed for divorce officially in 1794, but this time on the grounds of adultery. Because of their confusing and near-scandalous marriage, Jackson fought (often in duels) to defend his wife's reputation. Although they never had children of their own, Rachel and Jackson adopted two boys: Rachel's nephew and an orphaned Native American boy (an act of kindness contradictory to Jackson's anti-Native American political stances). During Jackson's presidential bid, Rachel's character and reputation were attacked viciously. She died of a heart attack on December 22, shortly after Jackson's presidential victory in 1829. It is reported that he clung so tightly to his wife's body that they had to pry her from his arms. Jackson blamed the vicious campaigning for his wife's death.

RACHEL JACKSON

BTW: Rachel Jackson smoked a pipe!

LIBERTY Language

Solicitor General: The chief lawyer under the attorney general, who represents law cases that are first heard in state courts and could possibly reach the Supreme Court.

CONGRESSIONAL CORNER
★★★★★★★★★★★★★★★★★★★★★★

1. **Indian Removal Act of 1830:** This act forcibly removed thousands of Native Americans from their homeland to territories created by the federal government.

2. **Treaty of Dancing Rabbit Creek, September 27, 1830:** This was the first removal treaty after the passage of the Indian Removal Act, negotiated with the Choctaw Indians.

3. **Tariff of 1832:** This tariff raised the national tariff rate and consequentially initiated the Nullification Crisis of 1832.

4. **Compromise Tariff of 1833:** This compromise worked to resolve the Nullification Crisis by lowering tariffs.

5. **Force Bill of 1833:** This bill allowed tax collectors to use arms and force when collecting tax revenue.

6. **Treaty of New Echota, December 29, 1835:** This treaty ceded all lands of the Cherokee Indians east of the Mississippi to the United States.

★★★★★★★★★★★★★★★★★★★★★★★★

Previous Political Career

- 1788: Solicitor general for the western territory of North Carolina, which would soon become Tennessee.
- 1796: Jackson helped draft the Tennessee Constitution, which led to Tennessee's admittance to the Union. He wanted all free men to be able to vote, not just those who owned land.
- 1796: Jackson became Tennessee's first representative to the U.S. House of Representatives.
- 1798: Appointed to the Tennessee Supreme Court.
- 1821: Served as military governor of Florida.
- 1822: Elected to the U.S. Senate.

Presidency

Andrew Jackson was elected mainly because of his appeal to the working class, farmers, and laborers. He was known as "the People's President," and during his presidency, the White House was known as "the People's House." Jackson's people-oriented approach led one observer to note, "It was the people's day, and the People's President, and the People would rule."

The National Bank

Jackson's terms in office were was marked by the controversy around renewing the charter for Alexander Hamilton's Bank of the United States. It regulated currency (monitoring how much was taken out, how much it was worth), and was controlled by the Department of Treasury.

Emily Dickinson is born, 1830

21st president Chester Arthur is born, October 5, 1829

The Indian Removal Act is passed, May 28, 1830

The French invade Algeria, 1830

Belgium declares independence from Great Britain, 1831

20th president James A. Garfield is born, November 19, 1831

The Nullification Crisis, November 19, 1832

Louisa May Alcott is born, 1832

The first Democratic Convention takes place, May 21, 1832

First Term in Office

| 1828 | 1829 | 1830 | 1831 | 1832 |

BTW: Andrew Jackson was the first president to ride on a train.

MILITARY CAREER

 BTW: Jackson was the only president to serve in both the Revolutionary War and the War of 1812.

Jackson in the War of 1812

During the War of 1812, America was fighting two fronts: the British at sea and on the East Coast and the Native Americans in the southeast. Jackson was there for both. Jackson fought in the Battle of Horseshoe Bend in March of 1814, in what is now modern-day Alabama and Georgia. He then moved to Pensacola, Florida, where he and his soldiers captured a British fort. Jackson achieved national fame after the Battle of New Orleans, where his army of 5,000 men defeated a British army of 9,000. American sharpshooters killed 300 British, wounded 1,200, and captured many more. Meanwhile, only thirteen Americans were killed. However, Jackson remained a humble leader, once lending his horse to wounded soldiers and walking alongside his foot soldiers.

Jackson and the Seminole Indians

Jackson became commander of the Southern District of the U.S. Army in 1815. During this time, southern Georgia was suffering from frequent attacks by Seminole Indians. Believing that the British were orchestrating the Native American attacks from Florida, Jackson led his soldiers in a retaliatory attack on the Seminoles, advancing into Florida territory and killing two British men. Their deaths at the hands of an American sparked international outrage between America, Britain, and Spain, causing Congress to censure Jackson. Ironically, it was Jackson's future presidential opponent and enemy, John Quincy Adams, who persuaded then current president James Monroe to dismiss the charges against Jackson. The matter was dropped and international turmoil was avoided.

Jackson continued serving his country in the army by protecting Americans from Seminole raids in southern Georgia. These raids and Jackson's involvement later led to the Adams-Onis Treaty, where America annexed the Florida Territory from Spain.

Upon Jackson's arrival into office, the bank had branches in twenty-nine cities, handled one in five of the country's loans, and handled one in three of all American bank deposits. Despite the bank's extreme influence on America's financial situation, it was largely unregulated by the government or federal laws, and eight million dollars were held by foreign investors. Jackson wanted to take away the bank's funding and distribute the money to smaller state banks.

Congress strongly opposed Jackson's idea for state banks, calling them "pet banks," and in 1832 Congress passed a bill for renewing the funding of the established National Bank. However, Jackson vetoed this bill, and he successfully removed the bank's funding in 1833.

Unfortunately, Jackson's idea backfired; the dollar lost value quickly because it was no longer federally regulated. The federal government could no longer monitor how much money was printed, and states started printing money with no actual value—there was not enough gold and silver to back the money being printed. This led to inflation.

BTW: Andrew Jackson was the first president without a college education. This lack of education made him more appealing to Middle America; likewise, Jackson found Middle America more appealing than the educated and sophisticated circles of society.

Slavery is abolished in Great Britain, 1833

The revolt in Spain, 1833

23rd president Benjamin Harrison is born, August 20, 1833

Edgar Degas is born, 1834

The second Seminole War begins, 1835

Mark Twain (Samuel Clemens) is born, 1835

The Battle of the Alamo, February 23–March 6, 1836

The Bank of the United States expires, March 1, 1836

The Texan War of Independence takes place, 1836

Arkansas becomes a state, 1836

Michigan becomes a state, 1837

Queen Victoria ascends to the throne in Great Britain, 1837

Second Term in Office

| 1833 | 1834 | 1835 | 1836 | 1837 |

ELECTION RESULTS!

After losing the election of 1824, Jackson was bitter and worked in every way possible to block any legislation with John Quincy Adams's name on it. In 1828, Jackson emerged as a political candidate with a vengeance, entering into one of the most aggressive, fierce, and competitive political campaigns of American history.

Jackson, still fuming over the previous election, accused Adams of corruption, elitism, and illegal activities (all false accusations). Adams in turn attacked Jackson's wife and fueled rumors against her reputation and character. Jackson won, taking every state south of the Potomac and west of the Alleghenies. Jackson was elected by a coalition of southern and middle-state voters that later developed into the Democrat Party.

Henry Clay emerged as Jackson's opponent in the election of 1832. The main campaign issue surrounded the Bank of the United States and Jackson's plan to revamp the entire treasury of the U.S. Although Jackson's reforms were radical, the American people supported them because of the scandals and corruption surrounding the current bank system. Jackson won in a landslide victory.

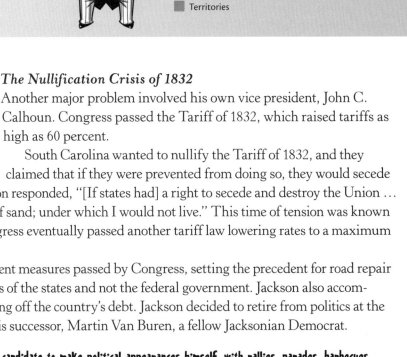

Election of 1828	Electoral Votes
1st Andrew Jackson	178
2nd John Quincy Adams	83

■ Andrew Jackson — Democrat Won
■ John Quincy Adams — Republican Won
■ Territories

Election of 1832	Electoral Votes
1st Andrew Jackson	219
2nd Henry Clay	49
3rd Other	18

■ Andrew Jackson — Democrat Won
■ Henry Clay — Republican Won
■ Other — Independant Democrat Won
■ Territories

FUN FACT!

On his inauguration day, Jackson opened the doors to the White House, but a mob of people flooded the house, broke or ruined thousands of dollars of furniture, and destroyed carpets with mud and food, forcing Jackson to escape through a side entrance and lodge at a room in the Gadsby's Hotel.

The Nullification Crisis of 1832

Another major problem involved his own vice president, John C. Calhoun. Congress passed the Tariff of 1832, which raised tariffs as high as 60 percent.

South Carolina wanted to nullify the Tariff of 1832, and they claimed that if they were prevented from doing so, they would secede from the Union. Jackson responded, "[If states had] a right to secede and destroy the Union … then indeed is our Constitution a rope of sand; under which I would not live." This time of tension was known as the Nullification Crisis of 1832. Congress eventually passed another tariff law lowering rates to a maximum of 20 percent.

He vetoed many national improvement measures passed by Congress, setting the precedent for road repair and canal upkeep to remain in the hands of the states and not the federal government. Jackson also accomplished the near-impossible task of paying off the country's debt. Jackson decided to retire from politics at the close of his second term, handpicking his successor, Martin Van Buren, a fellow Jacksonian Democrat.

 BTW: Jackson was the first candidate to make political appearances himself, with rallies, parades, barbecues, slogans, and more. Before this election, candidates had relied on stand-ins to campaign for them.

THOUGHTS ON THE CONSTITUTION

> The Constitution is still the object of our reverence, the bond of our Union, our defense in danger, the source of our prosperity in peace.

Post-Presidency

Jackson retired to "The Hermitage," where he bred racehorses and enjoyed his retirement. But the economic downturn in 1837, a direct result of his closing the National Bank, forced him to borrow money to avoid selling his property.

Jackson also suffered from ill health. He had many duels, even before becoming president, and he was dependent on a cane because of injuries he incurred. He even carried around a bullet that had been lodged an inch from his heart in one of his many duels over a horse racing bet. In the end, Jackson had back problems, and dropsy (edema) made his body swell so much that he could no longer lie flat in bed. Tuberculosis and heart failure took him at the age of seventy-eight. More than three thousand people attended his funeral procession.

POLITICAL PARTIES

★★★★★★★★★★★★★★★★★★★★★★★★★

The election of 1828 and Jackson's inauguration as president marked the start of the modern party system and the formation of the Democrat Party.

Jacksonian Democrats: The Democrat Party was formed primarily by political mastermind Martin Van Buren. Formed during Andrew Jackson's presidential campaign, the party believed in limiting federal spending and decreasing the size of government. They championed the middle and working sector of America. The Democrats also strongly supported separation of church and state. Andrew Jackson and the Democrats helped introduce the "spoils system" to the federal government, a system through which loyal party members were awarded government positions.

Anti-Jacksonians: This faction would become known as the Whig Party, a faction in Congress that organized in disagreement to Jackson's presidency and his policies.

What Has He Done for Me Lately?

The time from 1828 to 1848 is known today as "the Age of Jackson" or "the Jackson Era." Andrew Jackson was the first president elected by a modern-day political party, and he started the line of presidents who championed "the common man." He worked to balance the powers of the presidency and the views of the states, and supported expansion of America. However, history would have remembered Jackson even if he had failed to become president. His leadership in the Battle of New Orleans resulted in one of the major American victories in the War of 1812—a war that was neither a real American nor British victory. It gave the American people something to rejoice about in an otherwise anticlimactic war.

PLATFORM SPEECH

> The rich and powerful too often bend the acts of government to their selfish purposes [and could] destroy our republican institutions.

> Jackson wanted to protect America and persuade the people that a simple, democratic government free of corruption and patronage is the best government on earth.

ANDREW JACKSON

 BTW: Jackson's last words were. "Oh do not cry. Be good children and we shall all meet in heaven."

Presidential Times

★ ★ ★ ★ ANDREW JACKSON Terms in Office 1829–1837 ★ ★ ★ ★

Written by Juliette Turner

JACKSON'S VIEWS ON NATIVE AMERICAN SETTLEMENT

May 28, 1830—Jackson signed into law the Indian Removal Act, ordering the forced removal of tens of thousands of Native Americans to lands west of the Mississippi. This act has freed twenty-five million acres of land for white settlement. It also comes as another drastic action taken by Jackson in regard to Native American affairs. One congressman referred to the Indian Removal Act as "inconsistent with the plainest principles of moral honesty."

• • •

August 5, 1832—In early March of this year, the Supreme Court decided, in Worcester v. Georgia, that the individual states had no authority to intervene in affairs with Native Americans. The court ruled that Native American tribes must be viewed as nations, thus making Native American affairs the concern of the federal government. However, President Jackson has always believed that states should be in charge of dealing with the Native Americans within their borders. Sticking to his own personal beliefs, Jackson has decided to ignore this court ruling and instead follow his own beliefs on the issue.

A PRESIDENT OF THE PEOPLE

March 6, 1829—Andrew Jackson's inauguration was a sight to be seen. A great crowd gathered to hear him speak, and when he emerged (in solid black because of his wife's recent death), the people erupted in deafening applause. It seemed "to shake the very ground…ten thousands upturned and exultant human faces, radiant with sudden joy," said one observer. After taking his oath of office, Jackson kissed the Bible (the first to do so since President George Washington), causing the people to cheer even more. He delivered a short, ten-minute speech, mounted his white stallion, and led the crowd to the White House, their White House.

CENSORING THE PRESIDENCY

March 28, 1834—Censored not once but twice! Jackson was first censored for his rash actions in the Spanish Florida Territory, but today Congress moved to censor him again for his veto of the legislation creating the Second National Bank. However, Jackson has many allies in Congress, and they have successfully erased the second censor from the congressional record.

ASSASSINATION ATTEMPT!

January 30, 1835—Today, Andrew Jackson narrowly escaped death, after being attacked by Richard Lawrence. Thankfully, the bullet never reached Jackson. Always one to duel, after the shot was fired, Jackson actually confronted the man and chased him with his cane. Lawrence has been deemed insane and will not be criminally charged.

THE DEATH OF CHIEF JUSTICE JOHN MARSHALL

July 7, 1835—After serving on the nation's highest court for almost thirty-five years, Supreme Court Chief Justice John Marshall passed away yesterday. Rumor in Washington, D.C., is that he will be replaced by Roger Taney in the near future.

STATE OF THE UNION

POPULATION IN 1830
12,866,020,

$1 WORTH IN 1801
NOW WORTH
$25.00

$1 WORTH IN 1809
NOW WORTH
$24.38

UNITED STATES DEBT

Jan. 1 1829	$58,421,413.67
Jan. 1 1837	$336,957.83

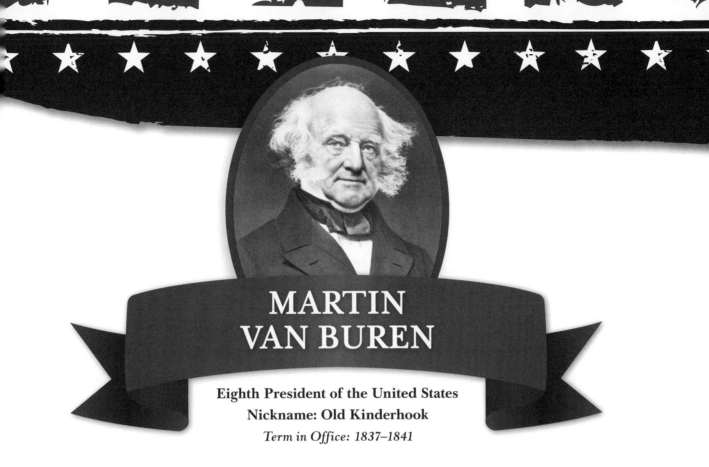

MARTIN VAN BUREN

Eighth President of the United States
Nickname: Old Kinderhook
Term in Office: 1837–1841

The Bottom Line

During Martin Van Buren's term in office, America suffered an economic collapse caused by the radical banking policies of previous president Andrew Jackson. This was known as the Panic of 1837.

What Was He Thinking?

Martin Van Buren was a Jacksonian Democrat, and he in fact helped form the party, which became the modern-day Democrat Party. He hoped this party would champion and preserve the ideals in which he believed: limiting the policies of the federal government and protecting the government and the people from interference by foreign countries. He believed states should be granted power over certain aspects of the country, such as banking. However, when he became president, he was forced to face the economic challenges of the day, and he worked to recentralize the banks under the control of the national government.

FAST STATS

★ Born December 5, 1782, in Kinderhook, New York
★ Parents: Abraham and Maria Hoe Van Alen Van Buren
★ Died July 24, 1862, in Kinderhook, New York; age 79
★ Age upon Start of Term: 54; Age upon Conclusion of Term: 58
★ Religious Affiliation: Dutch Reformed
★ Political Party: Democrat
★ Height: 5 feet 6 inches
★ Vice President: Richard Mentor Johnson

Why Should I Care?

Martin Van Buren's major accomplishment during his presidency lasted in America for almost a century. The Independent Treasury System,

 BTW: Van Buren was the first president born after the Declaration of Independence was signed.

which he helped form in response to the Panic of 1837, lasted until 1913. The Independent Treasury System took over Andrew Jackson's state banks and collected, stored, and disbursed public revenue. This treasury system was more regulated by the government. Van Buren initiated a heavy government regulation of the treasury system so that another episode of unchecked printing and loaning (which is what caused the Panic of 1837) could be avoided.

Breakin' It Down

Early Life

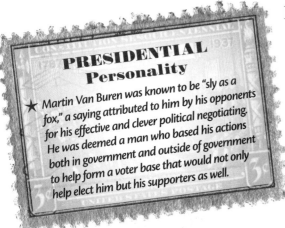

PRESIDENTIAL Personality

★ Martin Van Buren was known to be "sly as a fox," a saying attributed to him by his opponents for his effective and clever political negotiating. He was deemed a man who based his actions both in government and outside of government to help form a voter base that would not only help elect him but his supporters as well.

Martin Van Buren was born into a Dutch family in the Dutch village of Kinderhook, New York. In fact, Van Buren's first language was not English, but Dutch. His father was a farmer and an innkeeper for an inn frequently visited by politicians—such as Alexander Hamilton and Aaron Burr—on their way to political activities. He grew up among his seven siblings, three of whom were half siblings. He had little formal education but quickly became known as an impressive orator. He left his one-room schoolhouse at age thirteen and started working at a law office by fourteen. He even gave the closing arguments in front of a town judge at age fifteen. His political involvement began three years later when, at age eighteen, he campaigned for Thomas Jefferson.

First Couple

Martin Van Buren's wife never got to enjoy the White House. She died at age thirty-five and Martin never remarried. In 1807, Van Buren married Hannah Hoes, who was also Dutch and from his hometown. They spoke Dutch fluently and it was their main language of communication. Hannah bore five children, four of whom lived to adulthood, before she succumbed to tuberculosis in 1819. Van Buren became the third widower to assume the presidency, and with his four sons being bachelors when he became president, the post of first lady was vacant for quite some time. That was, however, until his oldest son, Abraham, married in 1838, giving the first lady duties to his wife, Angelica, who received a little help from the ever-present Dolley Madison.

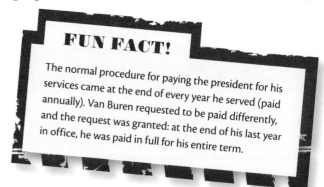

FUN FACT!

The normal procedure for paying the president for his services came at the end of every year he served (paid annually). Van Buren requested to be paid differently, and the request was granted: at the end of his last year in office, he was paid in full for his entire term.

The First Opium War between China and the British begins, 1839

Charles Dickens publishes *Oliver Twist*, 1838

Iowa Territory forms from Wisconsin Territory, 1838

Upper and Lower Canada are united, 1840

British Queen Victoria marries Prince Albert, 1840

Painter Claude Monet is born, 1840

Supreme Court Justice Oliver Wendell Holmes is born, 1841

Great Britain claims Hong Kong after winning the First Opium War, 1841

Term in Office

1836   1837   1838   1839   1840   1841

Previous Political Career

- 1812: Elected state senator in New York, working to abolish the debtors' prisons, which had existed for decades.
- 1816: Named New York's attorney general at age thirty-three.
- 1820: Founded a political group called the Albany Regency: the first political machine to emerge in Amercan politics, controlling the political elections of New York State for eighteen years through the "spoils system" and party discipline.
- 1821: Appointed to New York's second constitutional convention, which worked to modify and amend the state's constitution.
- 1821: Elected to the U.S. Senate. Van Buren was the key opponent to John Quincy Adams's national improvement measures, such as proposals for a national academy and promotion of sciences, and he used his influence to block them successfully.
- 1828: Resigned from the Senate after winning the election for governor of New York. As governor, he worked to create a coalition of supporters from the north and the south to help ensure Andrew Jackson's presidential victory.
- 1829: Secretary of state under Andrew Jackson. During this time he worked to open a trade route to the West Indies through successful treaty negotiations, gained repayment from the French for American naval ships destroyed during the Napoleonic Wars in Europe, and initiated the first peace treaty with the Ottoman Empire, which granted Americans access to the Black Sea.

LIBERTY Language

Debtors' prison: A prison established for individuals who were unable to repay their debts on time.

> As to the Presidency, the two happiest days of my life were those of my entrance upon the office and my surrender of it.

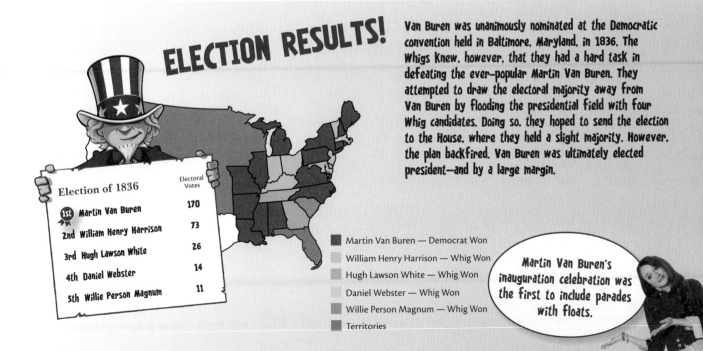

ELECTION RESULTS!

Van Buren was unanimously nominated at the Democratic convention held in Baltimore, Maryland, in 1836. The Whigs knew, however, that they had a hard task in defeating the ever-popular Martin Van Buren. They attempted to draw the electoral majority away from Van Buren by flooding the presidential field with four Whig candidates. Doing so, they hoped to send the election to the House, where they held a slight majority. However, the plan backfired. Van Buren was ultimately elected president—and by a large margin.

Election of 1836

		Electoral Votes
1st	Martin Van Buren	170
2nd	William Henry Harrison	73
3rd	Hugh Lawson White	26
4th	Daniel Webster	14
5th	Willie Person Magnum	11

- Martin Van Buren — Democrat Won
- William Henry Harrison — Whig Won
- Hugh Lawson White — Whig Won
- Daniel Webster — Whig Won
- Willie Person Magnum — Whig Won
- Territories

> Martin Van Buren's inauguration celebration was the first to include parades with floats.

Presidency

The unfortunate series of events that plagued Van Buren's term, and ultimately denied him a second term, was not directly his fault. Van Buren inherited many of the problems from the previous president, Andrew Jackson. However, Van Buren did contribute to the problems; his work as Jackson's advisor helped initiate the defunding of the national bank, which became the center of the country's economic woes. Van Buren had not been in office even a year when the Panic of 1837 spread throughout the country.

CONGRESSIONAL CORNER

1. Proclamations of Neutrality: To avoid a war with Canada, proclamations of neutrality were issued as tensions along the Canadian border rose in 1838.

2. Independent Treasury Act of 1840: This act called for a complete separation of the banks and the states with the establishment of an Independent Treasury, which was a system designed to hold government funds outside of the national banking system.

Panic!

The Panic, caused by state banks using federal money to make loans to customers who could not always pay back their loans, was the worst economic collapse the country experienced until the Great Depression almost a century later. Of the 850 banks in America at the time, 343 declared bankruptcy and 62 partially failed. Unemployment reached double digits and businesses began declaring bankruptcy as well. To make matters worse, New Yorkers began raiding food warehouses, which led to mob violence and protests over the lack of food.

This depression lasted six years. Van Buren struggled to correct the crisis, but to little avail. He succeeded in cutting the government's spending by twenty percent, but at the same time he opposed public work projects that would have remedied the growing unemployment numbers. He was forced to undo much of Jackson's bank reconstruction, because that appeared to be the only way to stop the economic collapse. The Independent Treasury System was signed into law in 1840 and lasted as the country's federal banking system until 1913.

THOUGHTS ON THE CONSTITUTION

For myself, therefore, I desire to declare that the principle that will govern me in the high duty to which my country calls me is a strict adherence to the letter and spirit of the Constitution as it was designed by those who framed it.

War Cries

To make matters worse, hostilities and tension arose between Americans and British Canadians over the border between Maine and New Brunswick. This period of increased tensions became known as the Aroostook War. Militias were formed and summoned on both sides of the border, but war acts did not occur until the Canadians seized the U.S. ship *Caroline* and killed an American citizen, Amos Durfee.

The American people called for all-out war, but Van Buren took the less popular route of diplomatic negotiations. The conflict was resolved by the Webster-Ashburton Treaty in 1842. The whole time, Van Buren's popularity and approval seemed to steadily decrease.

Native American Policies and Slavery

Van Buren followed in his predecessor's footsteps in regard to policies with the Native Americans. During his term in office, he supported the efforts to forcibly relocate the Cherokee Indians.

In regard to slavery, by Van Buren's inauguration, 274 abolitionist societies had been formed in New York State alone. However, Van Buren's personal stance on slavery seemed to vacillate throughout his political career. He grew up in a household with domestic slaves and once owned a slave himself (although the slave ran away and was not replaced). When campaigning during the presidential election of 1836, he promoted the gag rule in the U.S. House and even sent surrogates to break up New York abolitionist meetings to increase his standing in the south. During his tenure as president, he disregarded any abolitionist attempts, even staying neutral (and commanding his cabinet to do the same) during the controversial Amistad case. He believed the issue of slavery—and whether or not to allow slavery in new territories—would destroy the union. Van Buren even opposed the annexation of Texas to avoid the issue of slavery at all costs.

Up for Reelection

Though Van Buren's popularity seemed to steadily decrease during his presidency, the Democratic Convention unanimously nominated him again in the election of 1840. It was the first election where the two highly organized parties held political rallies, relied on surrogate and candidate speeches, and led torchlight parades to spread their candidate's message.

Despite gallant campaign efforts, Van Buren lost to William Henry Harrison, making him the third U.S. president to lose in a bid for reelection. Although Van Buren's actions were unpopular at the time, his actions benefited America. The reinstitution of the federal bank helped reverse the Panic, Van Buren's banking system supported America for almost a century, and avoiding war with Canada and Great Britain not only saved American lives but protected the country as a whole.

Post-Presidency

Van Buren remained active in politics despite his defeat for presidential reelection. In fact, he ran for president again in 1848, but this time as a candidate for the Free Soil Party. The Free Soil Party was the first real third party (not one of the two major political parties) in American history, and Van Buren won 10 percent of the vote. Before his third presidential run, however, he became the first former American president to tour Europe. He also authored an autobiography, which was published five years after his death: *An Inquiry into the Origin and Course of Political Parties in the United States.* Despite his neutrality and inaction on the issue of slavery during his time in America's political field, Van Buren later became an avid opponent of slavery. He even wrote "The Barnburner Manifesto," which explained his position against the expansion of slavery.

What Has He Done for Me Lately?

Martin Van Buren was the leader in forming the Democrat Party. This party has lasted in American politics since Andrew Jackson's candidacy all the way to political campaigns today. Although the party's vision has changed over the years, Van Buren can be credited with helping form the party system of today. His work in uniting political supporters formed the "Jacksonian Era," which elected Democratic presidents for almost twenty years.

PLATFORM SPEECH

Our forefathers were deeply impressed with the delicacy of [slavery] and they treated it with a forbearance so evidently wise that in spite of every sinister foreboding it never until the present period disturbed the tranquility of our common good.

In his State of the Union address, Van Buren recognized that if they had attempted to abolish the trade in the Constitution, the Constitution would never have been ratified.

MARTIN VAN BUREN

Written by Juliette Turner

CONGRESSIONAL GAG RULE OF 1837

December 4, 1844—After much pleading and advocating on behalf of John Quincy Adams and other pro-abolitionists, the gag rule has now been repealed. The U.S. House of Representatives adopted a gag rule, a regulation that prohibits discussing certain matters, on the subject of slavery in 1837. This meant that no member of Congress could "bring to the floor" or discuss the abolition of slavery or any discussion on the matter, whatsoever.

MARTIN VAN RUIN?

January 12, 1842—Sometimes known as "Little Magician" or the "Red Fox of Kinderhook" because of his sly politics and fox-like facial appearance, Martin Van Buren's list of nicknames didn't end when he became president. He used his most notable nickname, Old Kinderhook, to sign many of the bills placed on his desk while president; he would initial the bills "OK," a word not used frequently until after his leave from office. His most insulting nickname came during the Panic of 1837, when his opponent pegged him "Martin Van Ruin."

TRAIL OF TEARS

December 5, 1838—The process of Native American removal began under the presidency of Andrew Jackson when he ordered U.S. soldiers to forcibly remove them from their homelands in the American southeast to relocate them in "Indian Territory" west of the Mississippi.

The relentless and unforgiving process is set to continue until almost all Native Americans are relocated. One of these removals in a series of forced relocation has been called the Trail of Tears. Martin Van Buren sent 1,700 American soldiers to forcibly remove the Cherokees from the southeast region of the country.

Along the 1,200 mile march, an estimated 5,000 Native Americans died from whooping cough, dysentery, cholera, or starvation. This tragic episode is only one of the marches that have been forced upon the Native Americans by the government. It has added to a death toll that was already shockingly large.

WRONG TIMING

August 10, 1837—As the country suffers from economic instability and many Americans remain unemployed, Martin Van Buren has taken on the task of redecorating the White House.

He is pleased to introduce the "Blue Room," which is an oval-shaped salon that has been painted a royal blue color.

Many United States citizens have protested these house improvements, stating that they are opulent and indulgent. His presidential ratings have dropped quite a bit since the redesign plans were released.

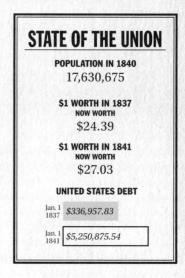

STATE OF THE UNION

POPULATION IN 1840
17,630,675

$1 WORTH IN 1837
NOW WORTH
$24.39

$1 WORTH IN 1841
NOW WORTH
$27.03

UNITED STATES DEBT

Jan. 1 1837	$336,957.83
Jan. 1 1841	$5,250,875.54

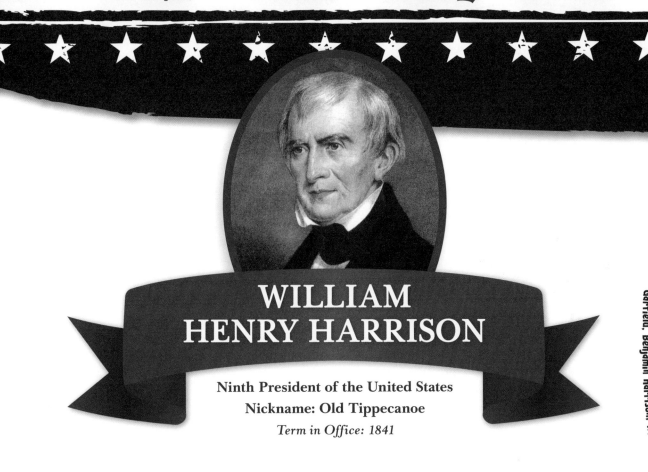

WILLIAM HENRY HARRISON

Ninth President of the United States
Nickname: Old Tippecanoe
Term in Office: 1841

The Bottom Line

William Henry Harrison was president for only one month before he died from pneumonia. He leaves very little mark on the presidency, and we don't know what kind of president Harrison would have been, but many speculate that Harrison would have proved himself a man who could hold his own despite an overbearing and controlling party.

What Was He Thinking?

Today, we probably know more about William Henry Harrison's beliefs than the people who actually voted for him. During his campaign, the Whig Party made sure Harrison's proslavery and high-tariff beliefs were kept quiet and away from voters' ears. However, despite these two controversial beliefs, Harrison believed in a limited federal government as well as in the importance of the constitutional checks and balances on leaders. He prioritized the needs of the people, because he aptly realized he was sent to represent the people's needs and desires, not his own or his party's.

FAST STATS

★ Born February 9, 1773, in Charles City County, Virginia
★ Parents: Benjamin and Elizabeth Bassett Harrison
★ Died April 4, 1841, in Washington, D.C.; age 68
★ Age upon Start of Term: 68
★ Religious Affiliation: Episcopalian
★ Political Party: Whig
★ Height: 5 feet 8 inches
★ Vice President: John Tyler

BTW: Harrison was the first of eight presidents to be born in Ohio. After him were Ulysses Grant, Rutherford Hayes, James Garfield, Benjamin Harrison, William McKinley, William Taft, and Warren Harding.

 BTW: Harrison was the first president to arrive in Washington, D.C., by train.

Harrison advised the people to always check their rulers and prevent them from abusing their power. We can only do this if we understand our Constitution and the limitations it places on our leaders.

Why Should I Care?

Harrison was the first president to die in office, he delivered the longest inaugural address, and he held the shortest term of office of any of the presidents. During his campaign and in his inaugural address, Harrison promised (although he never had a chance to fulfill his promises) that he would do much to help control the ever-growing government. He was the first president to pledge to limit his tenure of office to a single term, and he constantly battled to limit the government by denying the thousands of office seekers who sent unwarranted job applications every day. Had Harrison lived through his term, the course of history may have been altered. As it was, Harrison left his legacy and presidency to his successor, his vice president, John Tyler.

Breakin' It Down
Early Life

William Henry Harrison was born to a family of politicians and patriots. His father was a member of the First and Second Continental Congress, one of the fifty-six men who signed the Declaration of Independence, and who later became the governor of Virginia. William was born on his family's "Berkley Plantation," which was raided during the Revolutionary War in 1781. William had six siblings, but he was the baby of the family. He was privately tutored before attending the Hampden-Sydney College, where he studied history and literature. Considering entering the field of medicine, he transferred to University of Pennsylvania Medical School and studied under Dr. Benjamin Rush. However, his plans for a medical career changed

FUN FACT!

When British soldiers raided Harrison's birthplace in 1781, they killed the family's cattle and livestock, stole all of their slaves and horses, and plundered their mansion, leaving the once-thriving Virginia plantation barren.

LIBERTY Language

Aide-de-camp: The official name for a military officer who serves as an assistant to a higher-ranking official.

BTW: General "Mad" Anthony Wayne praised Harrison for his fighting, complementing his "conduct and bravery in exciting the troops to press for victory."

William Henry Harrison dies in office, April 4, 1841

Supreme Court Justice Oliver Wendell Holmes is born, 1841

William Henry Harrison delivers the longest presidential inaugural address, March 4, 1841

Britain claims Hong Kong in China, 1841

| 1840 | 1841 | 1842 | 1843 | 1844 | 1845 |

BTW: Harrison was the oldest to assume the presidency (sixty-eight) until Ronald Reagan became president at sixty-nine.

when he entered the military at age eighteen, joining the First Infantry of the Regular Army. He fought in the Northwest Indian War from 1791 until it ended in 1795. He fought in the Battle of Fallen Timbers and became aide-de-camp to General "Mad" Anthony Wayne. He later became commander of Fort Washington. Noticing his gallantry and ability as a soldier, the government in Washington D.C., as well as the American people, began considering Harrison for political roles in our government.

First Couple

William Henry Harrison married Anna Tuthill Symmes in 1795. Both of their parents were against the two young lovers marrying, but Anna and William married anyway, on November 25. They had nine children. One of their children, John Scott, made history when his son Benjamin Harrison became president in 1889. John Scott remains the only man whose father and son both became president of the United States.

FUN FACT!

Anna Harrison was the first president's widow to receive a congressionally approved pension.

ANNA HARRISON

Previous Political Career

- 1798: Appointed secretary of the Northwest Territory by President John Adams.
- 1799: Elected territorial delegate from the Northwest Territory to the U.S. Congress. Harrison proposed "The Harrison Land Act of 1800," to make it more affordable and easier for citizens to own and purchase land in territories.
- 1800: Appointed as the Indiana Territory's first governor by President John Adams, holding this position for twelve years.
- 1812: Military leader during the War of 1812. It was in this war that Harrison gained national exposure, especially at the Battle of Tippecanoe, where he led American troops to an unlikely victory.
- 1816: Elected to the U.S. House of Representatives to represent recently formed Ohio, and won.
- 1824: Appointed to the U.S. Senate. He served for just four years, until 1828, and promoted national improvement measures to help repair deteriorating road conditions across America.
- 1828: Appointed as the first minister to Colombia under John Quincy Adams. Yet, by the time Harrison arrived in the country, he was recalled by Andrew Jackson.
- 1836: Failed to win in the 1836 presidential election.

THOUGHTS ON THE CONSTITUTION

The broad foundation upon which our Constitution rests being the people—a breath of theirs having made, as a breath can unmake, change, or modify it—it can be assigned to none of the great divisions of government but to that of democracy.

Here, Harrison explains that the Constitution depends on the people. The people made the Constitution and can change or modify the Constitution. The Constitution was made solely for and can only work with a democratic government.

BTW: As governor of the Indiana Territory, one of Harrison's duties was to negotiate land treaties with the Native Americans. Harrison did so when he negotiated the Treaty of Fort Wayne, which gave 2.5 million acres of Native American land to the U.S.

ELECTION RESULTS!

Election of 1840	Electoral Votes
1st William Henry Harrison	234
2nd Martin Van Buren	60

■ William Henry Harrison — Whig Won
■ Martin Van Buren — Democrat Won
■ Territories

The presidential campaign of 1840 was the first between two highly organized political parties: the Democrats and the Whigs. More than actual substantive issues, Harrison's campaign was based on slogans, images, and behind-the-scenes string pulling. Harrison was ordered to keep his speeches short and his proslavery views to himself. The Democrats retaliated by claiming Harrison was a frontiersman who belonged in "a log cabin with a glass of hard cider." Although this was meant as an insult, the Whigs used this branding to further their cause and began holding rallies in log cabins. Democrats also called him "Granny Harrison" (because of his age), "General Mum" (because of his lack of political views), and "Nosirrah" (Harrison's name spelled backward). However, Harrison's strategy of style over substance worked, and he became the first president to receive more than one million votes. Eighty percent of Americans turned out to vote, making it the third-best voter turnout in history.

Presidency

William Henry Harrison holds the record for the shortest tenure of any president: exactly one month. However, in stark contrast, he holds the record for the longest inaugural address: 8,445 words, a speech lasting one hour and forty minutes. His inauguration took place on a frigid winter day in Washington, D.C., and his long inaugural address probably came out of his desire to shake the "backwoodsman" stereotype surrounding his campaign. He dressed lightly to prove his strength, then soon became ill with pneumonia. He eventually fell into a coma, where he stayed for a few days, muttering, among other things, "These applications, will they ever cease?" referring to the flood of applications from job seekers he had been forced to decline during his limited time in office.

BTW: Harrison's last words were, "Sir, I wish you to understand the true principles of the government. I wish them carried out. I wish nothing more."

PLATFORM SPEECH

A person elected to that high office, having his constituents in every section, State, and subdivision of the Union, must consider himself bound by the most solemn sanctions to guard, protect, and defend the rights of all and of every portion, great or small, from the injustice and oppression of the rest.

In this quote, Harrison stated that every representative and government leader is responsible for the care of the people they represent

WILLIAM HENRY HARRISON

What Has He Done for Me Lately?

Harrison's prepresidential work in America remains his longest-lasting achievement. His leadership helped his troops earn victory in the Northwest Indian War and the War of 1812. Without Harrison's "conduct and bravery," the army may have ultimately been defeated. Although his term as president remains almost inconsequential, Harrison was nonetheless a significant player in American history.

BTW: After returning to America at the start of Andrew Jackson's presidency, Harrison became a courtroom clerk to support his family.

Written by Juliette Turner

THE PROPHET'S CURSE

April 20, 1841—During the recent presidential election, some may have heard about "the Prophet" and the "curse" he placed on William Henry Harrison. At the Battle of Tippecanoe, Harrison defeated Shawnee Indian chief Tecumseh. Tecumseh had a brother known as "the Prophet," or Tenskwatawa, who was regarded by his tribe as a prophet who could predict the future. After his brother's defeat, the Prophet predicted that William Henry Harrison would not win in the presidential election of 1836—which Harrison in fact lost. The Prophet continued on to predict that if Harrison were to win in the future, he would die in office—which he now has, exactly one month to the day after his inauguration. Additionally, the Prophet predicted that every president elected on every twentieth year would also die while serving America as president. Two of the Prophet's predictions came true—will the third?

UNITED STATES V. THE AMISTAD

March 10, 1841—The Supreme Court published a decision yesterday that greatly impacts slavery in America.

Many view it as the first step taken by the federal government toward the abolition of slavery. The case discussed the fate of a group of slaves who had been illegally captured (the slave trade has been abolished and outlawed) by Spanish slave traders on their way to Spain.

The slaves mutinied and killed some of their captors before demanding the ship's crew sail them back to Africa. Instead of going to Africa, the ship entered American waters and was captured by the U.S. Navy. No one knew what to do with the Africans: were they free or enslaved? They were either free—this would be the case if they had been illegally captured from Africa in the slave trade—or they belonged to the Spaniards as slaves.

The case eventually reached the Supreme Court. The closing arguments were given by former president John Quincy Adams, a speech that ultimately swayed the justices to vote in favor of the Africans' freedom. The Africans are now free to sail back to their home in Africa, but has the question of slavery been settled in America for good?

HARRISON DELIVERS LONGEST INAUGURATION SPEECH TO DATE

March 4, 1841—President Harrison has outdone all his predecessors, having given the longest inaugural address today. The former general of the Indian campaigns delivered an hour-and-forty-five-minute speech in a snowstorm.

He gave a pledge "to discharge all the high duties of my exalted station according to the best of my ability, and I shall enter upon their performance with entire confidence in the support of a just and generous people."

The 68-year-old president stood outside for the entire inauguration, greeting crowds of his supporters at the White House later this afternoon, and will attend several celebrations this evening.

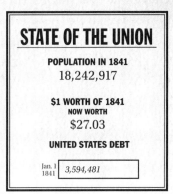

STATE OF THE UNION

POPULATION IN 1841
18,242,917

$1 WORTH OF 1841
NOW WORTH
$27.03

UNITED STATES DEBT

Jan. 1
1841 | 3,594,481

JOHN TYLER

Tenth President of the United States
Nickname: His Accidency
Term in Office: 1841–1845

The Bottom Line

John Tyler served as William Henry Harrison's vice president, but when Harrison died a month into his first year in office, Tyler assumed the presidency, as directed by the Constitution. During his term in office, Tyler struggled with a partisan and bitter Congress, but experienced significant foreign policy gains, including the annexation of Texas.

FAST STATS

★ Born March 29, 1790, in Charles City County, Virginia
★ Parents: James and Mary Marot Armistead Tyler
★ Died January 18, 1862, in Richmond, Virginia; age 71
★ Age upon Start of Term: 51; Age upon Conclusion of Term: 54
★ Religious Affiliation: Episcopalian
★ Political Party: Whig
★ Height: 6 feet
★ Vice President: none

What Was He Thinking?

John Tyler believed in the literal interpretation of the Constitution. Tyler was one to stick to his beliefs, even if it meant crossing party lines, resigning from a government position, or losing the support of his party. Furthermore, he was almost impeached for it! John Tyler believed in limited federal power, and in doing so, believed that the Missouri Compromise, rechartering of the National Bank, and protective tariffs infringed upon states' rights. Economically, John Tyler believed in the economic policies of Adam Smith, an economic philosopher, which promoted free enterprise and limited government regulation.

BTW: John Tyler was the first president born after the signing of the U.S. Constitution.

Why Should I Care?

Tyler was the first nonelected president. However, he proved himself an able president—despite his constant quarrels with Congress—especially in the international field. Tyler opened trade with China and sent American ships to prohibit illegal slave trading in Africa. Additionally, without Tyler's perseverance and persuasion, Texas may never have entered the Union to become a state.

Breakin' It Down

Early Life

John Tyler was born on his family's Greenway Plantation in Virginia. His mother died when he was only seven years old, leaving eight children — three sons and five daughters. John was the third youngest. He attended a local Virginia school until the age of twelve, when he transferred to a preparatory school for the College of William and Mary. John enjoyed writing poetry and playing the violin throughout his childhood. He graduated from the College of William and Mary in 1807 and became a lawyer.

First Couple

John Tyler married Letitia Christian in 1813. Together they had eight children. Letitia died in 1842 during Tyler's term as president, the first time a first lady died while in the White House. Tyler remained a widower for two years, until he met Julia Gardiner, who was thirty years younger. Tyler was the first president to remarry after his first wife's death. Julia was twenty-four when she married, making her the second-youngest first lady in history, and it was the first time a president wed while still in office. With Julia, John had seven more children. Tyler holds the presidential record for having the most children: fifteen.

Previous Political Career

- 1811: Elected to the Virginia state legislature. Tyler won all four of his reelection bids.
- 1812: During the War of 1812, he joined the "Charles City Rifles," the local militia group that took up arms to defend Richmond. However, he never saw any action. He left his position when his party requested he vote a certain way on the Missouri Compromise.

FUN FACT!

When John was ten years old, he led a class rebellion against the mean and strict schoolmaster. The children managed to lock the teacher in a closet, but only after John had succeeded in tying the man's hands. Needless to say, school was out for the day.

LETI TYLER

JULIA TYLER

The Second Seminole War between the U.S. and the Seminole Indians ends, 1842

The First Opium War ends with the signing of the Treaty of Nanjing, 1842

Gold and silver are discovered in Australia, 1842

American Noah Webster, author of the modern-day Merriam-Webster dictionary, dies, 1843

Samuel Morse sends the first message in Morse code, 1844

The Irish Potato Famine begins, 1845

The YMCA is formed, 1844

Florida becomes a state, 1845

Iowa becomes a state, 1845

Term in Office

1841　1842　1843　1844　1845　1846

PRESIDENTIAL Personality

★ John Tyler was known as a southern politician who held the notable character traits of charm, grace, and an appealing manner around his peers. He was a well-bred southerner with a Roman nose and blue eyes and whose demeanor warmed those he worked with, especially during his political negotiations.

FUN FACT!

John Tyler never gave an inaugural address, nor was he ever elected president!

- 1816: Elected to the U.S. House of Representatives, supporting states' rights and voting against the Missouri Compromise and the charter for the Second Bank of the United States.
- 1823: Elected to the Virginia House of Delegates once again.
- 1825: Elected governor of Virginia.
- 1826: Elected to the U.S. Senate, winning the position by just five votes. Tyler opposed national improvement legislation (such as repairing roads, funding national colleges, and funding federal work projects) as well as efforts by the federal government to regulate commerce and agriculture. When the Virginia state legislature pressured him to vote in favor of recalling Andrew Jackson's censure in 1836, he resigned from his position.

Presidency

John Tyler was the first vice president to assume the presidency after the death of a sitting president. In addition to this, Tyler, at fifty-one, was the youngest man to become president up to that point. However, becoming the president was far from seamless and easy for Tyler. Upon Harrison's death, a debate arose over the constitutional guidelines for presidential succession: What should happen if a president were to die in office? The Constitution clearly states that the vice president assumes the role of the presidency if it is vacated for any reason, but it doesn't stipulate how long the vice president is to remain the president. In other words, does the vice president remain president just until a special election can be held to replace the president, or does the vice president take on the full responsibilities of the president for the remainder of that term?

While Congress deliberated this question, Tyler settled the matter himself by taking the oath of office without waiting for congressional approval. This action settled the question surrounding the

THOUGHTS ON THE CONSTITUTION

For the first time in our history the person elected to the Vice Presidency of the United States, by the happening of a contingency provided for in the Constitution, has had devolved upon him the Presidential office.

John Tyler was the first serving vice president to unexpectedly become president—and it was all because of the U.S. Constitution.

BTW: While in the Senate, Tyler cast the only dissenting vote on the Force Bill.

guidelines for presidential succession and set the precedent for all future vice presidents. Popular with the people but not with politicians, Tyler faced an increasingly hostile Congress, to the point that his own party abandoned him.

Domestic Policy Woes
In domestic policy, Tyler had very little success. Washington was essentially in gridlock during his presidency. Whatever Congress passed, Tyler almost immediately vetoed. Congress passed laws that would have expanded the power of the federal government and Tyler vetoed them. Since Van Buren's Independent Treasury System had been dissolved by the Whigs in 1840, Congress, under Tyler's presidency, passed a law to recharter the second National Bank. Tyler vetoed this law. When Tyler vetoed the bank bill the second time, his entire cabinet (with the exception of Daniel Webster) resigned in protest. However, Tyler wasn't intimidated and continued vetoing, even vetoing the tariff passed by Congress. This time, Congress had enough of Tyler's politics and moved to impeach him, but they were not successful. Nevertheless, Tyler decided to consider not vetoing for a while and even signed the next tariff bill to reach his desk.

Foreign Policy Successes
In stark contrast to his domestic achievements, Tyler's foreign policy seemed to become his administration's strong point. The Webster-Ashburton Treaty was signed and ratified in 1842, resolving a quasi-war with Canada and Great Britain that started under Van Buren's presidency. Under Tyler's supervision, American naval ships were deployed to the African coast to monitor and prohibit any illegal slave trading. He also used the Monroe Doctrine to prevent Europe or Asia from colonizing and invading the Hawaiian Islands. Finally, he negotiated a trade treaty with China.

CONGRESSIONAL CORNER

1. **Bankruptcy Act of 1841:** This law permitted, for the first time, voluntary bankruptcy filing by debtors.

2. **Preemptive Act of 1841:** Citizens gained the right to buy government land after living on the land for fourteen years.

3. **Tariff of 1842:** This legislation lowered tariffs by 20 percent over a period of ten years. John Tyler vetoed this bill.

> This was the tariff John Tyler tried to veto twice, which almost turned him into an impeached president!

4. **Webster-Ashburton Treaty:** This treaty was signed in 1842, resolving a quasi-war with Canada and Great Britain that started under Van Buren's presidency.

5. **Presidential Election Day Act of 1845:** This law ordered a nation-wide election day for the president. It established the first Tuesday in November after the first Monday as the national "election day."

6. **Treaty of Wanghia:** This treaty, signed July 3, 1844, was the first diplomatic trade agreement between China and the United States.

FUN FACT!
Samuel F.B. Morse sent the first telegraph to be transmitted by wire in May 1844. The message was sent from the U.S. Capitol to the B&O Railroad in Baltimore, Maryland. The message? "What hath God wrought?"

Texas

Throughout his entire term, Tyler supported the annexation of Texas. This issue arose as the major issue during the election of 1844. Not surprisingly, the Whigs refused to nominate Tyler in that election. So Tyler formed a National Democrat Party. A short time into the campaign, he dropped out of the race and encouraged his supporters to back Democratic candidate James Polk, who also approved of the annexation of Texas. However, Polk never played a role in Texas's annexation because Tyler signed the congressionally approved resolution bringing Texas into the Union just days before he left office.

Slavery

John Tyler believed that slavery was an evil practice, but a necessary one for the economy of the south, which relied so heavily on slave labor. No gains, losses, or major debates over slavery occurred during Tyler's presidency. The only action Tyler took in regard to the infamous practice was one in favor of slavery: joining the Confederacy when Virginia seceded from the Union.

Post-Presidency

John Tyler had a controversial political life. This continued when Tyler joined the Confederacy and helped Virginia secede from the Union on the eve of the Civil War.

Tyler was appointed to the Confederate House of Representatives, but he never reached the Confederate capital and never served in the treasonous House of Representatives because he died before he could assume office. His death was not recognized by the Union or Congress because of his treason. They refused to lower flags or even issue a memorial stone (this was not done until 1915). Tyler's coffin was draped in a Confederate flag.

PLATFORM SPEECH

I am the president and I shall be held responsible for my Administration. I shall be pleased to accept your counsel and advice. But I can never consent being dictated to ... When you think otherwise, you resignations will be accepted.

Many times throughout his presidency, Tyler struggled to combat a rebellious and outspoken cabinet that attempted to control Tyler's actions. Tyler refused to listen to the cabinet and demanded they stay in line, or face a forced resignation.

JOHN TYLER

What Has He Done for Me Lately?

Like many presidents before him, Tyler stands as an example of a politician who wasn't afraid to stand up for his beliefs. His work in Congress before his presidency and as president helped prevent a rapid expansion of government, even though he had to break from his party to do it. Tyler's most lasting contribution to American politics was when he became president after Harrison's death. This action, controversial at the time, cemented the process of American presidential succession still in place today: when the office of the president is vacated, the vice president assumes the office of the president for the remainder of the term, not just for a short amount of time.

Written by Juliette Turner

TEXAS IS ANNEXED!

February 28, 1845—John Tyler couldn't leave office without having Texas become part of the Union under his watch. Today Congress passed the joint-resolution allowing Texas to join the Union. A joint-resolution is passed by both the U.S. House of Representatives and Senate, which becomes legal when signed by the president.

It has been a long, drawn-out process—ending in a rather unusual annexation. The time was right for Texas annexation just as Tyler was leaving office, yet the support in Congress was not behind the motion. Never discouraged, Tyler was determined to have this accomplishment take place under his presidency. As a way to bypass the need for a two-thirds majority in the Senate (as is required for any treaty), Tyler proposed Texas annexation as a "joint-resolution," which only requires a simple majority. When Tyler proposed the document both he and Sam Houston had signed in April 1844 to Congress, his wish was granted, and Texas became a state, although by slightly unusual means.

FIRST LADY DIES

September 11, 1842—First Lady Leticia Tyler passed away yesterday afternoon. She was fifty-one years old. Her cause of death is not known, but she suffered a stroke six years ago, which left her partially paralyzed.

Though she couldn't get around easily, most knew her as an amiable and loving first lady. She was confined to her bedchamber for most of her time in the White House, but made many charitable contributions and often weighed in on her husband's presidential duties and decisions.

VETO OVERRIDDEN

March 3, 1845—Congress overrode a presidential veto for the first time today, one day before John Tyler's term ends. Tyler recently vetoed a bill that prohibited the president from authorizing naval ships being built for the Coast Guard without first gaining congressional approval for the funding. Now Congress has voted to override the veto and the legislation has become a law.

STATE OF THE UNION

POPULATION IN 1845
20,691,887

$1 WORTH IN 1841
NOW WORTH
$27.03

$1 WORTH IN 1845
NOW WORTH
$30.30

UNITED STATES DEBT

Jan. 1 1841	$5,250,875.54
Jan. 1 1845	$15,925,303.01

85

JAMES POLK

Eleventh President of the United States
Nickname: Young Hickory
Term in Office: 1845–1849

The Bottom Line

James K. Polk, during his one term as president, managed to complete all four of his campaign promises: reforming the treasury, lowering tariffs, settling a border dispute with Great Britain, and acquiring California (and more states) from Mexico.

> Shocking, right? Keeping campaign promises? That's such a thing from the past. Just kidding, of course.

FAST STATS

★ Born November 2, 1795, in Pineville, North Carolina
★ Parents: Samuel and Jane Knox Polk
★ Died June 15, 1849, in Nashville, Tennessee; age 53
★ Age upon Start of Term: 49; Age upon Conclusion of Term: 53
★ Political Party: Democrat
★ Religious Affiliation: Presbyterian and Methodist
★ Height: 5 feet 8 inches
★ Vice President: George M. Dallas

What Was He Thinking?

Polk was a Democrat and, therefore, believed in the basic political beliefs of the Democrats before him: state sovereignty, lower tariffs, and a smaller federal government. However, what made Polk unique—and ultimately helped him win the Democrat nomination—was his belief in the concept of Manifest Destiny. As history shows, Polk accomplished nearly all of his goals and stuck to all of his beliefs for his four years in office.

 BTW: Polk remains the only president to win a presidential election without winning his home state.

Why Should I Care?

Polk worked every day during his presidency to breathe life into his campaign promises. He reformed and reinstated the Independent Treasury System formed under Martin Van Buren (it had been repealed when the Whigs gained power in the Congress), a system that lasted until 1913. He also achieved Manifest Destiny, through annexing or negotiating the purchase of the land that makes up America's current shape. America now reached "from sea to shining sea."

Breakin' It Down

Early Life

James was the eldest of Samuel and Jane Polk's ten children. Due to ill health and, apparently, stomach pains, James was unable to start school until age seventeen, causing him to be nearly illiterate until that point. His bad health continued to plague him until his father took him to Dr. Ephraim McDowell, who diagnosed James with gallstones. Recommending surgery as the only remedy, James underwent the extremely painful and dangerous operation to remove the stones. He was fully awake (anesthesia had not been developed at that time) and strapped to a table, holding his father's hand during the entire procedure. However, James's health was restored, making it possible to attend school and assume a social life.

He attended a school in Murfreesboro, Tennessee, becoming proficient in Latin, Greek, and English before enrolling at the University of North Carolina. He graduated in 1818 with a B.A. and honors in math and classical studies. After graduating, Polk became a lawyer but later became involved in politics.

First Couple

Polk married Sarah Childress on New Year's Day 1824 when he was twenty-eight and she was twenty. Their courtship was encouraged by Andrew Jackson, a friend of both the Polk and Childress families. James and Sarah

LIBERTY Language

Manifest Destiny: A doctrine and belief that American expansion of the land from the Atlantic Ocean to the Pacific Ocean was justified and inevitable.

FUN FACT!

While still in college, Polk studied and admired the works and political beliefs of Thomas Jefferson. He regarded Andrew Jackson as an inspiration to enter politics.

"No man and no administration was ever more assailed, and ever achieved more ... The United States were never in a more proud, peaceful, and prosperous condition than at present." —*New York Sun*, during Polk's presidency

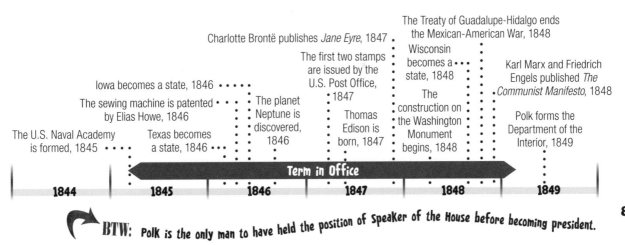

Term in Office

- The U.S. Naval Academy is formed, 1845
- Iowa becomes a state, 1846
- The sewing machine is patented by Elias Howe, 1846
- Texas becomes a state, 1846
- The planet Neptune is discovered, 1846
- Charlotte Brontë publishes *Jane Eyre*, 1847
- The first two stamps are issued by the U.S. Post Office, 1847
- Thomas Edison is born, 1847
- The Treaty of Guadalupe-Hidalgo ends the Mexican-American War, 1848
- Wisconsin becomes a state, 1848
- The construction on the Washington Monument begins, 1848
- Karl Marx and Friedrich Engels published *The Communist Manifesto*, 1848
- Polk forms the Department of the Interior, 1849

1844　1845　1846　1847　1848　1849

BTW: Polk is the only man to have held the position of Speaker of the House before becoming president.

87

had no children together. Some historians speculate whether or not the surgical procedure James underwent as a teen prevented him from having children. Sarah was a strict Presbyterian who forbade alcohol, card playing, and dancing during all political White House functions. She even forbade Polk from attending horse races! When he was president, Sarah worried about his propensity to overwork, sometimes helping him write speeches and letters or scanning his mail to prioritize those that needed urgent attention. Like many of the first ladies before her, Sarah received guidance from Dolley Madison.

SARAH POLK

Previous Political Career
- 1823: Elected to the Tennessee state legislature.
- 1825: Elected to the U.S. House of Representatives, representing Tennessee. As a leader of the Jacksonian-Democratic faction, he believed in the superiority of states' rights and the importance of lower tariffs, as well as a radical disbanding of the Electoral College. He became the chairman of the powerful Ways and Means Committee while in the House.
- 1835: Elected Speaker of the U.S. House of Representatives.
- 1839: Elected to become the governor of Tennessee by just two thousand votes.

FUN FACT!
Sarah Polk held the White House's first annual Thanksgiving dinner.

Presidency

James Polk assumed the office of the presidency with four goals that he wanted to achieve in his four years in office: (1) reestablish the federal bank and treasury, (2) lower tariff rates, (3) resolve the Oregon Territory dispute with Great Britain, and (4) negotiate the purchase of California from the Mexicans. The shocking thing is that Polk managed to keep his campaign promises and to accomplish all four goals.

Polk accomplished his first goal by working with the Democratic majority in Congress to reestablish the Independent Treasury System. The system, first passed under the Van Buren administration, had been repealed by the Whigs the following year, and Polk hoped to reestablish it. Polk didn't want the federal gov-

PRESIDENTIAL Personality

★ Polk was a man who wanted to get things done. When he set a goal, he met it, even if it meant working to his fullest capacity every day of his life. Biographer Charles G. Sellers summarized Polk's personality when he wrote that he "drove himself ruthlessly, exploiting the abilities and energies he did possess to an extent that few men can equal." Furthermore, Polk's hard-working personality left him quiet and shy among those around him, and he confided in very few people.

INDEPENDENT Treasury System

The Independent Treasury System set up under Martin Van Buren established an "independent treasury" that would be separate from state banks. Polk reestablished the bank in 1846. The system would pay its own funds (supply its own money) and be completely separate from the financial and banking system of the country. It would make all government payments in specie (coined money).

ELECTION RESULTS!

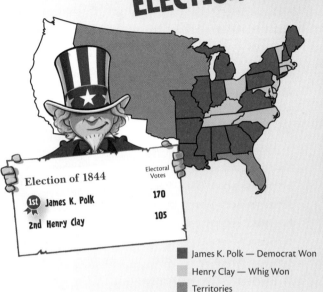

Election of 1844

Electoral Votes

1st James K. Polk — 170

2nd Henry Clay — 105

■ James K. Polk — Democrat Won
■ Henry Clay — Whig Won
■ Territories

The election focused mainly on the subject of expansionism — whether or not the U.S. should annex the Oregon Territory and Texas. Polk campaigned that the Oregon Territory, which should in turn become a state, should reach up to the 54th parallel, 40th minute border (a boundary that marks Alaska's southern border, meaning America would have annexed the majority of modern-day Canada as well). Polk's expansionist ideals won supporters in the south and the west, but victory still did not look decisive. Then Polk took a risk in campaigning. Polk promised at the party convention that he would only run for one term as a way to unite the various groups within the Whig party—hoping that by doing so those who supported other candidates could unite behind him and then focus on getting their chosen candidate elected in four years. The move worked, and Polk won the election, although by a very slim margin: 1.4 percent in the popular vote.

BTW: At the Democratic presidential convention, Polk emerged as a darkhorse candidate (a candidate with little recognition who surprisingly wins the election) and won unanimously on the ninth ballot.

ernment to have sole banking power, so he passed an act he called the "Constitutional Treasury Act," which distributed the government's money into state banks—much like Andrew Jackson had attempted.

Polk accomplished his second goal of lowering tariffs with the Walker Tariff Act. The lower tariffs helped the western states sell their excess produce to foreign countries.

Polk's third goal was accomplished through skillful diplomacy. Instead of rushing to war, Polk first attempted to negotiate with Great Britain, using diplomatic measures. The plan worked, and the treaty set the 49th parallel as the border between Canada and America, the border extending from the north border of modern-day Minnesota to the Pacific Ocean. The negotiations were successful and peace was achieved.

Polk's fourth goal proved to be the hardest. Texas believed her southern border to be marked by the Rio Grande. However, Mexico believed the border to be the northern Nueces River, a boundary that would have given the southern tip of Texas to Mexico. Polk tried to duplicate his success with Britain by sending ambassadors to negotiate, but both sides failed to agree on a treaty.

> *Though I occupy a very high position, I am the hardest-working man in this country.*

JAMES POLK and Andrew Jackson

Besides both becoming president of the United States, Polk and Jackson had other commonalities. Both men were born in North Carolina but moved to Tennessee to start their law and political careers. Both men believed in a limited federal government that put the power in the hands of the states. Furthermore, both men strove to create a banking system that would take power away from the national government. Both men were trailblazers, but, unfortunately, only one is very well known today: Andrew Jackson.

BTW: At the age of forty-nine, Polk was the youngest person to become president of the United States. He broke the record of his predecessor, John Tyler, who was fifty-one.

1. **District of Columbia Retrocession (1846): The city of Alexandria returned to Virginia. It had been ceded by the state to form a portion of the District of Columbia.**

2. **Walker Tariff Act (1846): This act reduced tariff rates from 32 to 25 percent.**

3. **Oregon Treaty is ratified (1846): This treaty established the border between Canada and America along the 49th parallel (between the Rocky Mountains and the strait of Juan de Fuca).**

4. **Treaty of Cahuenga (1847): This was the informal agreement between American and Mexican forces to stop Mexican-American War fighting.**

5. **Treaty of Guadalupe Hidalgo (1848) officially ends the Mexican-American War.**

6. **Department of the Interior (1849) established by Congress.**

7. **Gold Coinage Act (1849): This act created the first "gold dollar" and also created the "Double Eagle" twenty dollar gold piece.**

★★★★★★★★★★★★★★★★★★★★★★★★★

THOUGHTS ON THE CONSTITUTION

One great object of the Constitution was to restrain majorities from oppressing minorities or encroaching upon their just rights.

Polk believed the Constitution was designed to protect the rights of the minority and prevent their voices from being overshadowed by the majority.

JAMES K. POLK

Hail to the Chief
★★★★★★★★★★★★★★★★★★★★★★★★★

"Hail to the Chief" is the song that follows the president wherever he goes. It was first played at a celebration for what would have been George Washington's eighty-third birthday, then again when John Quincy Adams attended the groundbreaking of the Chesapeake and Ohio Canal in 1828. It became attached to the presidency when Julia Tyler requested that it be played at her husband's formal receptions. Sarah Polk requested that it be played whenever her husband appeared in public. The tradition has been broken only twice: during Chester Arthur's presidency—he despised the song, and during Gerald Ford's presidency—he chose to play the University of Michigan fight song instead. In 1954, under the presidency of Dwight Eisenhower, the song was made an official requirement for all presidential appearances.

Mexican-American War
Polk then ordered General Zachary Taylor to patrol the Rio Grande with troops. Events spiraled from bad to worse fairly quickly when Mexican General Mariano Arista attacked Taylor's forces, killing eleven of the American cavalry patrolmen. Polk wanted to declare war, but this upset the northern states, which feared acquiring new territory would agitate the issue of slavery. Yet war was declared, marking the beginning of the Mexican-American War that lasted for two years.

As a result of Polk's expansionist policies, 1.2 million square miles were added to the American landmass. However, the cost of the war with Mexico totaled $97 million (on top of the $15 million for the land sold by Mexico). These land gains consequently led to new political debates: what about slavery in the new territories? The Wilmot Proviso, proposed in the U.S. House of Representatives, banned slavery in all new states added. During these debates, Polk attempted to stay neutral,

BTW: Polk started as a clerk to the state senate, known as the Tennessee General Assembly, and also joined the state militia as a colonel.

yet this fueled anger among both the Whigs and the Democrats. This issue would bleed over into the hands of the next president.

Although Polk's presidency remains one of the most successful in history, he wasn't very popular at the time because of the controversy over the war and the political divide in Washington, D.C. Yet Polk left office having completed the concept of Manifest Destiny, a pretty high accomplishment.

Post-Presidency

Polk's hard labor during his term in office inflicted quite a toll on his health. Within three months of leaving office, he died. He had frequently suffered from stomach ailments, probably results of his poor health as a child. Polk was the last of the Jacksonian Democrats, leaving behind him a legacy and the shadow of a once-powerful party.

What Has He Done for Me Lately?

Because he died three months after leaving office, one could say that James Polk gave his life to achieving the goals he set forth during his campaign. He didn't do it for personal gain; rather, he did it to help create the ideal government and country in which he believed. Achieving Manifest Destiny stretched America to its current, mainland shape, adding areas of the West Coast and Southwest. He ensured economic stability with a system that lasted until 1913. He left office with America a safer, prospering nation, not to mention larger.

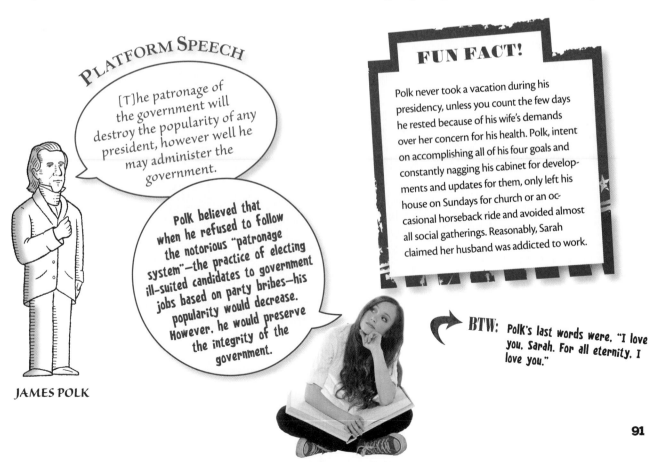

PLATFORM SPEECH

[T]he patronage of the government will destroy the popularity of any president, however well he may administer the government.

Polk believed that when he refused to follow the notorious "patronage system"—the practice of electing ill-suited candidates to government jobs based on party bribes—his popularity would decrease. However, he would preserve the integrity of the government.

JAMES POLK

FUN FACT!

Polk never took a vacation during his presidency, unless you count the few days he rested because of his wife's demands over her concern for his health. Polk, intent on accomplishing all of his four goals and constantly nagging his cabinet for developments and updates for them, only left his house on Sundays for church or an occasional horseback ride and avoided almost all social gatherings. Reasonably, Sarah claimed her husband was addicted to work.

BTW: Polk's last words were, "I love you, Sarah. For all eternity, I love you."

Written by Juliette Turner

SMITHSONIAN INSTITUTE ESTABLISHED

August 10, 1846—Almost twenty years after a grant was given to raise funds for the national science institution, the Smithsonian Institute opened its doors today for the first time. The institution was founded in 1829 by British scientist James Smithson, who donated $500,000. It was established for "the increase and diffusion of knowledge." Former president John Quincy Adams expresses his excitement, having long been the champion of the institution. He and the old Federalist Party championed the institution's birth, working to receive the grant from Mr. Smithson in 1829.

ON SLAVERY

June 16, 1849—Polk always believed that slavery should be left up to the states. He owned slaves himself, but ordered that, upon his death, all of his slaves be given to his wife, Sarah. She has now acquired his slaves, and upon her death, they are to be permanently freed.

IN MEMORIAM: SARAH POLK

August 30, 1891—Sarah Polk, who passed away two weeks ago, has been laid to rest next to her husband, the late President James Polk.

When Polk died, Mrs. Polk attempted to preserve his legacy in every way possible. In addition to wearing black from the day of her husband's death until the day of her own death, a span of forty-two years, Sarah Polk also worked to preserve his legacy of neutrality on the issue of slavery.

During the Civil War, Polk Place in Nashville, Tennessee, was considered neutral territory, and Sarah kept the doors open to soldiers and citizens on both sides of the war. She also perfectly preserved James's study, never moving one item after he had last entered the room. However, Polk Place was not only a place of preservation of the past. The first telephone in Nashville was installed there. Sarah Polk will be missed. She has left a legacy of political support and dignity.

THE MEXICAN-AMERICAN WAR IS FINALLY OVER

February 2, 1848—The Mexican-American War began when Mexican general Mariano Arista fired on American general Zachary Taylor's cavalry patrolmen, killing eleven. After the green light from Polk, Taylor advanced from the Rio Grande down to the city of Veracruz, a location just east of Mexico City. The American armies experienced victories against the Mexican armies, most notably at the battle of Mexico City. When the Americans captured the city in September 1847, it forced the Mexican army to surrender.

As a result of negotiations in the Treaty of Guadalupe Hidalgo, Mexico agreed to sell California and New Mexico, and establish the southern border of Texas at the Rio Grande. However, this came at a high price: $15 million, plus the cost of war damages the Mexicans inflicted upon America. The monetary toll may be high, but the war also resulted in thirteen thousand dead Americans, killed mainly by the diseases that spread through the army camps.

STATE OF THE UNION

POPULATION IN 1849
23,140,856

$1 WORTH IN 1845 NOW WORTH
$30.30

$1 WORTH IN 1849 NOW WORTH
$30.30

UNITED STATES DEBT

Jan. 1 1845	$15,925,303.01
Jan. 1 1849	$57,023,192.09

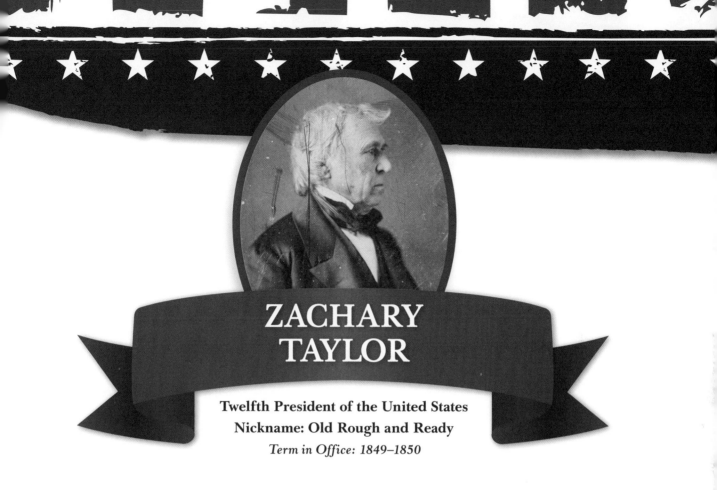

ZACHARY TAYLOR

Twelfth President of the United States
Nickname: Old Rough and Ready
Term in Office: 1849–1850

The Bottom Line

In his time as president, Zachary Taylor struggled to combat the rising tensions over the debate about whether or not to allow slavery in the new territories added as a result of the Mexican-American War. One year into his presidency, Taylor became the second U.S. president to die in office.

What Was He Thinking?

Although he campaigned and was elected on the Whig party platform, Taylor considered himself more of an independent. Having never before held political office, he had no strong ties to any of the parties in the American political field. Taylor favored a strong central banking system and disagreed with the actions of Jackson, Van Buren, and Polk. On slavery, he felt it unnecessary to expand the practice to new territories where cotton was not grown, even though he was a slave owner himself. Drifting away from his own party, Taylor opposed high tariffs and expensive national improvement measures and believed in the sovereignty of Congress

FAST STATS

★ Born November 24, 1784, in Montebello, Virginia
★ Parents: Richard and Sarah Dabney Strother Taylor
★ Died July 9, 1850, in Washington, D.C.; age 65
★ Age upon Start of Term: 64; Age upon Death: 65
★ Religious Affiliation: Episcopalian
★ Political Party: Whig
★ Height: 5 feet 8 inches
★ Vice President: Millard Fillmore

 BTW: Zachary Taylor was the last president to be born before the ratification of the U.S. Constitution.

FUN FACT!

During the Battle of Buena Vista Hacienda, Taylor was wounded when a bullet lightly grazed his left arm. Another time, a small cannonball almost hit Taylor, but he dodged it by standing up in his stirrups and letting it pass between his legs.

and a limited president. He was also a strong nationalist, or someone who believed in the unity of the Union and opposed any idea of secession.

Why Should I Care?

Like the presidents before him and all the presidents until Abraham Lincoln, Taylor struggled to keep the balance of power between the proslavery south and the proabolition north. Taylor was the first to threaten the south with military action when they almost moved to secede over the issue of slavery. Taylor's strong presidential actions kept the country together, delaying the Civil War for approximately another decade.

Taylor had unusually short legs, requiring the assistance of an orderly to mount "Old Whitney," the horse he used during the Mexican-American War. Whitney later grazed on the White House lawn.

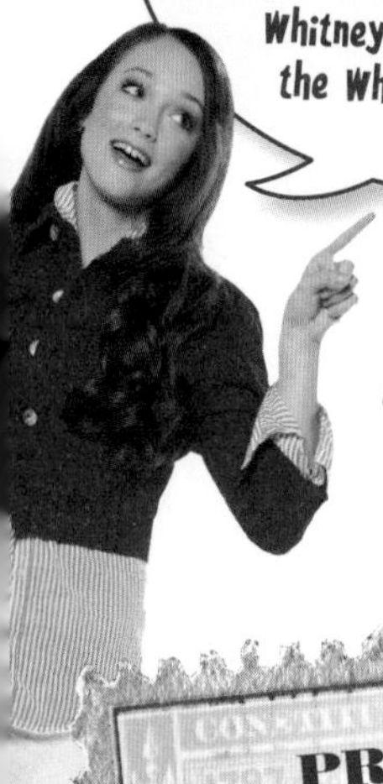

Breakin' It Down

Early Life

Zachary Taylor was born in Virginia as the third oldest of eight children. He had four brothers and three sisters. Zachary studied for a short time under private tutors, but his father, Richard, never forced an education on his children, even though he was educated at the College of William and Mary. More than formal learning, Zachary enjoyed the outdoors and worked on building strength and stamina through exercise—an easy thing to do in the Kentucky, frontier lifestyle.

PRESIDENTIAL Personality

★ *Zachary Taylor was known to be an independent-minded and brave soldier who led his men gallantly into battle. He never let his accomplishments go to his head, however, and remained humble in all his services. He was also known for his plain and blunt speech and his sometimes ragged clothing style.*

First Couple

MARGARET TAYLOR

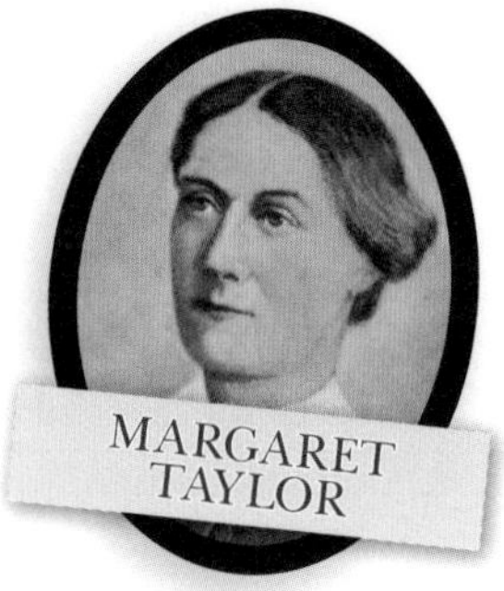

In 1810, Zachary Taylor married twenty-two-year-old Margaret Smith, whom he called Peggy. Together they had six children. Two of their daughters died of a rapidly spreading fever that sickened the family in 1820. The illness left Peggy in ill health for the majority of her life. One of their daughters, Sarah Knox, married

The Taiping Rebellion begins civil war in China, resulting in thirty million Chinese deaths, 1850

The Gold Rush begins, 1849

Robert Louis Stevenson is born, 1850

Henry Clay begins debate that leads to the Compromise of 1850, 1850

Term in Office

1848 | 1849 | 1850 | 1851 | 1852 | 1853

BTW: Zachary Taylor was the first president to have no previous political experience before becoming president of the United States. So how did he become president? Taylor served a forty-year career in the military, defending several parts of the country during four wars.

soldier and future Confederate president Jefferson Davis. Opposed to the marriage, Zachary and Peggy refused to attend the wedding, but the marriage was short-lived; Sarah died of malaria three years later. Taylor's only son, Richard, served in the Confederate Army.

LIBERTY Language

Brevet major: A "brevet" allows a military officer in the army to hold a position of higher ranks for a short period of time. So, if you are a brevet major, you are temporarily a major in the army.

FUN FACT!

Zachary Taylor's Inauguration day in 1849 fell on a Sunday, but he refused to be sworn in on the Lord's Day. Instead, he was sworn in on the following Monday (March 5, 1849). The term of the previous president, James Polk, ended on March 4, 1849, at midnight, so for one day, the President Pro Tempore of the Senate, David Rice Atchison, served as president of the U.S., as directed by the U.S. Constitution.

MILITARY CAREER

Zachary Taylor joined the Kentucky militia in 1806 and soon became a lieutenant in the Seventh Infantry after receiving an appointment from James Madison. In the War of 1812, Taylor and his regiment held off an army of four hundred Indians with just fifty soldiers. After the war concluded, Taylor was commissioned to settle the small land disputes between the Indians and the new American settlers, usually siding with the Indians. Taylor was then appointed by President James Madison to the Third Infantry at Green Bay, Wisconsin. In 1832 during the Black Hawk War, Taylor commanded an army of four hundred men and received a promotion to colonel. A short time later, Taylor served in the Second Seminole War in 1837, rising to brigadier general. Despite his already extensive service in the military, Taylor experienced his "claim-to-fame" during the Mexican-American war. News of Taylor's unlikely victories and leadership in battle caused his name to quickly spread across the country, making him a very likely candidate for president.

For his actions in battle during the War of 1812, Taylor was awarded the position of brevet major, the first time the position was ever awarded.

ELECTION RESULTS!

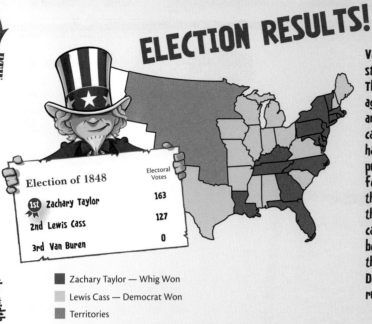

Election of 1848

		Electoral Votes
1st	Zachary Taylor	163
2nd	Lewis Cass	127
3rd	Van Buren	0

- ◼ Zachary Taylor — Whig Won
- ◻ Lewis Cass — Democrat Won
- ◼ Territories

Voters in this election had no clue where Taylor stood on either domestic issues or foreign issues. The only thing they did know was that Taylor agreed with the Wilmot Proviso, a stance that angered many of his southern supporters. Democratic candidate Lewis Cass argued that territories should have sovereignty on the issue, but Martin Van Buren pushed for the full abolition of slavery. The election fell primarily on one state: New York and her thirty-six electoral votes (the most of any state in the country). Shockingly, the Whig candidate (Taylor) carried the predominantly Democratic state, partially because Martin Van Buren (the country's first major third-party candidate) drew votes away from Democrat Lewis Cass. Had Van Buren not been in the running, Cass may well have become the president.

BTW: The election of 1848 was the first time the entire nation voted on the same day.

Presidency

The Gold Rush was underway when Taylor assumed the presidency. Preparing for the large migration of Americans to the region, Taylor and Congress asked the California and New Mexico territories to join the Union, and gave them the ability to choose whether or not they would adopt slavery. Both territories were against slavery.

> If elected, I would not be the mere president of a party—I would endeavor to act independent of party domination and should feel bound to administer the government untrammeled by party schemes.

Compromise of 1850

In the House of Representatives, Henry Clay proposed the Compromise of 1850, which was formed to calm the tensions arising from both sides of the issue. President Taylor came out in fervent opposition to the bill, promising to veto it. The government's disagreement and debate did not help the already tenuous situation. Tensions over the issue of slavery continued to escalate in Congress and throughout the country. Rumors began to spread about some of the southern states seceding, but Taylor announced he would send federal troops to the states if the talk of secession continued.

TAYLOR on the Battlefield

While fighting in the army, Taylor became a leader among his men and received many high-ranking promotions, but he refused any special treatment and only accepted provisions given to all the foot soldiers. He patched up his clothes when needed, and was described by another soldier as, "an old farmer going to market ... jovial and good natured."

Foreign Policy

In contrast to Taylor's struggles in domestic policy over the issue of slavery, Taylor experienced some achievement in the international field. The Clayton-Bulwer Treaty of 1850 opened the proposed Panama Canal to all nations. However, it would be decades before construction would start on the canal.

Unexpected Death

On July 4, 1850, Taylor attended a tedious ceremony celebrating the groundbreaking of the Washington Monument. As the hot sun beat down upon Taylor and the rest of the crowd, Taylor downed large quantities of ice-cold water, iced milk, and raw fruits and vegetables. Within days, Taylor was ill and worsening quickly. Of the four doctors who attended him, none were quite sure what happened to the nation's president: some said acute indigestion, some said gastroenteritis, and some said cholera. Nevertheless, Taylor died five days later on July 9, the last Whig to be elected to the presidency. One hundred thousand people lined the president's funeral route. Taylor was the second president in the course of ten years to die in office.

POLITICAL PARTIES

★★★★★★★★★★★★★★★★★★★★★★★★

Free Soil Party: **The Free Soil Party was first organized in 1848 and lasted until 1854. The party opposed the expansion of slavery into new territories, expressing the views of the pro-abolitionists of the day. Their slogan was "free soil, free speech, free labor, and free men," appealing to the small farmers, merchants, millworkers, and the common people. They first nominated Martin Van Buren to run for president in the election of 1848, but the party only gained 10 percent of the popular vote and no electoral votes. By 1854, the Free Soil Party merged with the enlarging and more popular Republican Party, which also condemned slavery and opposed expansion.**

THOUGHTS ON THE CONSTITUTION

Whatever dangers may threaten it, I shall stand by it and maintain it in its integrity to the full extent of the obligations imposed and the powers conferred upon me by the Constitution.

Zachary Taylor said this in his annual address to Congress in 1849. He was willing to protect the Constitution no matter what powers threatened its authority, and said he would only use the presidential powers given to him by America's governing document.

BTW: James Madison was Zachary Taylor's cousin.

What Has He Done for Me Lately?

Because Zachary Taylor was the first man to become president without previous political experience, he helped to enforce the maxim that any American can become the president of the United States. Just like George Washington before him and many after him, Taylor proved that military men were able men, suited for the office of the presidency, abiding by the limitations of the Constitution and to not become a dictator.

FUN FACT!

Taylor, a southerner, owned many slaves, but he believed slavery was purely an economic practice, and opposed slavery in regions where cotton was not grown. He believed states obtained a constitutional right to choose whether or not they would adopt the practice of slavery, but he declared that "the people of the North need have no further apprehension of the extension of slavery."

PLATFORM SPEECHES

> Our Government is one of limited powers, and its successful administration eminently depends on the confinement of each of its coordinate branches within its own appropriate sphere.

BTW: Taylor did not register to vote until after the Mexican-American War. He voted for the first time at age sixty-two, three years before he became president.

> By holding the representative responsible only to the people, and exempting him from all other influences, we elevate the character of the constituent and quicken his sense of responsibility to his country.

> Zachary Taylor said this in his State of the Union address to Congress in 1849. Taylor believed that American liberties were safest when each branch of government stayed within its constitutional confines. If the limited powers are overreached, monarchy or dictatorship can occur.

> Zachary Taylor feared representatives who held ties to party benefactors or the patronage system. According to Taylor, the best representative is one who only answers to the people who elect him.

ZACHARY TAYLOR

BTW: Last Words: "I am about to die. I expect my summons very soon. I have tried to discharge my duties faithfully. I regret nothing, but I am sorry that I am about to leave my friends."

BTW: Taylor's military résumé includes serving as colonel to an army of four hundred men in the Black Hawk War in 1832 and as brigadier general to eleven hundred men in the Second Seminole War in 1837.

Written by Juliette Turner

MONEY SCANDAL TAINTING WASHINGTON

February 25, 1850—There is no excitement in Washington unless there is a scandal surrounding the presidency. Zachary Taylor has experienced his fair share of scandal. News leaked that his secretary of war, George Crawford, has illegally solicited money from the government.

Crawford reportedly did so while representing the Galphin family, who was petitioning the government for a compensation payment of $191,000. While representing the family, Crawford secretly received a portion of the money awarded the family. Taylor has yet to request Crawford's resignation.

FOUL PLAY INVOLVED IN PRESIDENT'S DEATH?

July 9, 1850—Today America lost a humble and valiant leader. A man who served his country for over forty years, President Zachary Taylor offered his strength, brains, and guidance to the betterment of America. America now mourns her president for the second time in less than a decade.

Though doctors have said Taylor died because of massive consumption of iced-milk and cherries on an abnormally warm July day, many are requesting an autopsy to rule out foul play. Assassination has not yet been ruled out, but even though tensions have reached an all-time high over the increasingly delicate issue of slavery, most doubt that any ill will against the president resulted in an assassination.

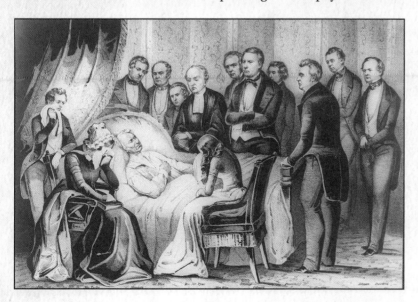

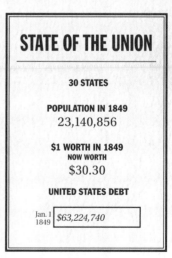

STATE OF THE UNION

30 STATES

POPULATION IN 1849
23,140,856

$1 WORTH IN 1849
NOW WORTH
$30.30

UNITED STATES DEBT

| Jan. 1 1849 | $63,224,740 |

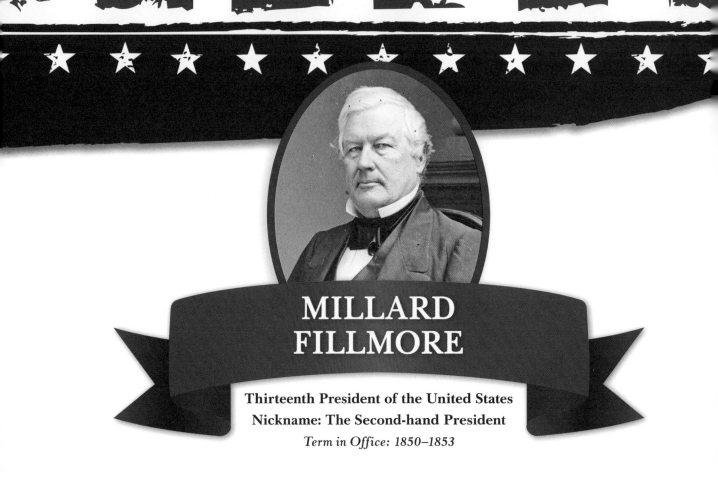

MILLARD FILLMORE

Thirteenth President of the United States
Nickname: The Second-hand President
Term in Office: 1850–1853

The Bottom Line

Millard Fillmore served the remainder of Zachary Taylor's term, until 1853, during which time he signed the controversial Compromise of 1850 bill and worked to appease the southern states. He also opened the first trade agreements with Japan.

FAST STATS

★ Born January 7, 1800, in Locke, New York (present-day Summerhill)
★ Parents: Nathaniel and Phoebe Millard Fillmore
★ Died March 8, 1874, in Buffalo, New York; age 74
★ Age upon Start of Term: 50; Age upon Conclusion of Term: 53
★ Religious Affiliation: Unitarian
★ Political Party: Whig
★ Height: 5 feet 9 inches
★ Vice President: none

What Was He Thinking?

Millard Fillmore believed in a limited presidency that answered to a more powerful Congress, not the other way around as some previous presidents had believed. He was against the expansion of slavery and wanted to preserve the Union. As shown by his support of the Compromise of 1850, he believed in using executive and government force when necessary to enforce the law. However, Fillmore also believed it was necessary to appease the southern states to prevent seccession.

 BTW: He was the nation's second "accidental president," the second to assume the presidency after the untimely death of a sitting president.

> God knows I detest slavery, but it is an existing evil, for which we are not responsible, and we must endure it, till we can get rid of it without destroying the last hope of free government in the world.

FUN FACT!

Fillmore was chosen as Taylor's vice presidential nominee to balance out the ticket. Taylor was a slave owner, but Fillmore adamantly opposed slavery. The two didn't meet until after the election, just before inauguration day, and Fillmore realized during this meeting that Taylor did not care about Fillmore or his views.

Why Should I Care?

Two of Fillmore's most lasting accomplishments were far from finished when he left office, but he remains known as the man who instigated them. The first was the beginning of the transcontinental railroad. This not only eased transportation throughout the country but also led to the mass population of the West Coast. (Of course, the California Gold Rush helped too.) The second was the beginning of trade agreements with Japan. It not only opened up a whole new market for American goods; it also marked the expansion of American influence around the world.

POLITICAL PARTIES

★★★★★★★★★★★★★★★★★★★★★★★

Anti-Masonic Party: **The Anti-Masonic Party was formed in 1826 as the first third party in American politics. The party was formed after many accused the masons of killing William Morgan, a former mason who planned to write a book exposing the secrets of the Masonic society. Appealing strongly to the poorer classes, the Anti-Masonic Party had a platform that focused on condemning the Masonic society as secretive, exclusive, and undemocratic.**

Know-Nothing Party: **The Know-Nothing Party was formed in the 1840s in response to the rising levels of German, Irish, and Roman-Catholic immigrants. The party believed in limiting immigration, preventing foreign-born individuals from voting, and forcing them to live in America for twenty-one years before they could be eligible for citizenship. The name of the party came from the fact that members were told to tell outsiders they "knew nothing" of the group. By 1860 the group merged with Whig politicians to form the Constitutional Union Party.**

Breakin' It Down
Early Life

Millard Fillmore had a unique first name; Millard was also his mother's maiden name. He was the second oldest of eight children and, as a young boy, worked on the family farm with his father before working in a textile mill. During that time, Millard received no formal education, but he learned to read by reading passages from the Bible. Additionally, he saved the money he earned at the textile mill to buy a dictionary, which he studied during his breaks at work.

At age nineteen, Millard enrolled in the newly established Hope Academy and met Miss Abigail Powers, the woman he later married. After studying law on his own, Millard clerked for a local attorney and took advantage of the open library at the firm to learn more. Mostly self-educated, Fillmore decided to test the waters of politics, starting first at the state level.

The New Mexico Territory is added, 1850
California becomes a state, 1850
The Texas borders are amended, 1850

The Utah Territory is added, 1850

The first modern bathtub is installed in the White House, 1851
The first kitchen stove is installed in the White House, 1851
Telegraph line connecting London, England and Paris, France is linked, 1851

The Washington Territory is formed from a portion of the Oregon Territory, 1853

Term in Office

| 1848 | 1849 | 1850 | 1851 | 1852 | 1853 |

BTW: Millard Fillmore's personal library contained more than four thousand books, and he supposedly read every one of them.

An honorable defeat is better than a dishonorable victory.

First Couple

ABIGAIL FILLMORE

Abigail Powers was a teacher at Hope Academy, where Fillmore attended. Their courting relationship took many years to fully develop, and they married seven years after they first met at the academy. They had two children: one son, Millard Powers, and one daughter, Mary Abigail.

When Fillmore became president, Abigail became the first "first lady" to have held a job after marrying. Always interested in promoting knowledge, Abigail asked for funds from Congress to start the first permanent White House library. She received the funds, and the library was established on the second floor in the Blue Room. True to their faith, Abigail and Millard banned smoking and drinking in the White House, much to the dismay of their guests.

Tragedy struck the happy family when, less than a month after he left the presidency, Fillmore's beloved wife died of pneumonia after attending the cold outdoor inauguration ceremony for his successor.

Previous Political Career

- 1829: Elected to the first of his three terms in the New York state assembly.
- 1832: Elected to the U.S. House of Representatives, refusing to run for a second term in 1834.
- 1836: Elected to the U.S. House of Representatives again, serving until 1843. In 1840: failed to become Speaker of the House, instead becoming the chairman of the House Ways and Means Committee.
- 1844: Failed in his attempt to become governor of New York.
- 1847: Elected as New York's state comptroller.
- 1848: Chosen by the Whig convention to serve as Taylor's vice presidential candidate.

PRESIDENTIAL Personality

★ Fillmore was a tall, blond, blue-eyed man known to his contemporaries as someone who stuck to his beliefs even if they were unpopular at the time. Fillmore strove to hold his own during the controversies about slavery during and even after his presidency. Despite the fact that his beliefs caused his popularity to decrease, he held true to his convictions.

Though I had no desire for the office and still less for the nomination, yet being nominated, I am not anxious to be defeated.

Fillmore spoke these words after his nomination for governor of New York.

The first books in the White House library were two copies of *Uncle Tom's Cabin*, a book written by Harriet Beecher Stowe after an uprising regarding the Fugitive Slave Law occurred in Maryland.

BTW: Fillmore won election as NY Representative as an Anti-Masonic candidate, but after serving one term in the position he switched to the Whig Party.

BTW: While in the U.S. House of Representatives, Fillmore championed higher tariffs to protect American businesses and even passed a bill to help Samuel F. B. Morse develop the telegraph.

CONGRESSIONAL CORNER

★★★★★★★★★★★★★★★★★★★★★★★

1. **Compromise of 1850:** Proposed by Henry Clay, the "Great Compromiser," this bill attempted to settle the slavery debate and appeal to both sides. It accomplished five things: (1) California was admitted as a free state. (2) Texas was compensated for withdrawing its claims over New Mexico. (3) New Mexico became a territory, and the issue of slavery was left to the territory to decide. (4) The slave trade (not the practice) was abolished in D.C. (5) The Fugitive Slave Law was enacted.

2. **Fugitive Slave Law:** This law gave slaveholders federal troops to track down escaped slaves. It suspended slaves' rights to habeas corpus and their right to testify in court. Additionally, anyone who helped runaway slaves could be jailed for six months or fined $1,000.

3. **Donation Land Claim Act of 1850:** promoted homestead settlements in the Oregon Territory. Under this law, 7,437 land grants were issued between 1850–1855.

★★★★★★★★★★★★★★★★★★★★★★★

FUN FACT!

While president, Fillmore bought a previously used carriage, yet he wondered if it was acceptable for the president to be riding around in a "secondhand carriage." Since Fillmore assumed the presidency after Taylor died, the salesman in the store said, "Mr. Fillmore, you are a secondhand president." Therefore, Fillmore decided, the secondhand carriage was fitting.

Presidency

Upon becoming president, Fillmore requested the resignation of Taylor's entire cabinet, and his request was granted. Before long, Fillmore was confronted with the biggest and most controversial bill to reach the president's desk in decades: the Compromise of 1850. As soon as Fillmore signed the bill into law, protests quickly arose all over the country. In Maryland, forty-one protesters gathered in sympathy for an escaped slave whose master was using the Fugitive Slave Law to recapture him. Fillmore authorized federal troops to go to Maryland and assist the slave owner in recapturing his slave and enforcing the new law. Fillmore then tried the forty-one protesters for treason. It was the largest treason trial in American history. This action appeased the southern states, who still, despite the Compromise of 1850, were grumbling about seceding from the Union.

Successes

Although slavery still topped the list of the most important and controversial issues of the day, Fillmore had other issues to solve during his presidency. One issue was the desperate need and demand for transcontinental railroads, which were increasingly needed because of the California Gold Rush. Fillmore and Congress approved funding for transcontinental railway construction in 1853, yet construction would not begin until after the Civil War. Despite his struggles with domestic policy, Fillmore did achieve at least one significant gain in the international field: he was responsible for initiating the first U.S. trade relations with Japan.

Reelection Defeat

Fillmore suffered the same fate as former vice-president-turned-president John Tyler when his party failed to nominate him for reelection during the Whig convention of 1852. However, Fillmore had made it clear that he would have refused the nomination anyway. Fillmore left office having delayed the Civil War for another

BTW: Fillmore was the last Whig to hold the office of the president. However, since he was not elected to the position, Zachary Taylor holds the title of the last Whig candidate to be elected president.

decade through his actions to appease the southern states. However, these political debates and the Union divide did not disappear.

Post-Presidency

Both Fillmore's wife and daughter died from illness within a year of his leaving the presidency. Despite those personal tragedies, Fillmore busied himself in politics once more, even running for president again in 1856 as a candidate for the Know-Nothing Party. After being soundly defeated, however, he retired from politics. He married Caroline Carmichael McIntosh in 1858, becoming the second president to remarry after the death of his first wife.

He remained politically active by openly declaring his views on the issues of the day. He branded Abraham Lincoln a military dictator when the Civil War began, causing fellow New Yorkers to brand him as a "Copperhead" (Confederate sympathizer). When Andrew Johnson became president, Fillmore supported his lenient Reconstruction plans in the south, earning further scorn from his northern kin.

Fillmore also became an active philanthropist, helping to create the Buffalo General Hospital, the Buffalo Fine Arts Academy, the Buffalo Historic Society, and the Buffalo chapter for the Society for the Prevention of Cruelty to Animals. On top of all that, he was the first chancellor of the University of Buffalo—modern-day New York State University at Buffalo. In 1874, Fillmore suffered a stroke and died shortly after. Because his son and daughter never had children, Fillmore had no other direct descendants.

What Has He Done for Me Lately?

Though he never intended to be president, it was because of Fillmore's leadership during the debate over the Compromise of 1850 that the legislation was passed by Congress and executed into law. This legislation calmed the issue of slavery, temporarily preventing the southern states from seceding. Fillmore's actions united the country at that time and avoided a civil war for another decade.

Reconstruction: The period after the Civil War dur[ing] which the southern states reentered the Union. Dur[ing] Reconstruction, the U.S. military occupied many southern states to ensure the abolition of slavery and that the new voting policies for African-Americans were thoroughly implemented.

THOUGHTS ON THE CONSTITUTION

Every power which [the Constitution] has granted is to be exercised for the public good; but no pretense of utility, no honest conviction, of what might be expedient, can justify the assumption of any power not granted.

MILLARD FILLMORE

PLATFORM SPEECH

Although we may sympathize with the unfortunate or the oppressed everywhere in their struggles for freedom, our principles forbid us from taking any part in such foreign contests. We make no wars to promote or to prevent successions to thrones, to maintain any theory of a balance of power, or to suppress the actual government which any country chooses to establish for itself.

In his first State of the Union address to Congress in 1850, Fillmore was saying that America should not intervene in the policies and affairs of other countries.

MILLARD FILLMORE

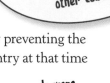

BTW: Millard Fillmore's last words were. "The nourishment is palatable" after accepting a spoonful of soup from a doctor.

Written by Juliette Turner

JAPAN AND U.S. BEGIN NEGOTIATIONS ON TRADE AGREEMENT

April 31, 1854—Last month, Commodore Matthew Perry signed the Convention of Kanagawa, a landmark agreement opening trade between Japan and the United States for the first time.

Two years ago, President Fillmore commissioned Perry to sail for Japan with a fleet of American ships to negotiate opening trade between the two countries. When he arrived, Perry demanded that the Japanese read a letter from Fillmore to create a trade treaty based on Fillmore's proposals.

Many saw Fillmore's standards as too demanding. Japan had refused to negotiate with any other country regarding trade for over two hundred years, except with the Dutch, who were allowed to bring one ship to their ports per year.

To Perry and America's surprise, when Perry sailed back to Japan with twice as many ships, he found a treaty complying with Fillmore's previous demands, marking the opening of American ports in Japan.

GOLD DISCOVERED IN CALIFORNIA!

December 10, 1849—Ever since gold was discovered in the Sacramento Valley in the California Territory early last year, the population of the region has continued to boom. In March of 1848, the population of the region was approximately 800 people and now the population is reaching 100,000. Gold extracted from the region is estimated to amount to $2 billion.

WHITE HOUSE LIBRARY

September 25, 1850—First Lady Fillmore's wish for a White House library has come true. Abigail, an avid reader who takes immense pleasure in teaching others, is the one who set this plan into motion.

Congress has recently approved the use of federal funds to supply a library, after denying Fillmore's first request. Two thousand dollars has been set aside for the acquisition of books for the new library.

Up until now, presidents residing in the White House have brought their own collection of books and removed them at the end of their time in office.

This new White House library will be an official collection of books on a variety of subjects for use by Fillmore and any future president.

Charles Lanman has been tasked with choosing reading material for the library, and the first lady is in charge of the decorations.

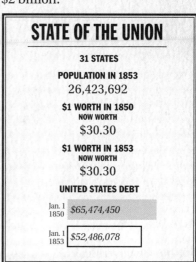

STATE OF THE UNION

31 STATES

POPULATION IN 1853
26,423,692

$1 WORTH IN 1850
NOW WORTH
$30.30

$1 WORTH IN 1853
NOW WORTH
$30.30

UNITED STATES DEBT

Jan. 1 1850	$65,474,450
Jan. 1 1853	$52,486,078

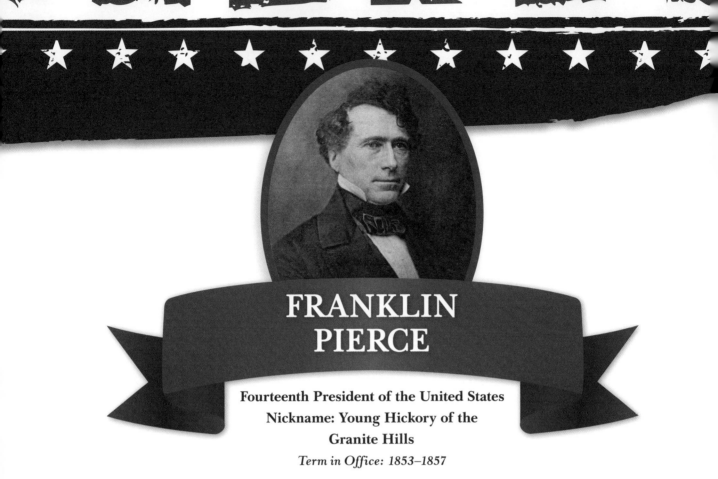

FRANKLIN PIERCE

Fourteenth President of the United States
Nickname: Young Hickory of the
Granite Hills
Term in Office: 1853–1857

The Bottom Line

During Franklin Pierce's term in office, he struggled with the increasing tension and violence that arose as a result of the warring proslavery and abolitionist forces. The one non-slavery-related issue that arose during his presidency seemed to be his only positive accomplishment: purchasing the southern portion of Arizona and New Mexico.

FAST STATS

★ Born November 23, 1804, in Hillsborough, New Hampshire
★ Parents: Benjamin and Anna Kendrick Pierce
★ Died October 8, 1869, in Concord, New Hampshire; age 64
★ Age upon Start of Term: 48; Age upon Conclusion of Term: 52
★ Religious Affiliation: Episcopalian
★ Political Party: Democrat
★ Height: 5 feet 10 inches
★ Vice President: William R. King (March–April 1853) and vacant (1853–1857)

What Was He Thinking?

Franklin Pierce advocated America's expansion beyond the American continent into new lands, and so he supported America's strong foreign policy position in world affairs. Pierce believed that the constitutional rights of the individual states and state sovereignty should be valued above all else. One of these constitutional rights, Pierce believed, was the states' ability to choose on the issue of slavery. This belief led him in many of his actions regarding slavery.

 BTW: Franklin received much of his Knowledge on politics from his father, Benjamin, who was a decorated Revolutionary War veteran and served two terms as New Hampshire governor.

Why Should I Care?

Franklin Pierce's term in office was far from successful. He served in a time when Americans wanted to prevent war, but heated passions seemed to overwhelm common sense. This made it difficult for Pierce to combat and control the south's belligerent attitude regarding slavery. Attempts at peace were futile, and war appeared more and more inevitable. Although Pierce achieved no success in domestic affairs, he did succeed in negotiating the 1854 Gadsden Purchase, which added the southern portion of New Mexico and Arizona to the U.S., giving America her full, modern-day continental shape.

Breakin' It Down
Early Life

Franklin Pierce was the first president born in the nineteenth century, and he was the only president to be born in the state of New Hampshire. As the fifth of eight children, Franklin had four brothers, two sisters, and one half sister.

Franklin attended local schools until he was twelve and then entered a private academy. At the age of fifteen, he entered Bowdoin College and joined a class that included Nathaniel Hawthorne and Henry William Longfellow. Franklin was at the bottom of his class and had the lowest marks of anyone in his grade by the end of his sophomore year. However, he soon began to work hard in school and graduated third in his class. Within a year of graduation, he already held his first political position.

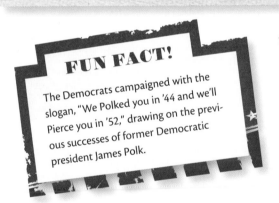

FUN FACT!

The Democrats campaigned with the slogan, "We Polked you in '44 and we'll Pierce you in '52," drawing on the previous successes of former Democratic president James Polk.

JANE PIERCE

The Washington Territory is formed from a portion of the Oregon Territory, 1853

Vincent van Gogh is born, 1853

The Crimean War begins between Russia and Britain, France, and the Ottoman Empire, 1854

The Republican Party is formed, 1854

Oscar Wilde is born, 1854

The Crimean War ends, 1855

Sigmund Freud is born, 1856

The Second Opium War between Great Britain and China begins, 1856

Term in Office

| 1852 | 1853 | 1854 | 1855 | 1856 | 1857 |

BTW: Franklin Pierce won every political position he ever sought.

FRANKLIN PIERCE
and the
Mexican-American War

Pierce fought under the command of Winfield Scott (his future political presidential opponent). Pierce experienced a chain of embarrassments, injuries, and setbacks during the war. For example, during the Battle of Contreras, he fell from his horse, injured his leg and groin, and fainted from the pain. The injuries he sustained were serious enough for the army to grant him a discharge, yet Pierce insisted on staying until the fighting ended. In spite of his hopes of gaining recognition through a war record like many before him, Pierce returned weary, ill, and accused of cowardice.

First Couple

Franklin Pierce married Jane Means Appleton in 1834 after a courtship that lasted nearly ten years. Jane was introverted, shy, and had a depressive personality—much like her husband—and it was obvious to friends and family that their marriage was often strained. They had three children together, though none of them lived to adulthood. Jane despised Washington, D.C., and the rancor of politics and, in fact, she fainted upon hearing the news of her husband receiving the Democratic nomination for president. Not emotionally or mentally stable enough to assume the duties of first lady, Jane often relied on her uncle's wife, Abigail Kent Means, to help with the few social gatherings the Pierces held.

Despite the claims by fellow soldiers that Pierce fainted due to fear of battle, Ulysses S. Grant later wrote, "Whatever General Pierce's qualifications may have been for the presidency, he was a man of courage."

Previous Political Career

- 1829: Elected to the New Hampshire state legislature and served four terms. While serving, he became the state Speaker of the House.
- 1833: Elected to the U.S. House of Representatives, representing New Hampshire at the age of twenty-nine, serving until 1837.
- 1837: Elected to the U.S. Senate, becoming the Senate's youngest member. He voted against any measure to limit slavery, believing that states should have the right to be free from government intervention, even on the subject of slavery.
- 1844: Elected as New Hampshire's chairman for the Democrat Party.
- 1845: Appointed by President James Polk to the position of Federal District Attorney.
- 1846: Joined the army to fight in the Mexican-American War.

THOUGHTS ON THE CONSTITUTION

The great scheme of our constitutional liberty rests upon a proper distribution of power between the State and Federal authorities ... The harmony and happiness of our people must depend upon a just discrimination between the separate rights and responsibilities of the States and your common rights and obligations under the General Government.

BTW: Franklin's term in the Senate was cut short when he resigned because his wife detested Washington society and asked him to step down. It was rumored that Pierce also suffered from a drinking problem that led to his resignation.

ELECTION RESULTS!

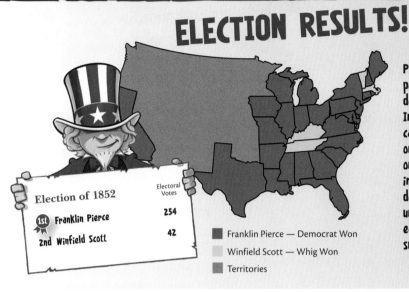

Election of 1852	Electoral Votes
1st Franklin Pierce	254
2nd Winfield Scott	42

■ Franklin Pierce — Democrat Won
□ Winfield Scott — Whig Won
■ Territories

Pierce did not gain the presidency because of political popularity, nor did he gain the presidency because of previous military victory. Instead, Pierce emerged as the dark-horse candidate at the Democratic Convention, winning on the forty-ninth ballot unanimously and based on his riding the wave of Democratic popularity in the country at the time. The Whigs' popularity declined in 1852 because of the lack of success under Zachary Taylor and Millard Fillmore. Pierce easily defeated his opponent and former military superior, Winfield Scott.

BTW: Franklin Pierce is the only president to have given a completely memorized inaugural address.

BTW: Franklin Pierce was the youngest man to become president up to that point. He was forty-eight.

Presidency

Whereas many inaugurations are times of celebration, Franklin Pierce's inauguration was a time of tragedy. During the Pierce family's train ride to Washington, the train cars randomly derailed, causing no injuries or harm to anyone on the train except for Pierce's eleven-year-old son, Bennie, who was crushed to death before his parents' eyes. This marked the death of the last of the three Pierce children. After the inauguration, the mood was anything but victorious. One visitor recorded that "everything in that mansion seemed cold and cheerless."

CONGRESSIONAL CORNER
★★★★★★★★★★★★★★★★★★★★★★★★★★★★

1. **Treaty of the Convention of Kanagawa, 1853: Opened U.S. trade with Japan.**

2. **Kansas-Nebraska Act of 1854: Proposed by Illinois senator Stephen Douglas, this act repealed the Missouri Compromise and gave the citizens of the Kansas and Nebraska territories the ability to choose whether or not they would adopt slavery.**

3. **March 3, 1855: The U.S. Congress appropriated $30,000 to create the U.S. Camel Corps.**

★★★★★★★★★★★★★★★★★★★★★★★★★★★★

Foreign Policy Hits & Misses

His first attempt at expansion failed when his cabinet and ambassadors did not secure the purchase of Cuba under the Ostend Manifesto. Pierce, however, did achieve an accomplishment when he signed the Gadsden Purchase.

A camel-mounted cavalry? Am I the only person having a hard time imagining that?

109

FRANKLIN
and Jefferson (not the founding fathers)

Franklin Pierce nominated Jefferson Davis to be his Secretary of War. During his term, Pierce relied heavily on his old friend from Congress, causing him to receive criticism in the newspapers. To avoid further criticism, Pierce would sometimes sneak out of the White House at night to visit Davis and ask his opinion on issues. Once, Davis requested that Congress fund the purchase of thirty-three camels to be used as a replacement for horses in the army being deployed to the deserts in the southwest.

National Problems

He attempted to continue the plans to build a transcontinental railroad, but there was a debate over whether the railway should be constructed in the north or in the south—the location of the railroad would benefit either the abolitionist north or the proslavery south. Then came the catastrophe of the Kansas-Nebraska Act. By repealing the Missouri Compromise, the Kansas and Nebraska Act gave the citizens of the newly formed Kansas and Nebraska territories the ability to choose whether or not they adopted slavery. The calamity that followed became known as "Bleeding Kansas" because of the violence and death that resulted.

Post-Presidency

As a Democrat, Pierce emerged as one of the biggest critics of Abraham Lincoln, arguing that it was a "fearful, fruitless, [and] fatal civil war." He even personally and verbally attacked Lincoln by claiming he had "limited ability and narrow intelligence." When Lincoln issued his Emancipation Proclamation, Pierce deemed the document unconstitutional.

Throughout the continuation of the Civil War, Pierce stood by the north, although he openly sympathized with the south, even corresponding regularly with Jefferson Davis. When Pierce's wife died in 1863, he recoiled into near seclusion and reportedly drank himself into oblivion for six years until dying from dropsy (edema) in 1869.

What Has He Done for Me Lately?

Franklin Pierce was a man ill-fit for the time he served as president. The passions that slowly ripped apart the country required a strong leader, but Pierce was no such leader. Efforts on behalf of Pierce and the politicians in Washington, D.C., seemed to make matters worse, but as history proved, nothing short of a civil war would be able to settle the debate on slavery.

Ostend Manifesto: A document written by the Pierce administration, outlining reasons why the U.S. should purchase Cuba from Spain. The document also recommended that America declare war on Spain if she refused to sell the island.

PRESIDENTIAL Personality

★ Franklin Pierce was an unlikely person to become president because of his tendency to follow on issues, not lead on them. Pierce was uncomfortable and ineffective in leading his peers. In attempts to appease both sides of the conversation and remain out of the limelight on issues, he failed to hold his ground on important issues. Pierce continually fought feelings of depression and boredom, causing him to turn to drinking. However, he was a likable person and had a casual manner, which made him popular among voters and boosted his popularity.

PLATFORM SPEECH

It must be felt that there is no national security but in the nation's humble, acknowledged dependence upon God and His overruling providence.

Pierce, a strongly religious man, accredited Providence for the many blessings Americans were enjoying in 1853, the year he gave his inaugural address.

FRANKLIN PIERCE

Written by Juliette Turner

THE OSTEND MANIFESTO

October 18, 1854—Republicans are branding the Ostend document as the Pierce administration's "manifesto" to appease the southern, proslavery states.

Last year, U.S. minister to Spain, Pierre Soule, failed to purchase Cuba from the Spanish government. Earlier this year, Pierce's secretary of state, William L. Marcy, encouraged Soule to meet with U.S. minister to Great Britain, James Buchannan, and U.S. Minister to France, John Y. Mason, in Ostend, Belgium, to compose a plan to seize Cuba if Spain refused to sell the island.

Marcy argued that the island should be seized before a slave revolt could take place—a revolt that could cause a subsequent slave revolt in the United States. Plus, the island would enlarge the American landmass.

This plan also called for military invasion if Spain refused to cooperate. However, the news of the secret "manifesto" was recently released to the public. News of the document has now reached Spain, who is no longer willing to discuss the issue. The chance to annex the Cuban island has seemingly disappeared forever.

KANSAS-NEBRASKA BILL AND BLEEDING KANSAS

September 30, 1857—Members of the Kansas territorial legislature is meeting in Lecompton, Kansas, to compose a state constitution—to favor slavery.

Months of fighting and bloodshed have ravished both the Kansas and Nebraska territories. This fighting resulted from the Kansas-Nebraska bill, which was proposed to repeal the Missouri Compromise.

The bill ordered not only that the territory stretching from the Missouri River to the Continental Divide in the Rocky Mountains be split into two territories, Kansas and Nebraska, but that the two new territories be able to choose whether or not they would adopt slavery.

The plan has failed miserably and cost many American lives. When the news of the legislation reached Missouri, proslavery Missourians quickly flooded into Kansas and set up a state legislature, which has passed proslavery legislation.

Free-soilers also have flooded into Kansas, and armed the native citizens. The governor has attempted to stop violence from occurring but passions were too high. The territorial leaders meeting in Lecompton are attempting to form a constitution so that Kansas can be accepted into the Union—an event that will hopefully stop the bloodshed and violence.

PROTESTS OVER THE FUGITIVE SLAVE LAW

May 24, 1854— Boston, Massachusetts, remains the epicenter of U.S. political rebellions and protests.

Today in central Boston, a group of abolitionists gathered to protest the capture of fugitive slave Anthony Burns. The protestors attempted to protect and rescue him from the courthouse where he is being held until his master can reclaim him.

In efforts to suppress the protest and prevent others from rising, Pierce has threatened to send the U.S. Army, the U.S. Marines, and twenty-two army companies to enforce the Fugitive Slave Law.

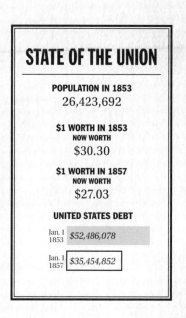

STATE OF THE UNION

POPULATION IN 1853
26,423,692

$1 WORTH IN 1853
NOW WORTH
$30.30

$1 WORTH IN 1857
NOW WORTH
$27.03

UNITED STATES DEBT

Jan. 1 1853 $52,486,078

Jan. 1 1857 $35,454,852

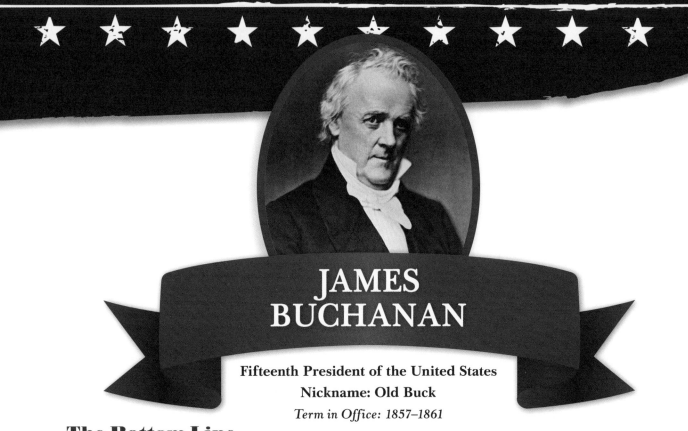

JAMES BUCHANAN

Fifteenth President of the United States
Nickname: Old Buck
Term in Office: 1857–1861

The Bottom Line

James Buchanan was president during a time of hostile sentiment between the north and the south over the increasingly prominent issue of slavery. Because he failed to address the growing hostilities between the North and South over the issue of slavery, seven southern states seceded from the Union during his presidency—resulting in the start of the American Civil War.

FAST STATS

★ Born April 23, 1791, in Cove Gap, Pennsylvania
★ Parents: James and Elizabeth Speer Buchanan
★ Died June 1, 1868, in Lancaster, Pennsylvania; age 77
★ Age upon Start of Term: 65; Age upon Conclusion of Term: 69
★ Religious Affiliation: Presbyterian
★ Political Party: Democrat
★ Height: 6 feet
★ Vice President: John C. Breckinridge

What Was He Thinking?

Above all, James Buchanan believed in the superiority of states' rights. He believed that the Constitution allowed the states to resolve the dispute over slavery and that there was no need for the federal government to take action. Like his fellow Democratic presidents, he believed that the American economy should be regional, not national. Although personally opposed to slavery, Buchanan made no moves while serving in Congress and the presidency to prevent the practice.

Why Should I Care?

As a Democrat, Buchanan was in a difficult position. States were pushing the limits of their rights and testing the presidency. When South Carolina moved to secede, Buchanan had two options: support the south in secession (he was warned this would be considered treason) or declare war (this, obviously, had severe consequences). Instead, Buchanan took a third route: inaction. Because of Buchanan's inaction, more southern states seceded. This inaction is considered the catalyst of the Civil War. The seceded states formed a larger and more powerful force—the Confederacy—that wished to wage war on the United States. Buchanan is blamed for failing to prevent the Civil War.

Breakin' It Down

Early Life

James Buchanan, the last president to be born in the eighteenth century, was the son of Irish immigrants. One of eleven children, he had four brothers and six sisters. His father died when James was a teenager. At age sixteen, he enrolled in Dickenson College and graduated in two years. After leaving college, he became a trial attorney. Soon, James decided to test his luck in politics.

First Couple

James Buchanan remains the only president to never marry. He did, however, once love a woman—a love that ended in tragedy. Young Ann Coleman and James Buchanan were close to being married, but Buchanan's marriage hopes ended when Ann died, possibly by her own hand. Thinking it was Buchanan's fault, Ann's parents denied his wish to attend her funeral. Buchanan vowed never to marry after that.

ANN COLEMAN

Previous Political Career

- 1814: Elected as a Pennsylvania state representative as a Federalist candidate.
- 1820: Elected to the U.S. House of Representatives, serving five terms. He was appointed to the House Judiciary Committee.
- 1831: Appointed minister to Russia by President Andrew Jackson, working to successfully negotiate the first peaceful trade treaty between the two nations.
- 1834: Elected to become a U.S. senator from Pennsylvania, holding office for eleven years and then be left to become Secretary of State in the Polk administration.
- 1837: Appointed to become the chairman of the Senate Foreign Relations Committee.

Charles Darwin publishes *On the Origin of Species*, 1859

Construction on the Suez Canal begins, 1859

Kansas becomes a state, 1861
The Colorado Territory is added, 1861
The Nevada Territory is added, 1861
The Dakota Territory is added, 1861

Minnesota becomes a state, 1858 · · · Oregon becomes a state, 1859

South Carolina becomes the first state to secede, 1860

The *Dred Scott v. Sandford* decision, 1857

Term in Office

| 1856 | 1857 | 1858 | 1859 | 1860 | 1861 |

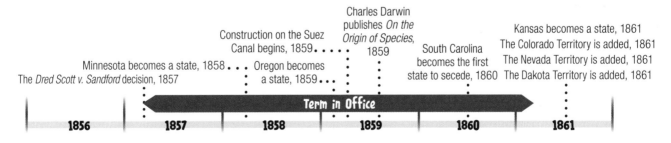

- 1845: Appointed to become secretary of state under President James Polk. He ensured negotiations over the treaty with Great Britain, which established the northern border between the U.S. and Canada. He attempted to negotiate with Mexico over the southern border of Texas (the dispute that eventually led to the Mexican-American War).
- 1848: Temporary retirement from politics at the age of fifty-seven. He left Washington, D.C., for his plantation, Wheatland, where he cared for his twenty-two nieces and nephews.
- 1853: Appointed to become minister to England by President Pierce.

CONGRESSIONAL CORNER
★★★★★★★★★★★★★★★★★★★★★★★★

1. **Harris Treaty: Signed July 29, 1858,** this treaty opened four Japanese ports to American traders and ships.

2. **Pacific Telegraph Act: Passed in 1860,** this act funded the project organized to construct a telegraph line that would enable communication between America's east and west coasts.

3. **Morrill Tariff: Passed in 1861,** this tariff increased tariff rates—increasing the cost of foreign goods—to promote American businesses.

★★★★★★★★★★★★★★★★★★★★★★★★

Presidency

Buchanan's first move as president was to appoint moderate Democrats and Republicans from both the north and the south to his cabinet. Buchanan tried to repair the divide in the country, but the gap was growing wider, especially after the Supreme Court decided in *Dred Scott v. Sandford* that slaves were not American citizens and had no rights under the Constitution. Ironically, in Buchanan's inaugural address just a few days before, he had claimed the issue of slavery should be settled in the federal courts. Indeed, the issue was settled in the Supreme Court,

THOUGHTS ON THE CONSTITUTION

There is nothing stable but Heaven and the Constitution.

ELECTION RESULTS!

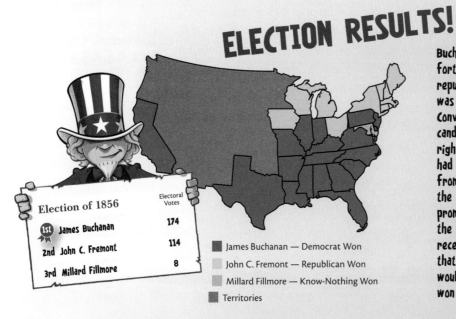

Election of 1856	Electoral Votes
1st James Buchanan	174
2nd John C. Fremont	114
3rd Millard Fillmore	8

- James Buchanan — Democrat Won
- John C. Fremont — Republican Won
- Millard Fillmore — Know-Nothing Won
- Territories

Buchanan appeared a likely candidate: he had forty years of political experience and the reputation of a highly skilled politician. He was unanimously chosen at the Democratic Convention of 1856, beating out two other candidates who shared his belief in states' rights. Unlike the other candidates, Buchanan had been out of the country and was free from any scandals or debates stemming from the current American turmoil. With the promise of "Save the Union," Buchanan and the Democrats campaigned against the recently formed Republican Party, claiming that if the Republicans were elected, war would be inevitable. As a result, Buchanan won every southern state except Maryland.

BTW: Although he was aligned with the northern states, he often sided with the south on fiscal issues, like tariffs, and gained the reputation of a fiscal moderate.

AMERICA'S Prewar Boom

Despite the divide between the north and the south, America was booming. Railroads were rapidly appearing, telegraphs expedited communication at a rate not seen before, advancements were being made in the field of science and technology, and religious revivals materialized across the country. This led not only to an increase in Americans' physical well-being but their spiritual well-being as well.

LIBERTY Language

Midterm election: The congressional election taking place two years into the president's term of office.

but it only made matters worse outside of America's court system.

Recession and War

On the domestic front, Buchanan's presidency could not have experienced a more tumultuous time. An economic recession hit in 1857. It led to falling gold prices and worsened the standing of the state banks, which operated without any federal control (a situation similar to the Panic under Martin Van Buren). On top of the economic instability of the country, developments in the south continued to suggest a civil war was on the horizon.

Foreign Policy

> I believe slavery to be a great political and great moral evil. I thank God my lot has been cast in a state where it does not exist.

Although he failed to achieve any great victories in America's domestic affairs, Buchanan drew on his experience as secretary of state and achieved many foreign policy successes. First, Buchanan saw the opening of trade agreements with Latin America. Second, he successfully opened ports on the west coast of America to supply the incoming shipments from Asia. Third, he prevented Great Britain from colonizing areas in Central America.

In spite of these achievements, the Republicans gained the majority in the 1858 midterm elections. This shift in the balance of power created a deadlock on all legislation proposed in the last half of Buchanan's presidency, even on legislation over a national railroad. At this time, the southern states were on the very edge of secession and vandalizing federal property in the south. Congress urged Buchanan to send troops to protect federal property, but Buchanan refused, thinking it would provoke them into full-out rebellion.

PRESIDENTIAL Personality

★ Although he was not considered a great orator or a great president, Buchanan was known by his peers as a courteous, faithful, and generous man. He often refused to accept gifts during his presidency and freely loaned money to friends and family in need. He conducted himself with dignity but was never pompous, often caring for and giving to the poor and secretly working in his personal life to free African slaves.

BTW: James Buchanan was the first president to send a transatlantic telegram.

BTW: Buchanan often bought slaves. Instead of keeping them for his own personal gain, he took them to his home state of Pennsylvania, where they were considered free. He immediately emancipated every slave he ever bought.

Failure at Reelection

Northern Americans were furious with Buchanan over his inaction with the seceding states, and southern Americans were furious with Buchanan because he faltered on supporting the states' rights to secede. If a Republican were to win in the next presidential election, the south swore they would secede. To make matters more complicated, however, the Democrat Party split into north and south because of debates over the slavery platform. Buchanan, though, refused to seek reelection, more than happy to leave the office that had been the center of so much turmoil during his stay in office.

Post-Presidency

Buchanan was happy to retire to his plantation just as he had planned to do twelve years earlier. This time the retirement was permanent, and Buchanan focused on writing his three-hundred-page book, *Mr. Buchanan's Administration on the Eve of Rebellion*, in which he blamed Republicans for the Civil War and the secession of the south. During this time, he cared for his nephew, James Buchanan Henry—who also served as Buchanan's personal secretary during his presidency—and paid for his Princeton education. At the age of seventy-seven, Buchanan fell ill with pneumonia. This, as well as his gout and other ailments, contributed to his death the same year. He divided his $300,000 estate among his relatives before he died.

What Has He Done for Me Lately?

Upon Buchanan's leave of office, the country was on the eve of civil war. The debate on slavery had escalated to secession and Buchanan had done nothing to stop it. However, would action on behalf of the federal government really have prevented further secession? Or was slavery an issue that could only be worked out through war? Regardless, Buchanan only succeeded in fanning the flame that consumed the country in civil war.

> My dear sir [Abraham Lincoln], if you are as happy on entering this house as I am leaving, you are a very happy man indeed.

PLATFORM SPEECH

> The different sections across the Union are now arrayed against each other, and the time has arrived, so much dreaded by the Father of this Country, when hostile geographical parties have been formed.

> Buchanan said this in his 1860 annual address to Congress. The division over slavery was exactly what our founders feared—the country divided based on party lines over the issue of slavery.

BTW: Last Words: "Whatever the result may be, I shall carry to my grave the consciousness that at least I meant well for my country. Oh Lord God Almighty, as thou wilt."

JAMES BUCHANAN

Presidential Times

Written by Juliette Turner

JOHN BROWN'S RAID ON HARPERS FERRY, VIRGINIA

October 17, 1859—Abolition activist John Brown led a raid today on the federal arsenal in Harpers Ferry, Virginia. Brown and his group of abettors captured prominent civilians and seized the federal armory in the town.

Brown hoped to spark a slave rebellion throughout the country after his success in capturing weapons. No slaves aided Brown in his actions.

U.S. Marines under the command of Robert E. Lee soon came to subdue Brown and his accomplices and actually killed many of the raiders. Brown was captured, charged with treason, and is sentenced to hang on December 2.

TREASON! THE SOUTH SECEDES!

February 1, 1861—Texas just became the seventh state to secede from the Union. On December 20, 1860, South Carolina was the first state to secede. Mississippi, Florida, Alabama, Georgia and Louisiana, have also seceded. These seven states now refer to themselves as the "Confederacy."

BUCHANAN PREVENTS SECESSION … IN UTAH?

June 19, 1858—Peace has finally been established in the Utah territory. After years of tension, the Mormons of the Utah desert are now allowed to return home. Brigham Young, however, is not. Starting in 1847, the Mormons who settled in the Utah Territory governed themselves. In 1851, however, Utah became a U.S. territory and Brigham Young was appointed its governor. Rumors in Washington, D.C., began to circulate about a Mormon theocracy with Young at its head. Installing religious leaders in an American territory is strictly prohibited. These rumors remained rumors until Young and his men began defying American laws and regulations, frequently driving federal officials off Utah land.

In response, President Buchanan ordered 2,500 soldiers to advance into Utah while accompanying a new governor to the territory. This is referred to as the "Mormon War." Simultaneously, Young declared Utah a free and independent territory and organized his own two-thousand-man army. While they nervously waited to protect their land from the insurgence of American troops, they lashed out at a group of 120 innocent pioneers.

This event is called "Massacre at Mountain Meadows." Buchanan then ordered four more regiments to advance from Washington, D.C., to Utah, but bad weather slowed the army and they did not arrive until this spring. When the troops arrived, however, Young surrendered and submitted to federal authority.

BUCHANAN: APPEASER OF THE SOUTH

December 20, 1860—Many Americans are now accusing President Buchanan of treason. South Carolina has seceded from the Union only seventeen days after Buchanan addressed Congress, stating that neither the president nor congress "ha[d] the power to coerce a State into submission which is attempting to withdraw or has actually withdrawn from the [Union]." Many are claiming Buchanan figuratively waved the green flag in his address, signaling the south to begin the secession process.

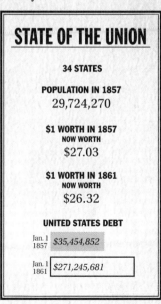

STATE OF THE UNION

34 STATES

POPULATION IN 1857
29,724,270

$1 WORTH IN 1857
NOW WORTH
$27.03

$1 WORTH IN 1861
NOW WORTH
$26.32

UNITED STATES DEBT

Jan. 1 1857	$35,454,852
Jan. 1 1861	$271,245,681

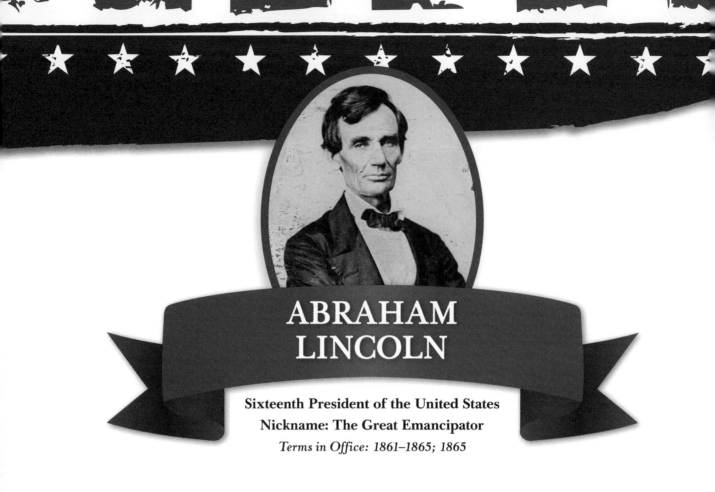

ABRAHAM LINCOLN

Sixteenth President of the United States
Nickname: The Great Emancipator
Terms in Office: 1861–1865; 1865

The Bottom Line

Abraham Lincoln remains the only man to serve as president during a civil war on American soil. The Civil War turned American against American and eventually claimed approximately 650,000-850,000 American lives. Lincoln served one full term and a month into his second term, before he was fatally shot on Good Friday, April 14, 1865, making him the first president to be assassinated.

FAST STATS

★ Born February 12, 1809, in Hodgenville, Kentucky
★ Parents: Thomas and Nancy Hanks Lincoln; step-mother: Sarah Bush Johnston Lincoln
★ Died April 15, 1865, in Washington, D.C.; age 57
★ Age upon Start of First Term: 52; Age upon Conclusion of First Term: 56
★ Age upon Start of Second Term: 56; Age upon Assassination: 57
★ Religious Affiliation: Christian
★ Political Party: Republican
★ Height: 6 feet 4 inches
★ Vice President: Hannibal Hamlin (1861–1865) and Andrew Johnson (1865)

What Was He Thinking?

Abraham Lincoln began as a politician who was against the complete abolition of slavery but became the president responsible for ending slavery in America for good. He supported a strong federal government and believed in free-homestead legislation, establishing a daily mail service, constructing a transcontinental railroad, and higher tariff rates to protect American businesses.

 BTW: Lincoln's father, skillful at carpentry, was nearly illiterate, as was his mother.

THOUGHTS ON THE CONSTITUTION

Don't interfere with anything in the Constitution. That must be maintained, for it is the only safeguard of our liberties.

PRESIDENTIAL Personality

★ Lincoln was an honest man and a powerful speaker, yet he also fought depression. Ironically, his depression may have helped him become such a great leader. To help himself, he read poetry, literature, and the Bible, which helped form his impressive writing skills. His depression also influenced his sense of humor. He once wrote that jokes "are the vents of my mood and gloom."

Why Should I Care?

Abraham Lincoln served as president during one of the most dangerous, turbulent, and aggressive time periods in American history.

The issue of slavery, finally leading to the American Civil War, dominated the political landscape and influenced all Lincoln's actions as president. As a man who issued the proclamation to free all slaves, he governed the country during its first and only war between brethren and championed the Thirteenth Amendment, which officially ended slavery in America. Lincoln fundamentally changed the United States into a country that finally upheld the decree set forth in the Declaration of Independence: "All men are created equal."

Breakin' It Down

Early Life

Abraham Lincoln lived the American Dream. Though he grew up in a log cabin with a dirt floor in Kentucky and his family lived in a pole shed the first winter they lived in Indiana, he managed to make his way to the highest office in the land and, above all, become one of the most cherished American presidents of all time.

His family eventually settled in Indiana, where his mother died when he was only nine. She was only thirty-four and died from drinking poisonous cow's milk which occured after the cow ate a plant called "white snakeroot," a common cause of death back then.

Abe's younger brother, Thomas, died in infancy, and Abe became very close with his only other sibling, his older sister, Sarah. The two were almost inseparable. Soon their father remarried, and Abe gained three stepsiblings. Abe loved his stepmother, also named Sarah, and considered her his best friend. She encouraged Abe to educate himself by reading. He only received one year of formal education his entire life.

The Commissioner of Internal Revenue is established, 1862

The Department of Agriculture is formed, 1862

The Emancipation Proclamation is issued, 1862

Victor Hugo publishes *Les Miserables*, 1862

The Nevada Territory is added, 1861

The Colorado Territory is added, 1861

Beginning of Civil War, April 1861

West Virginia becomes a state, 1863

Henry Ford is born, 1863

The Battle of Gettysburg is fought, 1863

Nevada becomes a state, 1864

Louis Pasteur perfects the process of pasteurization, 1864

Robert E. Lee surrenders at Appomattox Court House, VA; the Civil War ends, 1865

The 13th Amendment abolishes slavery, 1865

First Term in Office

1860   1861   1862   1863   1864   1865

Lincoln's first job came after the family moved to Illinois in 1830. He captained a ferryboat that carried passengers and their luggage to the riverboats on the Ohio River. Lincoln took several other jobs, including blacksmithing, sailing a flatboat from Illinois down to New Orleans, and clerking at a general store in town.

> I do the very best I know how, the very best I can; and I mean to keep on doing it to the end. If the end brings me out all right, what is said against me will not amount to anything. If the end brings me out all wrong, then a legion of angels swearing I was right will make no difference.

> If I ever get a chance to hit [slavery], I'll hit it hard.

First Couple

MARY TODD LINCOLN

Abraham Lincoln met Mary Todd through his law partner in Springfield. The two quickly became engaged and planned to marry in 1840, but Lincoln failed to show up for the wedding. Nevertheless, the two reconciled and married in 1842. Mary was known for her impulsive attitude, unstable personality, and indulgent spending practices. (She even overspent on the White House renovations she ordered during the Civil War.) Mary was an unlikely match for a northern antislavery politician, since she was from the south and a proslavery family. All but two of Mary and Abraham's four children died a premature death. Tad lived to be eighteen and died in 1871. Robert was their only child to live into adulthood.

Previous Political Career

- 1832: Became captain during the Black Hawk War.
- 1832: Failed attempt to win a place in the Illinois state legistature. He finished eighth in the race.
- 1834: Elected to the Illinois House of Representatives; served as chairman of the finance committee.
- 1847: Elected to the U.S. House of Representatives.
- 1858: Selected as the Republican candidate for U.S. Senate. This began the series of famous debates between Lincoln and the incumbent Democratic candidate, Stephen Douglas. Although Lincoln lost the election 54 to 46, the debates gave him national exposure.

ABE the Lawyer

In 1836, Lincoln received his license to practice law in front of the Illinois Supreme Court in Springfield, Illinois. Lincoln spent six months out of the year riding the circuit even though he oftentimes rejected cases he did not believe in. Lincoln quickly garnered the reputation of a dynamic and exciting speaker, often filling the court's balconies with people gathering simply to hear him speak.

Lincoln Debates Douglas

★★★★★★★★★★★★★★★★★★★★★★★★

The debates taking place in 1858 between Abraham Lincoln and Stephen Douglas are known today as hallmarks of the American political system. In a series of seven heated and intense debates that sometimes lasted over three hours, Lincoln and Douglas debated in front of crowds as large as fifteen thousand people. The candidates and their political views received nationwide newspaper coverage. They debated not only slavery but also the future of the country. Lincoln's view of gradual emancipation of the slaves became the platform for the Republican Party in his presidential bid.

ELECTION RESULTS!

Lincoln entered the Republican presidential convention behind William Seward, who held the lead, but with help from his supporters. Lincoln won and became the second Republican candidate to run for president. Lincoln's election to the presidency had much to do with the Democrat Party dividing. Had the Democrats not divided, Lincoln would have come in a distant second. Because there were so many Democrats and third-party candidates, the election went to Lincoln.

Abraham Lincoln handily won the popular vote by 10 percentage points and a staggering 93 percent of the electoral college. Instead of Hannibal Hamlin, a staunch abolitionist, Lincoln chose southerner and Democrat Andrew Johnson to help pull some of the northern democratic vote to the Lincoln camp. The emergence of absentee voting also ensured Lincoln's victory—120,000 of the 154,000 soldiers who voted in the election of 1864 voted for Lincoln. He won every free state except New Jersey but received no southern support.

BTW: The election of 1860 has the second highest voter turnout in history with approximately 81% of Americans voting.

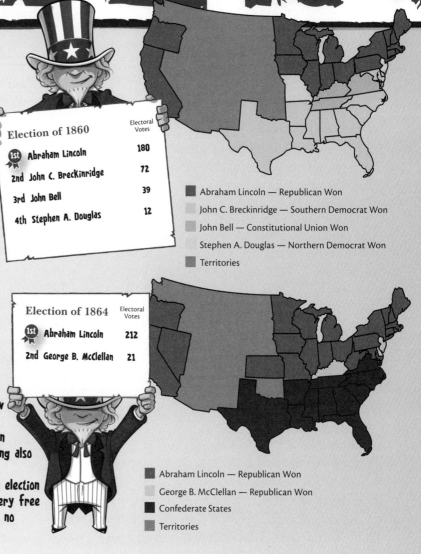

Election of 1860

		Electoral Votes
1st	Abraham Lincoln	180
2nd	John C. Breckinridge	72
3rd	John Bell	39
4th	Stephen A. Douglas	12

- ■ Abraham Lincoln — Republican Won
- ■ John C. Breckinridge — Southern Democrat Won
- ■ John Bell — Constitutional Union Won
- ■ Stephen A. Douglas — Northern Democrat Won
- ■ Territories

Election of 1864

		Electoral Votes
1st	Abraham Lincoln	212
2nd	George B. McClellan	21

- ■ Abraham Lincoln — Republican Won
- ■ George B. McClellan — Republican Won
- ■ Confederate States
- ■ Territories

Peoria Speech

★★★★★★★★★★★★★★★★★★★★★★★★

The Peoria Speech marked Lincoln's rise in politics. In this speech, he first expressed his radical views on slavery, calling it a moral issue, not just a political issue. He also urged that slavery become a national issue, not merely a regional issue. After giving this speech, Lincoln was unanimously chosen by the Illinois Republican State Convention to run for U.S. Senate opposite incumbent Democrat Stephen Douglas.

Presidency

Abraham Lincoln's inauguration was the most highly policed of any up to that point, with sharpshooters lining the rooftops. Lincoln's hopes and pleadings for peace vanished into thin air with the Crisis of Fort Sumter. Fort Sumter was federally controlled land surrounded by Confederate South Carolina. The U.S. army wanted to surrender the fort because it proved too hard to supply, much less defend. The only other option was to send armed U.S. naval ships to resupply the fort, forcing the U.S. army to be the first to advance. However, Lincoln created a third option. He decided to send an unarmed ship loaded with simple food provisions. With this plan,

 BTW: Did you know that the eleven confederate states that seceded did not vote in the election of 1864?

121

the Confederacy would have to be the first to fire, and thus would be to blame for the war.

The Civil War Begins

Confederate president Jefferson Davis ordered Fort Sumter be taken by force, and the first shots of the Civil War were fired on April 12, 1861. With the start of war, Lincoln made difficult decisions, some of which remain constitutionally questionable. Most notably, he claimed he had the right to suspend the writ of habeas corpus, a power expressly granted to Congress. Lincoln also greatly expanded the executive branch's power by claiming that he had the power to protect the Union with military force without the approval of Congress, bypassing the normal judicial and constitutional proceedings. With his war declaration, Lincoln called for 7,600 volunteers. Lincoln claimed that his declaration of war did not concern slavery, but rather the preservation of the Union.

Emancipation Proclamation

Then, on September 22, 1862, Lincoln issued the Emancipation Proclamation and freed all slaves in the Confederate states. Slave owners in the Union states were not required to free their slaves; rather, it was simply encouraged. The declaration also allowed African-

POLITICAL PARTIES

The split of the Democrat Party: **In 1860, the Democrat Party split over the issue of slavery. When it did, the once-powerful party formed two smaller and not as powerful parties, the Northern Democrats and the Southern Democrats. The difference between the two parties was simple: the Northern Democrat Party opposed the expansion of slavery and the Southern Democrat Party believed slavery should exist in every area of the United States.**

Constitutional Union: **This party hoped to compromise the ideals of the Northern Democrats and the Southern Democrats by reinstating the age-old Missouri Compromise and extending the dividing line across the United States. Under this plan, states formed north of the line would be prohibited from adopting slavery and states south of the line would be permitted to enter into the Union as slave states.**

LIBERTY Language

Wilmot Proviso: A proposal by David Wilmot that declared, "neither slavery nor involuntary servitude shall ever exist" in lands won in the Mexican-American War.

On Slavery

At the start of his political career, Lincoln believed slavery to be immoral but did not believe it could be immediately ended. Lincoln dreaded the wrath of the slave owner, fearing the attempts to do good by forcing emancipation may, by accident, "increase its evil." In the U.S. House, Lincoln voted for the Wilmot Proviso and publicly branded slavery a hypocrisy, proclaiming his belief that the practice of slavery had no place in a country based on equality and freedom. When the Wilmot Proviso failed, Lincoln proposed his own policy, which freed all slave children born on or after January 1, 1850, and required the free children to learn a trade through apprenticeship. Lincoln argued that slavery should be considered a moral issue instead of a political one, not merely an issue of the north or south. He said, "A house divided against itself cannot stand. I believe a government cannot endure permanently half-slave and half-free." Upon becoming president, the only thing to which Lincoln committed himself was prohibiting slavery in the new territories. On September 22, 1862, however, Lincoln issued his Emancipation Proclamation, which freed all southern slaves on January 1, 1863. After doing so, Lincoln pressed for the passage of the Thirteenth Amendment to the Constitution, which solidified the abolition of slavery forever.

CONGRESSIONAL CORNER

★★★★★★★★★★★★★★★★★★★★★★★★★★

1. **Homestead Act of 1862:** This act ordered 160-acre plots of land to be given to settlers for a small fee if they agreed to stay on the farm land for five years. It also freed aspects of federal lands to states to establish agricultural and technological institutes.

2. **Pacific Railway Act of 1862 and 1864:** These bills provided federal assistance to the Union Pacific and Central Pacific Railroads to build a transcontinental railroad from Missouri to the Pacific Ocean.

3. **National Banking Act of 1863:** This act, passed February 25, 1863, changed America's banking system from state-based to nation-based by initiating a national charter for banks and establishing a national currency.

4. **Thirteenth Amendment:** Passed by Congress and ratified by the states in 1865, this amendment constitutionally abolished slavery in every state in America.

★★★★★ ★★★★★★★★★

> My paramount objective is to save the Union.

LIBERTY Language

Writ of habeas corpus: A Latin term meaning "you shall have the body." In practice, the right to habeas corpus means that you cannot be held in jail without facing legitimate charges of some kind. Learn more about it in *Our Constitution Rocks!*

> I never in my life, felt more certain that I was doing the right thing than I do in signing [the Emancipation Proclamation].

Americans to join the army for the first time.

Lincoln did not stop at the Emancipation Proclamation. He immediately turned his attention to the passage of the Thirteenth Amendment, which would permanently and constitutionally outlaw slavery and involuntary servitude. It was not until late 1865 and after Lincoln's death that the amendment was ratified.

Economy and National Affairs

Meanwhile, there was still a nation to run outside of the war. On the economic front, Congress passed the National Banking Act, which created a national currency for the first time. Additionally, in an attempt to pay for the war, Lincoln launched the first national income tax. When Great Britain came close to entering the war on the side of the Confederacy, Lincoln dispatched Charles Francis Adams, John Adams' grandson, to negotiate a treaty that kept Britain safely on the sidelines.

As the war continued and after the midterm elections of 1862, a group called the "Radical Republicans" gained increasing influence in Congress. This group later pushed for harsher measures to be taken against the south. Despite the increasing political tensions, Lincoln kept Congress in check. Together, the executive and legislative branches passed the Homestead Act, which encouraged settlers to travel to new lands. Then in 1862 and 1864, Congress passed the Pacific Railway Acts and opened new railroads in the West.

War Ends

Barely a month after his second inaugural address, the Civil War ended (April 9, 1865). In celebration of the event, Lincoln requested the presidential band play the southern anthem, "Dixie." Lincoln also pushed for generous terms of surrender and ordered that there be no harsh punishments. He prohibited hanging Confederate leaders, fearing it would promote more bloodshed throughout the country.

BTW: Lincoln constantly tended to things himself, expressing his avid dislike whenever he had to rely on someone else to do work for him.

Assassination

On the evening of Good Friday, April 14, 1865, Abraham Lincoln planned to celebrate the end of the war by seeing the comedy play *Our American Cousin*, in Ford's Theater with his wife, Mary. Earlier, Lincoln had met with his cabinet, reinforcing his views that the surrender and readmittance of the southern Confederate states to the Union must be marked by leniency.

Lincoln's trip to Ford's Theater that night ended in tragedy when John Wilkes Booth entered the theater, approached the president's theater box, gave his card to the White House footman who sat guard outside, was allowed entrance, and fired a bullet into the back of Lincoln's head just as the audience erupted in the biggest laugh of the evening. Lincoln was quickly taken from the box and transferred to a nearby boarding house, where a surgeon declared Lincoln close to death. About nine hours later, at 7:22 a.m. on April 15, Abraham Lincoln died.

The White House Animals

Newly inaugurated presidents often received gifts, and Lincoln received a living bald eagle, in good health but with one missing foot. Lincoln was also the first president to keep a menagerie of animals at the nation's house. Two favorites were Tad's pet goats. Once Tad hooked up a sled to the goats and led them through the East Room in the middle of a White House guest reception.

What Has He Done for Me Lately?

Lincoln stretched the bounds of the presidency to unprecedented levels. Because of his strict leadership, however, and the risks he took to use his power for the betterment of the country, the Union in the end won the war and all slaves received their inalienable freedom.

PLATFORM SPEECHES

> Fondly do we hope, fervently do we pray, that this mighty scourge of war may speedily pass away. Yet if God wills that it continue until all the wealth piled by the bondsman's two hundred and fifty years of unrequited toil shall be sunk, and until every drop of blood drawn with the lash shall be paid by another drawn with the sword, as was said three thousand years ago, so still it must be said, "The judgments of the Lord are true and righteous altogether."

> With malice toward none, with charity for all, with firmness in the rights as God gives us to see the right, let us strive on to finish the work we are in, to bind up the nation's wounds, to care for him who shall have borne the battle and for his widow and his orphan, to do all which may achieve and cherish a just and lasting peace among ourselves and with all nations.

> In his 1865 State of the Union address, Lincoln compares the wealth lost because of the war to the wealth gained by the slave owners. Likewise, he compares the bleeding of the slaves because of whipping to the bloodshed on the battlefield. In Lincoln's view, this was repayment and justice.

> Lincoln wanted to bind the nation together and embrace the south when they lost—to maintain peace and unity.

ABRAHAM LINCOLN

Written by Juliette Turner

LINCOLN'S SECOND INAUGURAL ADDRESS

March 4, 1865—Today could not have been more symbolic. It was dreary and rainy when Lincoln stepped to the podium, but then the rain stopped and clouds cleared, almost in divine representation of the American storm that was slowly passing. Also symbolic, the Capitol building, which had been only half completed at Lincoln's first inauguration, now stood finished behind him as he spoke. Thirty-five thousand people gathered to hear Lincoln deliver the second shortest inaugural address in history. The address entitled by Lincoln's hand "Meditations on the Divine Will," of which Lincoln destroyed all rough drafts, used "I" only once and instead used "we" and "both." Lincoln mentioned the name of God fourteen times and called for prayer three times.

A COMMEMORATIVE ARTICLE: THE AMERICAN CIVIL WAR

April 10, 1865—"In your hands, my dissatisfied fellow-countrymen, and not in mine, is the momentous issue of civil war."

Four months after President Lincoln spoke those words to a dividing country, the Civil War officially began. Forty percent of the ten-thousand engagements would be fought in Chickamauga and Shiloh, Tennessee, and Fredericksburg, Virginia. In late 1862, it appeared that the south, under the command of Robert E. Lee, had the upper hand. The decisive battle of Antietam—the bloodiest engagement in the war—switched the power into the hands of the north.

After this battle, Lincoln issued his Emancipation Proclamation, which went into effect January 1, 1863, freeing all slaves in the Confederate states. In 1863, the Battle of Gettysburg resulted in 51,112 American casualties. Lee lost this battle and the south was forced to a major retreat for the first time. Lincoln appointed Ulysses S. Grant as chief commander of the Union army in early 1863. The north won the Battle of Vicksburg in July of 1863. By the spring of 1865, General Grant had crushed the Confederate Army in a long series of battles, forcing General Lee to surrender at the Appomattox Court House in Virginia on April 9, 1865.

The death toll of the war has been estimated to reach 850,000, making it by far the worst American war in history. The average soldier stood at 5'8.25" and weighed 143.5 pounds. Five hundred thousand foreign-born soldiers and 166 regiments of black troops fought for the Union Army alone.

LINCOLN'S ASSASSIN IS IDENTIFIED

April 16, 1865—A shocking revelation is that John Wilkes Booth, Lincoln's assassin, was standing just ten yards away from Lincoln as he delivered his inaugural address.

John Wilkes Booth was known as a brilliant actor who came from a line of great theatrical actors. Had he continued his career, which was still young in the making, Booth may have been known in history as a beloved stage actor rather than an assassin. However, before the end of the Civil War, Booth had planned with several other men to kidnap the president and members of his cabinet to use as a negotiation tool for a Union surrender.

These plans changed when the south was defeated, and

Booth turned for blood. Booth organized a plan in which he and his coconspirators would kill Lincoln, Vice President Andrew Johnson, and Secretary of State William Seward, and by doing so, throw the Union into disarray. Booth's coconspirators, however, failed to act in their mission, and ultimately Lincoln was the only one killed.

After shooting Lincoln with his .44 caliber derringer at 10:15 p.m. on Good Friday, Booth jumped from the president's box and onto the stage, wielding a bloody knife he had used to slash Lincoln's friend and army officer Henry Rathbone. He yelled "Sic Semper Tyrannis"—Latin for "Thus always for tyrants." Booth fled the nation's capital.

After his death, it was found that Lincoln received more than his fair share of threatening letters, yet he never threw even one of them them away, keeping all threats in a large manila envelope he labeled "Assassination."

PROFILE OF AN ASSASSIN AND HIS COCONSPIRATORS

July 7, 1865—Today, John Wilkes Booth's coconspirators were hung for treason: David Herold, the man who led Booth in his escape from Washington, D.C.; George Azterodt, the man who was assigned to assassinate Vice President Johnson but failed to do so and instead became intoxicated at a hotel bar; and Lewis Powell, the man assigned to assassinate Secretary of State William Seward. In addition, Mary Surratt, who had aided

the abettors by allowing them to use her house to form their assassination plots, was the first woman to be executed by the U.S. government.

DEVELOPING: THE PONY EXPRESS!

Sacramento Union Newspaper —March 19, 1860—Men Wanted: The undersigned wishes to hire ten men or a dozen men, familiar with the management of horses, as hostlers, or riders on the Overland Express Route via Salt Lake City. Wages $50 per month and found.

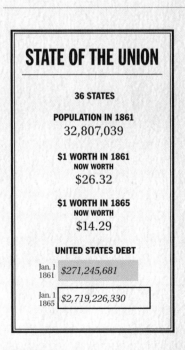

STATE OF THE UNION

36 STATES

POPULATION IN 1861
32,807,039

$1 WORTH IN 1861
NOW WORTH
$26.32

$1 WORTH IN 1865
NOW WORTH
$14.29

UNITED STATES DEBT

Jan. 1 1861	$271,245,681
Jan. 1 1865	$2,719,226,330

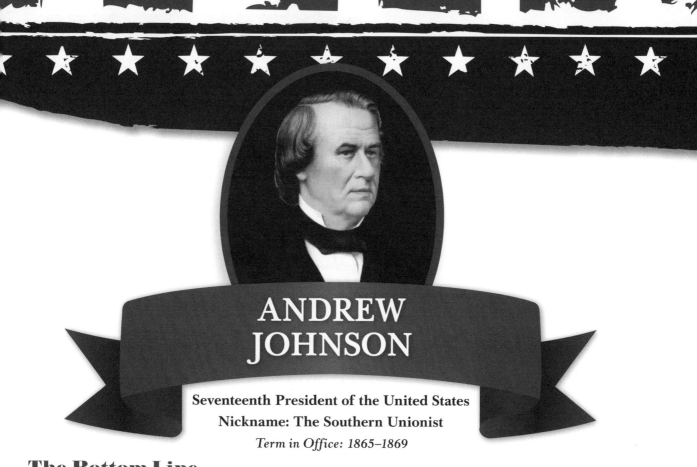

ANDREW JOHNSON

Seventeenth President of the United States

Nickname: The Southern Unionist

Term in Office: 1865–1869

The Bottom Line

Andrew Johnson was the first man to assume the presidency after the assassination of his predecessor. Johnson served the remainder of Abraham Lincoln's term of office, during which time he struggled to balance the process of Reconstruction. Johnson didn't favor providing federal protection for the newly freed slaves and after much wrangling with the Republicans in Congress, he was the first American president to be impeached.

FAST STATS

★ Born December 29, 1808, in Raleigh, North Carolina
★ Parents: Jacob and Mary McDonough Johnson
★ Died July 31, 1875, in Carter's Station, Tennessee; age 66
★ Age upon Start of Term: 56; Age upon Conclusion of Term: 60
★ Religious Affiliation: Christian
★ Political Party: Democrat
★ Height: 5 feet 10 inches
★ Vice President: none

What Was He Thinking?

Johnson related well to the working class and considered himself the advocate and guardian of the farmers, lower classes, and laborers. Serving as president after America's bloodiest war, Johnson's views on slavery contrasted greatly with Abraham Lincoln's. Johnson believed that the passage of civil legislation—mainly granting rights to the newly freed African-Americans—infringed upon state rights, and he advocated against them. As a Democrat, Johnson believed in state sovereignty and a limited government—a political stance that came as a shock and disappointment to the Radical Republicans in Congress.

POLITICAL PARTIES

★★★★★★★★★★★★★★★★★★★★★★★★

War Democrats: A faction of the Democrat Party that denounced the idea of secession and broke from the Copperheads-controlled Democratic base. These War Democrats also demanded stricter action toward the Confederacy and supported Abraham Lincoln in his efforts in the Civil War.

Copperheads: A faction of Northern Democrats that was opposed to the Civil War and instead suggested peaceful negotiations with the Confederacy.

Radical Republicans: A faction within the Republican Party that strongly opposed slavery, supported the Civil War, and urged harsher punishment for the ex-Confederate states. This group was also responsible for emphasizing civil rights and suffrage for African-Americans, including championing the passage of the Civil Rights Act of 1866 and the formation of the Freedman's Bureau.

Why Should I Care?

When Lincoln was assassinated, his job was only half done. Lincoln succeeded in winning the war and defeating the Confederacy, but his death left Johnson with the monumental and crucial task of reuniting the Union. Though it did not appear so at the time, Johnson helped to bind the gaping wounds of the nation.

Breakin' It Down
Early Life

Andrew Johnson was born the youngest son of a poor family. When he was only three years old, his father died after diving into an icy river to try to save two drowning men. After his death, the family became destitute, even labeled "white trash" by the townspeople. To provide enough money for food, Andrew's mother worked as a spinner and a weaver.

At a young age, Andrew and his brother worked at a tailor shop rather than going to school, and Andrew became an apprentice at age ten. He worked at the trade until he was seventeen and then moved to Greenville, Tennessee, and opened his own tailor shop. It was quickly successful, becoming the gathering

Diamonds are discovered in South Africa, 1868

The Alaska Territory is purchased from Russia, 1867

William Gladstone is named prime minister of Great Britain, 1868

Henri Matisse is born, 1869

Tennessee is readmitted to the Union, 1866

Nebraska becomes a state, 1867

Karl Marx publishes *Das Kapital*, 1867

Leo Tolstoy publishes *War and Peace*, 1869

The Secret Service is established, 1865

Mahatma Gandhi is born, 1869

Term in Office

| 1864 | 1865 | 1866 | 1867 | 1868 | 1869 |

THOUGHTS ON THE CONSTITUTION

[T]he Constitution is to be made the nation's safe and unerring guide.

place for people to discuss politics and issues of the day. During the debates and conversations, Andrew became known as a forceful speaker and often sided with the small farmers. Soon, nearly everyone in the town knew about tailor Andrew Johnson. This recognition helped Andrew win his first run for political office at the young age of twenty.

First Couple

Andrew Johnson married Eliza McCardle in 1827, when he was nineteen and she was seventeen. Among all the first ladies, Eliza holds the record for being the youngest to marry. Eliza gave birth to four children in seven years but gave birth to her youngest child eighteen years later. Eliza had a basic education and was responsible for teaching her husband reading, writing, and the basics of mathematics.

ELIZA JOHNSON

Previous Political Career

- 1829: Elected a member of a city court at the age of twenty.
- 1833: Elected mayor of Greenville, Tennessee.
- 1834: Elected to the Tennessee state legislature. He lost reelection in 1837 but won in the subsequent 1838 election.
- 1841: Elected to Tennessee's state senate.
- 1843: Elected to the U.S. House of Representatives, where he would serve for the next ten years, becoming known as an independent-minded politician who was always armed with the facts.
- 1853: Elected to become Tennessee's governor, serving two terms. He promoted taxes to support education, equal pay for male and female workers, and regulations for schoolteachers.
- 1857: Elected to the U.S. Senate to represent Tennessee.
- March 27, 1861: Became the leader of a faction called the War Democrats—the congressional Democrats from the south, who stayed loyal to the Union.
- 1862: Appointed military governor of Tennessee after Abraham Lincoln installed a temporary military government.

Presidency

Andrew Johnson had served as vice president for barely six weeks when Abraham Lincoln was assassinated. In their last meeting, just days before Lincoln's murder, Lincoln cautioned Johnson not to be too lenient in how he approached the former Confederate states and citizens, although Lincoln strictly forbade his other cabinet members from enforcing harsh punishment on Confederate states.

Almost immediately upon his promotion to president, Johnson was forced to negotiate with the Republican majority in Congress over the treatment of the confederates as well as the newly freed slaves. This congressional faction constantly pushed for harsher punishment of the south, an effort which Johnson attempted to block. However, there was only so much he could do.

BTW: Eliza and Andrew were married by the Reverend Mordecai Lincoln, Abraham Lincoln's cousin.

Reconstruction period: The period after the Civil War when the southern states reentered the Union. During Reconstruction, the U.S. military occupied many southern states to ensure the new abolition and voting policies for African-Americans were thoroughly implemented.

The Radical Republicans eventually restricted full participation of representatives from former Confederate states in matters regarding foreign affairs, among other things. Instead of working to reconcile and negotiate between the two forces, Johnson attacked the situation with his naturally combative attitude, only making things worse. Immediately, the relationship between Johnson and Congress hardened. Congress blocked nearly all of Johnson's proposals for Reconstruction, forming their own Committee on Reconstruction, which wanted punishment instead of peaceful leniency. The Committee then proposed and Congress passed the Fourteenth Amendment to the Constitution. Johnson was opposed to the Fourteenth Amendment, but because of the powerful Republican majority in Congress, Johnson's views mattered little.

Shortly before Lincoln's assassination, Congress had formed the Freedmen's Bureau, an agency designed to send federal aid to freed slaves. Johnson disliked the bureau and deemed it unconstitutional, because, he reasoned, it invaded the sovereignty of the southern states by dictating policy they had no say in forming. (Representatives from the Confederate states had not yet reentered Congress.) Congress then passed the Civil Rights Act, which Johnson vetoed, but Congress overrode the veto.

In the midterm election of 1866, Johnson attempted to campaign for moderate candidates through his disastrous "Swing Around the Circle" nationwide speaking campaign. Because of his low popularity across the country, however, his appearances did more harm than good.

Impeachment Attempt

Congress finally had enough of the stubAndrew Johnson, and in 1867 they passed Tenure of Office Act, making it illegal for

CONGRESSIONAL CORNER

★★★★★★★★★★★★★★★★★★★★★★★★★★★★

1. **Civil Rights Act of 1866: Guaranteed that all African-Americans would be able to enjoy the same rights as all white Americans, making all forms of discrimination illegal.**

2. **Freedmen's Bureau Bills of 1866: Established the Freedmen's Bureau, an organization created under Abraham Lincoln's presidency to help freed slaves transition into their new life of freedom.**

3. **Judicial Act of 1866: Reduced the number of members on the Supreme Court from nine to seven. This was passed by Congress to prevent Andrew Johnson from nominating any justices to the Supreme Court.**

4. **The Four Reconstruction Acts: March 2, 1867; March 23, 1867; July 19, 1867; March 11, 1868— These acts organized and commanded the readmittance of the Confederate states into the Union. These acts also divided the former Confederate states into five military zones, each commanded by a military government and military governor (a U.S. general) to ensure all freed slaves were treated with equality in their transition into freedom.**

5. **Fourteenth Amendment: This amendment, ratified July 9, 1868, established four things: all people born in the U.S. are legally citizens and receive all benefits of citizenship, the threefifth's clause was repealed, former Confederate leaders couldn't vote or hold office, and no Confederate states, or Americans who aided the Confederate Army, would get any compensation from the federal government for Civil War debts.**

★★★★ ★★★★★

It is treason, nothing but treason, and if one State, upon its own volition, can go out of this Confederacy without regard to the effect it is to have upon the remaining parties to the compact, what is your government worth?

In this quote, Johnson is scolding the southern states that had seceded for their rash actions. In his view, they seceded without any regard for how it would impact the nation and their fellow states.

LINCOLN'S Ten Percent Plan

On December 8, 1863, Lincoln announced his Proclamation of Amnesty and Reconstruction—his "Ten Percent Plan"—that required only 10 percent of the Confederate states' populace to swear to uphold the Constitution in order for the state to be readmitted. In May 1865, Johnson adapted Lincoln's already lenient policies to lean more toward complete amnesty and only light requirements for readmittance. For example, Johnson pardoned all southern whites except for Confederate leaders. Johnson held that the states could reenter the Union after passing the Thirteenth Amendment and then nullifying all state debts incurred as a result of the war.

LIBERTY Language

Amnesty: An official governmental pardon for American citizens who have committed grave political offenses.

Johnson to remove any officeholder or cabinet member without congressional approval. Johnson understandably vetoed the bill, but Congress overrode his veto. Tempted to test the act and see what reaction he would receive from Congress, Johnson suspended Secretary of War Edwin Stanton after he discovered Stanton and Ulysses S. Grant were implementing policy behind his back. Congress was outraged and moved to impeach Johnson. Eleven charges of misconduct (mostly violations of the Tenure of Office Act) were drawn against him. Even though it appeared the impeachment measure would suceed in the Senate after easily passing in the House, it failed to win the two-thirds majority necessary for Johnson's removal by a single vote.

Johnson failed to win his party's nomination for the next presidential election. Yet he did not let this discourage him from acting until the very last day of his presidency. One of Johnson's most controversial actions came on Christmas Day, 1868, when he granted amnesty to all former Confederate citizens. This time, Johnson had nothing to lose.

Post-Presidency

During the Panic of 1873, Johnson lost most of his investments. Now, no longer in the mood to retire after losing so much of his nest egg, Johnson decided to run for political office yet again. He won his bid for U.S. Senate in 1874, becoming the only president to serve in the Senate after leaving office. Johnson's stay in the position was short-lived, however. On July 31, 1875, he suffered a severe stroke and died on the same day. Johnson was buried wrapped in the U.S. flag with his personal copy of the Constitution placed under his head, per his request.

What Has He Done for Me Lately?

Andrew Johnson fulfilled his duties as president—reuniting the north and south after a bloody war. By the time he left office, seven of the eleven Confederate states had reentered the Union. After almost being impeached and experiencing a four-year-long battle with Congress, Johnson initiated the process that also granted official pardons for almost all former members of he Confederacy.

PLATFORM SPEECH

[T]he greatest wrongs inflicted upon a people are caused by unjust and arbitrary legislation, or by the unrelenting decrees or despotic rulers, and ... the timely revocation of injurious and oppressive measures is the greatest good that can be conferred upon a nation.

Andrew Johnson said this in his 1868 State of the Union address to Congress. He believed that big government and laws that restrict the people's liberties are the biggest threats to the American people. He believed that only through careful reversal of those laws and the shrinking of the government can a nation's freedoms be truly restored.

ANDREW JOHNSON

BTW: Last Words: "I need no doctor. I can overcome my troubles."

Presidential Times

Written by Juliette Turner

VICE PRESIDENT JOHNSON OFF TO A BAD START

March 4, 1865—An awkward silence fell over the crowd today as they observed Vice President Andrew Johnson stumbling to the podium during Abraham Lincoln's second inauguration.

Train passengers who traveled with Johnson on his trip to Washington, D.C., observed the vice president constantly sipping from his flask of whiskey. By the time he arrived at the inauguration ceremonies, he was clearly intoxicated. He began a barely audible, rambling address, which caused many to brand him as a southern, no-good drunk.

In an attempt to save his dignity, some of Lincoln's cabinet members led Johnson away from the podium only several minutes into his incoherent address.

Later, President Lincoln claimed to the press, "I've known Andy a great many years, and he ain't no drunkard."

We now know that Johnson was sick with typhoid fever and had asked to miss the ceremonies. Lincoln persuaded him to come anyway, and the vice president had been drinking to ward off the pain.

SEWARD'S FOLLY

March 30, 1867—President Johnson's secretary of state, William Seward, has negotiated the purchase of the Alaskan Territory from the Russians for $7.2 million. Because this unchartered land is unknown to most Americans, many are wondering why such a large amount of money was spent on it.

It has also been reported that Seward also purchased the Midway Islands—a string of small islands most Americans have never heard of—through the same treaty. Many have deemed the mysterious purchase "Seward's Folly."

MONROE DOCTRINE RESURFACES

November 15, 1867—Napoleon III of France has agreed to enter the final stages of withdrawal from Mexico this month. During Mexico's civil war, France intervened, beginning in 1861, installing princes and leaders in Mexico who operated under the control of Napoleon III. As soon as the Civil War ended and Johnson assumed office, he invoked the age-old Monroe Doctrine to prevent France from further colonizing areas in Mexico and permanently installing a French prince in the region. Secretary of State William Seward sent fifty thousand troops to the Mexican-American border and demanded that Napoleon III withdraw his troops from the region. Napoleon III first ordered the withdrawal on January 1, 1866.

SHH! IT'S A SECRET

June 4, 1865—Sadly, it takes an assassination to persuade Washington, D.C., to revamp its security system. Today it was announced that a secret security service known as the secret service has been formed to protect the president. The service claims it was formed to suppress the printing of fake and illegal currency, but it will be widely known that it is a presidential security squad.

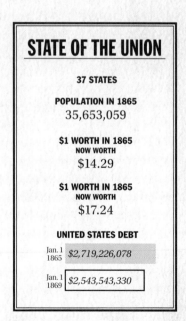

STATE OF THE UNION

37 STATES

POPULATION IN 1865
35,653,059

$1 WORTH IN 1865
NOW WORTH
$14.29

$1 WORTH IN 1865
NOW WORTH
$17.24

UNITED STATES DEBT

Jan. 1 1865	$2,719,226,078
Jan. 1 1869	$2,543,543,330

ULYSSES S. GRANT

Eighteenth President of the United States
Nickname: Unconditional Surrender Grant
Terms in Office: 1869–1873; 1873–1877

BTW: Grant called the Mexican – American War "one of the most unjustified ever waged by a stronger nation against a weaker one."

The Bottom Line

Ulysses S. Grant, the youngest president to date, was president during a time when America struggled to regain her footing after the Civil War. During his first term, Grant struggled to restore the south after the devastation caused by the Civil War. His second term was characterized by five major government scandals, hurting Grant's effectiveness in office.

FAST STATS

★ Born April 27, 1822, in Point Pleasant, Ohio
★ Parents: Jesse Root and Hannah Simpson Grant
★ Died July 23, 1885, in Wilton, New York; age 63
★ Age upon Start of First Term: 46; Age upon Conclusion of First Term: 50
★ Age upon Start of Second Term: 50; Age upon Conclusion of Second Term: 54
★ Religious Affiliation: Methodist
★ Political Party: Republican
★ Height: 5 feet 8 inches
★ Vice Presidents: Schuyler Colfax (1869–1873) and Henry Wilson (1873–1877)

What Was He Thinking?

Although he was known as a Republican and ran as a Republican in his election bid for president, Ulysses S. Grant really considered himself an independent. He supported Lincoln, but he sometimes agreed with the politics of James Buchanan and Stephen Douglas. As president, Grant pushed for a return to the gold standard and also believed in controlling the actions of the southern states by force (although he favored using local militias instead of the national army).

Why Should I Care?

Although economic instability and government scandals plagued the nation, Grant left the presidency having instituted several Reconstruction plans that helped protect African-Americans and quicken America's emergence from the Reconstruction era. Unlike his predecessor, Andrew Johnson, Grant was unafraid to use force in the southern states to protect the rights of former slaves, and because of it, Grant's successor, Rutherford B. Hayes, was able to call an end to the process of Reconstruction.

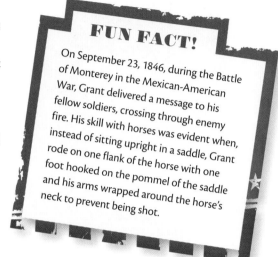

FUN FACT!

On September 23, 1846, during the Battle of Monterey in the Mexican-American War, Grant delivered a message to his fellow soldiers, crossing through enemy fire. His skill with horses was evident when, instead of sitting upright in a saddle, Grant rode on one flank of the horse with one foot hooked on the pommel of the saddle and his arms wrapped around the horse's neck to prevent being shot.

Breakin' It Down
Early Life

Hiram Ulysses Grant, called HUG as a child, was the oldest of six children and grew up in a two-room log cabin. As a young boy, Ulysses attended a local schoolhouse, where he enjoyed learning math. He also joined an outside-of-school debating society. Ulysses began to show a special talent for training and caring for horses, a task he enjoyed very much. Before long, Grant's father realized that his eldest son would never be a businessman, so he prepared to send him to the U.S. Military Academy at West Point. Ulysses enrolled in the school at the age of seventeen. An average student except for excelling in math, Ulysses graduated from West Point in 1843, twenty-first in a class of thirty-nine.

JULIA GRANT

First Couple

In 1848, Ulysses S. Grant married Julia Dent. Grant's avid antislavery, abolitionist family refused to attend the wedding because Julia's father was a slaveholder. Together the couple had four children.

BTW: Before the Civil War, Grant began to build a home on his plantation which he called, "Hardscrabble" because of its bad crop soil. Because of his failure as a farmer, Grant decided to entered real estate, which also proved unsuccessful. Grant was then forced to work at his father's tanning shop where his siblings nicknamed him "Useless."

The Wyoming Territory grants women the right to vote, 1869

The first U.S. continental railroad is completed, 1869

The Black Friday U.S. financial panic takes place, September 24, 1869

The Department of Justice is formed, 1870

The Fifteenth Amendment is added to U.S. Constitution, 1870

Orville Wright (of the Wright Brothers) is born, 1871

The Great Chicago Fire kills 250 individuals and leaves $196 million in damages, 1871

The German Empire is recognized, 1871

The Brooklyn Bridge opens, 1872

Yellowstone National Park is founded by Ulysses S. Grant, 1872

First Term in Office

| 1868 | 1869 | 1870 | 1871 | 1872 |

BTW: In mid-April 1865, Grant and his wife, Julia, received an invitation from first lady Mary Lincoln to accompany her and the president to see the play *My American Cousin* at Ford's Theater. Grant declined—a decision that most likely saved his life.

Ulysses S. Grant dedicated his life to the service of America through the army. In 1846, Grant entered the Mexican-American War, fighting in major battles under the command of Winfield Scott and Zachary Taylor, rising to second lieutenant. After the conclusion of the war, Grant was sent to patrol the Oregon Territory, but resigned his position in April of 1854. It is speculated that during this time Grant suffered from a drinking problem and that his resignation occurred just before the problem ruined his military career. In 1860, as the Civil War began, Grant recruited soldiers and organized, trained, and lead an army of volunteers in Galena, Illinois. Two years later, Grant led this volunteer army to win a major Union Army victory at the capture of Fort Donelson in Tennessee and the bloody battle of Shiloh and the Battle of Vicksburg. On March 8, 1864 Abraham Lincoln commissioned Grant to become lieutenant general, making him the first man to hold to position since George Washington. In April of 1865, Grant accepted Robert E. Lee's surrender at the Appomattox Courthouse after Lee's defeat at the Battle of Five Forks. With the conclusion of the war, Grant toured the south and sent reports on the updated situation in the region to then President Johnson.

Presidency

At his inauguration ceremony, Grant declared, "Let us have peace"—an interesting request for a former war general. Calling for an end to regional divisiveness, Grant attempted to fix the problems in the Reconstruction and reunification process, which came as a result of Johnson's bickering with Congress. Grant strongly supported the Fifteenth Amendment to the Constitution (which prohibited voter discrimination based on race or color) and the other civil rights efforts that occurred under his presidency.

PRESIDENTIAL Personality

★ Ulysses S. Grant, the military leader and president, seems to contradict Ulysses S. Grant, the private man. He was modest, polite, formal, soft-spoken, and gentle. He hated dirty jokes and was extremely superstitious. Grant became one of the greatest military leaders in history.

BTW: Grant smoked seven to ten cigars a day, a habit that later led to the throat cancer that killed him soon after his presidency.

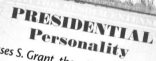

Color photography is invented, 1873 •

Between 1866 and 1873, 35,000 miles of railroad track are added across America

The U.S. Financial Panic of 1873 takes place, 1873

Gertrude Stein is born, 1874 •

Grant's daughter Nellie marries in the White House, May 21, 1874

The first Kentucky Derby is run, 1875

The Battle of Little Big Horn is fought, 1876

Alexander Graham Bell invents the telephone, 1876

Colorado becomes a state, 1876

Second Term in Office

| 1873 | 1874 | 1875 | 1876 | 1877 |

ELECTION RESULTS!

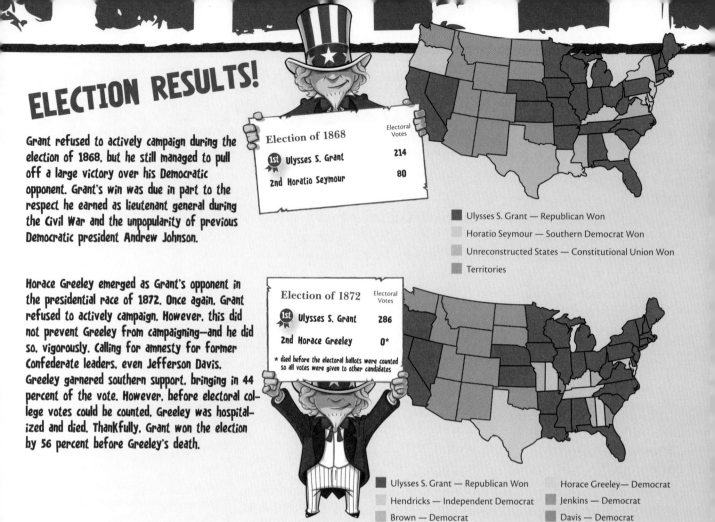

Grant refused to actively campaign during the election of 1868, but he still managed to pull off a large victory over his Democratic opponent. Grant's win was due in part to the respect he earned as lieutenant general during the Civil War and the unpopularity of previous Democratic president Andrew Johnson.

Horace Greeley emerged as Grant's opponent in the presidential race of 1872. Once again, Grant refused to actively campaign. However, this did not prevent Greeley from campaigning—and he did so, vigorously. Calling for amnesty for former Confederate leaders, even Jefferson Davis, Greeley garnered southern support, bringing in 44 percent of the vote. However, before electoral college votes could be counted, Greeley was hospitalized and died. Thankfully, Grant won the election by 56 percent before Greeley's death.

Election of 1868

	Electoral Votes
1st Ulysses S. Grant	214
2nd Horatio Seymour	80

- Ulysses S. Grant — Republican Won
- Horatio Seymour — Southern Democrat Won
- Unreconstructed States — Constitutional Union Won
- Territories

Election of 1872

	Electoral Votes
1st Ulysses S. Grant	286
2nd Horace Greeley	0*

* died before the electoral ballots were counted so all votes were given to other candidates

- Ulysses S. Grant — Republican Won
- Horace Greeley— Democrat
- Hendricks — Independent Democrat
- Jenkins — Democrat
- Brown — Democrat
- Davis — Democrat
- Territories

Economic Woes

During Grant's two terms in office, the economic repercussions of the war resulted in heavy financial problems for the country, and he dealt with two financial panics. The first occurred on September 24, 1869, and was known as Black Friday. Grant narrowly avoided a complete economic collapse by releasing gold from the federal treasury to help stabilize the dollar. In 1875, Grant signed the Specie Resumption Act, which attempted to remedy the financial crisis by reducing the number of greenbacks in circulation, thus increasing the value of the dollar.

Trouble with the South

After the passage of the Fifteenth Amendment in 1870, the south reacted with vengeance. With the Enforcement Act of May 1870, Congress authorized the installation of federal soldiers in nearly all of the southern states to protect the voting rights of African-Americans. The radical plan worked to a degree, but it led to the formation of the infamous Ku Klux Klan. To combat the radical and deadly group, Grant signed the Ku Klux Klan Act of April 1871, which used federal courts to stop "radical supremacy" groups from forming. Federal courts indicted approximately three thousand members of the Klan, and many of those were convicted. Then Grant signed the Civil Rights Act of 1875, which, among other things, prohibited racial segregation in housing and transportation. However, this act was declared unconstitutional eight years later.

The framers of our Constitution firmly believed that a republican government could not endure without intelligence and education generally diffused among the people.

—ULYSSES S. GRANT—

CONGRESSIONAL CORNER

★★★★★★★★★★★★★★★★★★★★★★★★★★★★

1. **Public Credit Act of 1869:** Passed on March 18, 1869, this act established that individuals who helped finance the Civil War (on the Union side) would be repaid in gold.

2. **Civil Rights Act of 1870:** This act, also known as the Force Act or the Ku Klux Klan Act, gave the president and the federal government power to, using force if necessary, implement the fifteenth amendment to prevent racial supremacy groups from forming.

3. **Currency Act of 1870:** This act helped restabilize the U.S. economy after the economic panic of 1869.

4. **Indian Appropriation Act:** This act granted Native Americans citizenship, gave them educational and medical aid, and moved tribes to reservations where they could receive education and the opportunity to learn about Christianity.

5. **Civil Rights Act of 1871:** Passed April 20, 1871, this act gave the president the power to suspend the writ of habeas corpus to combat racist groups like the Ku Klux Klan.

6. **Amnesty Act of 1872:** This act provided amnesty for all who had been members of the Confederacy, except for five hundred Confederate military leaders.

7. **Specie Payment Resumption Act of 1875:** This act, as a result of the Panic of 1873, restored the gold standard.

8. **Civil Rights Act of 1875:** This act ensured that newly freed slaves would be treated equally in public accommodation and public transportation. However, the Supreme Court declared the act unconstitutional in 1883.

★★★★★★★★★★★★★★★★★★★★★★★★★★★★

Native American Policy

During his presidency, Grant also addressed U.S. relations with Native Americans. The issue had remained on the sidelines for many years, but Grant—who stated that Native Americans were "the most harmless people you ever saw"—worked to help them. In reality, it resulted in a large restriction upon the free will of the Native American population. In March, 1871, Grant signed the Indian Appropriation Act. Although this plan was not ideal, it was a great improvement. Previous presidents and administrations failed to keep nearly all of the 370 treaties the government made with the Native Americans.

Scandal and Crisis

Grant was reelected in 1872, but his second term was even more chaotic than his first. The first of five scandals that would rock Grant's presidency leaked during the election. The Crédit Mobilier Scandal, as with the four subsequent scandals, never involved Grant directly, but involved friends he had appointed to his executive cabinet. Others scandals were the Sanborn Contract Incident (1874), the Whiskey Ring (1875), the Delano Affair (1875), and the Indian Trader Post Scandal (1876). On top of the scandals, America once again experienced an economic crisis worse than during Grant's first term. The Panic of 1873 was a financial crisis that triggered a depression in Europe and the United States that lasted from 1873 to 1879, and even longer in some countries. This time, Grant would not be as lucky. Grant was unable to stabilize the U.S. economy while in office, but he did greatly reduce the national debt, which had grown to unprecedented heights during the Civil War.

Post-Presidency

Four years after he left office, Grant almost won the Republican nomination for a third run for the presidency, but he lost to James Garfield. Instead, Grant became president of the Mexican Southern Railway and invested his retirement money in his son's New York banking firm. However, it went bankrupt, and Grant lost all his money. One day Grant was worth 1.5 million dollars, the next day he was in debt. Then Grant met Samuel Clemens, aka Mark Twain, who encouraged Grant to write a memoir. Grant soon found out that he was ill with throat cancer. Nevertheless, Grant worked eight hours a day, refusing pain killers so his thinking would not be clouded, and he finished the book within a year. Grant died at age 63. Grant's funeral procession was seven miles long and took hours to pass by. Over 300,000 people watched in observance of a man who led the country in war and in peace.

> I never wanted to get out of a place as much as I did to get out of the presidency.

What Has He Done for Me Lately?

Grant's brilliant military strategy, determination, and leadership as lieutenant general during the Civil War led to the Union victory and put an end to the bloodshed. As general and as president, Grant remained selflessly committed to his duties, effectively expediting America's process of reconstruction and protecting the rights of the newly freed African-Americans who still struggled for equality.

PLATFORM SPEECH

> Treat the Negro as a citizen and voter, as he is and must remain, and soon parties will be divided not on the color line, but on principle.

> Grant said this in his 1874 state of the union address. Even though the Civil War had ended, some political beliefs and parties were still based on the issues of the war, including Reconstruction and racism. Grant hoped that soon political beliefs would instead be based on principles.

BTW: While Grant was serving as president, he received a ticket from the Washington, D.C., police with a $20 fine. Grant supposedly was riding his horse too fast.

ULYSSES S. GRANT

BTW: Last Word: "Water."

Written by Juliette Turner

BLACK FRIDAY

September 24, 1869—Gold prices are plummeting for the fourth day in a row. On Monday, two New York financiers—Jay Gould and Jim Fiske—attempted to gain considerable profits by buying large quantities of gold in the American gold market, increasing prices due to a decreasing supply and then selling the gold for profit. Once the transaction occurred, the gold prices skyrocketed by 20 percent. Now the worth of greenbacks—money printed without silver or gold backing—has collapsed further, all gold-based foreign trade has halted, and the stock market has been forced to close. Many individual banks are closing across the country, and investors are hurting.

You may remember that, during the Civil War, greenbacks were issued in large quantities by the federal government to help farmers and workers purchase necessary goods during the war. Since these greenbacks, or dollars, were not backed by gold, their value was highly unstable. When Grant entered office, he expressed his views that the American dollar should again be backed by gold. Now the plummeting gold prices are pulling the worth of the dollar down as well. In a statement to the press, the Grant administration said they are planning to release four million dollars' worth of gold into the market.

SCANDAL!

October 23, 1872—The Crédit Mobilier Scandal is bad timing for Ulysses S. Grant, who is up for reelection this year. However, opponent Horace Greeley must be pleased to hear that the press is now covering a major scandal that is rocking the Grant administration. The Crédit Mobilier Scandal started when Thomas Durant chartered a company during the Lincoln administration. Named Crédit Mobilier, the company allowed individuals to invest in the railroad construction business without being liable—or legally responsible—for their investments. The deal was offered to some congressmen, who took the bait and dishonestly approved federal funding for the construction so they themselves would benefit from it. Although Grant was not engaged in these illicit activities, critics are saying it may hurt his reelection chances.

BAD FAMILY CONNECTION

September 30, 1869—White House aides are reporting that President Grant is furious after hearing the news that his own brother-in-law, Abel Corbin, was involved in the recent Panic of 1869. Corbin reportedly gave background information on the president to Jay Gould and Jim Fiske to help them plan their gold purchases. Additionally, the assistant to Grant's secretary of treasury, Daniel Butterfield, was bribed by Gould with $10,000 for inside information on the nation's gold exchanges.

PANIC OF 1873

October 18, 1873—Over ten thousand banks across the country have now closed their doors after last month's financial panic. New York firm Jay Cooke and Company declared bankruptcy and closed its doors on September 18, causing a financial panic across the nation. After the Civil War, banks and investors began investing in the booming railroad construction business. Jay Cooke and Company was one of the major investors in the railroad industry. Now one in every four railroad companies have declared bankruptcy. Unemployment is predicted to reach 15 percent and is expected to remain at that high level for several years, perhaps as late as 1879.

THE PROBLEM WITH GRANT'S CABINET

May 14, 1874—When Grant entered office, he selected his cabinet based on friendship, not on who could do the job well. He is now feeling the consequences. After two financial panics, the last thing Grant needs is another scandal—but now he has one. The Sanborn Incident involves Grant's secretary of treasury, William Adams Richardson, who commissioned John D. Sanborn, a private citizen, to collect unpaid taxes from various businesses and companies that had evaded certain taxes. Yet the commission came with a bribe: Sanborn would be able to keep half of the taxes he collected, an amount that equaled $427,000. When Sanborn completed his task, he had obtained the tidy sum of $213,500, distributing $156,000 of it to various assistants.

GRANT INVESTIGATES THE WHISKEY RING SCANDAL

March 13, 1875—Grant authorized his secretary to investigate the members of the so-called Whiskey Ring Scandal today, and many arrests are now taking place. The scandal was recently uncovered, just one year after the Sanborn Incident. A group of Republican congressmen and politicians accepted millions of dollars' worth of bribes from whiskey distilleries in exchange for granting them exemption from the whiskey tax. The tax money was instead being used by the distilleries to fund Ulysses S. Grant's reelection campaign, without the president's knowledge.

This scandal is one in a long list of scandals occurring

ANOTHER SCANDAL!

March 2, 1876—Secretary of War William Worth Belknap has become the first member of a presidential cabinet to be impeached. President Grant accepted Belknap's resignation at 10:20 a.m. but this did not stop the House of Representatives from voting to impeach Belknap, who was receiving bribes from traders wanting to do business at Indian trading posts.

GET TO KNOW YOUR PRESIDENT

As a special feature in today's news, we have a couple fun facts about President Grant. Did you know that he is disgusted by blood? Even though he became a general in America's bloodiest war, young Ulysses refused to work in his father's tanning shop, claiming the blood-soaked environment sickened him. He also hates dealing with dead animals and is revolted at the idea of killing them.

JUST DON'T TAKE THE BRIBE

October 15, 1875—In the fifth scandal of his presidency, Grant is again forced to root out corruption from his own cabinet. Today Grant accepted the resignation of his secretary of the interior, Columbus Delano. Earlier this year, Delano was accused of accepting a $1,200 bribe over land grants and land patents from a Colorado banker. It was also reported that Delano's son was receiving partnerships and surveying contracts through illicit means.

during Grant's presidency. His time in office is easily the most scandal-ridden of any presidency. Many Americans consider Grant a man of honesty and integrity, and his reputation has remained mostly intact; however, the scandals keep coming from the friends he selected to serve in his cabinet.

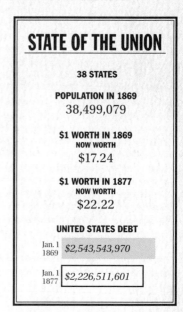

STATE OF THE UNION

38 STATES

POPULATION IN 1869
38,499,079

$1 WORTH IN 1869
NOW WORTH
$17.24

$1 WORTH IN 1877
NOW WORTH
$22.22

UNITED STATES DEBT

Jan. 1 1869	$2,543,543,970
Jan. 1 1877	$2,226,511,601

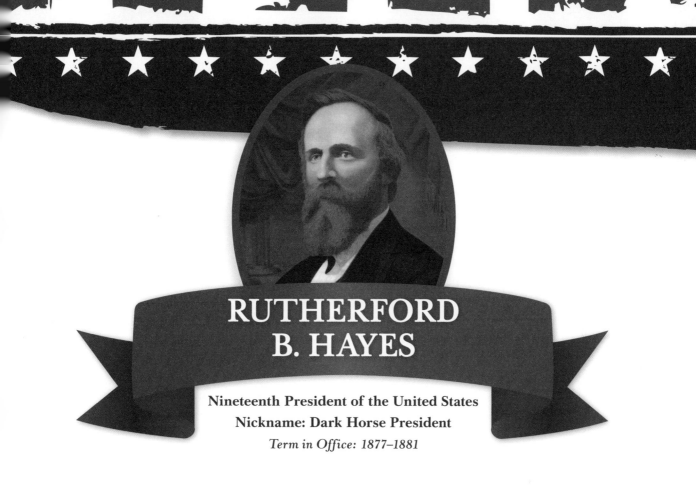

RUTHERFORD B. HAYES

Nineteenth President of the United States
Nickname: Dark Horse President
Term in Office: 1877–1881

The Bottom Line

Rutherford B. Hayes ended the process of postwar Reconstruction and instituted a civil service system for executive appointments.

What Was He Thinking?

Throughout his political career, Hayes championed social reform. He was passionate about education for children, proper treatment of prisoners and the mentally ill, and supported the civil reforms occurring in the nation. Hayes also believed economic stability was imperative to the success of the working class and worked to stabilize the economy after the Panic of 1873 by returning America to the gold standard.

FAST STATS

★ Born October 4, 1822, in Delaware, Ohio
★ Parents: Rutherford and Sophia Birchard Hayes
★ Died January 17, 1893, in Fremont, Ohio; age 70
★ Age upon Start of Term: 54; Age upon Conclusion of Term: 58
★ Religious Affiliation: Methodist
★ Political Party: Republican
★ Height: 5 feet 9 inches
★ Vice President: William A. Wheeler

Why Should I Care?

Hayes ended the Reconstruction era in America and turned the page to a different battle for civil rights. Throughout his political career, Hayes championed social reforms like universal high school education, temperance, and black voting rights. Although removing soldiers and the military governments from the southern states seemed like a good idea, it actually tremendously

slowed the process of achieving equality for African-Americans. Hayes also worked to reform the appointment system in the executive branch by installing a civil service system that ended a series of corrupt appointments.

Breakin' It Down

Early Life

Rutherford (Rud) was raised by his single mother, Sophia, because his father died of malaria two months before the future president was born. The redheaded, blue-eyed Rud was a sickly young boy, but he grew into a strong, able young man. He attended private schools starting at age nine, his tuition paid by his uncle Sardis. In 1842, Rutherford graduated from Kenyon College first in his class and enrolled in Harvard Law School. He would be the first president to graduate from a formal law school. Shortly after graduating in 1845, Hayes began serving as a volunteer attorney for the Underground Railroad. He first entered the political field when he began to give speeches that supported a temperance society and opposed the anti-Catholic and anti-immigrant Know-Nothing Party. He helped form the Republican branch in Ohio and joined the Literature Club of Cincinnati, where he established connections with powerful Ohio politicians and benefactors. It was these political connections that helped Hayes win his first political position in 1858.

LUCY HAYES

First Couple

On December 30, 1852, Rutherford Hayes married Lucy Ware Webb. The two had met when Lucy was fourteen, but they did not start "dating" until after she graduated from Wesleyan Female College in Ohio. Lucy was the first of any first lady to have graduated from college. The couple courted for three years and finally married in 1852, beginning a nearly fifty-year marriage. Together they had eight children.

Lucy was an opinionated, smart, and witty woman, openly expressing her avid opposition to alcohol and slavery. With strong and avant-garde beliefs on women's rights, Lucy once stated, "Woman's mind is as strong as man's—equal in all things and is superior in some."

Reconstruction officially ends and Jim Crow segregation laws arise, 1877

Frederick Douglass is named the first black marshal for Washington, D.C., March 30, 1877

Thomas Edison patents the phonograph, 1877

The Second Afghan-British War begins, 1878

The Great Railroad Strike of 1877 takes place, 1877

The first commercial telephone exchange occurs in New Haven, Connecticut, 1878

Thomas Edison invents the electric light, 1879

A U.S.-China treaty limits Chinese immigration to America, 1880

Term in Office

1876   1877   1878   1879   1880   1881

Previous Political Career

- 1858: Appointed Cincinnati city solicitor to fill the vacant position after the death of the sitting solicitor, winning reelection twice.
- 1861: Joined the 23rd Ohio Infantry as a major during the Civil War.
- 1864: Elected to the U.S. House of Representatives as a Republican even though he still fought in the Civil War. He served as chairman of the Committee on the Library of Congress, while serving in the House. He worked to add two new wings to the library.
- 1868: Elected governor of Ohio, winning despite ebbing Republican influence and popularity.
- 1872: Defeated in an attempt to run for Congress.
- 1874: Temporary retirement to his new home, Spiegel Grove, Ohio, which his deceased uncle Sardis had left him.
- 1876: Elected to an unprecedented third term as governor of Ohio.

During the Civil War Hayes fought in fifty engagements, was wounded five times, and had four horses shot out from under him. One time he was shot in the elbow, leading to a serious loss of blood that impeded his ability to walk and nearly caused him to pass out. Although he was forced to sit down in the middle of the battle, Rutherford continued to give commands until his men were forced to retreat. In November of 1864, Hayes was promoted to brevet major general for his "distinguished and gallant services in the Campaign of 1864."

BTW: Hayes refused to serve alcohol at White House functions.

ELECTION RESULTS!

Election of 1876

Electoral Votes

1st Rutherford B. Hayes — 185

2nd Samuel J. Tilden — 184

■ Rutherford B. Hayes — Republican Won
■ Samuel J. Tilden — Democrat Won
■ Territories

This election remains one of the most disputed in history and the only presidential election to be decided by a congressional commission. There was proof of fraud on both sides: Democrats intimidated African-Americans to prevent them from voting and Republicans duplicated the ballots cast by those African-Americans who did vote.

To resolve the issue, a bipartisan congressional commission was established. In the end, Hayes was declared the winner, but only after a deal that was pegged the Compromise of 1877. The Democrats agreed to allow Hayes to win the presidency as long as (1) all federal troops were withdrawn from the southern states, (2) southern Democrats were appointed to Hayes's cabinet, and (3) Democrats were guaranteed congressional funding for the Texas and Pacific Railroads, a railway that would connect New Orleans to the West Coast.

Although the Constitution is explicit in the guidelines for an election that ends in a tie or an election where no candidate receives the electoral majority, the Constitution gives no guidelines for when electoral votes are disputed and the winner of the popular vote in states is unclear.

1. **Bland-Allison Act of 1878:** This act required the federal treasury to purchase a set amount of silver and release it to the market as silver dollars for purchase. It was vetoed by President Hayes, but Congress overrode the veto.

2. **Timber and Stone Act:** This act, passed in 1878, ordered all land unfit for farming be sold for $2.50 per acre in 160-acre plots for the purposes of timbering and mining.

★★★★★★★★★★★★★★★★★★★★★★★★★

LIBERTY Language

Jim Crow segregation laws: A set of forceful anti-African-American laws established in the south that deepened the divide between white and black and slowed African-Americans' progress for civil rights.

Presidency

True to his campaign promise and the promise of the congressional commission, Hayes's first act as president was to end Reconstruction. When he took office, South Carolina and Louisiana were governed by two state governments, one of which was a military government policed by federal troops. Hayes met with the governors of South Carolina and Louisiana and negotiated the removal of federal troops and the abolition of the military government, reinstating a single government for each state. Although these actions were good for the sovereignty of the southern states, it hurt the African-Americans' struggle for equal rights. Shortly after federal troops left the south, the Jim Crow segregation laws were installed.

Social Reform

Hayes continued to fulfill his second campaign promise: initiating a civil service system for executive officeholders. He signed an executive order in 1877 that prohibited government officials from engaging in the "management of political organizations, caucuses, conventions, or election campaigns." Hayes did this to end the infamous "patronage system," which he despised. In regard to promoting civil rights, Hayes supported having elections supervised by federal troops to eliminate fraud—an issue close to home after his own fraud-plagued election. Hating racism of every kind, Hayes vetoed a bill that would have restricted Chinese immigration.

International Accomplishments

On the international scene, Hayes gained approval from Congress in 1881 to partner with a French firm on the construction of the Panama Canal. However, construction on the canal would not begin for another two decades.

Monetary Reform

On the economic front, Hayes stabilized the faltering economy, still suffering from the Panic of 1873, by resuming the practice of backing the dollar with a federal gold reserve. Hayes received push back from Congress on this issue because it limited their ability to print more money and issue more silver and gold coins. As a result, Congress passed the Bland-Allison Act of 1878, which went directly against

PRESIDENTIAL Personality

★ Rutherford B. Hayes was known as a social man with an air of modesty and humility. He made those he met feel special and important, possessing the remarkable ability to remember the faces and names of even the briefest acquaintances. As a politician, he respected his opponents and welcomed constructive criticism, genuinely expressing interest in people's thoughts, opinions, and even problems. His friends from childhood remained his friends for life, and Hayes is remembered as a solid man of good character who served his country well.

BTW: Hayes was the first sitting president to travel to the West Coast.

THOUGHTS ON THE CONSTITUTION

It will be the duty of the Executive, with sufficient appropriations for the purpose, to prosecute unsparingly all who have been engaged in depriving citizens of the rights guaranteed to them by the Constitution.

BTW: Last words: "I know I am going where Lucy is."

Hayes's requests and demanded that the federal treasury buy two to four million dollars' worth of silver coins each month. The coins were to be used to pay off national debts. Hayes expressed his support of the Resumption of Specie Act, which had been passed four years earlier and allowed individuals across the country to redeem their "greenbacks" with gold.

Post-Presidency

When Hayes left the presidency, he retired to his home in Spiegel Grove, Ohio, and almost immediately began to work in the philanthropic field. Using his influence, Hayes helped to promote proper treatment of war veterans, championed education, and advocated for underprivileged children. Hayes became the president of the National Prison Association and served on the board of trustees for Ohio State University, Ohio Wesleyan College, and the Western Reserve University. He also served on the boards of many veterans organizations and on the board of the Peabody Fund, which helped underprivileged children in the south receive education. Twelve years after he left the presidency, Hayes died peacefully on January 17, 1893, in his home in Spiegel Grove.

What Has He Done for Me Lately?

Rutherford B. Hayes, like Ulysses S. Grant, served his country both in the Civil War and as the president. Although Hayes was a Republican, he ended the Reconstruction period in America, helping the country to take another step in the healing of the Civil War's wounds. Additionally, Hayes's efforts to reform the presidency helped to move the executive branch from one of fraud to one of ability, integrity, and responsibility.

PLATFORM SPEECH

[H]ere we are, Republicans, Democrats, colored people, white people, Confederate soldiers, and Union soldiers, all of one mind and one heart today ... Let each man make up his mind to be a patriot in his own home and place. You may quarrel about the tariff, get up a sharp contest about the currency, about the removal of the state capitals and where they shall go to, but upon the great question of the Union of the states and the rights of all the citizens, we shall agree forevermore.

Rutherford B. Hayes said these words in his speech on the end of Reconstruction in 1877. As a former solider in the Civil War, Hayes wanted nothing more than unity among all Americans.

RUTHERFORD B. HAYES

Written by Juliette Turner

RAILROAD STRIKERS CLASH WITH FEDERAL TROOPS

July 18, 1877— Railroad strikes are erupting all across the country, greatly interrupting travel for thousands of Americans. Today in Ohio, strikers blocked branches of the railroad and destroyed several lines, preventing any trains from passing. In Martinsburg, West Virginia, yesterday, the workers on the Baltimore & Ohio Railroad initiated a workers' strike because the railroad company has reduced their wages twice over the previous year. The strike quickly spread to other states, including Maryland.

West Virginia's governor attempted to organize militia forces to end the strike, but the militia sympathized with the workers, refusing to act. This prompted the governor to contact President Hayes, who sent federal troops to reopen the railroad. Outside West Virginia, events quickly became dangerous: in Baltimore, Maryland, violence erupted between the strikers and state militia; in Pittsburgh, Pennsylvania, and St. Louis, Missouri, strikers captured several cities before federal troops could gain control; and in Chicago, Illinois, twenty thousand people gathered to support the strikers.

LUCY HAYES HOLDS THE FIRST WHITE HOUSE EASTER EGG ROLL

April 22, 1878—The White House lawn was a festive sight today as children from all across the Washington, D.C., area gathered to celebrate Easter. It was the first time the annual Easter Egg Roll was held on the White House Lawn. In the 1870s, the first Easter Egg Roll was held on the Capitol lawn, but it was discontinued this year because of the destruction to the lawn caused by so many children. President and Mrs. Hayes pitied the children and opened up the White House Lawn.

STATE OF THE UNION

37 STATES

POPULATION IN 1877
47,118,638

$1 WORTH IN 1877
NOW WORTH
$22.22

$1 WORTH IN 1881
NOW WORTH
$22.73

UNITED STATES DEBT

Jan. 1 1877	$2,226,511,601
Jan. 1 1881	$2,006,221,663

JAMES A. GARFIELD

Twentieth President of the United States
Nickname: The Preacher President
Term in Office: 1881

The Bottom Line

James Garfield's presidency did not last long. He was assassinated only six months into his term, ending his lifelong service to his country.

What Was He Thinking?

Much of what is known today about James Garfield's political beliefs comes from his time in Congress and his 1880 presidential campaign. Garfield refused to vote for national projects that would increase the federal debt, an issue he considered a high priority. He believed in a strong federal government and an "independent presidency," meaning a president with power to act without the consent of Congress.

FAST STATS

★ Born November 19, 1831, in Orange, Ohio
★ Parents: Abram and Eliza Ballou Garfield
★ Died September 19, 1881, in Elberon, New Jersey; age 49
★ Age upon Start of Term: 49; Age upon Assassination: 49
★ Political Party: Republican
★ Religious Affiliation: Disciples of Christ
★ Height: 6 feet
★ Vice President: Chester A. Arthur

Why Should I Care?

Because the presidency today is protected by high security, surveillance, and secret service agents, it is easy to take for granted that the job is relatively safe. This was far from true in the days of James Garfield. President Garfield lacked the technology and manpower today's presidents enjoy. James Garfield risked his life for his country not once, but twice: in

 BTW: Garfield's first act as president came immediately after he took the oath of office: he turned and kissed his aging mother, who sat behind him during the inauguration ceremonies.

> *A brave man is one who dares to look the devil in the face and tell him he is a devil.*

the Civil War and as president. Although he survived the hostilities of war, he was the second president to be assassinated and the fourth to die in office.

Breakin' It Down
Early Life

James Garfield was the youngest of five children and grew up in a small log cabin with his impoverished family. When he was just eighteen months old, his father, Abram—a man who had worked as a farmer and canal construction supervisor—died fighting a nearby forest fire. His mother eventually remarried, but James never warmed toward his stepfather. Despite the hardships he faced, he began to show his brilliance at age three when he could read as well as any adult. As a child, Garfield experienced constant stomach pains and headaches, so he turned to books like Robinson Crusoe to escape his day-to-day life.

Garfield attended a cabin school, and excelled in his studies and in debate. As a young man, he attended Ohio Western Reserve Eclectic Institute, later renamed Hiram College, before transferring to Massachusetts' Williams College, where he became president of the school's literary society. When Garfield graduated second in his class in 1858, he was known as a good athlete and left the school with honors in both Latin and literature.

Garfield was raised in a devoutly religious household and attended a religious grade school. Temporarily becoming a traveling preacher for the Disciples of Christ, he preached across Ohio and spoke on the evils of slavery and the necessity of abolition. He later became a teacher at his old college, the Western Reserve Eclectic Institute, lecturing on classical languages. Even in the classroom, however, Garfield continued to champion abolition. At age twenty-six, he became the college's president, and young Garfield emerged as a prominent figure in the community, ready for the political stage.

First Couple

Lucretia Randolph and James Garfield were childhood friends, attending both grade school and the Western Reserve Eclectic Institute together. They were married in 1858 and had seven children together. The marriage was shaken in 1863 when Lucretia discovered James was having an affair with a New York widow. The family suffered again when three-year-old daughter Eliza died from diphtheria, but James and Lucretia came together after the tragic loss and renewed their marriage, remaining together until James's death in 1881. Lucretia was known as a wonderful public speaker and worked as a schoolteacher. She outlived her husband by thirty-six years.

LUCRETIA GARFIELD

BTW: As part of the Radical Republican faction in Congress, Garfield voted in favor of impeaching President Andrew Johnson.

Booker T. Washington founds the Tuskegee Institute for African-American higher education, 1881

The Zionist movement begins in Palestine, 1881

Garfield is shot by Charles J. Guiteau, 1881

Garfield succumbs to his injuries and Chester Arthur becomes president, September 19, 1881

The Sudan War begins, 1881

| 1879 | 1880 | 1881 | 1882 | 1883 | 1884 |

BTW: Garfield served in the state Senate during the presidential election of 1860 and campaigned vigorously for Abraham Lincoln, making more than fifty speeches on his behalf.

Previous Political Career

- 1859: Elected state senator in the Ohio state legislature.
- 1861: Appointed colonel of the 42nd Ohio Volunteer Infantry in the Civil War.
- 1863: Elected U.S. Representative from Ohio, where he served twenty-two years. While in Congress, served as chairman of the Military Affairs Committee, which founded the Reserve Officers' Training Corps (ROTC), the Banking and Currency Committee, and the Appropriations Committee.
- 1874: Elected House minority leader, using his influence to support the policies of President Hayes, although he personally disagreed with Hayes's actions toward the south.
- 1876: Served on the congressional commission that decided the outcome of the election, voting in favor of Republican Rutherford Hayes.

THOUGHTS ON THE CONSTITUTION

Under this Constitution the boundaries of freedom have been enlarged, the foundations of order and peace have been strengthened, and the growth of our people in all the better elements of national life has indicated the wisdom of the founders and given new hope to their descendants.

JAMES A. GARFIELD

BTW: This election had the highest voter turnout in American history with 81% of Americans voting for president.

Presidency

James Garfield's presidency lasted just over six months—the second shortest presidency in history, after William Henry Harrison. His legacy as president remains in what he had hoped to accomplish. He campaigned mainly on civil service reform and the end of patronage appointments, following the lead of his predecessor, Rutherford Hayes. It was this promise that led to Garfield's death.

FUN FACT!

When Garfield heard the news of his unsolicited election to Congress, he almost did not go. Garfield believed his place was in the army and intended to remain there until a Union victory. It was only after Abraham Lincoln contacted him and requested that he join Congress to increase the Republican force there that Garfield decided to depart for Washington, D.C.

ELECTION RESULTS!

Election of 1880

		Electoral Votes
1st	James A. Garfield	214
2nd	Winfield Scott Hancock	155

James A. Garfield — Republican Won
Winfield Scott Hancock — Democrat Won
Territories

Garfield arrived in Chicago, Illinois, for the 1880 Republican convention with no intention of running for president. Rather, he planned to serve as friend John Sherman's campaign manager and deliver his nomination speech. Things did not work out very well for Sherman, however, and he eventually dropped out of the race. On the sixth day of the convention, Garfield's name was added to the ballot, and a day later he clinched the election. Garfield chose Chester Arthur as his running mate, a New York politician who had the support of a major Republican faction. When the polls closed and votes were counted, Garfield won by only 0.1 percent.

BTW: Garfield is the only president to simultaneously be a sitting congressman, senator-elect, and president-elect. He had been elected to the U.S. Senate earlier in 1880.

JAMES GARFIELD and Crédit Mobilier Scandal

During Ulysses S. Grant's presidency, Garfield was accused of being part of the Crédit Mobilier Scandal. He accepted ten shares in the illicit railroad company, and also received a $300 loan from a company involved in an illegal business venture with Union Pacific Railway. Somehow, Garfield emerged from the scandal unscathed and referred to the incident as a "lapse in judgment."

★ Today, James Garfield would be described as a "people person," always talkative, inclusive, and amiable to those he met. As a politician he was a gifted public speaker, able to persuade and captivate his audiences. He regularly led his peers, and treated them with dignity and friendliness. Garfield admitted to suffering from a period of depression during his young-adult life, referring to this prolonged time as his "years of darkness." However, Garfield worked through his illness and became a great leader of his day, in war and as president.

BTW: During Garfield's six-month presidency he investigated the Star Route Scandal. After the Civil War, postal officials schemed to steal funds and tax collections on their way to the capital.

Assassination

Refusing to grant any requests for patronage appointments, Garfield rejected the job application of a man named Charles J. Guiteau. Guiteau believed his moderate efforts to elect the president—consisting of rambling speeches to small groups of people who quickly lost interest—made him deserving of a presidential appointment to an ambassador position. When Guiteau found his application rejected, he schemed to kill the president.

On July 2, 1881, just four months into his presidency, Garfield planned to travel by train to his twenty-fifth college class reunion at Williams College in Massachusetts, but he never made it. At 9:30 a.m. Guiteau approached him and shot him multiple times in the abdomen. He was tended by several doctors, who located the bullets thanks to the newly developed metal detector designed by Alexander Graham Bell. Although several of the bullets were removed, one had lodged in the president's pancreas and remained undetected because of interference from the metal bedframe around Garfield. In addition, the bullets were extracted with unsanitary surgical utensils and bare hands. The procedure ultimately led to Garfield's decline in health when infection spread throughout his body, with help from the hot, muggy Washington, D.C., air. Garfield lingered for two more months until he breathed his last on September 19, leaving his legacy and presidency to the unassuming Chester Arthur.

PLATFORM SPEECH

I have, in many ways, shown my desire that the wounds of the war should be healed; that the grass which has grown green over the graves of the dead of both armies might symbolize the returning spring of friendship and peace between citizens who were lately in arms against each other.

After seeing the horrors and toll of the Civil War, Garfield was eager for peace among Americans.

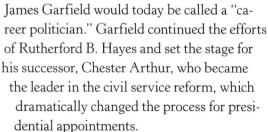

JAMES GARFIELD

What Has He Done for Me Lately?

James Garfield would today be called a "career politician." Garfield continued the efforts of Rutherford B. Hayes and set the stage for his successor, Chester Arthur, who became the leader in the civil service reform, which dramatically changed the process for presidential appointments.

BTW: Right before his presidency, Garfield complained of a sense of foreboding over his upcoming task, experiencing nightmares and headaches.

Presidential Times

Written by Juliette Turner

ASSASSIN CHARLES GUITEAU HUNG

July 30, 1881—Twenty-eight days after pulling the trigger, Guiteau was hung by federal police. Since Garfield's assassination, the call for civil-service reform has escalated. If only Garfield had accepted Guiteau's job application. When Guiteau found his application rejected, he immediately planned to kill the president. Although Guiteau later claimed he fired his pistol to "[unite] the Republican Party and save the Republic," it was clear that the deranged man was simply angered over rejection. When questioned by police as to why he committed the heinous crime, Guiteau rambled on about how "God" prompted him to do it. Anger quickly spread among Ameri-

cans and Guiteau himself was almost killed during his trial.

ROBERT TODD LINCOLN: A BAD LUCK CHARM?

September 30, 1881—If you were president, you might not want to be around Robert Todd Lincoln. Outside of the people in Ford's Theater, Robert Lincoln was the first person notified of his father being shot. And he was just feet from James Garfield at the train station the day Garfield was shot. Government officials are starting to feel uncomfortable whenever they see Robert Lincoln.

Robert Todd Lincoln

STATE OF THE UNION

38 STATES

POPULATION IN 1881
51,979,622

$1 WORTH IN 1881
NOW WORTH
$22.73

UNITED STATES DEBT

| Jan. 1 1881 | $2,006,221,663 |

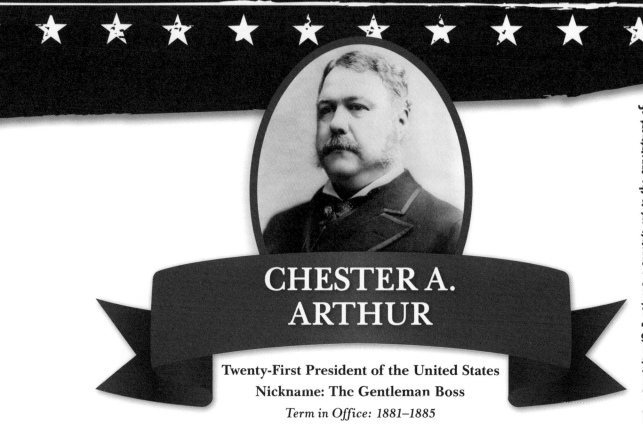

CHESTER A. ARTHUR

Twenty-First President of the United States
Nickname: The Gentleman Boss
Term in Office: 1881–1885

The Bottom Line

Chester Arthur was the fourth vice president to assume the presidency after the death of his predecessor. During his presidency, Arthur abolished the patronage system and significantly lowered corruption in America's government by establishing a civil service system that remained for years to come.

What Was He Thinking?

Chester Arthur did not mind crossing party lines, as was apparent during his presidency. In addition to working to end corruption and patronage appointments, Arthur vetoed many pieces of legislation that would have added to the national debt and opposed any attempts to limit immigration to America, especially limitations placed on the Chinese. Arthur also worked to increase America's national defense by adding sixty-eight steel ships to the U.S. naval fleet.

FAST STATS

★ Born October 5, 1829, in Fairfield, Vermont
★ Parents: William and Malvina Stone Arthur
★ Died November 18, 1886, in New York, New York; age 57
★ Age upon Start of Term: 51; Age upon Conclusion of Term: 55
★ Political Party: Republican
★ Religious Affiliation: Episcopalian
★ Height: 6 feet
★ Vice President: none

Why Should I Care?

America's government has come a long way from the mid-1800s when fraudulent appointments and illegal activities were so prevalent.

Pop Quiz! Do you remember the definition of a patronage appointment? A patronage appointment is the appointment of an individual to a government position based on party favors and bribes instead of merit and ability.

   **BTW:** The position of vice president was the first national political position Arthur held before becoming president.

The improvement started with Rutherford Hayes and ended with Chester Arthur, who broke from his own political background and defeated the monster of corruption that had nearly ruined America's political system.

Breakin' It Down
Early Life

Chester Alan, the firstborn child of seven in the Arthur family, was a bit of a rebel child. "Chet" and his family lived in upstate New York, where Chester attended school. He admitted later in life to fistfighting with a schoolmate who criticized his presidential choice, Henry Clay. Chester, chastised frequently for skipping chapel services, once even led a school rebellion, when he dumped the school's bell into the Erie Canal.

Arthur later attended Union College, regarded as one of the finest colleges at the time, and graduated in 1848 in the top third of his class. He was also a member of Phi Beta Kappa. Following his graduation, Arthur became an attorney in New York City and quickly earned a reputation as one of the best attorneys in the city. He represented many African-Americans in civil rights cases and played a key role in ending the segregation of New York City's transportation system.

At the outbreak of the Civil War, Arthur was appointed to be engineer in chief of the New York militia. Quite a powerful position at the time, Arthur was commissioned to supply every solider passing through New York with clothing, armament, and supplies.

First Couple

Chester Arthur married Ellen Lewis Herndon in 1859 when she was twenty-two and he was thirty. Arthur loved his wife deeply, and together they had three children. Their marriage only lasted twenty years, for at age forty-two, Ellen caught a cold that led to pneumonia and eventually killed her one year before Arthur assumed the presidency. Yet it was as if Ellen had never left. During his presidency, Arthur placed a fresh flower by her portrait every morning. At each White House dinner, he left an empty seat always at his side in memory of his wife. After retiring from the presidency, Arthur presented a stained glass window to the church where Ellen sang in the choir.

ELLEN LEWIS ARTHUR

Previous Political Career

• 1871: Appointed collector for the New York Customs House, collecting 79 percent of all American taxes on imported goods. He supervised over one thousand workers and their payroll of a combined two million dollars.

POLITICAL PARTIES
★★★★★★★★★★★★★★★★★★★★★★★★★★★★

The Stalwarts: A Republican faction emerging at the end of the 1800s led by Senator Roscoe Conkling. The faction opposed the civil service reform policies of Presidents Hayes and Garfield, and subsequently President Arthur, and also sought a third term for Ulysses S. Grant in 1880.

Arthur authorizes the construction of the first all-steel ships for the U.S. Navy, 1883 • •

France presents the U.S. with the Statue of Liberty, 1884 •

Samuel Clemens (Mark Twain) publishes *The Adventures of Huckleberry Finn*, 1884

The Bank of Japan is established, 1882 • • •

Édouard Manet dies, 1883 • • •

Karl Marx dies in London, 1883 •

The Washington Monument is dedicated, 1885

Term in Office

| 1880 | 1881 | 1882 | •1883• | • 1884 | 1885 |

BTW: Some of Arthur's political opponents claimed he was born in Canada because of his father's job there, thus arguing he was ineligible for the presidency.

- 1878: Fired from the Customs House after President Hayes issued his executive order for civil service reform and Chester Arthur refused to stop his patronage appointments or his backing of the Republican Party through corrupt venues.
- 1880: Chosen as James Garfield's vice presidential candidate to draw votes from the Stalwarts faction and the East Coast states.

> *I hope ... my God, I do hope it's a mistake.*

> When Garfield was suffering from his gunshot wounds, Arthur tried desperately to meet with him, but doctors refused Arthur entrance into Garfield's room. When he finally heard of Garfield's death, he uttered these words and wept openly, not so much for the deceased president, but for the new one.

LIBERTY Language

Customs House: A government office monitoring the import and export of all goods into and out of America as well as monitoring taxes on the exports and imports.

Presidency

Arthur worked hard to serve his country from the day he took office to the day he left. Arthur first worked at continuing the civil service reforms set in place by Hayes and Garfield.

Since Arthur was a man who rose to the presidency through the patronage system, his efforts to abolish it shocked those around him. Even though support from the public wavered at the beginning of his term, Arthur quickly won public approval for his ardent attempts to end corruption in the government.

CONGRESSIONAL CORNER

★★★★★★★★★★★★★★★★★★★★★★★★★★

1. **Chinese Exclusion Act, 1882:** This act prohibited all immigration of Chinese laborers, becoming known as the biggest restriction on free immigration. It would be renewed in 1892, made permanent in 1902, but finally repealed in 1943.

2. **Pendleton Civil Service Reform Act, 1883:** This act established a series of competitive exams that would decide who received what government position. It prevented appointments from being based on political affiliation.

3. **Tariff of 1883 (Mongrel Tariff):** Although the act was intended to significantly reduce tariff rates, it in fact only reduced rates marginally.

★★★★★★★★★★★★★★★★★★★★★★★★★★

Reforms

Arthur first signed the Pendleton Civil Service Reform Act in 1883, fulfilling his predecessors' attempts to end corruption in the government. Then Arthur turned to reigning in congressional spending. Arthur vetoed several pieces of spending legislation, including a bill calling for nineteen million dollars in national improvements. Arthur's fiscal policies often defied party lines, ignored special interest groups, and held the government accountable for their actions—which irritated Congress. In an attempt to lower tariff rates, Arthur signed the Tariff Act of 1883, called the Mongrel Tariff Act by its opponents. The legislation only succeeded, however, in lowering overall rates by less than 2 percent.

International Affairs

During Arthur's tenure in office, Congress passed the Chinese Exclusion Act, which limited Chinese immigration to America and prevented any Chinese immi-

 BTW: Chester Arthur's presidency was the last in a long line of Republican presidents that served from 1860 to 1885, excluding Andrew Johnson.

THOUGHTS ON THE CONSTITUTION

The wisdom of our fathers, foreseeing even the most dire possibilities, made sure that the Government should never be imperiled because of the uncertainty of human life... Though the chosen of the people be struck down, his constitutional successor is peacefully installed without shock or strain except the sorrow which mourns that bereavement.

Arthur experienced firsthand the "backup system" set in place by the Constitution if a sitting president dies. The fragility of human life cannot endanger America's government.

grants from becoming American citizens. Arthur vetoed the bill, but once again, his veto was overridden. Regarding national defense, Arthur supported improving the existing U.S. Navy, including the construction of several new naval ships. Arthur's actions on this front would help the U.S. Navy emerge as the world's most powerful and important naval force.

The End of His Term

At the end of his presidency, Arthur dedicated the newly completed Washington Monument on February 21, 1885, a memorial that took nearly two and a half decades to complete. Chester Arthur did seek reelection, but he lost the nomination at the Republican convention to James G. Blaine, who was Arthur's secretary of state for a short period of time.

Post-Presidency

Chester Arthur did not get a chance to enjoy his retirement from political office. Just over a year and a half after leaving the presidency, Arthur died of Bright's disease (a kidney disease) on November 18, 1886. Shortly before his death, Arthur demanded that all of his personal papers be burned, and he faded into American history as one of the most forgotten and underestimated presidents. Samuel Clemens (aka Mark Twain) commented, however, "It would be hard indeed to better President Arthur's administration."

What Has He Done for Me Lately?

Chester Arthur had more courage and determination than many people in our government today. Arthur's actions to end the patronage system in the government took away the majority of his political supporters and ended any chances he had for reelection. If the system had continued, there is no saying how much damage certain appointed "friends" could have inflicted on our government.

PLATFORM SPEECH

I trust the time is nigh when, with the universal assent of civilized people, all international differences shall be determined without resort to arms by the benignant process of civilization.

Chester Arthur believed that soon the world would be able to settle their differences without war to better society. Sadly, this has yet to be.

CHESTER A. ARTHUR

★ ★ ★ ★ ★ ★ ★ ★ ★ ★ ★ ★ ★ ★ ★ ★ ★ ★ ★

Presidential Times

★ ★ ★ CHESTER A. ARTHUR Term in Office 1881–1885 ★ ★ ★

CHESTER ARTHUR AND HIS GRANDIOSITY

Written by Juliette Turner

June 5, 1884— Many have dubbed President Chester Arthur as "Elegant Arthur" for his high style and involvement in high society. Exceptionally notable is Arthur's extensive wardrobe: his closet is said to be home to eighty pairs of trousers. Additionally, "Chet" changes his clothes several times a day in order to perfectly suit every occasion. During his years in New York City high-society, Arthur frequented hundreds of lavish dinner parties, contributing to Arthur's weight of 225 pounds.

Now that Arthur is president, the White House parties are among some of the most lavish the house has ever seen, despite the absence of a first lady. Arthur's personal chef and butler accompanied him to the White House, and he is the first president to have a valet. No one doubts that Arthur works hard as the nation's leader, but White House aides have revealed that he keeps his working hours to a minimum: White House work begins at 10:00 a.m. and ends at 4:00 p.m.

CHESTER ARTHUR ORDERS THE CREATION OF 68 NEW STEEL NAVY SHIPS

December 17, 1883—President Chester Arthur recently authorized the first all-steel ships to be constructed and added to the U.S. Navy. Because of his efforts in this field, many are calling Arthur the "Father of the American Navy."

THE WASHINGTON MONUMENT IS DEDICATED

February 27, 1885—In one of his last acts as president, President Arthur dedicated the Washington Monument today. If you are wondering why it took thirty-six years to construct the white obelisk in memory of George Washington's service, you are not alone. Construction occurred in two major stages, 1848 to 1856 and 1876 to 1884, which is the reason behind the color change in the stone halfway up the monument.

John Marshall first proposed that a monument be constructed in the nation's capital in remembrance of George Washington. Action did not begin until James Madison formed the Washington National Monument Society in 1833. The cornerstone was laid on July 4, 1848, and construction continued until 1856. Construction was halted during the Civil War because of lack of funds and the turmoil in the country during the war. When construction resumed in 1876, the U.S. Army Corps of Engineers of the War Department finished the task. The monument will officially open to the public on October 9, 1888. The Washington Monument is the tallest building in Washington, D.C., at 555 feet tall. It weighs 81,120 tons.

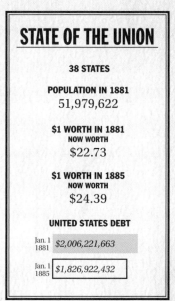

STATE OF THE UNION

38 STATES

POPULATION IN 1881
51,979,622

$1 WORTH IN 1881
NOW WORTH
$22.73

$1 WORTH IN 1885
NOW WORTH
$24.39

UNITED STATES DEBT

Jan. 1 1881	$2,006,221,663
Jan. 1 1885	$1,826,922,432

GROVER CLEVELAND

Twenty-Second and Twenty-Fourth President of the United States
Nickname: The Veto President
Terms in Office: 1885–1889; 1893–1897

The Bottom Line

Grover Cleveland remains the only president to serve two nonconsecutive terms. In his first term (1885–1889), he worked to balance federal spending. In his second term (1893–1897), he struggled to restore the American economy after the Panic of 1893.

FAST STATS

★ Born March 18, 1837, in Caldwell, New Jersey
★ Parents: Richard and Anne Neal Cleveland
★ Died June 24, 1908, in Princeton, New Jersey; age 71
★ Age upon Start of First Term: 47; Age upon Conclusion of First Term: 51
★ Age upon Start of Second Term: 55; Age upon Conclusion of Second Term: 59
★ Political Party: Democrat
★ Religious Affiliation: Presbyterian
★ Height: 5 feet 11 inches
★ Vice Presidents: Thomas A. Hendricks (1885) and Adlai E. Stevenson (1893–1897)

What Was He Thinking?

As the first Democrat to win the presidency in twenty-four years, Cleveland remained true to his Democratic platform by representing the concerns of workers and the rights of laborers. Cleveland also pushed for tariff revision and further limitations on Chinese immigration. Like the Republican presidents before him, Cleveland believed in appointing jobs based on merit instead of patronage. Cleveland also believed in a strong central government and a strong presidency that should be able to act independently from Congress.

157

> *While the people should patriotically and cheerfully support their Government, its functions do not include the support of the people.*

> *Cleveland wished to travel west, but traveling required money he did not have. He borrowed twenty-five dollars from a neighbor to fund his travels, but ended up settling in Buffalo, New York. Regardless, Grover Cleveland paid his old neighbor back, even with interest.*

Why Should I Care?

Grover Cleveland worked to transform the federal government from one that spent unnecessary money on a variety of projects to a government of frugality. Cleveland realized the danger of instability in the federal treasury and worked cautiously to restore Americans' confidence in the economy. He initiated no federal aid to businesses or the American people during the collapse of 1893, setting a precedent that the federal government should not intervene in the free market economy.

Breakin' It Down

Early Life

Stephen Grover was the fifth of nine children born to Richard and Anne Cleveland. Though he did not enter formal school until age eleven, Stephen, who wished to be called Grover, enjoyed his education, especially debate, and hoped to attend Hamilton College. However, when Grover's father died in 1853 just as Grover turned sixteen, the family could no longer afford his college tuition. Instead, Grover accepted a teaching position at the New York Institution for the Blind and sent his paychecks to his mother to help her during the economic struggles. He left the position after one year to travel west, stopping in Buffalo, New York, on his way, but Grover never left. In Buffalo, he worked on the construction of the Erie Canal and as a store clerk for a time, but eventually he joined a law firm, where he quickly developed his skills as a lawyer, impressing judges and juries with his eloquent, memorized arguments.

When the Civil War began, Cleveland did not join the army but paid a Polish immigrant $300 to go in his place (a completely legal action under the Federal Conscription Act, which allowed men solely providing for their family to pay other men to go in their place).

FUN FACT!

Cleveland proposed to Frances by letter after she and her mother (recently widowed) visited the White House several times. Newspapers speculated that Cleveland would propose to the older Ms. Folsom, but Cleveland responded to the speculations by asking why the press kept marrying him to old ladies.

First Couple

While president in 1886, Grover Cleveland married Frances Folsom who was twenty-one at the time and twenty-seven years his junior, making her the youngest first lady to ever occupy the White House.

FRANCES CLEVELAND

The Statue of Liberty dedicated, 1886

Cleveland marries Frances Folsom in the White House, 1886

Sir Arthur Conan Doyle publishes his first Sherlock Holmes story, *A Study in Scarlet*, 1887

Queen Victoria of Great Britain celebrates her Golden Jubilee, 1887

The Great March snow blizzard hits northwest U.S., leaving $25 million in damages, 1888

The Department of Agriculture is formed, 1889

George Eastman develops his Kodak camera, 1888

Term in Office

1884   1885   1886   1887   1888   1889

BTW: While governor of New York, Cleveland signed a bill approving a one and a half million acre park around Niagara Falls.

THOUGHTS ON THE CONSTITUTION

On this auspicious occasion we may well renew the pledge of our devotion to the Constitution, which, launched by the founders of the Republic and consecrated by their prayers and patriotic devotion, has for almost a century borne the hopes and the aspirations of a great people through prosperity and peace and through the shock of foreign conflicts and the perils of domestic strife and vicissitudes.

GROVER CLEVELAND

He was the second president (after John Tyler) to get married while president. He and his wife yearned for a place of their own out of the limelight of the Presidential Palace. They purchased a twenty-seven-acre plot of land three miles from the White House in an isolated area near George-town.

While first lady, Frances held two receptions a week. One was held on Saturday afternoons and was open to the public. At the public reception, Frances welcomed any woman who held a job, and once greeted over eight thousand guests at a single reception. They were married for over twenty years — until Cleveland died in 1908. Together they had five children.

Previous Political Career

- 1863: Appointed assistant district attorney by the district attorney for Erie County, New York.
- 1865: Won the Democratic nomination for district attorney of Erie County NY, but lost to the Republican candidate.
- 1870: Appointed Erie County sheriff.
- 1881: Elected mayor of Buffalo, New York.
- 1882: Elected governor of New York, winning the position by 190,000 votes.

LIBERTY Language

Federal pension bill: A piece of legislation appropriating the amount of money to be paid to individuals working for the federal government.

Presidency

Cleveland's tasks as president were not easy. First, he continued the civil service reform implemented by the Republican presidents before him and actually doubled the number of federal workers who met the requirements under the Civil Service Commission. Cleveland carefully examined each federal pension bill placed on his desk—often staying up late into the night to do so—and rejected more than two hundred he believed to be fraudulent attempts by veterans to receive aid from ailments they suffered after the Civil War concluded. Cleveland also used his veto to decline

New Zealand becomes the first country to grant women the right to vote, 1893

The Panic of 1893 takes place, 1893

Cleveland's second inauguration, 1893

The Supreme Court rules that "separate but equal" is indeed constitutional, 1894

The Pullman Railroad strike takes place, 1894

Wilhelm Röntgen discovers the first X-rays, 1895

J.P. Morgan bails out the federal government, 1895

Utah becomes a state, 1896

Term in Office

1892   1893   1894   1895   1896   1897

BTW: While serving as county sheriff, Cleveland once had to personally hang two men for their crimes—becasue the executioner got cold feet.

ELECTION RESULTS!

Cleveland was an ideal candidate for the Democrat Party in 1884: he was a spotless reformer and could easily win the vital state of New York. He campaigned on his old motto, "Public Office Is a Public Trust." But during the campaign, it was discovered that Cleveland, a bachelor, had fathered a child out of wedlock. A political cartoon illustrated a baby crying, "Ma, Ma, where's my pa?" in front of Cleveland. Voters waited for Cleveland to react to the rumor, and, shocking the whole nation, Cleveland told the truth and explained the whole matter: he had fathered the child and sent financial aid to the boy until he was adopted.

When Cleveland came out on top in 1884 after the ballots were cast, the Democrats finally replied to "Ma, Ma, where's my pa?" with "Gone to the White House, ha, ha, ha!"

In stark contrast to Cleveland's first presidential campaign experience, the campaign of 1892 remained surprisingly peaceful and well-tempered. It was the first time that both presidential candidates had previously held the presidency and were vying to regaining it.

Election of 1884

		Electoral Votes
1st	Grover Cleveland	219
2nd	James G. Blaine	182

- Grover Cleveland — Democrat Won
- James G. Blaine — Republic Won
- Territories

Election of 1892

		Electoral Votes
1st	Grover Cleveland	277
2nd	Benjamin Harrison	145
3rd	James B. Weaver	22

- Grover Cleveland — Democrat Won
- Benjamin Harrison — Republic Won
- James B, Weaver — Populist
- Territories

bills he considered unneeded legislation and public waste that would cost the working class unnecessary tax money.

Relations with Native Americans

This topic had not been majorly addressed since Ulysses S. Grant's presidency. Cleveland supported the Dawes Act of 1887, an act that encouraged Native Americans to buy plots of land sectioned off by the federal government. However, this act led to a major reduction in the size of Indian reservations, for the land the Native Americans could purchase was carved out of the reservations, leaving less room for the natives who wanted to remain on communal land.

Monetary Reforms

Then arose the great debate over silver and gold, an issue that had plagued the presidency since the Civil War. Cleveland wanted to repeal the Bland-Allison Act of 1878. By repealing this act he wished to decrease the

LIBERTY Language

Bimetallism movement: A movement that supported making both gold and silver the national currency.

BTW: Grover Cleveland delivered his inaugural address in 1885 without the aid of any notes—the second and last president to do so.

amount of money (and silver) that left the Federal Treasury. Cleveland understood that the Federal Reserve was having a hard time because it had been working to pay off the large U.S. debt. In Cleveland's view, the Bland-Allison Act made matters worse by making the nation's treasury release money into the markets every month—money the treasury could have been spending on its bills. Congress refused to repeal the act. Cleveland did manage to prevent excessive spending in other areas, however, and created a large budget surplus in the Federal Reserve. Cleveland was also against the bimetallism movement, calling it "a dangerous and reckless experiment."

Interim
In 1888, although he won the majority of the popular vote by a very slight margin, Cleveland failed to secure enough states for an Electoral College win, making Benjamin Harrison the president-elect. During the term of Benjamin Harrison, Cleveland watched helplessly as the budget surplus which he had fought so hard for slowly dwindled away because of Congress and Harrison's spending.

The Panic of 1893
One month before Cleveland took office for the second time, the economy began to collapse in what would be one of the worst economic depressions until the Great Depression—the Panic of 1893. Cleveland shocked the nation when he refused to give federal aid to banks and railroads or even organize public works efforts. Deemed "His Obstinacy" for sticking to his beliefs, Cleveland thought the economy should be able to fix itself naturally, believing that federal interference would violate the Constitution. Congress worked to repeal the Sherman Silver Purchase Act, a bill Cleveland also opposed, believing it harmed the nation's economy and drained the federal gold supply.

Becoming a Global Power
Cleveland believed the U.S. should avoid staking a permanent claim on Hawaii, convinced that it would be an act of American imperialism. Additionally, when rebellion arose in Cuba, Cleveland strove to

CONGRESSIONAL CORNER
★★★★★★★★★★★★★★★★★★★★★★★★

1. **Presidential Succession Act of 1886:** This act established the line of presidential succession if both the president and vice president are unable to assume the duties of the presidency.

2. **Interstate Commerce Act of 1887:** This act, passed in February of 1887, established the Interstate Commerce Commission, which would regulate railroad rates.

3. **Dawes Act of 1887:** This act allowed the president of the United States to divide land in Indian Reservations to sell to Native Americans.

4. **Edmunds-Tucker Act:** This act, passed in 1887, seized Mormon church property that was not used exclusively for worship. It also required Mormons to take an "oath of loyalty" before gaining voter eligibility and declared women as competent witnesses in Mormon trials.

5. **Chinese Seclusion Act (Scott Act):** This act, passed on May 6, 1888, banned Chinese workers from immigrating or returning to the United States.

6. **Nelson Act of 1889:** This act forcibly relocated the Native Americans of Minnesota to Indian reservations.

7. **Wilson-Gorman Tariff of 1894:** This act lowered the tariff rates set in place by the McKinley Tariff and imposed a 2 percent income tax.

★★★★★★★★★★★★★★★★★★★★★★★★

Pop Quiz! Do you remember the Bland-Allison Act? This act, passed in 1878, called for the federal government to purchase and coin millions of dollars in silver each month.

remain neutral. The Senate disagreed with Cleveland's stance and the issue remained unresolved until the end of his term in office. On the other hand, when Venezuela requested American assistance in settling a border dispute with Great Britain, Cleveland agreed. War almost ensued between America and Great Britain when Cleveland ordered U.S. naval ships to confront British ships off the coast of Venezuela. However, after the show of force, Britain came to the negotiation table, and war was avoided. Nevertheless, his actions over the border dispute in Venezuela remained one of Cleveland's most controversial foreign policy decisions.

PRESIDENTIAL Personality

★ *Grover Cleveland was a determined and stubborn man who was known to have limited patience and a quick temper. When he was not working, he was jovial, carefree, and outgoing. However, when he was in his office, his mood and attitude drastically changed: he was stern and highly dedicated to finishing his work.*

Post-Presidency

In 1897, Cleveland retired to New Jersey with his wife and three children. He and Frances had two more children after leaving the White House. Cleveland became the trustee of Princeton University, earning the nickname "Sage of Princeton." He also authored three books: *Presidential Problems* (1904), *Fishing and Shooting Sketches* (1906), and *Good Citizenship* (1908). In 1908, Cleveland died of heart failure.

What Has He Done for Me Lately?

Grover Cleveland vetoed more legislation than any other two-term president: over 584 vetoes. That makes his veto tally close to 50 percent larger than the second highest record holder, Harry Truman. The vetoes he issued were meant to protect the nation's treasury and reign in unnecessary spending, but they also set a precedent for future presidents: the executive branch could veto as many pieces of legislation as they wanted, most of the time without consequences.

PLATFORM SPEECH

A government for the people must depend for its success on the intelligence, the morality, the justice, and the interest of the people themselves.

The law of nations is founded upon reason and justice and the rules of conduct governing individual relations between citizens of subjects of a civilized state are equally applicable as between enlightened nations.

Grover Cleveland believed that the people, to protect their rights, must be educated in their government's affairs.

Cleveland said this in his message to Congress opposing the annexation of Hawaii in 1893. He opposed annexing Hawaii because he believed it was an unjust action of a powerful country oppressing a weaker country. He believed foreign affairs should always be founded on reason and justice.

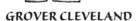

GROVER CLEVELAND

Presidential Times

Written by Juliette Turner

PANIC OF 1893

March 18, 1893—America is still experiencing the aftermath of last month's economic collapse. In February, the Reading Railroad and Philadelphia lines declared bankruptcy, sparking a railroad collapse across the country.

Soon, five hundred banks failed, millions were unemployed, and an additional thousand railroad workers initiated a nationwide strike, hurting the nation's coal and transportation industries.

Unemployment is now at 19 percent—more than four million unemployed, with one in every five factory workers out of a job and farm prices are plummeting. The stock market collapse alarmed European investors, who began to withdraw their involvement in the American market.

The federal gold reserves have also reached a near all-time low with only $100 million in gold reserves. Cleveland worked to return America to a solely gold standard (instead of gold and silver), contradicting the views of his Democrat Party as well as the views of the majority of the American people in the south and west.

THE SECRET OPERATION

July 2, 1893—President Cleveland underwent a secret dental operation yesterday aboard his private yacht. The press was alerted that Cleveland would be spending the day on the yacht, but it was not known that Cleveland would spend the day tied to the mast of the yacht under anesthesia while five doctors and a dentist worked to remove a cancerous growth. The tumor was so large that the doctors removed several teeth and the entire left side of his jaw. To replace the missing bone, Cleveland was fitted with an artificial jaw. The president is said to be recovering well.

HAYMARKET RIOT

May 4, 1886, Chicago, Illinois —Today Chicago police advanced on a labor protest, where the laborers demanded eight-hour workdays. One of the protesters threw a bomb at the police force, causing the police to open fire on the protesters. Seven police and one civilian have now died as a result of the violence. Eight labor protesters have been arrested and are being convicted of connection with the violence, despite a lack of evidence.

PULLMAN RAILROAD STRIKE

July 4, 1894—President Cleveland sent 2,500 federal soldiers to Chicago, Illinois, today to combat a local strike at the Pullman Place Car Company. Earlier this year, on May 11, 1894, a local strike ensued after the company cut workers' pay by 25 percent as a result of the Panic of 1893. After the workers received no pay raise, the Union's national council president, Eugene Debs, called for a national boycott, sparking strikes in twenty-seven states. Now that the federal soldiers have been deployed to control the situation, the strike is predicted to end within a week.

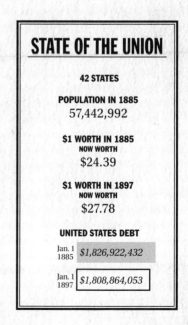

STATE OF THE UNION

42 STATES

POPULATION IN 1885
57,442,992

$1 WORTH IN 1885
NOW WORTH
$24.39

$1 WORTH IN 1897
NOW WORTH
$27.78

UNITED STATES DEBT

Jan. 1 1885	$1,826,922,432
Jan. 1 1897	$1,808,864,053

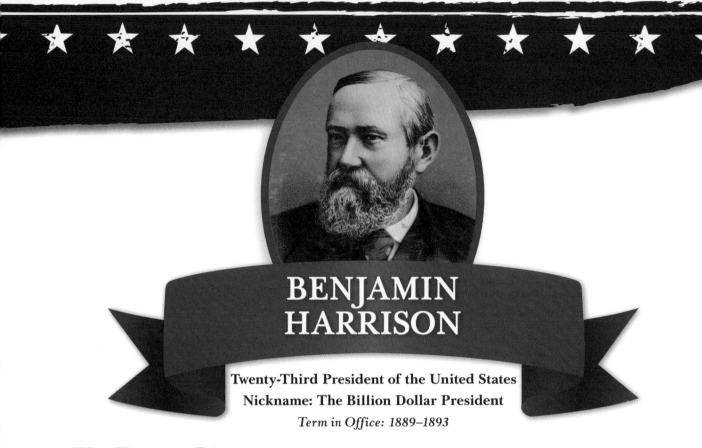

BENJAMIN HARRISON

Twenty-Third President of the United States
Nickname: The Billion Dollar President
Term in Office: 1889–1893

The Bottom Line

During his one term in office, Benjamin Harrison oversaw the first billion dollar federal budget during peacetime in America's history. Under his presidency, six new states were added to the U.S., and he funded pensions for Civil War Union veterans.

What Was He Thinking?

Most of what Harrison believed was shaped by his work in Congress: he supported expansionism, higher tariffs to protect American businesses, and funding pensions for Union Civil War veterans. Harrison also supported civil rights protection for African-Americans and opposed limiting immigration to America.

FAST STATS

★ Born August 20, 1833, in North Bend, Ohio
★ Parents: John and Elizabeth Irwin Harrison
★ Died March 31, 1901, in Indianapolis, Indiana; age 67
★ Age upon Start of Term: 55; Age upon Conclusion of Term: 59
★ Religious Affiliation: Presbyterian
★ Political Party: Republican
★ Height: 5 feet 6 inches
★ Vice President: Levi P. Morton

Why Should I Care?

Grover Cleveland helped the federal government achieve a budget surplus, but it did not last for long. Benjamin Harrison gave veterans pensions for their wartime service, paid for various national improvements, and then funded a renovation of the navy. Under Harrison, the government spent more than a billion dollars. Also during his term was the Panic of 1893, the

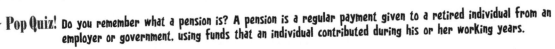

Pop Quiz! Do you remember what a pension is? A pension is a regular payment given to a retired individual from an employer or government, using funds that an individual contributed during his or her working years.

worst U.S. economic collapse until the Great Depression of the twentieth century.

> The law, the will of the majority [of Americans] ... is the only king to which we bow.

Breakin' It Down
Early Life

Benjamin came from a long line of politicians and great leaders. Most notably, his great-grandfather signed the Declaration of Independence, his grandfather was the ninth president of the United States, and his father served in Congress from 1853 to 1857. Despite his political blood, Benjamin spent a normal childhood with his five full siblings and two half siblings on a six-hundred-acre farm called "the Point" near North Bend, Ohio.

In school, he was an excellent student and participated in debate. Benjamin considered studying theology to become a Presbyterian minister but ended up choosing law instead and attended the Miami University in Ohio, graduating third in his class in 1852.

> John Adams and John Quincy Adams could say they were the first father-son team to become president, but William Henry Harrison and Benjamin Harrison could say they were the first and only grandfather-grandson team to assume the presidency.

After graduation, Harrison assumed several small political roles: city attorney of Indianapolis in 1857 and the leader of the local Republican Party in 1858. In 1860, he became a Supreme Court reporter in Indiana, transcribing judicial opinions and trial records. Then, in 1861, war came. Young Harrison was commissioned as second lieutenant for the 70th Indiana Regiment. In this position, he and his men patrolled the Union railroad tracks and trains, but they also entered a few battles, including the battle at the Kennesaw Mountains and the Battle of Nashville. At the Battle of the Kennesaw Mountains, Harrison served as the regiment's surgeon after the official surgeon became separated from the rest of the men. By the war's end, Benjamin had risen to brigadier general.

First Couple

CAROLINE HARRISON

In 1853, Benjamin Harrison married Caroline Lavinia Scott, and together they had three children. The Presidential Palace (as the White House was called in the day) was a busy place when Caroline and Benjamin resided there. Caroline oversaw the installation of electricity in the White House, and the family underwent an extreme scare when Benjamin received an electrical shock when he touched a light switch. All of Benjamin and Caroline's children and their grandchildren lived there for the entirety of Harrison's term, but the happy family was torn apart

Sir Arthur Conan Doyle publishes *The Adventures of Sherlock Holmes*, 1891

The Homestead Strike in Homestead, Pennsylvania, between laborers and the Carnegie Steel Company, takes place, 1892

Coup d'etat takes place in Hawaii against Queen Lili'uokalani, 1893

Henry Ford creates the first automobile, 1893

Oscar Wilde publishes *The Picture of Dorian Gray*, 1890

The Sioux Indians are defeated in the Battle of Wounded Knee, 1890

Tchaikovsky creates *The Nutcracker Suite*, 1892

Harrison hands the presidency back to Grover Cleveland, 1893

North Dakota, South Dakota, Montana, and Washington become states, 1889

Ohio and Wyoming become states, 1890

Walt Whitman dies, 1892

The First Pan-American Conference, 1889

Term in Office

| 1888 | 1889 | 1890 | 1891 | 1892 | 1893 |

in 1892 when Caroline died of tuberculosis shortly before Harrison lost his reelection bid.

Previous Political Career

- 1872: Sought the Republican nomination for Indiana governor—but lost.
- 1876: Won the nomination for governor of Indiana but lost to his Democratic opponent.
- 1879: Appointed head of the Mississippi River Commission.
- 1881: Elected U.S. Senator from Indiana. He favored civil rights for the still newly freed African-Americans. He supported raising tariffs to support American businesses. As a former war veteran, he believed the government should supply more pensions for war veterans. He supported the Pendleton Act, which increased the pensions for Union veterans. Having worked as the Mississippi River Commissioner, he moved to allot funds to improve Mississippi River navigation. Served as chairman of the Territories Committee.
- 1887: Lost reelection, which ended his time in the Senate.

Presidency

Improvements

True to his campaign promises, Harrison signed the Dependent and Disability Pensions Act, which appropriated $160

POLITICAL PARTIES

★★★★★★★★★★★★★★★★★★★★★★★★★★★★

Populist Party: **The Populist Party became powerful in the 1880s and the 1890s. The party's base of supporters came from the country's farmers and laborers, supporting an income tax, eight-hour workdays, and popular-vote elections for senators. The party also called for unlimited silver coinage and government ownership and regulation of railroads, businesses, and industries.**

I want it to be understood that I am the grandson of nobody. I believe that every man should stand on his own merits.

FUN FACT!

During the Civil War, Harrison was given a variety of nicknames: "Little Ben" from his fellow soldiers for his small stature; "Kid Gloves" for his mild temperament; and "Human Iceberg" for his rigidity and formality around others. Later in life, Harrison was be nicknamed "the centennial president" because he assumed the presidency one hundred years after George Washington.

ELECTION RESULTS!

Election of 1888	Electoral Votes
1st Benjamin Harrison	233
2nd Grover Cleveland	168

■ Benjamin Harrison — Republican Won

■ Grover Cleveland — Democrat Won

■ Territories

Benjamin Harrison's family name (and the fact that his grandfather had served as president) did help him at the Republican Convention in 1888. During the campaign, Harrison supported a protective tariff while incumbent Cleveland did not, and he also favored pensions for Civil War veterans, making him popular in the east and midwest, where the majority of the veterans resided. The race was close, to say the least, and Harrison became the third of the four presidents to win the seat of the presidency despite losing the popular vote.

CONGRESSIONAL CORNER

★★★★★★★★★★★★★★★★★★★★★★★

1. **Dependent and Disabilities Act of 1890:** This act provided pensions for all Americans who had served on the side of the Union Army for at least ninety days during the Civil War and who suffered some physical disability that prevented them from working.

2. **Sherman Antitrust Act of 1890:** This act prohibited businesses from taking certain actions that would limit competition in their field of business.

3. **Sherman Silver Act of 1890:** This act required the federal treasury to buy 4.5 million ounces of silver monthly, which was designed to boost the economy and help individuals pay off their taxes—the dollar was worth less now, and thus debts were worth less as well.

4. **McKinley Tariff of 1890:** This bill raised tariff rates by almost 50 percent to protect American businesses. It would later be replaced with the Wilson-Gorman Tariff in 1894.

5. **Land Revision Act of 1891:** This act allowed the president to set aside land for national parks, so Harrison was able to set aside land for Yellowstone Park in Wyoming later in his presidency.

6. **Geary Act of 1892:** This act extended the Chinese Exclusion Act, which had been passed in 1882. It also added more requirements for Chinese immigrants.

★★★★★★★★★★★★★★★★★★★★★★★

million for the pensions of disabled Union veterans, even if their injuries occurred after the Civil War. Congress also appropriated funds to improve the navy, thus creating the first peacetime billion-dollar budget. In 1890, Harrison signed the Sherman Antitrust Act, making it illegal for major companies to block competition in their field. (For example, a major toy company trying to prevent a new toy company from forming, because the two companies would then compete for business.) If business leaders did this, they would be fined five thousand dollars and suffer a one-year prison sentence. The act was later used by William McKinley and Theodore Roosevelt to break up large business monopolies.

Attempts at Monetary Reforms

Also in 1890, Harrison signed the McKinley Tariff, which placed an all-time high tariff of 48 percent on businesses and supported the Sherman Silver Act of 1890—an act that would lead to the Panic of 1893. The Sherman Silver Act forced the federal treasury to buy 4.5 million ounces of silver per month and caused the gold reserves to reach dangerously low quantities. This led to its repeal three years later.

Expansion

Six states and three territories entered the Union under Harrison's presidency. Near the end of his term, events in Hawaii quickly caused a debate over annexation. When a Hawaiian rebellion overthrew Queen Lili'uokalani, Harrison refused any action on behalf of the rebels or the queen, hoping the island would soon be independent for American annexation. Harrison also hoped to establish naval bases on the island. When the rebellion successfully overthrew the queen, a civil government was installed, a government Harrison backed.

Thoughts on the Constitution

> Unlike many other people less happy, we give our devotion to a government, to its Constitution, to its flag, and not to men.

Foreign Policy

Harrison did not enjoy many successful foreign policy achievements. During his presidency, relations were strained with both Great Britain and Italy. The United States disagreed with Great Britain over fishing rights around Alaska, although, fortunately, the dispute was resolved peacefully. Relations hardened between the U.S. and Italy after one policeman and eleven Italians were killed in New Orleans. Additionally, American anti-Italian groups lynched several Italian-Americans, causing the Italian government to demand federal prosecution of the perpetrators. Harrison apologized to the Italian government for the events, but explained that the criminals would be tried by state and local courts, as was their constitutional right.

Post-Presidency

After he left the presidency at the age of fifty-nine, Harrison had an active post-presidential career. In 1896, four years after his first wife died, Harrison married Mary Scott, a woman twenty-five years younger than him. At the age of sixty-five, Harrison fathered a daughter, who was younger than any of his grandchildren. In 1897 he authored *This Country of Ours*, in which he explained his opinion on how the federal government should operate, and in 1901 he authored *Views of an Ex-President*. Harrison also lectured on constitutional law at Stanford University in addition to giving speeches across the country—in one thirty-day period, he delivered 140 speeches. While Grover Cleveland was in office, he appointed Harrison to serve as council to Venezuela, where he helped resolve the border dispute with British Guiana. When William McKinley won the presidency, he appointed Harrison to the Permanent Court of Arbitration. In 1901, Harrison fell ill with influenza, which turned into pneumonia, leading to his death in March. His second wife, Mary Scott, survived him by fifty years.

Platform Speech

> The indiscriminate denunciation of the right is mischievous. It perverts the minds, poisons the heart, and furnishes an excuse to crime. No poor man was ever made richer or happier by it. It is as illogical to despise a man because he is rich as because he is poor. Not what a man has, but what he is, settles his class. We cannot right matters by taking from one what he has honestly acquired to bestow upon another what he has not earned.

> Benjamin Harrison believed that causing strife for others based on class or wealth is petty and unnecessary, and that those views seem to excuse unwarranted violence and corruption. For Harrison, a man's status should be based on who he is and not what he has. Harrison also opposed taking from the wealthy to give to the poor.

BENJAMIN HARRISON

BTW: Benjamin Harrison was the first president to attend a baseball game: on June 6, 1892, the Cincinnati Reds defeated the Washington Senators 7 to 4.

What Has He Done for Me Lately?

Under the presidency of Benjamin Harrison, six states were added to the Union, more than any previous president. Annexation of Hawaii was also debated during this time. Under Benjamin Harrison, America grew significantly closer to her present-day fifty-state status.

168

Presidential Times

Written by Juliette Turner

DAM COLLAPSE KILLS THOUSANDS IN PENNSYLVANIA!

June 1, 1889—In Johnstown, Pennsylvania, the collapse of a major dam led to a forty-foot wall of water and debris sweeping through the city, killing more than 2,200 people yesterday. The newly formed Red Cross, led by Clara Barton, conducted the relief efforts in the region.

Johnstown is one of many towns that experienced a heavy rain surge, which resulted in the massive flooding that caused the dam to collapse. Government officials are calling this one of the worst American natural disasters in history.

MASSACRE AT WOUNDED KNEE, SOUTH DAKOTA

December 30, 1890—An accidental but ghastly massacre has taken place in South Dakota. Yesterday, Major General Nelson Miles and the 7th Cavalry marched into Wounded Knee, South Dakota, to remove 350 Sioux and take them back to their reservation in Pine Ridge, South Dakota. The majority of the Indians being removed consisted of women and children. While the army led the removal, unintended shooting broke out, leaving 150 Sioux Indians dead. Major Miles has apologized for the event as Americans try to fathom the horrors that occurred during the relocation effort.

POPULATION BOOM!

June 17, 1890—After the recent release of the 1890 census, it appears that America has experienced an extreme boom in population. Between 1880 and 1890, the American population has increased by 25.5 percent. New York City still remains America's most populous city with over 1.5 million people, and Chicago, Illinois, is close behind with just over one million people.

SCENES OF 1891.
BATTLE OF WOUNDED KNEE.

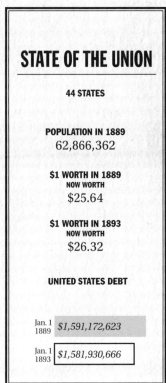

STATE OF THE UNION

44 STATES

POPULATION IN 1889
62,866,362

$1 WORTH IN 1889
NOW WORTH
$25.64

$1 WORTH IN 1893
NOW WORTH
$26.32

UNITED STATES DEBT

Jan. 1 1889	$1,591,172,623
Jan. 1 1893	$1,581,930,666

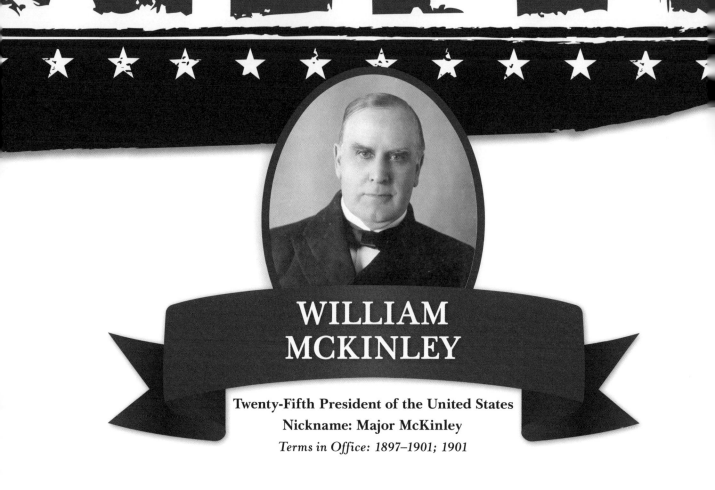

WILLIAM MCKINLEY

Twenty-Fifth President of the United States
Nickname: Major McKinley
Terms in Office: 1897–1901; 1901

The Bottom Line

William McKinley served two terms in office, during which he oversaw the beginning and conclusion of the Spanish-American War and worked to resolve the bimetallism issue in America at the time. His second term was cut short when he was assassinated just over seven months into his term in office.

FAST STATS

★ Born January 29, 1843, in Niles, Ohio
★ Parents: William and Nancy Campbell Allison McKinley
★ Died September 14, 1901, in Buffalo, New York; age 58
★ Age upon Start of First Term: 54; Age upon Conclusion of First Term: 58
★ Age upon Start of Second Term: 58; Age upon Assassination: 58
★ Religious Affiliation: Methodist
★ Political Party: Republican
★ Height: 5 feet 7 inches
★ Vice President: Garret Hobart (1897–1899) and Theodore Roosevelt (March–September 1901)

What Was He Thinking?

William McKinley believed in preserving the limited nature of the government, which came in handy during the start and end of the Spanish-American War. McKinley also wanted to ensure the stability of America's economy by preserving the value of its currency. This belief prompted McKinley to end the bimetallism debate that was threatening to destabilize the U.S. economy.

Why Should I Care?

The Spanish-American War was a major war in the history of the United States. By winning this

BTW: William McKinley was the first president to ride in an automobile.

war, America acquired Puerto Rico, Guam, and the Philippines—the first time American land extended outside the North American continent. Also, McKinley returned America's economy to the gold standard (with much help from the Klondike/Alaskan Gold Rush), preventing an economic collapse.

Breakin' It Down
Early Life

William McKinley was the seventh of eight children born to William and Nancy McKinley in Niles, Ohio. As a youth, William attended the Poland Academy, where the other students considered him unusually shy. His shy personality was not a reflection of his intelligence, however, which became obvious when the schoolteachers required William to sit in the back of the class to allow "slower" students time to catch up. Eventually, William outgrew his shyness, joined the school's debate club, and became a great public speaker and even the president of the local community debating club.

> That is all a man can hope for during his lifetime—to set an example—and when he is dead, to be an inspiration for history.

William attended Allegheny College, but withdrew within a month of enrollment because of exhaustion, illness, possible depression, and a lack of funds. After abandoning higher education for the time being, he became a postal clerk and a part-time schoolteacher. At the outbreak of the Civil War, he enlisted in the Twenty-Third Voluntary Ohio Regiment at the age of eighteen. At the Battle of Antietam, McKinley was commissioned to deliver supplies through enemy fire to isolated Union units and barely escaped death when his wagon was hit with a Confederate cannonball. Later in the war, McKinley fought under future president Rutherford B. Hayes and eventually rose to the position of second lieutenant.

After the Confederate surrender, McKinley attempted to continue his education by enrolling in Albany Law School, but he failed to graduate. During the presidential election of 1864, McKinley campaigned for Ulysses S. Grant. Intrigued by his first taste of politics, McKinley decided to run for office himself.

First Couple

In 1871, William McKinley married Ida Saxton during an extravagant wedding ceremony attended by more than one thousand friends, relatives, and guests. Ida and William had two daughters, but neither of them lived to adulthood: their first daughter succumbed to typhoid fever and their second daughter died shortly after her premature birth. After the death of both of her children, Ida herself became ill and never mentally or physically recovered. Among other illnesses, she fell victim to epileptic seizures, depression, and phlebitis (the painful swelling of the veins). Despite her constant near invalid state, William remained true to his wife and never left her side for more than a few days. William wasn't embarrassed by his wife's condition, and

The Newland Resolution orders the U.S. annexation of Hawaii, 1898

Spanish-American War, April–August 1898

The USS *Maine* sinks in Havana Harbor, Cuba, February 15, 1898

The Second Boer War begins in South Africa, 1899

The Philippine-American War begins, 1899

A hurricane hits Galveston, Texas, leaving six to eight thousand dead, 1900

The Gold Standard Act is passed, 1900

McKinley is shot by Leon Czolgosz and dies eight days later, September 6, 1901

Queen Victoria of Great Britain dies; Edward VII becomes king, 1901

Term in Office

1896　　1897　　1898　　1899　　1900　　1901

she frequently accompanied him to White House dinner parties or socials. When Ida had a seizure in public, William would hold a large handkerchief over her face to hide her from embarrassment.

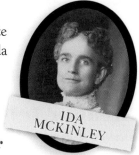

IDA McKINLEY

Previous Political Career

- 1867: Elected county chairman for the Republican Party.
- 1876: Elected to the U.S. House of Representatives, holding the position until 1883.
- 1885: Elected to Congress again, holding the position until 1891. During his time in Congress, two major issues arose: bimetallism and the raising/lowering of tariffs. McKinley supported bimetallism by voting for the Bland-Allison Act in 1878 and later the Sherman Silver Purchase Act in 1890. McKinley wanted to raise tariffs to protect businesses, even forming his own tariff legislation: the McKinley Tariff Act of 1890, which raised tariffs to such extremes that he was voted out of the House.
- 1889: Appointed the chairman of the House Ways and Means Committee until 1891.
- 1892: Elected governor of Ohio, earning reelection two years later. He served until 1896.
- 1892: Chairman of the Republican convention, increasing his recognition in the Republican Party.

Presidency

The American economy was on the upswing after the Panic of 1893 when McKinley assumed the presidency. McKinley relaxed government interference in businesses, allowing them to prosper in the economic recovery, and increased tariff rates (though not as dramatically as his McKinley Tariff) to protect American businesses even further. The bimetallism issue, so long at the center of American politics, finally came to an end when the Alaskan Gold Rush supplied enough gold for the federal treasury to become solely dependent on the gold standard.

The Spanish-American War

Americans across the country opposed Spanish occupation of the Cuban island, especially after the major newspapers began spreading awareness of (and sometimes overexaggerating) the despicable and inhumane treatment of the people on the island, including concentration camps. Two events occurred within the following months, which practically forced McKinley to declare war on Spain.

First, William Randolph Hearst printed a letter supposedly from the Spanish ambassador to America. Its validity was questioned because of Hearst's reputation of printing anything that would sell more papers. In the letter, Enrique Dupuy de Lome called McKinley "weak and a bidder for the admiration of the crowd, [and] a would-be politician who tries to leave a door open behind himself while keeping on good terms with the jingoes [a prowar faction] of his party." Americans—and McKinley—were infuriated.

BTW: William McKinley was the first president to campaign using the telephone.

 BTW: McKinley usually wore a red carnation in his jacket buttonhole for good luck.

ELECTION RESULTS!

McKinley notably switched his views to match the party he represented in the election: instead of favoring bimetallism, McKinley favored the gold standard. This flip led many businesses to support the Republican candidate, which they would not have done if McKinley had remained true to bimetallism. In turn, gold businesses gave somewhere between $3.5 million and $16 million to the McKinley campaign to ensure his election. McKinley also printed two hundred million campaign pamphlets in fourteen different languages and distributed them across the United States.

William McKinley campaigned once again from his own home, promising a "full dinner bucket" for everyone. He expressed his plans to increase America's involvement in international trade as well as his concern about the growing business-monopolies. McKinley chose Theodore Roosevelt to serve as his vice president, bringing Theodore's unique personality and recognition as a war hero to the ticket.

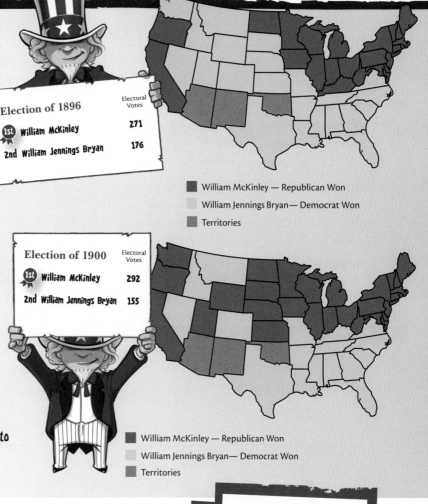

Election of 1896 — Electoral Votes

1st	William McKinley	271
2nd	William Jennings Bryan	176

William McKinley — Republican Won
William Jennings Bryan — Democrat Won
Territories

Election of 1900 — Electoral Votes

1st	William McKinley	292
2nd	William Jennings Bryan	155

William McKinley — Republican Won
William Jennings Bryan — Democrat Won
Territories

Then, an unexpected explosion occurred on the USS *Maine* while it was docked in a Cuban harbor, killing 266 American sailors. Although no one knew what caused the explosion, Americans used it as proof that Spain was out to attack the United States. In April, McKinley asked Congress to declare war, which they did by an overwhelming majority in the House (310 to 6) and a slightly narrow margin in the Senate (42 to 35).

China, the Philippines, Hawaii, and Panama

The U.S. negotiated the Open Door Policy with China, which encouraged trade between the two nations. After winning the war against Spain, McKinley ordered seventy thousand troops to maintain order in the Philippines, where the people had begun to rebel against the recent American takeover. McKinley hoped to secure the string of islands, because they proved an ideal location for the new China-America trade policies. Battles in the Philippines continued until 1902—a series of skirmishes sometimes referred to as the Philippine-American War—but finally the rebellion was controlled and America moved to officially take the region.

FUN FACT!

The inauguration of William McKinley in 1896 was the first recorded by a gramophone and a motion picture camera.

I have never been in doubt ... that I would someday be president.

1. **Declaration of War on Spain:** This declaration was issued on April 25, 1898, and officially approved the Spanish-American War.

2. **Newlands Resolution:** This resolution was approved by Congress on July 4, 1898, and authorized the annexation of Hawaii.

3. **Treaty of Paris:** This treaty, ratified on February 6, 1899, officially ended the Spanish-American War. Guam, the Philippines, and Puerto Rico came under U.S. control.

4. **Gold Standard Act of 1900:** This act made gold the only medium of exchange in the national government and all national banks.

★★★★★★★★★★★★★★★★★★★★★★★★★★

THOUGHTS ON THE CONSTITUTION

I shall use the authority vested in me by the Constitution and the statutes to uphold the sovereignty of the United States in those distant islands as in all other places where our flag rightfully floats. Aiming only at the public good, we cannot err.

WILLIAM MCKINLEY

The United States continued to expand its borders elsewhere in the Pacific. McKinley believed that the long-standing American policy of Manifest Destiny called for the annexation of Hawaii, and this occurred after the signing of the Newlands Resolution.

Assassination

Shortly after winning reelection in 1901, McKinley planned a transcontinental tour. However, once the tour began, it took a terrible turn. First, Ida McKinley fell terribly ill. Then, at the Temple of Music in Buffalo, New York, McKinley was shot by Leon R. Czolgosz. Immediately after the shot was fired, McKinley begged his guards not to hurt his assassin, crying, "Don't let them harm him." McKinley then thought of his wife and her unstable health, and pleaded, "My wife—be careful … how you tell her—oh, be careful." Only then did McKinley think of himself. The doctors used an X-ray machine to attempt to locate the bullets so they could remove them, and the president seemed to recover. However, after a week, gangrene set in. McKinley died eight days after Czolgosz fired his gun.

PLATFORM SPEECH

The credit of the Government, the integrity of its currency, and the inviolability of its obligations must be preserved. This was the commanding verdict of the people, and it will not be unheeded.

McKinley said this in his first State of the Union address in 1897. He believed that preserving the United States' good financial credit was vital to the success of America.

What Has He Done for Me Lately?

William McKinley accomplished the rare and difficult task of starting and ending a war within a four-year term. The Spanish-American War was a success, and an American victory increased America's power in the world.

WILLIAM MCKINLEY

BTW: William McKinley demanded to be a part of every stage of the Spanish-American War. He was directly involved in the diplomatic negotiations before the war, demanded firsthand accounts of the war operations, and personally oversaw the peace negotiations.

Written by Juliette Turner

THE KLONDIKE GOLD RUSH

August 17, 1896—Gold has been found in the Klondike and Yukon Rivers in the Yukon Territory in Canada. It is expected that close to thirty thousand people will be rushing to the site in an attempt to make a quick fortune.

USS *MAINE* EXPLODES! WAR CRIES ERUPT!

February 16, 1898—The U.S. battleship USS *Maine* exploded in Havana Harbor, Cuba, yesterday at 9:40 p.m. The explosion is being blamed on the Spanish and is calling many to advocate declaring war, though no substantial facts point to the Spanish as the perpetrator of the explosion.

It is speculated that underwater mines placed by the Spanish in the harbor exploded beneath the bottom of the ship. A more realistic cause is that a spontaneous combustion of coal in a storeroom next to the ammunitions storeroom on the ship caused the explosion.

THE SPANISH-AMERICAN WAR BEGINS . . . AND ENDS

August 14, 1898—The Spanish-American War lasted less than four months, ending just two days ago. Our great country took possession of lands outside the North American continent for the first time in history: Puerto Rico, Guam, and the Philippines.

The first American war presence in the Asian theater occurred on May 1 in the Philippines in Manila Bay, when Admiral George Dewey destroyed the entire Spanish fleet without a single American casualty.

American forces had many successes in this war, winning quick and decisive battles in Cuba, Puerto Rico, and the Philippines. Many feel that this is America's entry into world affairs.

MCKINLEY ASSASSIN EXECUTED

October 29, 1901—William McKinley's assassin Leon Czolgosz was executed for treason early this afternoon. Last month, McKinley died eight days after being shot during his transcontinental tour. Czolgosz, a self-proclaimed anarchist (person advocating the abolition of government, and instead self rule), declared he believed McKinley to represent an oppressive government. It is believed Czolgosz was inspired by the recent assassination of Italy's King Umberto I, carried out by Gaetano Bresci. Despite McKinley's pleas for his assassin to not be harmed, Czolgosz was executed by electrocution. Czolgosz's last words? "I killed the president because he was the enemy of the good people— the good working people. I am not sorry for my crime."

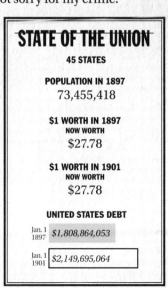

STATE OF THE UNION

45 STATES

POPULATION IN 1897
73,455,418

$1 WORTH IN 1897
NOW WORTH
$27.78

$1 WORTH IN 1901
NOW WORTH
$27.78

UNITED STATES DEBT

Jan. 1 1897 $1,808,864,053

Jan. 1 1901 $2,149,695,064

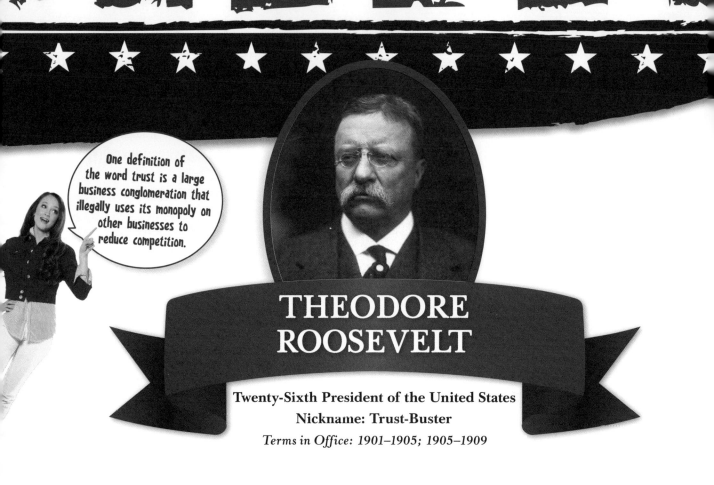

One definition of the word trust is a large business conglomeration that illegally uses its monopoly on other businesses to reduce competition.

THEODORE ROOSEVELT

Twenty-Sixth President of the United States
Nickname: Trust-Buster
Terms in Office: 1901–1905; 1905–1909

The Bottom Line

Theodore Roosevelt became president following the assassination of sitting-president William McKinley. During his first term, he began his "trust-busting" reforms and oversaw the construction on the Panama Canal. In his second term, Roosevelt continued his reforms to improve the lives of Americans by implementing the Pure Food and Drug Act, by creating national parks under the Forest Reserve Act, and by setting rail travel rates under the Hepburn Act.

FAST STATS

★ Born October 27, 1858, in New York, New York
★ Parents: Theodore and Martha Bulloch Roosevelt
★ Died January 6, 1919, in Oyster Bay, Long Island, New York; age 60
★ Age upon Start of First Term: 42; Age upon Conclusion of First Term: 46
★ Age upon Start of Second Term: 46; Age upon Conclusion of Second Term: 50
★ Religious Affiliation: Dutch Reformed
★ Political Party: Republican
★ Height: 5 feet 10 inches
★ Vice President: none (1901–1905) and Charles W. Fairbanks (1905–1909)

What Was He Thinking?

Although Theodore Roosevelt is known as a man who used government power to dismantle big-business corruption, he by no means believed the government should take over and control businesses. Roosevelt was opposed to full government control and wanted capitalism and businesses to be free to thrive and advance—as long as regulations were in place to prevent corruption.

THE SLOGANS
of Theodore Roosevelt

If you have ever heard the terms "bully pulpit" or "square deal," you can thank Theodore Roosevelt for that. Other terms first coined by the twenty-sixth president include "trust-buster," "muckraker," "Bull Moose," and "good to the last drop"—the Maxwell House Coffee slogan. Roosevelt drank up to a gallon of coffee every day.

Why Should I Care?

Theodore Roosevelt, known to some as "Teddy," is among the most well-known presidents of the United States. He greatly expanded the role of government in the daily lives of American citizens. His regulations improved the lives of Americans and continue to do so today. Among the most prominent of his reforms was the Pure Food and Drug Act, which regulated businesses that sold produce and increased the safety and reliability of America's pharmaceutical companies. You can also thank Roosevelt that cocaine is no longer used in Coca-Cola products!

FUN FACT!

Roosevelt had many "firsts" as president: He was the first president to stage photo ops and press events, to begin strategically releasing information to the press (whether or not it was favorable to his causes), to call the presidential residence the White House, to ride in an airplane and a submarine, and to travel overseas while in office.

Breakin' It Down
Early Life

As the second of four children in a wealthy New York family, Theodore refused to let anything hold him back—that is, except his poor health. Throughout his childhood, Theodore struggled with a constant state of ill health: he suffered everything from bronchial asthma, to upset stomachs, to chronic headaches. His parents tried every possible remedy—vaccinations, sulfur baths, lancing of lymph glands (without anesthesia, mind you), electrical charges, mustard plasters for his chest, late-night walks, and high-speed buggy rides to encourage air into his lungs. His health did not begin to improve until Theodore heeded his father's advice to begin exercising. Using everything from dumbbells to horizontal bars and even private boxing lessons from an ex-prizefighter, Theodore constantly pushed himself to try new things. In time, his health improved, and he became a strong, healthy, and fearless young man.

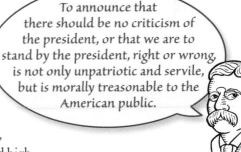

To announce that there should be no criticism of the president, or that we are to stand by the president, right or wrong, is not only unpatriotic and servile, but is morally treasonable to the American public.

Young Theodore was also an avid reader and nature observer. He loved great literary works and books on U.S. history, and he quickly became an expert on birds, flowers, and animals. Theodore recorded his observations in a nature journal, where he sketched pictures of mice, birds, and insects. He even stuffed and preserved birds, starting at age eleven.

BTW: Roosevelt actually hated the nickname Teddy, calling it "an outrageous impertinence." He much preferred T.R.

The foundation stone of national life is, and ever must be, the high individual character of the average citizen.

Theodore aspired to attend Harvard University, but even though he spoke fluent French and German, he failed the entrance exam. Two years later, however, after private tutoring, he passed and enrolled at Harvard. Theodore became the editor of the school paper, was a member of the Art and Rifle Club, qualified for Phi Beta Kappa, and graduated in 1880, magna cum laude. After graduating from Harvard, Theodore attended Columbia Law School, but he dropped out within a year, finding law boring and slow. Instead, Theodore decided to enter the realm of politics.

First Couple

Theodore Roosevelt was the fifth U.S. president whose wife died before he was inaugurated. In 1880, Roosevelt married Alice Hathaway Lee, with whom he had one daughter, also named Alice. Tragically, his wife died from kidney failure four years later. It only took two years for Roosevelt to remarry, however, and in 1886 he wed Edith Kermit Carow, a woman to whom he remained married for the rest of his life. Theodore and Edith had five children, four of whom lived to adulthood.

ALICE ROOSEVELT

EDITH ROOSEVELT

Previous Political Career

- 1882: Elected to the New York Assembly (the state legislature) to represent the twenty-first district at the age of twenty-three, winning reelection twice.
- 1886: Ran for mayor of New York, but lost, finishing a distant third place.
- 1889: Appointed to the U.S. Civil Service Commission by President Benjamin Harrison. He worked to eliminate fraud, rewrote the Civil Service examination to better regulate the government, and opened more jobs for women.
- 1895: Elected one of the four police commissioners of New York City and the President of the Board of Police Commissioners. He moved for more women to be hired, organized a police academy to better train

The Wright brothers make the first successful airplane flight in Kitty Hawk, North Carolina, 1903 • • • •

Jack London publishes his *Call of the Wild*, 1903

Construction on the Panama Canal begins, 1904

Roosevelt pardons all Filipinos who participated in the Philippine-American War, 1902 • • • •

Auguste Rodin completes *The Thinker* sculpture, 1902

Henry Ford organizes the Ford Motor Company, 1903

The New York City subway opens, 1904

Antitrust suits against Northern Securities (J. P. Morgan) and Standard Oil Company (John D. Rockefeller) were filed, 1902 •

The Boston Red Sox win their first World Series, 1903

First Term in Office

1900	1901	1902	1903	1904

BTW: The American Museum of Natural Sciences obtained a stuffed bat, twelve stuffed mice, a preserved turtle, a squirrel's skull, and four bird eggs from a certain thirteen-year-old boy named Theodore Roosevelt.

ELECTION RESULTS!

Election of 1904

		Electoral Votes
1st	Theodore Roosevelt	336
2nd	Alton B. Parker	140

Theodore Roosevelt — Republican Won

Alton B. Parker — Democrat Won

Territories

In 1903, Roosevelt announced he would run for a second term, but that he would not run again in 1908. In the campaign, both Roosevelt and his opponent ran on almost identical platforms (they had different views of the gold standard and the independence of the Philippines) and both chose to campaign from home. Roosevelt ultimately won over the American people with his charisma and successful record from his past three years as president, becoming the first accidental president to win a subsequent election.

FUN FACT!

Roosevelt's actions in the Spanish-American War are known by historians today to be more than worthy of a Medal of Honor, but he did not receive the medal at the war's conclusion because he criticized the army's slow withdrawal from Puerto Rico. In 2001, however, Roosevelt was duly awarded the medal by President Bill Clinton.

New York's police force, standardized weapons, and developed squads trained in certain specialties.

- 1897: Served as assistant secretary of the Navy under President William McKinley. Roosevelt increased the number of naval ships in the U.S. fleet.
- 1898: Resigned his post to join the First Volunteer U.S. Cavalry after the explosion of the USS *Maine*. He entered as lieutenant colonel, leading his band of "Rough Riders" through Cuba to fight for his country in the Spanish - American War.
- 1898: Elected governor of New York, winning by a narrow margin of just over seventeen thousand votes.
- 1900: Selected as vice president under William McKinley, playing a key role in McKinley's successful reelection bid.

Theodore Roosevelt remains the youngest man to hold the office of the president. He was forty-two. However, he was not elected until he was forty-six. The youngest man elected president was John F. Kennedy, who was forty-three.

Presidency

Following the common thought of the day, Roosevelt enforced regulations on big business trusts. These regulations established standard guidelines and procedures for all businesses. Additionally, Roosevelt worked to

Great Britain builds the powerful naval ship the HMS *Dreadnought*, 1906 •

San Francisco's earthquake and three-day fire occurs; five hundred individuals die, 1906

Oklahoma becomes a state, 1907

Henry Ford produces the first Model-T car, 1908

Einstein releases his Theory of Special Relativity, 1905

Roosevelt is awarded the Nobel Peace Prize, 1906

The Panic of 1907 and the stock market crash occur, 1907

Second Term in Office

1905	1906	1907	1908	1909

CONGRESSIONAL CORNER
★★★★★★★★★★★★★★★★★★★★★★★★★★

1. **Hay-Pauncefote Treaty of 1901:** This treaty and the previous agreement that the Panama Canal would be under international control. The treaty gave the canal and its construction to the United States.

2. **Expediting Act of 1903:** This act allowed the government to break up business trusts in steel, meat packing, oil, and railroad industries.

3. **Platt Amendment of 1903:** This amendment allowed U.S. forces to use military action in Cuba if necessary.

4. **Elkins Act of 1903:** This act allowed the Interstate Commerce Commission to impose heavy fines on railroad and shipping businesses that accepted or granted rebates for overpayment.

5. **Antiquities Act of 1906:** This act allowed the president to set aside public land for federal use, such as the creation of national parks.

6. **Hepburn Act of 1906:** This act gave the Interstate Commerce Commission the ability to set railroad rates for the entire railroad industry.

7. **Pure Food and Drug Act of 1906:** This act allowed the federal government to oversee the production of food and drugs to ensure the purity of the products that were put on the market. This bill was beneficial to the country because it prevented frauds and quacks from distributing medicine, and it also banned the use of cocaine in drugs and foods (such as Coca-Cola).

8. **Meat Inspection Act of 1906:** This act allowed the government to regulate the meat industry to prevent contaminated or mislabeled meat from being sold on the market.

9. **Federal Employers Liability Act of 1908:** This act forced railroad businesses to provide money to railroad workers who were injured while working on railroads.

★★★★★★★★★★★★★★★★★★★★★★★★★★

LIBERTY Language

Monopoly: The result of one large industry in a certain field of business controlling the distribution and creation of a certain good because of their power and control over smaller and less-formed businesses.

increase government influence in disputes between labor and business management. Despite Roosevelt's record and legacy as a "progressive" reformer, he used his position as President to enforce regulations on big business trusts.

Foreign Policy
Roosevelt achieved many foreign policy successes, ranging from the groundbreaking of the Panama Canal, to doubling the size of the U.S. Navy to successfuly invoking the Monroe Doctrine to limit European presence in Latin America. Roosevelt worked to peacefully resolve conflicts and issues, but he was prepared to act if necessary, believing military strength served as a deterrent to war. At the same time, Roosevelt was against the unnecessary expansion of American influence, including the annexation of Cuba and other islands.

Economic Problems
During his second term, the U.S. suffered an economic nosedive when the Knickerbocker Trust (one of the nation's major banks) collapsed. Yet, recovery was rapid, and Roosevelt's reputation was spared.

Post-Presidency
Roosevelt by no means "retired" after leaving office. After a tour of Europe, he returned to find his successor, William Howard Taft, unraveling many of

BTW: Last Words: "Please put out the light."

  BTW: After winning the election in 1904, Roosevelt said to his wife: "My dear, I am no longer a political accident."

THOUGHTS ON THE CONSTITUTION

> The Constitution was made for the people and not the people for the Constitution.

> Theodore Roosevelt believed that a loose interpretation of the Constitution was best to protect Americans and their well-being.

Roosevelt's achievements and taking Roosevelt's "trust-busting" tactics to an extreme. When the Progressive Republican Party asked him to run for president once again in 1912, Roosevelt replied, "My hat is in the ring." Roosevelt's third party became known as the "Bull Moose Party" and gained wide recognition throughout the country. Although Roosevelt was unable to pull off a second win, he did prevent Taft from winning.

After the election, Roosevelt—true to his adventurous spirit—toured Brazil, a trip that soon turned into a disaster. While traveling the "River of Doubt," one man drowned, another went insane and killed himself, and Roosevelt himself became terribly ill with jungle fever, to the point of hallucination! Roosevelt survived his journey and returned home. In 1919, at the age of sixty, the great warrior and trailblazer Theodore Roosevelt died from a coronary embolism.

What Has He Done for Me Lately?

On top of beginning the construction of the Panama Canal—which greatly expedited oceanic trade—Roosevelt also increased America's standing in the eyes of many foreign countries, particularly in Asia. Through his "naval exercises," which paraded U.S. Navy strength before other countries, and by expanding the United States Navy, Roosevelt intimidated the Japanese. Both Japan and the U.S. were contending for the Pacific empire, though no action was taken until World War II (when Theodore's cousin, Franklin, was president).

PLATFORM SPEECH

> There is mighty little good in a mere spasm of reform. The reform that counts is that which comes through steady, continuous growth; violent emotionalism leads to nothing.

> Roosevelt said this in his 1906 "Man with a Muck Rake" speech. He believed that reform should be steady and continuous, not rash and shortsighted.

THEODORE ROOSEVELT

Written by Juliette Turner

THE SQUARE DEAL

October 3, 1902—Earlier today, President Roosevelt met with representatives of the labor unions and coal businesses engaged in the recent nationwide coal worker strike. The administration is hoping to end the strike, which has lasted since May of this year.

In the first pro-labor move of any president, Roosevelt is proposing a deal that will result in a 10 percent increase in the wages of the coal miners and a reduction of the work day to nine hours. The management would in turn receive more leverage for their Washington, D.C., lobbyists. The deal was pegged the "Square Deal" after Roosevelt declared no one side would receive special treatment.

In a statement to the press, the president said, "The rights and interest of the laboring man will be protected and cared for."

THE PANAMA CANAL

November 18, 1903—The governments of Panama and the U.S. signed the Hay-Bunau-Varilla Treaty today. This treaty grants America a ten-mile strip of land along the isthmus for the creation of the Panama Canal; however, this temporary "land grant" was in exchange for an annual ten million dollars and an annual rent cost of two hundred and fifty thousand dollars.

This development occurred after the overthrow of the previous Panamanian government, which had refused any negotiations with the U.S. over the canal.

CRUISE OF THE GREAT WHITE FLEET

February 22, 1909—The Great White Fleet returned to Virginia today after its fourteen-month trip around the globe. In 1907, twenty-six battleships embarked on their voyage, not to return until today. Although Roosevelt claimed this to be an exercise of a new naval fleet, the countries of the Pacific understood the hidden meaning of the "exercise": as the naval fleet passed by the various countries, the countries saw the strength and power of the American Navy, giving them second thoughts about any belligerent actions.

THE NATURE PRESIDENT

January 11, 1908—President Roosevelt has made the Grand Canyon in Arizona a national monument. This act comes at the end of a long string of actions Roosevelt has taken to preserve America's land and natural habitats. Since 1905, Roosevelt has increased the amount of federally owned land from 42 million to 170 million acres. To date, twenty-one forest reserves have been created and eleven have been enlarged. This translates into sixteen million acres of national forests, five national parks, fifty-one wildlife refuges, and eighteen national monuments, including Crater Lake, a rain forest, Sequoia Stands, and, now, the Grand Canyon.

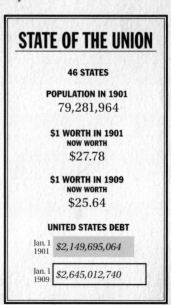

STATE OF THE UNION

46 STATES

POPULATION IN 1901
79,281,964

$1 WORTH IN 1901
NOW WORTH
$27.78

$1 WORTH IN 1909
NOW WORTH
$25.64

UNITED STATES DEBT

Jan. 1 1901	*$2,149,695,064*
Jan. 1 1909	*$2,645,012,740*

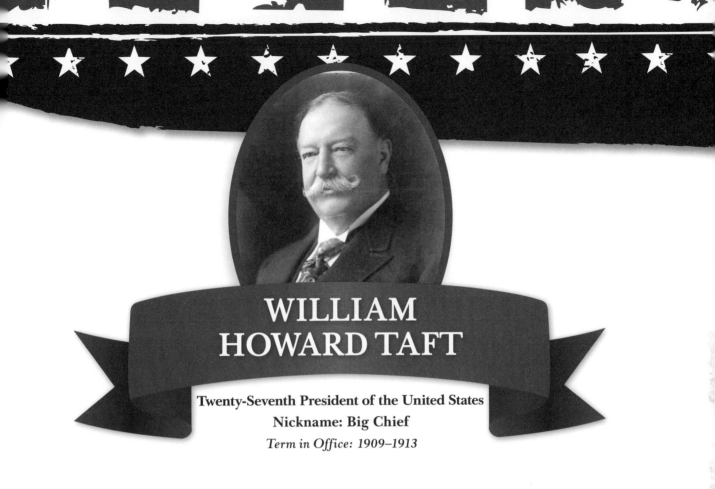

WILLIAM HOWARD TAFT

Twenty-Seventh President of the United States
Nickname: Big Chief
Term in Office: 1909–1913

The Bottom Line

William Howard Taft helped stabilize the American economy, continued and expanded many of the progressive reforms begun by Theodore Roosevelt, and instated his "Dollar Diplomacy" approach to foreign policy.

What Was He Thinking?

William Howard Taft worked to expand government regulation. On the economic front, Taft believed in having a national budget to prevent overspending and out-of-control debt. He also worked to lower tariff rates. Taft saw foreign policy differently than his predecessor and promoted peace by helping countries financially rather than brandishing American military strength.

FAST STATS

★ Born September 15, 1857, in Cincinnati, Ohio
★ Parents: Alphonso and Louisa Torrey Taft
★ Died March 8, 1930, in Washington, D.C.; age 72
★ Age upon Start of Term: 51; Age upon Conclusion of Term: 55
★ Religious Affiliation: Unitarian
★ Political Party: Republican
★ Height: 6 feet 2 inches
★ Vice President: James S. Sherman (1909–1912)

Why Should I Care?

Taft was influential in changing the scope and expanse of government. Although some of his acts were repealed later, Taft was responsible for approving legislation that allowed government regulation of private businesses (unlike Roosevelt, who wanted to regulate only corrupted corporations). Additionally, he created a great number of new committees, departments, and boards that were deployed to investigate, monitor, or regulate various aspects of American life.

Breakin' It Down
Early Life

William was born to Alphonso and Louisa Taft in 1857 as a happy and somewhat plump baby. Being overweight from his earliest days, William was not only self-conscious about his weight, he also suffered from weight-related health issues throughout his youth.

William attended local schools as a child and proved to be a smart and able student—although he tended to procrastinate. He began to show his progressive, "new world" way of thinking in high school when he wrote an essay arguing why women should have equal educational opportunities and the right to vote. After graduating second in his class, William attended Yale University, where he was awarded many prizes in all fields of study, was voted class orator, and graduated second in his class of 132 students in 1878. Two years later, he also graduated from Cincinnati Law School.

We are all imperfect. We cannot expect perfect government.

From a young age, William dreamed of becoming a chief justice for the Supreme Court. To begin his journey, he first became a courthouse reporter and served as assistant prosecuting attorney for Ohio's Hamilton County. Although Taft started his own private law practice, it wasn't long before he entered the world of politics, beginning a lifelong career of service to his country.

First Couple

William Howard Taft married Helen Herron (known as Nellie) in 1886—although Nellie rejected his marriage proposal twice. Together they had three children. William had Nellie to thank for his presidential success. She was the driving force behind Roosevelt's decision to choose Taft as his successor and she campaigned vigorously for her husband in 1908. Why was Nellie so driven? Maybe it stemmed from her childhood visit to the White House during Hayes's presidency, when she had promised to return to the mansion for a "longer stay."

HELEN TAFT

Previous Political Career

- 1882: Appointed as internal revenue collector for Ohio's first district by President Chester Arthur.
- 1887: Appointed to fill a vacancy on the Superior Court of Ohio at the age of thirty-five.
- 1888: Elected to the Superior Court of Ohio.

BTW: William was known to be a very good dancer in high school.

The sixteenth amendment is introduced, 1909

The National Association for the Advancement of Colored People (NAACP) is formed, 1909

Robert Peary reaches the North Pole, 1909

The rebellion in China overthrows the Qing Dynasty; the Republic of China is formed, 1911

The Mexican Revolution begins, 1910

The Great Fire of 1911 takes place in Maine, 1911

Arizona and New Mexico become states, 1912

The Titanic sinks in the North Atlantic, 1912

Great Britain organizes their Royal Flying Corps, 1912

The seventeenth amendment is introduced, 1912

Term in Office

| 1908 | 1909 | 1910 | 1911 | 1912 | 1913 |

- 1890: Appointed solicitor general by President Benjamin Harrison.
- 1892: Appointed judge of the Sixth Circuit U.S. Court of Appeals.
  - 1900: Appointed head of the "Philippine Commission" by President William McKinley, which monitored the Philippine islands after the Spanish-American War. He was offered a position on the Supreme Court by President Theodore Roosevelt, but Taft turned down the offer, feeling he should finish his duties in the Philippines before becoming involved in other jobs.
  - 1904: Appointed Roosevelt's secretary of war. Taft was key in monitoring one of Roosevelt's major successes—the Panama Canal—and also negotiated with Cuba to prevent American intervention in a rebellion taking place on the island.

BTW: While in the Philippines, Taft's wife, Nellie, founded the Drop of Milk Program, which educated the islands' natives about milk sterilization.

Pop Quiz! Do you remember what a solicitor general does? The solicitor general is the chief lawyer under the attorney general, who represents law cases that are first heard in state courts and could possibly reach the Supreme Court.

POLITICAL PARTIES

★★★★★★★★★★★★★★★★★★★★★★★★★★

Bull Moose (Progressive) Party: **The National Progressive Republican League was formed in 1911, by Wisconsin senator Robert M. La Follette. The group became the Progressive Party the following year. The party believed in forming welfare programs and making them the government's priority. Leaders also wanted to create an easier way to amend the Constitution, more business regulations, protection for labor forces, formation of the Department of Labor, and abolition of child labor.**

Anyone who has taken the oath I have just taken must feel a heavy weight of responsibility.

Presidency

For the first time since Andrew Jackson restarted the tradition of holding outdoor inaugurations, Taft's inauguration ceremonies were held indoors because six inches of snow and frigid temperatures had hit Washington, D.C., the night before the oath.

Trust-Busting and Reforms

First, Taft appointed his cabinet members, taking caution to choose moderate politicians, and continued many of Roosevelt's reforms, including the "trust-busting" suits against major business corporations. During Taft's presidency alone, seventy antitrust lawsuits were filed against American

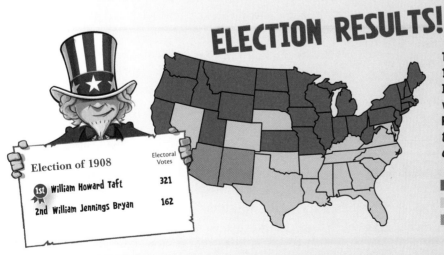

ELECTION RESULTS!

Election of 1908	Electoral Votes
1st William Howard Taft	321
2nd William Jennings Bryan	162

Taft did little to win the presidency in 1908, only speaking on very rare occasions. In fact, Taft hoped he would not emerge the victor of the election. Between Theodore Roosevelt's endorsement and the determination of Nellie Taft, however, William did clinch the presidency—and by a large margin.

■ William Howard Taft — Republican Won
■ William Jennings Bryan — Democrat Won
■ Territories

BTW: William Howard Taft was one of the first presidents to regularly play golf, a sport considered effeminate during that time. Nonetheless, with a president's endorsement, golf boomed in popularity and the number of golfers doubled.

1. **Payne-Aldrich Act of 1909:** This act signed into law by taft, was primarily a measure to lower tariffs. However, it also contained a provision that created the first corporate income tax. It affected all corporations that had annual revenue of more than $5,000.

2. **Mann-Elkins Act of 1910:** This act strengthened the Interstate Commerce Commission (created in 1887) by allowing it to regulate private railroad companies by setting railroad rates. The act also allowed the Interstate Commerce Commission to regulate the telephone and telegraph industries. The Commission continued until 1995, when it was abolished by Congress.

3. **Mann Act of 1910:** This act made it a federal felony to engage in human trafficking or the kidnapping of women for prostitution.

4. **Public Law 62-5:** Congress passed this law on August 8, 1911, setting the number of House representatives to 435. It first took effect in the election of 1913.

5. **Webb-Kenyon Act of 1913:** This act placed regulation on the sale of alcohol in an attempt to promote and support statewide prohibition movements.

6. **Burnett Act of 1913:** This act allocated $40 million of federal money for the construction of buildings in Washington, D.C.

7. **Labor Department Bill of 1913:** This bill separated the Department of Labor and Commerce into two separate departments. The Department of Labor included the Bureau of Labor Statistics, the Bureau of Immigration and Naturalization, and the United States Children's Bureau.

★★★★★★★★★★★★★★★★★★★★★★★

THOUGHTS ON THE CONSTITUTION

> We have a government of limited power under the Constitution, and we have got to work out our problems on the basis of law.

corporations, including the American Tobacco Company. Taft also expanded the government further by signing the congressionally approved Mann-Elkins Act of 1910. Additionally, Taft divided the Department of Commerce and Labor into two departments (the Department of Commerce and the Department of Labor), created the Bureau of Mines, and formed the Commission on Economy and Efficiency, which would later become the Budget and Accounting Office. Although the United States experienced a period of economic growth during Taft's tenure in office, his attempts to lower tariff rates backfired dramatically. In 1909, Taft signed the Payne-Aldrich Act into law, but the rates actually increased because of multiple Senate amendments. Taft's popularity suffered as a result.

Dollar Diplomacy

On the international scale, Taft began to implement his "Dollar Diplomacy" plan, which he claimed would replace bullets with dollars. The plan combined financial aid or investment and increased trade between the United States and a given foreign country to stabilize the economy of that country. Instead of using military deterrence as Roosevelt had, Taft used America's economic strength to promote peace while at the same time opening up new economic markets for American businesses in other countries through new trading routes. Taft's critics claimed the plan exploited impoverished foreign countries for America's economic gain, but Taft continued, and the plan succeeded.

Reelection Failure

Taft and Roosevelt seemed to follow the same belief system, but at the 1912 Republican Convention, two factions emerged: one side defending Taft and another vying for former president Theodore Roosevelt's reelection. Things quickly got out of hand, with fistfights breaking out on the convention floor. The Republican Party split in two, with Taft on the Republican ticket and Roosevelt on the Progressive ticket. Taft was reportedly dumbfounded when he discovered his old friend would be

BTW: Taft was the first president to reside over all forty-eight continental states.

BTW: Nellie Taft planted the first of the famous Japanese cherry trees along the Potomac River in Washington, D.C.

running and campaigning against him, with all the Roosevelt-style vigor. In the end, because Roosevelt drained votes that might have otherwise been for Taft, Taft was defeated.

Post-Presidency

It took a while—nine years—but William Howard Taft eventually achieved his dream of serving as chief justice on the Supreme Court of the United States. During the presidency of Warren Harding in 1921, Taft's appointment to the Supreme Court was approved in a 60 to 4 Senate vote.

Taft authored more than 250 opinions, translating into one-sixth of that court's opinions. In 1928, Taft ruled in Olmstead v. United States that the wiretapping of personal telephones by the federal government without a court warrant did not violate the fourth and fifth amendments in the Constitution. However, this ruling was reversed in 1967. Taft supported the Judiciary Act of 1925, which would give the Supreme Court the ability to decide which cases they would hear and which cases they would reject in addition to creating more than twenty new federal courts. Taft was also influential in calling for the court to have its own building; however, construction did not begin until 1932, two years after Taft retired. Although Taft retired after a mere eight years on the court, he claimed his time there was one of the happiest, as well as one of the most important accomplishments of his life. A little over a month after resigning, Taft died at the age of seventy-two, due in part to the high blood pressure and heart disease that stemmed from his struggle with obesity.

What Has He Done for Me Lately?

Do you or your parents pay income taxes? You know, those pesky forms your parents complain about every year? Well, not only was the sixteenth amendment passed during Taft's presidency (allowing the government to tax individuals and businesses based on their levels of income), but Taft signed into law the very first corporate income tax. Additionally, the seventeenth amendment was passed by Congress under Taft's presidency, changing the way senators were elected. This new method is still in place today. Instead of having our U.S. senators appointed by our state legislatures, the seventeenth amendment calls for all senators to be elected directly by the people. Thus, every six years the people, not the state legislature, directly vote for senators.

FUN FACT!

Taft threw the first presidential pitch at the Washington Senators and Philadelphia Athletics baseball game at Griffith Stadium on the opening day of the baseball season in 1910. Every president since Taft has thrown at least one "first pitch."

PRESIDENTIAL Personality

★ William Howard Taft was an amiable and happy man who put those around him quickly at ease. He was a cautious leader, often uncomfortable with the national spotlight and more comfortable behind a law desk or arguing cases in front of the Supreme Court. For the most part, Taft was unhappy in the White House, especially because he had no close advisors after Theodore Roosevelt turned against him. It wasn't until 1921, when Taft joined the Supreme Court, that his friends once again saw the jovial and happy William Howard Taft.

PLATFORM SPEECH

I don't much believe in a president's interfering with the legislative department while doing its work. They have their responsibility and I have mine.

Tafthe agreed that the legislative branch and the executive branch should remain separate. As President, he didn't want to interfere in the law-making process.

WILLIAM HOWARD TAFT

Presidential Times

Written by Juliette Turner

FORMER PRESIDENT THEODORE ROOSEVELT SHOT WHILE CAMPAIGNING IN MILWAUKEE

October 14, 1912— After announcing he would run for the office of president again in 1912, not everyone was swayed, including thirty-six-year-old John Flammang Schrank. While speaking in Milwaukee, Wisconsin, former president Roosevelt was shot by Schrank. Amazingly, Roosevelt did not even know he had been shot until someone commented on the hole in his shirt. If not for the glasses case and the thick copy of his speech Roosevelt held in his shirt pocket, the bullet would have punctured his lung. As it was, the bullet lodged into his skin just above his left lung. Yet, with typical "Roosevelt style," Roosevelt believed his lung was not punctured because he was not coughing up blood, and so continued his ninety-minute speech before retiring to the hospital.

Schrank was captured immediately and taken into custody. As Roosevelt was rushed to the hospital following his speech, his wife, Edith, attempted to prevent reporters from following him, but Roosevelt welcomed them and continued taking interviews. Sitting in the hospital bed, Roosevelt told one reporter, "It takes more than one bullet to kill a Bull Moose."

INCOME TAXES! THE SIXTEENTH AMENDMENT

July 2, 1909—Congress has passed the sixteenth amendment to the Constitution today, establishing a national income tax on all Americans. This amendment comes after the Supreme Court decided that income taxes were unconstitutional. The court ruled that, since personal income taxes are a direct tax and not apportioned by population, there is no clause in the Constitution allowing for such a tax. Congress then moved to pass an amendment to make an income tax constitutional. The amendment still must be ratified by the states before it becomes law, but congressional members are confident it will be passed.

THE SEVENTEENTH AMENDMENT

May 13, 1912—Congress has now passed another amendment to the U.S. Constitution. This time, the amendment has nothing to do with money. Instead, Congress has fundamentally changed how some government officials are elected. Since the signing of the Constitution in 1787, members of the U.S. Senate have been appointed by individual state legislatures. Now this recently proposed and passed amendment changes this structure so senators will be directly elected by the people (as congressmen are).

Many critics are claiming that this amendment will greatly disturb the system of checks and balances in our government and will take away much of the states' powers. They argue that the states will no longer have a representative in the national government and, subsequently, the federal government will become larger and more powerful. But congressional members believe there will be no problems in the state-ratification process.

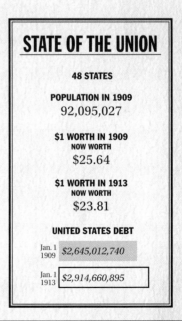

STATE OF THE UNION

48 STATES

POPULATION IN 1909
92,095,027

$1 WORTH IN 1909
NOW WORTH
$25.64

$1 WORTH IN 1913
NOW WORTH
$23.81

UNITED STATES DEBT

Jan. 1 1909	$2,645,012,740
Jan. 1 1913	$2,914,660,895

WOODROW WILSON

Twenty-Eighth President of the United States
Nickname: The Progressive President
Terms in Office: 1913–1917; 1917–1921

The Bottom Line

Woodrow Wilson aggressively pushed his progressive reforms on American society and law—notably the banking system—and also struggled to pacify relations with Mexico during his first term as President. As he began his second term in 1917, the United States entered the First World War.

FAST STATS

★ Born December 28, 1856, in Staunton, Virginia
★ Parents: Joseph and Jessie Woodrow Wilson
★ Died February 3, 1924, in Washington, D.C.; age 67
★ Age upon Start of First Term: 56; Age upon Conclusion of First Term: 60
★ Age upon Start of Second Term: 60; Age upon Conclusion of Second Term: 64
★ Religious Affiliation: Presbyterian
★ Political Party: Democrat
★ Height: 5 feet 11 inches
★ Vice President: Thomas R. Marshall

What Was He Thinking?

Woodrow Wilson is known as one of the most progressive of the American presidents. His views, in hindsight—especially those outlined in the two books he published before his presidency—seem to voice the opinions of a man who wished to change the United States Constitution and America's republican form of government. Indeed, Wilson worked from the executive branch to expand the power of the national government during his time in office, bypassing the normal limitations of Congress and the judicial branch.

What was Wilson thinking? Several of the acts and commissions established under his command during the war violated the Constitution and endangered some of the rights of the American citizens. Maybe he was thinking this was another form of government.

Why Should I Care?

If you are a woman, you should appreciate Wilson's efforts and success in the arena of women's suffrage, for it was during Wilson's time in office that the nineteenth amendment was passed by the Republican majority in Congress, granting women the right to vote. Additionally, Wilson ably guided America through the nation's largest military engagement since the Civil War: World War I.

Breakin' It Down
Early Life

> My life would not be worth living if it were not for the driving power of religion, for faith, pure and simple... Never for a moment have I had one doubt about my religious beliefs.

The third of four children born to Joseph and Jessie Wilson, Thomas Woodrow Wilson was born in Virginia in the winter of 1856. During his youth, Woodrow was known to his friends as a mama's boy and suffered from frequent ill health. Because he was unable to read until around the age of twelve, scholars debate today whether or not Woodrow suffered from dyslexia. Woodrow worked to overcome his struggle, often writing in shorthand to help with his reading disability. Due to his illnesses and his late start on education, he was schooled mainly at home until he entered Davidson College in 1873. He left the school the following year after several bouts of illness.

Still eager for education, Woodrow self-educated by reading many of the multitudes of books in his family library. In 1875, he entered the College of New Jersey (now Princeton). While there, Woodrow remained busy with baseball, football, the debate team, theater productions, and writing columns, which were published in several journals. Woodrow graduated thirty-eighth in a class of 167 in 1879. He then attended the University of Virginia Law School but left the school in 1881. He went on to obtain a PhD from Johns Hopkins University in 1886, making him the only president to have earned a doctoral degree.

During this time, he also taught college courses at a women's college. He made his way up the ladder, eventually becoming Princeton's first non-clerical president. In this position, Wilson's leadership and administrative skills became apparent, and members of the community soon encouraged him to run for public office.

FUN FACT!

Woodrow Wilson wrote two books: *Congressional Government* in 1885, and *The State: Elements of Historical and Practical Politics* in 1889.

First Couple

Woodrow and his first wife, Ellen, married in 1885 and had three children. Ellen served as first lady for approximately one year,

---

The sixteenth and seventeenth amendments to the Constitution are ratified by the states, 1913

Henry Ford organizes the first assembly line, 1913

Mother's Day becomes a national holiday, 1914

Germany declares war on Russia; World War I begins, 1914

Archbishop Franz Ferdinand of Austria is assassinated, 1914

Einstein publishes *Theory of General Relativity*, 1915

The Coast Guard is created, 1915

The *Lusitania* is sunk by German U-boats, 1915

The Battle of Verdun is fought (WWI), 1916

The Battle of the Somme is fought (WWI), 1916

The National Parks Service is established, 1916

First Term in Office

1912   1913   1914   1915   1916

BTW: While serving as the president of Princeton University, Wilson suffered from severe hypertension in his left eye, which led to temporary blindness.

during which time she arranged two weddings in the White House for her daughters and also oversaw the first national Mother's Day celebration. She tragically died from Bright's disease (a disease of the kidneys) in 1914. A year later, Woodrow Wilson became the third president to marry while serving as president of the United States. He married Edith Galt, to whom he remained married until his death. They had no children together.

ELLEN WILSON

EDITH WILSON

Pop Quiz! Which former president died from the same disease that claimed the life of Wilson's first wife? Chester Arthur also died from Bright's disease, just over a year after he left office.

Previous Political Career

- 1910–1912: Elected governor of New Jersey, winning by a landslide. Wilson pushed for the direct election of U.S. senators and for ending outside influences (like political donors) on the governor. Enacted reforms by placing public utilities under state regulation, reorganizing and reforming public school systems, and also working to break up corporate monopolies. He supported and signed the state's first workman's compensation bill.

Presidency

Wilson's victory ended a Republican dominance on the presidency; other than Grover Cleveland, a Democrat had not held the office of the presidency since Andrew Johnson. Wilson did not delay his reforms, introducing his agenda— "New Freedom"—shortly after assuming office. On March 15, 1913, Wilson became the first president to hold an official press conference. He realized the importance of having the people's support to successfully implement his agendas. His stratagem worked, and a large influx of mail flooded Congress in support of Wilson.

PRESIDENTIAL Personality

★ Woodrow Wilson was a completely different man with his friends than he was as president. Among his contemporaries, Wilson was reserved and quiet, not one to lead a crowd. As president, however, he was an effective speaker with a firm voice, using colorful language and promoting progressive ideas. Wilson referred to his own personality once as a dormant volcano: cold and unresponsive on the outside but bubbling with lava and life within.

Federal Reserve System

Congress created the Federal Reserve System, a banking system owned, regulated, and controlled by the federal government. The Federal Reserve Act of 1913 created a new Federal Reserve

---

The Treaty of Versailles is signed, officially ending World War I, 1919

The League of Nations holds their first meeting in Geneva, Switzerland, 1920

The Department of Justice conducts its "red hunt" to capture American communist radicals, 1920

U.S. purchases the Danish West dies (U.S. Virgin Islands), 1917

Germany requests an armistice; World War I ends, 1918

The eighteenth amendment is ratified; Prohibition begins in America, 1919

Wilson is awarded the Nobel Peace Prize, 1920

U.S. declares war on Germany and her allies, 1917

Daylight savings time is established, 1918

The nineteenth amendment is ratified; women gain the right to vote, 1920

Second Term in Office

1917   1918   1919   1920   1921

ELECTION RESULTS!

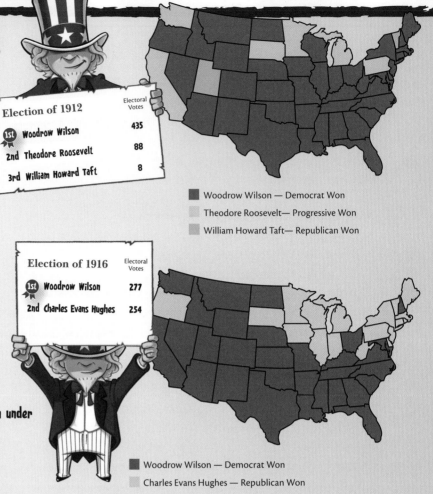

This election marked the beginning of state primaries. It helped Wilson that Roosevelt and Taft split the Republican Party and spent the majority of their efforts campaigning for the presidency against each other. As part of his platform, Wilson called for a "new nationalism" program, which would enforce federal regulations on businesses to increase government control of the economy. It was the only time in history that a past president (Roosevelt), an incumbent president (Taft), and a future president (Wilson) all ran in the same election.

America was on the brink of being drawn into the war that was ravaging the European continent. The only question was when. Luckily for Wilson, during the time of his political campaign America was safe in her neutrality proclamation. Thus, Wilson was able to campaign under the slogan, "He Kept us out of war."

Election of 1912

		Electoral Votes
1st	Woodrow Wilson	435
2nd	Theodore Roosevelt	88
3rd	William Howard Taft	8

- Woodrow Wilson — Democrat Won
- Theodore Roosevelt— Progressive Won
- William Howard Taft— Republican Won

Election of 1916

		Electoral Votes
1st	Woodrow Wilson	277
2nd	Charles Evans Hughes	254

- Woodrow Wilson — Democrat Won
- Charles Evans Hughes — Republican Won

FUN FACT!

During World War I, Wilson allowed sheep farmers to graze their sheep on the White House lawn. The wool was then donated to the American Red Cross.

System. The Federal Reserve replaced the Independent Treasury System in 1920 when Congress voted to close the system's various subtreasuries. This new centralized bank would have great influence over the American economy through its power to control money flow and adjust interest rates. The people would have little control over what it could and could not do. Following his predecessor, William Taft, Wilson continued to support the presence of income taxes in the lives of individual Americans by approving higher national income tax levels. Congress passed the Underwood Tariff Act, which lowered tariff rates, and Wilson signed it into law.

A Reform President

Wilson was also instrumental in creating the Federal Trade Commission, which was able to investigate and prosecute businesses for unfair trade practices. Social reforms set in place during this time include intro-

 BTW: In 1920, Wilson became the second American president within ten years to be awarded the Nobel Peace Prize.

ducing the forty-hour work week, banning child labor, establishing a crude federal highway system, and funding vocational and agricultural schools separate from colleges.

First-Term Foreign Affairs

The first area of concern came from Mexico after several American sailors were arrested. To make matters worse, Mexico was in the middle of their 1910 revolution. Wilson's efforts to negotiate peace with Mexico and also capture the infamous Pancho Villa failed after three years of negotiations and escapades. Success came when Wilson signed several alliance treaties of cooperation with dozens of foreign countries, leading to U.S. involvement and shipment of aid and military assistance to countries such as Haiti, the Dominican Republic, and the Virgin Islands. Then began the worldwide calamity that would engulf the entirety of Wilson's second term in office: World War I.

War!

While Wilson campaigned for reelection in 1916, America was officially neutral regarding the atrocities occurring in Europe, but it was evident that the United States favored the Allies. American involvement almost transpired before Wilson had secured re-election, when a German U-boat torpedoed the *Lusitania*, a British cruise liner, killing 1,170 passengers, including 128 Americans. War was temporarily avoided, however, when the Germans agreed to "diplomatic negotiations" — negotiations that never transpired. Instead, nearly a month after Wilson took his second oath of office, Germany sank an American merchant ship. In April 1917, Wilson asked Congress for a declaration of war against Germany and her allies, believing that there were no other means of defending America's rights. The country was at war.

Wartime Government

Wilson's actions at home were equally as important as the actions he ordered abroad. While thousands of men

CONGRESSIONAL CORNER

1. **Federal Reserve Act of 1913: This act established the United States Federal Reserve—America's central banking system—which has the sole ability to print U.S. currency.**

2. **Clayton Antitrust Act of 1914: This act allowed the government to regulate prices set by businesses on goods and produce, oversee the merging of businesses, and protect strikers and unions.**

3. **National Defense Act of 1916: This act reorganized the army, expanded the army and national guard, and formed the ROTC and Officers' and Enlisted Training Corps.**

4. **Federal Farm Loan Act of 1916: This act allowed the government to give more credit to rural farmers so they could purchase more farmland.**

5. **Espionage Act of 1917: This act made any anti-war views illegal and an action of dissent punishable as a crime.**

6. **International Emergency Economic Powers Act: This act passed in 1917, gave the president full powers to regulate commerce in America after declaring a national emergency.**

7. **Alien Naturalization Act of 1917: This act forcefully deported thousands of immigrants and noncitizen residents on the accusation of being "insufficiently patriotic."**

8. **Sedition Act of 1917: This act criminalized Americans' right to "willfully utter, print, write, or publish any disloyal, profane, scurrilous, or abusive language about the form of government of the United States, the Constitution ... or the flag."**

9. **Immigration Act of 1918: This act allowed the federal government to detain and deport immigrants they viewed as antiwar or anarchist.**

10. **National Prohibition Act of 1919: This act enforced the eighteenth amendment by prohibiting the sale of alcohol.**

were fighting in Europe, Wilson established a quasi-military state that stretched the limits of his constitutional authority as president. First, in 1917, Wilson signed the Espionage Act, making any antiwar views illegal and any action of dissent punishable. Second, Wilson enforced the Sedition Act. As a result, hundreds of Americans were imprisoned, including one clergyman who faced fifteen years' imprisonment for stating his opinion that Jesus Christ was a pacifist.

Furthermore, Wilson allowed the Department of Justice to send men—known as the "slacker brigade"—to stop, question, and arrest draft-age men on the streets suspected of possible draft evasion. The Department of Justice also formed the American Patriotic League, composed of a quarter of a million spies who were sent to spy on individual families and their own neighbors and report them if they found their actions "patriotically insufficient." The Alien Act of 1918 greatly marred Wilson's record by forcefully deporting thousands of immigrants and noncitizen residents. Then there was the infamous wartime propaganda, set in place by the Committee on Public Information formed during the Wilson administration. This propaganda was used to increase support for the war. The governement pushed patriotism and launched campaigns to sell war bonds, promote efficiency in factories, and maintain morale.

A Dream Deferred

Wilson's greatest contribution on the global scale came from the Fourteen Point Plan he introduced to the Treaty of Versailles at the war's end, which was meant to ensure peace among the European nations. Wilson's plan was not adopted by the council at Versailles, however, because Great Britain and France were intent on severely punishing Germany for their actions (an element of the negotiations that eventually led to World War II).

Back in America, Wilson hoped his plan would fare better. For the United States to enter the League of Nations, Wilson needed congressional approval for the peace treaty. Wilson was unable to negotiate with Congress, which requested amendments to the treaty. The treaty was not approved by the Senate as a result, and the U.S. never joined the League of Nations. Even though that aspect of his Fourteen Points was declined, several other points were implemented.

Series of Strokes

Wilson decided his last chance lay with the people, so he embarked on a nationwide tour, making several speeches a day. On September 25, 1919, a short time into the tour, Wilson collapsed of a stroke while speaking in Pueblo, Colorado. Unable to function, let alone publicly speak, Wilson returned to the White House, where his wife, Edith, cared for him. The treaty's process continued without Wilson, however, and twice it was rejected by the Senate. He had another stroke in October, leaving him paralyzed on his left side.

As a result of these strokes, America saw little of their president during his remaining time in office, and many began to wonder if Wilson's wife, Edith, was in fact running the White House—and America. Al-

BTW: Wilson's last words were spoken to his wife: "I am a broken piece of machinery. When the machine is broken ... I am ready."

though rumors spread that she was running the presidency, she in fact never initiated any programs or executed any major decisions without her husband's approval.

Post-Presidency

Despite the debilitating stroke Wilson suffered while still in office, he lived four more years as a private American citizen. He and his wife, Edith, retired to a mansion on D.C.'s "S Street," where Wilson worked diligently to finish his book, *President Wilson's Case for the League of Nations*. Even in the final years of his life, Wilson never gave up on his fourteenth point: that the U.S. should join the League of Nations.

LIBERTY Language

League of Nations: An international organization attended by the countries engaged in the First World War and other major world powers. The organization was formed to promote cooperation and prevent war from occurring between the nations in the League. It was dissolved in 1946, though the League had already become obsolete before the start of World War II.

What Has He Done for Me Lately?

The size and power of the federal government greatly increased during the presidency of Woodrow Wilson. The government also expanded its involvement in the affairs of private businesses through the protection of labor unions, the regulation of prices and product consumption, and new laws that limited how long and hard workers were allowed to work. The greatest expansion occurred during World War I, however, when Wilson allowed several government departments to infringe upon the rights of individual Americans, both the right to speech and the right to privacy.

PLATFORM SPEECH

Armed neutrality is ineffectual enough at best ... it is worse than ineffectual: it is likely only to produce what it was meant to prevent; it is practically certain to draw us into the war without either the rights or the effectiveness of belligerents.

Wilson realized that neutrality was no longer an option, and he gathered members of Congress and declared these words in 1916. The point of neutrality was to protect American lives, but after Germany torpedoed the *Lusitania*, Wilson believed that American involvement in the war was now inevitable.

WOODROW WILSON

THE GREAT WAR IS OVER

Written by Juliette Turner

November 11, 1918—On the eleventh hour of the eleventh day of the eleventh month, the Great World War ended. Although the U.S. entered the war just over a year and a half ago, Europe has experienced this bloody and ghastly war for the last four years.

The war took a total of ten million soldiers. Additionally, millions of civilians were killed, making this the bloodiest war to date. It all began with the assassination of Austria's Franz Duke Ferdinand and his pregnant wife by Serbia's Black Hand movement.

Austria initially declared war on Serbia, but many other countries got involved to protect alliances and assist comrade countries.

Russia declared war on Austria to protect their ally, Serbia. Germany—a staunch ally of the Austrian government—declared war on Russia. Germany then declared war on France and implemented their Schlieffen Plan, intended to defeat France before Russia was able to mobilize her forces.

Germany made a mistake by invading France through neutral Belgium—an ally of Great Britain. This caused Great Britain to enter the war in 1914 and the Great War ensued. The U.S. remained neutral, though supporting the Allies by sending money and weaponry. After German U-boats torpedoed the steam liner *Lusitania*, President Wilson appeared before Congress on April 2, 1917, asking them to approve a declaration of war on Germany and the Axis powers.

The most recent battle, the Second Battle of the Marne, forced a major Germany retreat. Shortly thereafter, Germany requested an armistice and the Allies declared victory. President Wilson will now travel to France to negotiate the peace accords.

WILSON'S ATTEMPTS AT PEACE: HIS FOURTEEN POINT PLAN

January 8, 1918—Wilson presented his Fourteen Point Plan to Congress today. He will be taking this plan to the peace negotiations in Paris, France. His goal is to reduce corruption and conspiring between countries. Wilson's plan consists of:

1. Keeping international diplomatic relations in public view
2. Nations being able to navigate the seas freely
3. Trade conditions being equalized among consenting countries
4. National arms and protections being lowered to a bare minimum to protect the citizenry's safety
5. Adjustment to the colonial claims of countries
6. The evacuation of Russian territory captured during the war
7. The evacuation and rebuilding of Belgium, whose neutrality had been infringed upon during the war
8. The restoration and evacuation of French lands
9. Reinstitution of the boundaries and borders of Italy
10. Ensured autonomy for Austria-Hungary
11. All occupied countries and territories being restored
12. Turkish Ottoman Empire to be sovereign and the Dardanelle strait open to all countries for trading purposes
13. The creation of independent Polish states
14. The construction and formation of the League of Nations

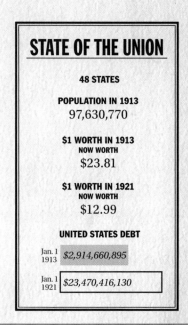

STATE OF THE UNION

48 STATES

POPULATION IN 1913
97,630,770

$1 WORTH IN 1913
NOW WORTH
$23.81

$1 WORTH IN 1921
NOW WORTH
$12.99

UNITED STATES DEBT

Jan. 1 1913	$2,914,660,895
Jan. 1 1921	$23,470,416,130

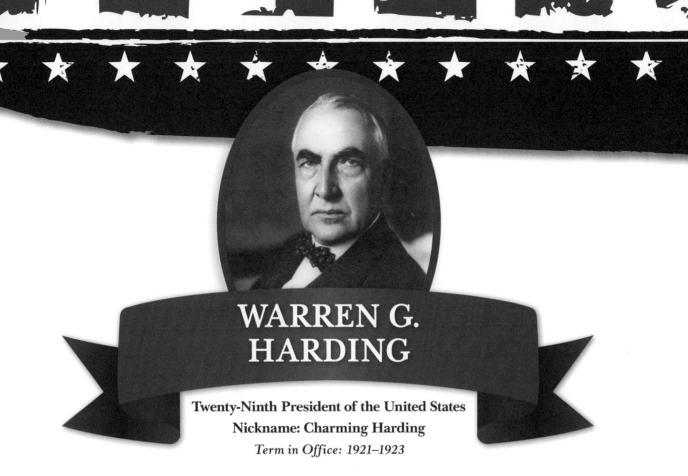

WARREN G. HARDING

Twenty-Ninth President of the United States
Nickname: Charming Harding
Term in Office: 1921–1923

The Bottom Line

Warren Harding died from illness (possibly a heart attack) two years into his first term. During his time in office, Harding worked tirelessly to reverse the government takeover of the private sector in America, including reversing regulations on businesses, reducing taxes, and limiting government spending. He also worked to improve the status of blacks and women in American society.

FAST STATS

★ Born November 2, 1865, in Blooming Grove, Ohio
★ Parents: George Tryon and Phoebe Elizabeth Dickerson Harding
★ Died August 2, 1923, in San Francisco, California; age 57
★ Age upon Start of Term: 55; Age upon Death: 57
★ Religious Affiliation: Baptist
★ Political Party: Republican
★ Height: 6 feet
★ Vice President: Calvin Coolidge

What Was He Thinking?

Warren Harding very much wanted to please his constituents, listening to their needs and often compromising his own views to better serve the people. He won support from women in America by supporting their right to vote. As president during the era of alcohol prohibition, Harding outwardly supported the amendment, but he still drank at the White House by subtly bending the rules.

Why Should I Care?

The Roaring Twenties were all about flapper girls, jazz music, crazy parties, and dancing out on the town. Warren Harding's pro-business policies

America's need is not heroics but healing, not nostrums but normalcy; not revolution but restoration; not agitation but adjustment; not surgery but serenity; not the dramatic but the dispassionate; not experiment but equipoise.

HARDING the Orator

Warren Harding was all about presentation. His speaking was known for two distinguishing characteristics: his frequent use of alliterations and his knack for creating words on the spot. What is alliteration? Well, look at this line from one of Harding's speeches and count the Ps: "Progression is not proclamation nor palaver. It is not pretense nor play on personal pronouns, not perennial pronouncement. It is not the perturbation of a people, passion-wrought, nor a promise proposed." One of the original words Warren created was *bloviating*, meaning speaking for a long time without really saying anything.

FUN FACT!

In 1920, during his address at the Republican convention, Warren Harding coined the phrase "Founding Fathers."

removed government regulation from the American private sector. Additionally, Harding worked hard to limit federal spending and balance the budget. As a result, the government was able to pass measures that enabled an economic boom and sense of stability that enhanced the American way of life.

Breakin' It Down
Early Life

Warren Harding was the first president to be born after the Civil War. The oldest of eight children, Warren attended school in small, one-room schoolhouses in rural Ohio, but he was soon working as an errand boy for the city newspaper. He attended Iberia College (now Ohio Central College) and after graduation became a teacher—a job he later claimed proved to be the most challenging of his life.

At age eighteen, Harding took on the job of reporter for one of the local newspapers, though his Republican political beliefs soon cost him his position. After unhappily selling insurance for a while, Warren attempted a risky business venture: he joined with two friends to buy the bankrupt *Marion Star* newspaper for three hundred dollars. Warren's investment paid off, and soon the paper became well known and eventually overshadowed the other newspapers in the region. The key to his success lay in the publication's content: instead of printing the same Democrat-leaning positions popular among newspaper owners, Warren played to his consumers by printing more Republican-leaning views while still remaining cautious to not offend Democrats. Warren's newspaper became the moderate voice that sought common ground for both parties. After success in the private sector, Warren decided to move into the public eye by entering politics.

A bomb explodes on Wall Street, 1921

The German economy begins to collapse because of war reparations, 1921

William Howard Taft is appointed Supreme Court chief justice, 1921

The USSR is formed in Russia by the First Congress of Soviets, 1922

The White House police force is established, 1922

The Lincoln Memorial is dedicated, 1922

Benito Mussolini occupies Rome, Italy, 1922

Warren Harding dies and Vice President Calvin Coolidge becomes president, August 2, 1923

An earthquake destroys a third of Tokyo, Japan, 1923

Adolf Hitler fails to overthrow the German government, 192

U.S. Secretary of State Charles Dawes forms a plan for restructuring Germany's war debt, 1923

Term in Office

1920 | 1921 | 1922 | 1923 | 1924 | 1925

First Couple

In 1891, Warren Harding married Florence Mabel Kling DeWolfe. They met through Warren's younger sister, who was Florence's piano student. Florence was five years older than Warren, and at the time of their marriage, she was a divorced, single mother. Although the couple never had children together, it was rumored that Warren had two children with another woman during one of his two extramarital affairs. Florence forgave her husband for his unfaithfulness, and his affairs were not publicized until after his death. As first lady, Florence began a new tradition for future first ladies to follow: she held her own press conferences and openly displayed her own beliefs on issues, a rarity for that day.

FLORENCE HARDING

Previous Political Career

- Spent twelve years campaigning for Republican candidates in national and state elections and speaking and promoting party unity.
- 1895: Lost his election for county auditor.
- 1899: Elected to the Ohio State Senate. He served two terms in the position and became known as a peacemaker who stuck to Republican ideals. He was appointed the state senate's majority leader and even wrote the state eulogy after the assassination of sitting president William McKinley.

FUN FACT!

Since the election of 1920 was the first in which women could vote, Florence Harding played a crucial role in garnering the women's vote for her husband. Florence obviously appealed to the American woman, especially by talking about racial equality and religious tolerance as well as a possible increase in female executive appointments.

ELECTION RESULTS!

Election of 1920	Electoral Votes
1st Warren G. Harding	404
2nd James M. Cox	127

■ Warren G. Harding — Republican Won

■ James M. Cox — Democrat Won

At the Republican convention, an underhanded private meeting occurred in a nearby hotel room, later referred to as "the smoke-filled room." In this meeting, the political donors and "bosses"—as they were called—met to discuss the pool of candidates. Evidently, Warren Harding was declared the best possible option, and he won the nomination.

Travel campaigning was still rather unpopular during this time, and Harding was placed under further restrictions by the Republican Party to hush certain beliefs. He delivered prewritten speeches from his home in Marion, Ohio, a setting that avoided on-the-spot questions for which Harding was not prepared to answer. Harding spoke about a "return to normalcy," which appealed to the war-weary American people.

CONGRESSIONAL CORNER
★★★★★★★★★★★★★★★★★★★★★★★★★

1. **Budget and Accounting Act of 1921:** This act established the first modern-day federal budget. The act also created the Bureau of the Budget (now the Office of Management and Budget), which oversees and regulates the monetary transactions of the government and helps the president in forming a budget.

2. **Federal Aid Highways Act of 1921:** This act set aside funding for a large network of national highways. The plan for the highways was designed by the National Highway Commission.

3. **Agricultural Appropriations Act of 1922:** This act formed the Bureau of Agriculture Economics, which reported on foreign agricultural developments and trade.

4. **Federal Narcotics Control Board of 1922:** This board established the Federal Narcotics Control Board, which strictly regulated the import and export of opiates.

5. **Washington Naval Treaty of 1922:** This treaty was among the major powers of World War I, which established measures to prevent an arms race among those nations.

★★★★★★★★★★★★★★★★★★★★★★★★★

> *Government rests upon the body of citizenship; it cannot maintain itself on a level that keeps it out of touch and understanding with the community it serves.*

LIBERTY Language

Red Scare of 1919: The Red Scare refers to the fear of communism threatening the stability of democratic governments worldwide. This first Red Scare occurred after the Bolsheviks (Communist Party) took over the Russian government in 1917.

- 1903: Elected Ohio's lieutenant governor, serving one term before he retired from the position to return to his newspaper business.
- 1910: Lost race for Ohio governor to Grover Cleveland's former attorney general, Judson Harmon, after a three-year break from politics.
- 1914: Elected to the U.S. Senate, winning by 100,000 votes. He remained in the Senate until 1920.
- 1916: Asked to speak at the Republican National Convention in 1916.

Presidency

Harding's presidency ushered in the period known as the Roaring Twenties because of the boom in economic growth, relatively peaceful foreign relations, and the generally excited mood of the American people. As his first act as president, Harding reversed many of the antibusiness regulations Wilson had placed on various corporations, leading to a new vitality in American enterprise. This was a part of Harding's "America First" plan, which included five main points: (1) tariffs on imports would be raised; (2) immigration would be restricted; (3) the Budget Accounting Act would create a strict federal budget that would end in surplus; (4) taxes on businesses would be lowered; and (5) federal expenditures would be cut to rates lower than prewar levels. In addition, Harding also freed the socialist and labor leaders who had been imprisoned either under the Sedition Act of 1918 or during the Red Scare of 1919.

BTW: Warren Harding was the first president to visit Alaska.

BTW: Harding engaged in at least two extramarital affairs. Proof of these affairs was found in the dozens of love letters between the two women and Harding.

International Affairs

In the international arena, Harding withdrew American participation in the Treaty of Versailles, leaving the European nations to resolve their disputes without American intervention. Second, Harding deployed his secretary of state, Charles Evans Hughes, to negotiate the Washington Naval Treaty, which reduced arms in nearly all major countries across the globe (the United States, France, England, Japan, and Italy) and thus ended the quasi-arms race erupting as a result of World War I.

Ours is a constitutional freedom where the popular will is the law supreme and minorities are sacredly protected.

Death

To celebrate the halfway point in his term, Harding embarked on a nationwide tour he pegged the "Voyage of Understanding." The trip did not go as planned, for before long Harding began complaining of fatigue and abdominal pain. The family's personal physician was called and he refused to allow any other doctors to tend to Harding. After inspecting the president, the doctor diagnosed food poisoning as the culprit, but in fact the president had most likely suffered a heart attack. Because of lack of treatment, Warren Harding died in San Francisco at the Palace Hotel, leaving his vice president, Calvin Coolidge, in control of the country.

Harding was quite the party man. Besides bending the rules to serve alcohol in the White House, he also played golf and cards almost constantly. Once, Harding bet a set of White House china on a single hand in a card game ... and lost.

What Has He Done for Me Lately?

Because Warren Harding released many of the American citizens who had been imprisoned during the Wilson administration, he inadvertently proved the illegality of much of Wilson's legislation. Consequently, the Constitution and Americans' rights and freedoms were reinforced. Harding was also influential in the creation of the Budget Accounting Office, which is still in existence in our government today, charged with the task of balancing the budget of the United States government.

[I]n the mutual tolerance, understanding, charity, recognition of the interdependence of the races, and the maintenance of the rights of citizenship lies the road to righteous adjustment.

Warren Harding spoke these words in a special session of Congress in 1921. He understood that the nation could not survive or thrive while still divided along racial lines. United, we would be stronger.

BTW: Last Words: "That's good. Go on. Read some more" in response to his wife, who was reading a newspaper article favoring the president.

WARREN G. HARDING

Presidential Times

WOMEN AT THE POLLING BOOTH!

Written by Juliette Turner

November 2, 1920—as printed in Pittsburgh Press—"A storming of the polling places by men and women in the early hours was the response to the appeals for early voting. The belief in political circles is that probably a larger per cent of the registered women than of registered men will cast ballots today, due to the enthusiasm among women over their first opportunity to vote. [...]

The crowd extended so far that it backed into Oliver Avenue for half a block, [with] hundreds being forced to crane their necks for a glimpse at the lighted bulletin board. [. . .] Nearby at the Republican Women's headquarters, "Every available inch of space was taken. [A] woman telegraph operator handled returns over a special wire [...] From a platform in front of a building,

they sang campaign songs; then they wheeled down Smithfield street, making the thoroughfare resound with the strains of 'John Brown's Body.' [...] When the Republican men swarmed about their headquarters, their red torchlights flaring and their band blaring its loudest marches, the women [again] hurried outside, [and] joined in cheers for Harding and Coolidge.

SCANDAL!

December 4, 1923—Scandals keep emerging from the late Warren Harding's administration. Although Harding served as president for only two years, three scandals have now been released to the press. The situation reminds many of Grant's term in office, when he struggled to keep his cabinet in line.

Today, in the third scandal to come to light, Attorney General Harry M. Daugherty awaits trail for illegal activities

in bootlegging and accepting bribes. President Coolidge is forced to clean up the mess. The first scandal surrounded the director of the Veterans' Bureau, Charles Forbes. He illegally sold government medical supplies to private businesses in return for money on the side. As a result, Forbes will spend more than a year in prison.

The second scandal came from the secretary of the interior Albert Fall and became known

as the Teapot Dome Scandal. Fall leased federal oil deposits in California to businesses in Wyoming. Fall was convicted of conspiracy, bribery, and defrauding the government and served a year jail sentence and paid $100,000 in fines. Fall was the first cabinet member to serve time in jail for political actions.

HARDING'S "FRAYED NERVES"

July 24, 1920—The *Times* recently investigated President Harding's past medical records, and shocking new developments on Harding's health have been revealed. Starting in the 1890s, it is documented that Harding began to complain about experiencing nervous breakdowns or

suffering from "frayed nerves." Harding actually checked himself into a sanitarium in Battle Creek, Ohio, after his first major nervous breakdown in 1890. Over the course of his lifetime, he returned to the sanitarium five times.

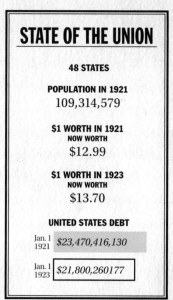

STATE OF THE UNION

48 STATES

POPULATION IN 1921
109,314,579

$1 WORTH IN 1921
NOW WORTH
$12.99

$1 WORTH IN 1923
NOW WORTH
$13.70

UNITED STATES DEBT

| Jan. 1 1921 | $23,470,416,130 |
| Jan. 1 1923 | $21,800,260177 |

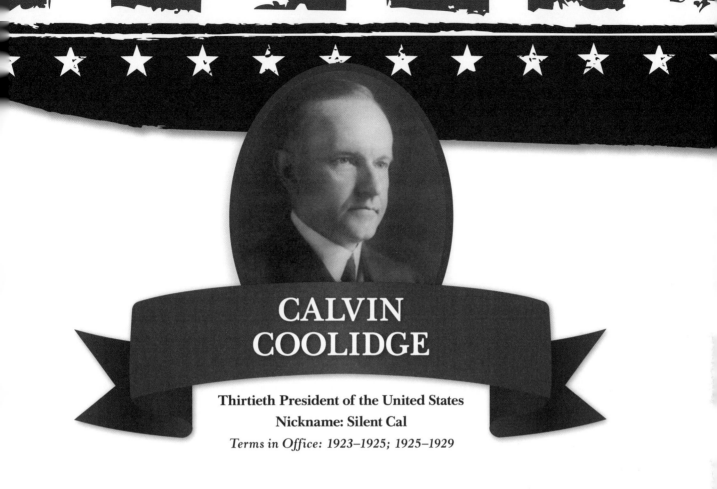

CALVIN COOLIDGE

Thirtieth President of the United States
Nickname: Silent Cal
Terms in Office: 1923–1925; 1925–1929

The Bottom Line

Calvin Coolidge served half a term after the death of President Harding in 1923 and then won reelection in 1924. During his time in office, Coolidge limited federal control of American businesses and let the country drive itself through the prosperity of the Roaring Twenties.

FAST STATS

★ Born July 4, 1872, in Plymouth Notch, Vermont
★ Parents: John and Victoria Moor Coolidge
★ Died January 5, 1933, in Northampton, Massachusetts; age 60
★ Age upon Start of First Term: 51; Age upon Conclusion of First Term: 52
★ Age upon Start of Second Term: 52; Age upon Conclusion of Second Term: 56
★ Religious Affiliation: Congregational
★ Political Party: Republican
★ Height: 5 feet 10 inches
★ Vice President: none (1923–1925) and Charles G. Dawes (1925–1929)

What Was He Thinking?

Calvin Coolidge believed the smaller the government, the better. This was evident in his consistent efforts to limit government control of businesses by cutting back regulations, penalties, and taxes. Coolidge also believed in lower taxes for the average American, working to reduce income tax and other taxes during his time in office.

Why Should I Care?

During Coolidge's term in office, many innovations, advances, and enhancements were made in the life of the American individual. This came

 BTW: Calvin Coolidge was the last president to write the majority of his speeches on his own.

CALVIN COOLIDGE'S Schedule

Calvin Coolidge was not only quiet, but organized. His schedule was the same every day:

6:30—wake up
8:00—begin work at presidential desk
12:30–2:30—shake hands with White House visitors
2:30—lunch and two-hour nap
Resume work well into the evening

> [T]hose who have the greater authority ought to have the greater knowledge.

mainly as a result of the freedom American businesses had from overbearing regulations from the federal government. Had any other individual served as president during this time and not allowed the country to "run itself" as Coolidge did, the United States likely would not have reached the level of accomplishment she did during this time.

Breakin' It Down
Early Life

Calvin Coolidge, whose first name was John, remains the only president to be born on the Fourth of July. There is little chance, however, that Calvin's parents knew their patriotic baby (who was in fact quite frail and suffered from asthma) would one day become president of the United States. Calvin's early education came primarily from his mother, who instilled in him a desire for learning and knowledge. Unfortunately, she died when Calvin was only twelve years old. For the rest of his life, he carried a small portrait of her in his breast pocket—he even had it the day he died. Within six years, tragedy struck the Coolidge family again with the death of Calvin's fifteen-year-old sister, Abbie, from acute appendicitis. Despite the sorrows in his life, Calvin enjoyed the life of a normal young boy in Vermont, who loved to fish and walk his dogs. For his early schooling, Calvin attended the Black River Academy in Ludlow, Vermont.

When Calvin first applied for college, he failed the entrance exam, but then he attended a preparatory school and entered Amherst College shortly thereafter. Calvin was a serious student, not much of a socializer, and graduated in 1895. He then became an attorney, clerking at a local law firm, where he simultaneously studied law. At age twenty-five, Calvin moved to Massachusetts and opened his own law firm in Northampton.

BTW: Calvin Coolidge's sixteen year old son died from blood poisoning from an infected blister—which he had contracted while playing tennis without socks. Young Coolidge is buried in the south lawn of the White House where a memorial plaque and a Vermont spruce tree mark his grave.

George Gershwin composes *Rhapsody in Blue*, 1923

Hitler is imprisoned in Germany and writes *Mein Kampf*, 1924

First Term in Office

| 1920 | 1921 | 1922 | 1923 | 1924 |

BTW: Calvin Coolidge became the first president to have his inauguration broadcast on the radio and the first to broadcast his congressional address over the radio.

First Couple

In 1905, Calvin Coolidge married Grace Anna Goodhue. Together they had two children, although only one lived to adulthood. Grace was the first of the American first ladies to have graduated from a public university; additionally, she was a member of Phi Beta Kappa. It appears Coolidge was just as quiet in his personal relationships as he was in his public appearances, for Grace once commented that she first heard her husband's viewpoints when she read them in the newspapers. Coolidge wasn't removed from his family, however. On the contrary, he loved to take time away from his busy presidential schedule and play baseball with his sons.

GRACE COOLIDGE

Previous Political Career

- 1899: Elected to the Northampton, Massachusetts state council, holding the position until 1900.
- 1904: Elected as the local Republican Party chair.
- 1906: Elected Massachusetts state congressman.
- 1909: Elected mayor of Northampton.
- 1911: Elected senator to the Massachusetts State Senate, holding the position until 1915.
- 1915: Elected lieutenant governor of Massachusetts, holding the position until 1918.
- 1918: Elected governor of Massachusetts.
- 1920: Chosen to run on the Republican Party's presidential ticket as vice president under Warren Harding.

Prohibition & Bootlegging

★★★★★★★★★★★★★★★★★★★★★★★★★★★

Today's image of the Roaring Twenties is one of parties, excitement, and a little excess drinking, courtesy of the book *The Great Gatsby*. Prohibition and the eighteenth amendment, however, were in effect until 1933. Enter bootlegging (the illegal selling and distribution of intoxicating liquors), the Mafia, gangs, violence, and speakeasies (the private, hidden, and clandestine saloons—the home of illegal drinking). Thanks to bootlegging, Americans were able to drink alcohol almost as much as they had before Prohibition.

Presidency

Little did the soft-spoken Calvin Coolidge know that running as vice president in the election of 1920 would land him in the seat of the presidency within two years. Coolidge became the nation's sixth "accidental president" on August 3, 1923.

America was booming: automobiles toured American streets and the constant, steady rise of the stock market made millionaires almost by the hour. American pride was at an all-time high. Baseball was the new

Rēza Shāh Pahlavi establishes the Pahlavi dynasty in Iran, 1925

Mount Rushmore is dedicated, 1927

Nellie Tayloe Ross of Wyoming becomes America's first female governor, 1925

U.S. Marines enter Nicaragua to suppress rebellion, 1926

Charles Lindbergh flies nonstop from New York to Paris, 1927

Mickey Mouse appears in his first Walt Disney film, *Plane Crazy*, 1928

Hitler publishes volume 1 of *Mein Kampf*, 1925

Germany is accepted into the League of Nations, 1926

Painter Claude Monet dies, 1926

American Gertrude Ederle becomes the first woman to swim the English Channel, 1926

Philo T. Farnsworth demonstrates the first working television model, 1927

Babe Ruth becomes the first baseball player to hit sixty home runs in one season, 1927

Alexander Fleming discovers penicillin, 1928

The final version of the *Oxford English Dictionary* is published, 1928

Second Term in Office

| 1925 | 1926 | 1927 | 1928 | 1929 |

ELECTION RESULTS!

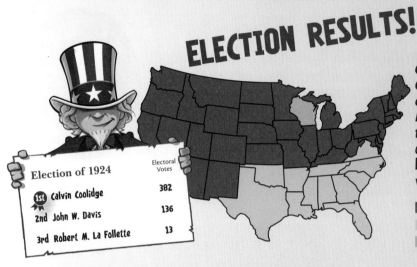

Election of 1924

		Electoral Votes
1st	Calvin Coolidge	382
2nd	John W. Davis	136
3rd	Robert M. La Follette	13

Coolidge campaigned with the slogan "Keep Cool with Coolidge." He attracted voters among the middle class because of the steady economic growth America was experiencing. though the prosperity of the time had its downside—that of apathy. Because of the "golden age" of prosperity. Americans became apathetic to politics. causing the lowest voter turnout rates in the history of the country.

- Calvin Coolidge — Republican Won
- John W. Davis — Democrat Won
- Robert M. La Follette — Progressive Won

Silent Cal

★★★★★★★★★★★★★★★★★★★★★★★★★

It soon became a jest throughout Washington that the sitting president never said more than two words at dinner parties. One White House dinner guest made a bet with her friend that she would be able to make the president speak more than two words. Throughout the evening, she watched Coolidge, but he said nothing. At the end of the evening, as she was leaving, Coolidge shook her hand and said, "You lose."

> You hear a lot of jokes every once in a while about "Silent Cal Coolidge." The joke is on the people who make the jokes. Look at his record. He cut taxes four times. We had probably the greatest growth and prosperity that we've ever known. I have taken heed of that, because if he did that by doing nothing, maybe that's the answer.

> Ronald Reagan admired Coolidge's political feats - he got things done but he also took time to relax. Coolidge enjoyed having the press photograph him in seemingly "un-presidential" situations—everything from sitting on the lawn with his dog to fishing and even wearing a Native American headdress.

American sport with the emergence of Babe Ruth, and American aviation took the world by storm with Charles Lindbergh's solo New York–Paris flight. One thing was missing, however: the people's faith in their government. With all of the scandals from the Harding administration still coming to light and requiring explanation, Coolidge had his work cut out for him to earn the trust of the American people. He did so effectively by firing the corrupted officials and also appointing a bipartisan counsel to investigate the wrongdoings.

Watch and Learn

Coolidge, like Harding, believed the government should interfere in the world of American business as little as possible. Under Coolidge, Congress cut taxes to help businesses grow and also limited government regulations. Interestingly, during the Roaring Twenties, the American economy essentially drove itself, free of government assistance or restriction. Coolidge recognized this and focused on running the presidency without forceful leader-

★ BUYING HOUSES
on Credit

Credit, put simply, is your record of how well you have paid your bills—if you paid them on time, in full, and so on. When you buy houses on credit, you take out a loan from your bank to pay for part of your house, and the bank determines how much they will give you based on your past credit. Since the money you used to buy the house wasn't yours in the first place, the house you buy is not really your property until you make the last payment on your loan. If you can't make your payments, the bank can take your house.

ship; instead, he stayed out of the way and watched as America boomed without government interference.

Reelection

In 1924, Coolidge began campaigning for reelection and won an overwhelming majority in both the popular vote and the electoral vote. His second term mirrored that of his first: he kept corporate business taxes low—also lowering income tax and abolishing the "gift tax"—and maintained the near nonexistent levels of government regulation. For the first time in American history, electricity, cars, radios, and refrigerators were available to the average American. Additionally, Americans could now buy houses on credit.

Problems

While domestic policy thrived under Coolidge's presidency, foreign policy encountered some glitches, including American relations with Mexico. The first problem occurred when the Mexican government seized the land belonging to American oil companies in the region. Though Coolidge resolved this through diplomatic negotiations, Mexican-American

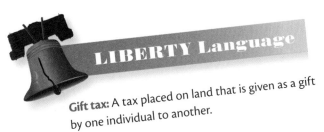

LIBERTY Language

Gift tax: A tax placed on land that is given as a gift by one individual to another.

CONGRESSIONAL CORNER
★★★★★★★★★★★★★★★★★★★★★★★★

1. **World War Adjusted Compensation Act of 1924:** Passed on May 19, this bill gave benefits to American military veterans who served in World War I.

2. **Immigration Act of 1924:** This act limited the annual immigration rate of individuals from every country to 2 percent of the people in America from that said country. For example, if one thousand Irish immigrants lived in the U.S. in 1924, then only twenty could immigrate to the U.S. the following year.

3. **Indian Citizenship Act of 1924:** This act granted citizenship to all Native Americans born within the territorial limits of the United States.

4. **The McNary Haugen Bill:** This bill was passed by Congress to protect farmers in the midwest from fluctuating crop prices by allowing the federal government to purchase crop surpluses. The government would then sell the crops abroad rather than let them enter the American market and deflate prices. Coolidge vetoed this bill twice, however, and farmers did not experience the same economic boom as other industries did the 1920s.

5. **The Federal Radio Commission:** The Federal Radio Commission was in charge of regulating radio use, including licensing and assigning frequencies, during this boom in the popularity of radios.

6. **Railway Labor Act of 1926:** This act allowed the federal government to oversee labor relations in the railroad and airline industries.

7. **Flood Control Act of 1928:** This act gave the Army Corps of Engineers the authority to design and construct dams and levees on the Mississippi and Sacramento Rivers to prevent major flood disasters.

8. **Kellogg-Briand Pact of 1928:** This pact was signed by eighty-four countries on August 27, 1928, and renounced any acts of war.

★★★★★★★★★★★★★★★★★★★★★★★★

 BTW: America's first motion picture with sound was released on October 6, 1927. *The Jazz Singer* marked the beginning of Hollywood's "golden age."

GNP (Gross National Product): The total market value of all the goods and services produced in one year by a country. This would include the price of all the cars produced by the Ford Motor Company as well as the income of the workers who made them.

THOUGHTS ON THE CONSTITUTION

The Constitution is the sole source and guaranty of national freedom ... To live under the American Constitution is the greatest political privilege that was ever accorded to the human race.

CALVIN COOLIDGE

relations were still turbulent. In 1926, Nicaragua (which was under American control at the time) encountered a quasi-civil war in which the rebels were supported by the Mexican government. Coolidge, in response, sent American marines to help suppress the guerrilla warriors, who were using Mexican-supplied arms. Coolidge did oversee several foreign policy successes, however, including the Kellogg-Briand Pact, a law signed by eighty-four other countries on August 27, 1928, forbidding any act of war.

Despite the relatively minor hardships in foreign policy, America continued to thrive—within three years the GNP increased by nearly 50 percent. Coolidge most likely would have won a third-term reelection, but he declined to run in 1928 and retired from politics after six successful years as the president of the United States.

Post-Presidency

Calvin Coolidge followed many of his predecessors and wrote a memoir, *The Autobiography of Calvin Coolidge*, published in 1929. Coolidge continued writing in a newspaper column he called "Thinking Things Over with Calvin Coolidge"—also sometimes called "Calvin Coolidge Says …"
In 1933, Coolidge died from a heart attack at the age of sixty. Sitting president Herbert Hoover declared thirty days of national mourning.

What Has He Done for Me Lately?

Although the lack of government regulation helped American businesses boom during the Roaring Twenties, it later became one of the factors leading to the Great Depression. Because businesses and the stock market were allowed to do whatever they pleased with prices and money, the American economy overextended itself and soon collapsed. Coolidge did what worked for the time, but ultimately the economy continued full throttle for too long.

CALVIN COOLIDGE

PLATFORM SPEECH

Government is and ought to be thoroughly committed to every endeavor of production and distribution which is entitled to be designated as true business. Those who are so engaged, instead of regarding the Government as their opponent and enemy, ought to regard it as their vigilant supporter and friend.

Calvin Coolidge said this in his speech on government and business in 1925. He wanted the government to be the champion of private businesses, not the enemy. During his term, Coolidge wanted business to begin to trust the government as its protector and supporter.

BTW: Coolidge's last words were to a carpenter working in his house: "Good morning, Robert."

MISSISSIPPI RIVER FLOOD

Written by Juliette Turner

April 15, 1927—In just eighteen hours, the New Orleans area has seen over fifteen inches of rain. Four feet of water now stands on the city streets, inflicting hundreds of millions of dollars in damages. It comes after the devastating flooding last Christmas Day in Nashville, Tennessee, as the Cumberland River rose to 56.2 feet.

This flooding in New Orleans caused the Mississippi River levee to burst in 145 places, further flooding 27,000 square miles. The area was covered in thirty feet of water in some places. Four hundred million dollars in damages resulted, and 246 people lost their lives in seven states. President Coolidge was at first opposed to sending federal aid to Mississippi, believing private businesses should be in charge of the humanitarian and relief efforts. After the flooding of New Orleans, however, Coolidge is pushing for legislation that would give the Army Corps of Engineers the job of taking measures to avoid future flooding disasters.

ST. VALENTINE'S DAY MASSACRE IN CHICAGO

February 14, 1929—A shootout occurred today on the streets of Chicago, leaving dead several men who belonged to the Irish bootlegging gang led by George "Bugs" Moran. Witnesses claim the shooters were dressed as policemen, but Chicago police say the men were frauds, not real policemen. Many are speculating that the shooting was organized by the notorious Al Capone because George Moran is his chief rival; the two have been viciously competing since Prohibition began. However, no official charges have been made against Capone at this time. This shootout, the most recent of a string of violent and deadly encounters between bootlegging gangs, is causing many to wonder if Prohibition is helping crime rates in America or hurting them.

COOLIDGE AND PROHIBITION

November 30, 1925—Presidents Coolidge and Harding may have held the same views on most government issues, but when it comes to Prohibition, the two are very different. Unlike his predecessor, Calvin Coolidge is not trying to bypass Prohibition; in fact, he rarely drinks at all. Coolidge, however, opposes Prohibition because he views the amendment as an unnecessary government intrusion into the lives of the American people.

STATE OF THE UNION

48 STATES

POPULATION IN 1923
112,750,796

$1 WORTH IN 1923
NOW WORTH
$13.70

$1 WORTH IN 1929
NOW WORTH
$13.70

UNITED STATES DEBT

Jan. 1 1923	$21,800,260,177
Jan. 1 1929	$16,558,199,158

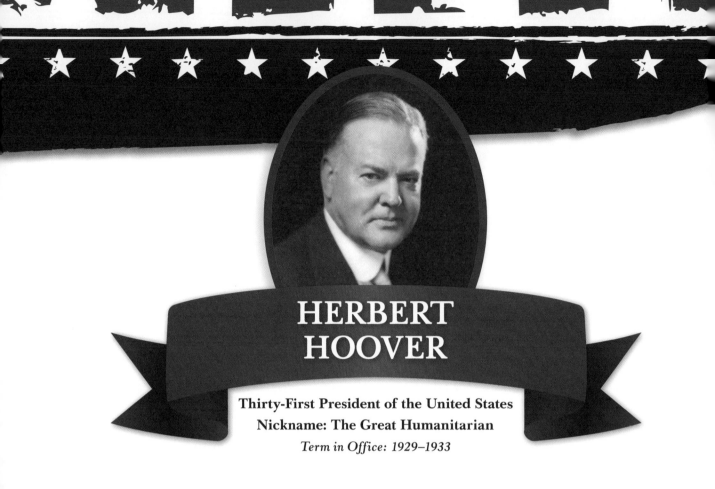

HERBERT HOOVER

Thirty-First President of the United States
Nickname: The Great Humanitarian
Term in Office: 1929–1933

The Bottom Line

Herbert Hoover served one term, during which he struggled to combat the Great Depression that began the first year he was in office.

FAST STATS

★ Born August 10, 1874, in West Branch, Iowa
★ Parents: Jesse Clark and Hulda Randall Minthorn Hoover
★ Died October 20, 1964, in New York City, New York; age 90
★ Age upon Start of Term: 54; Age upon Conclusion of Term: 58
★ Religious Affiliation: Society of Friends (Quaker)
★ Political Party: Republican
★ Height: 6 feet
★ Vice President: Charles Curtis

What Was He Thinking?

Herbert Hoover believed in limited government—a belief that did not serve him well during the Great Depression. Rather than sending government workers and departments to solve situations, Hoover preferred encouraging private, volunteer relief organizations.

Why Should I Care?

Herbert Hoover served as president at the start of one of America's darkest and bleakest periods. The Great Depression caused millions of Americans to lose their jobs and resulted in a substantial loss of the fortunes amassed during the Roaring Twenties. Hoover's policies were too weak for the crisis, and as a result the economy only worsened.

Breakin' It Down
Early Life

Herbert was born to a devout Quaker family, where he learned the values of hard work, community, cooperation, spirituality, and nonviolence. His father died at age thirty-four, when young "Herb" was only six years old. Three years later, his mother died, leaving Herbert and his two siblings orphaned and penniless. The Hoover children were sent to Oregon to live with their uncle, Henry Minthorn.

When Herbert reached college age, he enrolled at the newly established Stanford University, and became the youngest member of the first graduating class.

Hoover's first postcollege job was pushing carts of ore at a gold mine. The work was treacherous, but before long he landed an engineering job in San Francisco. This turned into the chance of a lifetime for Hoover, for he soon transferred to London's Bewick, Moreing, and Company, who hired him to inspect various mine sites across the globe. In 1899, Hoover and his wife moved to Beijing, China, where he continued to inspect coal mines. While there, Hoover amassed a large fortune and earned substantial gains for the Bewick, Moreing, and Company. By 1908, Herbert Hoover was worth four million dollars, and later he was worth much more.

First Couple

Herbert Hoover married Lou Henry in 1899. They met at Stanford, where Lou became the first woman in the United States to earn a degree in geology. Together the couple had two children. Lou was a trailblazing and progressive woman. She believed women could have active careers while caring for their children—and she did just that. Lou served as president of the Girl Scouts of America and was a member of the League of Women Voters, the National Women's Athletic Association, the American Association of University Women, and the National Geographic Society. She was also the only woman to serve as a board member for the National Amateur Athletic Federation. And she delivered her own radio addresses, encouraging people to share their resources when the Depression began.

Herbert Hoover lived the American dream. He began his life as a penniless orphan but became a self-made millionaire who used his money to help people all around the globe. On top of all that, he became president of the United States.

LOU HOOVER

Edwin Hubble introduces the idea of an expanding universe, 1929

The U.S. stock market collapses on Black Tuesday, 1929

Great Britain, the United States, Japan, Italy, and France sign a naval disarmament treaty, 1930

Construction begins on the Hoover Dam, 1930

Al Capone is sentenced to eleven years in prison for tax evasion, 1931

Hoover suspends France's and Germany's war debts to the U.S., 1931

Amelia Earhart becomes the first woman to fly solo across the Atlantic, 1932

The twentieth amendment to the Constitution is passed, 1932

Adolf Hitler is appointed the chancellor of Germany, 1933

Germany and Japan withdraw from the League of Nations, 1933

The twenty-first amendment to the Constitution is passed, February 20, 1933

Term in Office

1928   1929   1930   1931   1932   1933

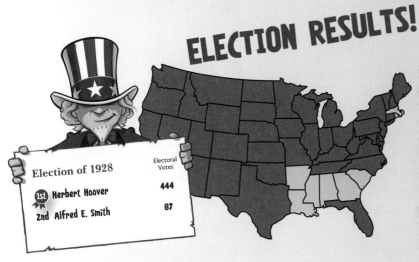

ELECTION RESULTS!

Election of 1928

	Electoral Votes
1st Herbert Hoover	444
2nd Alfred E. Smith	87

It was the first time Hoover had ever run for office—talk about starting big. Campaigning was still very different then than it is now: Hoover only made seven speeches during his whole campaign. His promotion of big business, capitalism, and limited government was opposed by the working and farming classes, but Hoover still managed to pull off a large electoral college win.

■ Herbert Hoover — Republican Won
□ Alfred E. Smith — Democrat Won

Previous Political Career

- 1917: Appointed head of the newly formed U.S. Food Administration by President Woodrow Wilson.
- 1919: Director of the American Relief Administration, which helped fight famine in the European war zones.
- 1921–1928: Served as secretary of commerce under both presidents Harding and Coolidge. In this position, Hoover instituted one of the first manufacturing codes for businesses and regulated manufacturing standards for everyday items such as nuts and bolts, paper, tires, and milk bottles.

Presidency

While Herbert Hoover served as president, the U.S. suffered the worst economic collapse it has ever known. The Great Depression and the effects of the collapse were not Hoover's fault, and had the man served during any other time, he might have been considered one of America's greatest leaders. The catastrophic recession came mostly as a result of Americans being irresponsible with their money—whether borrowing money based on "future income" they would never have or investing large amounts of money on risky corporations.

Stock Market Crash

> I have no fears for the future of our country. It is bright with hope.

> Sadly, Hoover would be regretting those words from his inauguration come October and the Stock Market Crash of 1929, which cost $26 billion in private money.

It all began on October 24, 1929, with the biggest stock market crash America has ever seen. Hoover attempted to soften the blow on the middle class by meeting with business moguls and begging them to keep workers' wages the same even if that meant a decline in their profits.

Although Hoover opposed sending government money into the situation, he urged local and state governments to begin public works projects to employ some of the grow-

 BTW: "The Star-Spangled Banner" became the official national anthem in 1931.

CONGRESSIONAL CORNER
★★★★★★★★★★★★★★★★★★★★★★★★

1. **Agricultural Marketing Act of 1929:** This act stabilized crop prices for farmers across America by allowing the government to buy surpluses from farmers. The act also provided loans to farmers who decided to pool their crops and resources in agricultural cooperatives.

2. **Smooth-Hawley Tariff Act of 1930:** This act greatly increased tariff rates on over twenty thousand imported goods.

3. **Reconstruction Finance Corporation Act of 1932:** This act created the Reconstruction Finance Corporation, which gave two million dollars in aid to state governments to help restart businesses and banks and refund mortgages and loans.

4. **Norris-LaGuardia Anti-Injunction Act of 1932:** This act stopped federal bans against strikes. It also prohibited judges from issuing court orders to limit peaceful striking.

5. **Revenue Act of 1932:** This act raised taxes on corporations and large estates.

6. **Federal Home Loan Bank Act of 1932:** This act lowered the cost of home ownership and formed the Federal Home Loan Bank, which helped finance home mortgages.

7. **Buy American Act of 1933:** This act required the federal government to buy only American-made products (if they were available) to help failing American businesses.

★★★★★★★★★★★★★★★★★★★★★★★★

BTW: Like almost every president, Hoover wrote his fair share of books: The Challenge to Liberty in 1934, The Basis of Lasting Peace in 1945, The Memoirs of Herbert Hoover in 1951, and The Ordeal of Woodrow Wilson in 1958. His final book even became a bestseller!

ing number of unemployed men across the United States. Nevertheless, as February approached and the depression slowly worsened, Hoover called for Congress to pass a $150 million bill to supply money for public works projects and tax cuts.

Hoover worked endlessly to fix the situation. Rising at dawn each day, he slowly made his way through an endless string of meetings with leaders from across America. Hoover also transformed the White House from a place of fanfare and custom to a house that provided only the most basic utilitarian needs. He canceled all ceremonies, celebrations, and celebratory presidential appearances. Despite Hoover's actions, Americans began to blame him for the decline in the economy.

By the summer of 1931, eight million Americans were unemployed. The homeless began camping in city parks, and several riots flared around the country as a result of the scant food supplies. Within a year, unemployment increased by 50 percent, and small cardboard structures housing penniless American families popped up all over the country.

Foreign Affairs

After the conclusion of World War I, France and Great Britain were deeply indebted to America. During Hoover's presidency, the two countries struggled to make their payments, and the payments eventually came at such sporadic rates that Hoover suspended them. The only other notable foreign policy event during this time period was the signing of the Stimson Doctrine, which proclaimed that any nation whose government was overthrown by a rebellion would still be able to develop diplomatic relations with the U.S.

 BTW: The Hoovers paid their secretaries and all their staff members out of their own pocket during their time in the White House.

Thoughts on the Constitution

> Our Constitution is not alone the working plan of a great Federation of States under representative government. There is embedded in it also the vital principles of the American system of liberty. That system is based upon certain inalienable freedoms and protections which not even the government may infringe and which we call the Bill of Rights. It does not require a lawyer to interpret those provisions.

FUN FACT!

The Hoover Dam on the Colorado River was named after Herbert Hoover!

Reelection Attempt

Hoover did attempt reelection, but it became apparent early on that a second term was unachievable. At Hoover's campaign stops, he often found himself at the mercy of angry and disgruntled crowds throwing rotten eggs and tomatoes. Twice Hoover's travels were disturbed by sabotaged and destroyed train tracks. As the election results came in, Hoover received just over 40 percent of the popular vote, a large margin for a man who was president during one of the darkest times in U.S. history.

Post-Presidency

Hoover did not retreat into hiding after his not-so-successful term in office. Rather, he remained as active as ever in the philanthropic field—worldwide and nationwide. At the outbreak of World War II, he headed the Polish Relief Commission. Later, President Truman commissioned Hoover to head the Food Supply for World Famine as well as the Commission on Organizations of the Executive Branch of the Government (more commonly known as the Hoover Commission). Hoover also established the Hoover Library on War, Revolution, and Peace at Stanford University, and for eight years served as the chairman of the Boy's Clubs of America. Hoover died at the age of ninety from internal intestinal bleeding.

What Has He Done for Me Lately?

Hoover's achievements before and after his presidency left a much greater legacy than his presidency itself.

A penniless orphan turned millionaire turned philanthropist, Hoover used his fortune and his leadership abilities to save millions of lives across the globe. From his actions to help stranded American travelers at the beginning of World War I, when he funded their safe travel back to America, to his efforts to supply food to starving countries across Europe during both world wars, Hoover spent nearly all of his time serving others. However, he failed to save America from the Great Depression during his presidency because of his belief the government should not control U.S. economic recovery efforts.

HERBERT HOOVER

Platform Speech

> [T]he American System ... is founded upon the conception that only through ordered liberty, freedom, and equal opportunity to the individual will his initiative and enterprise spur on the march of progress.

Hoover said this in his "Rugged Individualism" campaign speech of 1928.

BTW: Hoover responded to every letter he received (approximately twenty thousand a month) because he believed anyone determined enough to write him a letter deserved a response.

BTW: Last Words: "Levi Strauss was one of my best friends."

Written by Juliette Turner

BLACK TUESDAY: THE STOCK MARKET COLLAPSES!

October 24, 1929—Wall Street opened today to business as usual, but everything went downhill very quickly. Values of stocks in the New York Stock Exchange began to steadily and rapidly fall. A panic ensued as stock market brokers frantically traded their customers' stocks to prevent a massive loss. This made matters worse. This stock market collapse is the worst in American history. Banks across the country are already warning of foreclosures, and individuals are unable to obtain their cash, which has vanished over the course of twelve hours. Economists are warning people about a huge spike in unemployment.

THE GREAT DEPRESSION

February 27, 1930—In just over four months since the stock market crash, five million Americans have lost their jobs and that number is rising. Banks are foreclosing on mortgages, forcing thousands of Americans out of their homes. Farmers are going bankrupt, starting a spike in food prices. Banks are failing in every state. President Hoover attempted to curb the unemployment spike, but businesses are already laying off people to keep paychecks relatively stable. Additionally, people are no longer spending money on unnecessary goods and are cutting back on consumption, causing the economy to decline further. This is also making a quick recovery impossible. Many economists are predicting that twelve million Americans, one in four, will be out of work by the time Hoover leaves office.

THE BONUS ARMY MARCH

July 28, 1932—The Bonus Army's month-long camp-out in front of the White House came to a violent end today. After consistently refusing to speak to the group, President Hoover issued an order for the U.S. Army and the capital police to gently disperse the group.

However, the cardboard huts that the fifteen to twenty thousand veterans had lived in were burned and chaos ensued. A civilian mob charged the group, and one individual was accidentally shot and killed. An infant was also killed in the disarray, and many were harmed by tear gas. After the conclusion of World War I, the veterans were promised a bonus, due in 1945. This latest trouble began with the veterans' plea for their war bonuses to be released early so they could provide for their starving families. Congress did pass a bill allowing 50 percent of the whole amount due to be issued early. However, Hoover vetoed the bill last year. The Hoover administration is refusing to talk about the unintended violence. Presidential candidate Franklin Roosevelt commented, stating, "Well . . . this elects me."

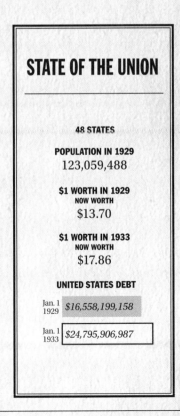

STATE OF THE UNION

48 STATES

POPULATION IN 1929
123,059,488

$1 WORTH IN 1929
NOW WORTH
$13.70

$1 WORTH IN 1933
NOW WORTH
$17.86

UNITED STATES DEBT

| Jan. 1 1929 | $16,558,199,158 |
| Jan. 1 1933 | $24,795,906,987 |

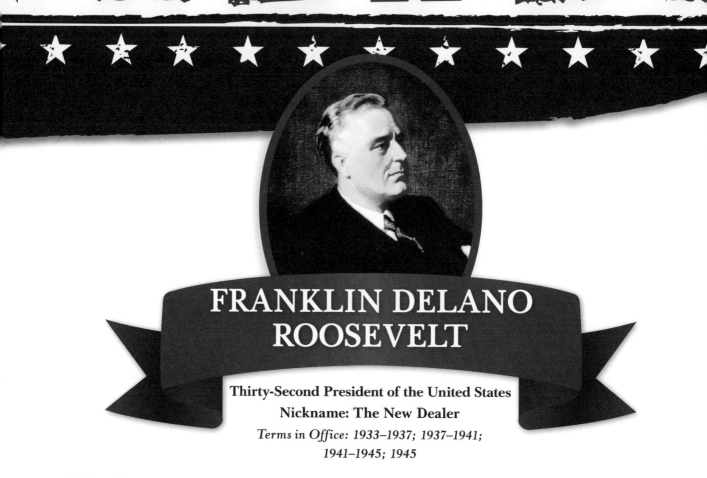

FRANKLIN DELANO ROOSEVELT

Thirty-Second President of the United States

Nickname: The New Dealer

Terms in Office: 1933–1937; 1937–1941;
1941–1945; 1945

The Bottom Line

Franklin Delano Roosevelt remains the only president to serve more than two terms. He struggled to combat the Great Depression and addressed the tensions in Europe that led to World War II, which actually helped end the Great Depression. Although Roosevelt was elected to a fourth term in office in 1945, he died within months as a result of failing health.

FAST STATS

★ Born January 30, 1882, in Hyde Park, New York
★ Parents: James and Sara Delano Roosevelt
★ Died April 12, 1945, in Warm Springs, Georgia; age 63
★ Age upon Start of First Term: 51; Age upon Conclusion of First Term: 55
★ Age upon Start of Second Term: 55; Age upon Conclusion of Second Term: 59
★ Age upon Start of Third Term: 59; Age upon Conclusion of Third Term: 63
★ Age upon Start of Fourth Term: 63; Age upon Death: 63
★ Religious Affiliation: Episcopalian
★ Political Party: Democrat
★ Height: 6 feet 2 inches
★ Vice President: John Nance Garner (1933–1941), Henry A. Wallace (1941–1945), and Harry S. Truman (1945)

What Was He Thinking?

Franklin Delano Roosevelt is undoubtedly one of the most progressive presidents. His belief in a strong central government resulted in a great increase in government-funded work projects and government control over the private business sector during the Depression.

Why Should I Care?

Roosevelt not only remains the only president to serve twelve years as president of the United States, he left his imprint heavily on the lives of

Americans then and now. He worked tirelessly to help workers and labor unions gain more rights in factories and other workplaces, and also pushed for racial and gender equality. Roosevelt raised income taxes for wealthier Americans to fund various stimulus spending legislation, such as public works initiatives. As much as he tried to avoid getting involved in World War II, it was inevitable.

BTW: Roosevelt appointed the first woman to serve in a presidential cabinet, Francis Perkins, as Secretary of Labor.

[W]hen there is no vision, the people perish.

Breakin' It Down
Early Life

Franklin Delano Roosevelt was the first president who did not have siblings. He did have one half brother, but all presidents before him had at least one blood sibling. Franklin was educated by private tutors and was cared for by a governess until the age of fourteen. He spoke fluent French and German and also enjoyed swimming, exploring nature, and collecting stamps—the latter his personal hobby.

As a teen, Franklin attended Groton, a prestigious Massachusetts preparatory school, where he learned about the virtues of public service. Franklin didn't receive high grades, and graduated the school as a "fair" student. In 1903, Franklin graduated from Harvard University, majoring in political science and government—once again not making very high grades. For a short period of time, he attended Columbia Law School; however, he left the school before graduating.

First Couple

Franklin Roosevelt and Anna Eleanor Roosevelt were married in 1905. Yes, their last names were the same, but they were so distantly related (fifth cousins once removed) that marriage was acceptable. Together they had six children. Observers noted that the relationship between Franklin and Eleanor Roosevelt was much more like a supportive friendship and companionship than marriage.

Maybe the lack of emotional connection stemmed from the affairs Franklin had, most notably, with Eleanor's personal secretary. The marriage stayed intact mostly due to Franklin's mother—a very opinionated and strong-willed woman who dominated her son's life until the day she died.

ANNA ELEANOR ROOSEVELT

FUN FACT!

Because Eleanor's father died before her wedding day, Theodore Roosevelt walked Eleanor Roosevelt down the aisle. He was her uncle and Franklin's cousin.

The twenty-first amendment is ratified; Prohibition ends, December 5, 1933

The Dust Bowl, 1933–1939

Adolf Hitler becomes president of Germany, 1934

The Communists' Long March takes place in China, 1934

The U.S.S.R. joins the League of Nations, 1934

Nuremberg Laws emerge in Germany, 1935

Amelia Earhart disappears over the Pacific Ocean during her around-the-world solo flight, 1937

King George V of Britain dies, 1936

Japan invades China, 1937

First Term in Office

1932   1933   1934   1935   1936   1937

BTW: By the time of his death, Roosevelt had collected 25,000 rare stamps.

ELECTION RESULTS!

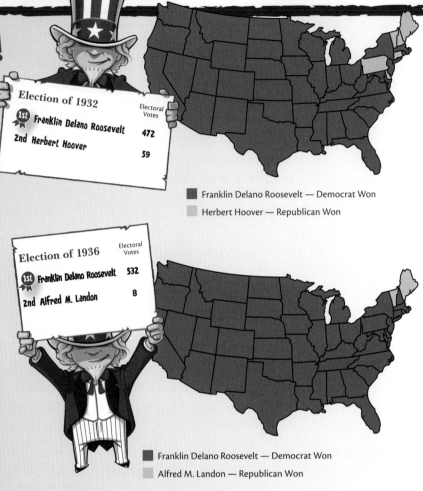

Election of 1932

	Electoral Votes
1st Franklin Delano Roosevelt	472
2nd Herbert Hoover	59

■ Franklin Delano Roosevelt — Democrat Won
□ Herbert Hoover — Republican Won

Election of 1936

	Electoral Votes
1st Franklin Delano Roosevelt	532
2nd Alfred M. Landon	8

■ Franklin Delano Roosevelt — Democrat Won
□ Alfred M. Landon — Republican Won

When running for president in 1932, Roosevelt offered his Democratic rival, John Nance Garner—Speaker of the U.S. House of Representatives and Texas native—the opportunity to run as his vice president. This took an opponent out of the running and also pulled the southern Democratic vote into the Roosevelt camp. Roosevelt campaigned in favor of an aggressive response to the Depression, including providing federal relief for the unemployed, remedying the overproduction of farms, instigating a government takeover of public utility industries, solidifying pensions for workers, and regulating the stock exchange.

Despite the fact that the economy had not recovered and his recovery measures had not notably helped America, Roosevelt won by a landslide over his opponent, Kansas governor, Alfred Landon.

Eleanor redefined not only the role of the first lady but also the role of the American woman. After her marriage to Franklin, Eleanor took a job (rare and even unsophisticated for the day) teaching the underprivileged children in New York's poorest neighborhoods. Upon becoming first lady, Eleanor remained just as active, holding weekly press conferences and often writing newspaper and magazine columns. She was a constant advocate for civil rights as well as job equality, equal pay, racial desegregation, and promotions for women. She was responsible for two of the "New Deal" programs, served as one of the first delegates to the United Nations, and was an activist against poverty and child labor.

BTW: FDR issued 635 vetoes.

> Progressivism with the brakes on [is preferable to] conservatism with a move on.

NBC makes the first official network television broadcast, 1940

Germany invades Poland; World War II officially begins, 1939
The film version of *The Wizard of Oz* premieres, 1939
Kristallnacht occurs in Germany, 1938

The film version of *Gone with the Wind* premieres, 1939

Winston Churchill becomes the prime minister of Great Britain, 1940

Second Term in Office

| 1936 | 1937 | 1938 | 1939 | 1940 |

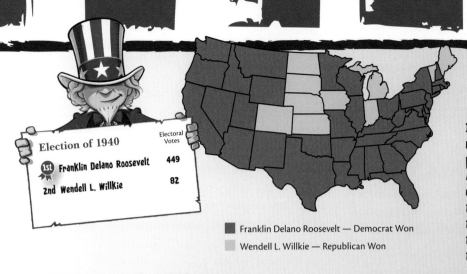

Election of 1940

		Electoral Votes
1st	Franklin Delano Roosevelt	449
2nd	Wendell L. Willkie	82

■ Franklin Delano Roosevelt — Democrat Won

■ Wendell L. Willkie — Republican Won

In 1940, Roosevelt ran for reelection and became the first president to win a third term. Although his popularity waned during this time period because of the still-struggling economy and the threat of war, Americans hesitated to change their leader so close to the brink of war.

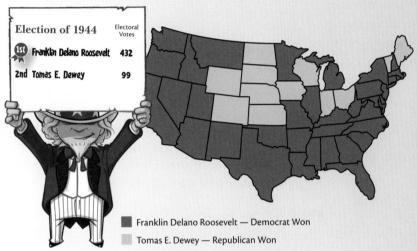

Election of 1944

		Electoral Votes
1st	Franklin Delano Roosevelt	432
2nd	Tomas E. Dewey	99

■ Franklin Delano Roosevelt — Democrat Won

■ Tomas E. Dewey — Republican Won

During the election, Roosevelt's health slowly declined, making campaigning difficult. Much of the campaigning was left in the hands of Roosevelt's new vice presidential pick, Harry Truman.

Previous Political Career

- 1911: Elected state senator in New York.
- 1913: Appointed assistant secretary of the Navy by President Woodrow Wilson.
- 1914: Failed to win the Democratic presidential nomination.
- 1920: Chosen to run as the vice presidential candidate under James Cox on the Democratic ticket; however, the ticket lost to Warren Harding and Calvin Coolidge.

FUN FACT!

Eleanor Roosevelt said of her husband, "Anyone who has gone through great suffering is bound to have a greater sympathy and understanding of the problems of mankind."

The Wannsee Conference in Germany begins the Holocaust, 1942

Japan attacks Pearl Harbor, Hawaii, 1941

Germany and Italy declare war on the U.S., 1941

Thanksgiving is declared a national holiday for the last Thursday in November, 1941

The U.S. declares war on Japan, 1941

The Battle of Midway between Japan and United States is fought, 1942

The Jefferson Memorial is dedicated on the two hundredth anniversary of Thomas Jefferson's birth, 1943

American forces defeat Japan at the battle of Guadalcanal, 1943

Penicillin is first used to treat a patient, 1943

Italian leader Benito Mussolini is overthrown, 1943

The Yalta Conference takes place, 1945

A proposal is made to form the United Nations, 1944

Allied forces invade Normandy on D-Day, June 6, 1944

Third and Fourth Term in Office

| 1941 | 1942 | 1943 | 1944 | 1945 |

The Socialist Party: **The Socialist Party was formed in 1901, but it did not gain popularity until the late 1920s. The party believed in the principles of socialism—public instead of private ownership of money, land, and property. Socialists believe a capitalist society favors the wealthy and is unfair to the disadvantaged members of society.**

Communist Party: **The Communist Party USA was formed in 1919. Communism was founded by Karl Marx and based on the belief that government should control and possess every aspect of society. In the elections of 1932 and 1936, the Socialist Party and Communist Party candidates received a combined two hundred thousand popular votes.**

PRESIDENTIAL Personality

★ Ironically, it was the most difficult hardship of Franklin Roosevelt's life that made him such a great man. His time suffering from the effects of polio and his paralysis added a layer of sensitivity and humility to a man who had before been pegged as somewhat distant and conceited. He did his best to put others around him at ease, even if he wasn't at ease himself, as was often the case because of his leg braces and dependency upon others to carry him.

- 1924: Attended the Democratic Convention and received national exposure.
- 1929: Won his election bid for governor of New York, and served in this position until 1932. Upon assuming office, Franklin began implementing his five-point plan: (1) reforest land ruined by overuse; (2) begin state-financed pensions; (3) create insurance plans for the unemployed; (4) regulate working hours for laborers; and (5) establish state control of New York's energy industry.

Presidency

The time of American history when Roosevelt took office was discouraging indeed. Between 1930 and 1933, nine thousand banks had failed in thirty-eight of the forty-eight American states. Thirteen million Americans were out of work, but this bleak news and the rising unemployment numbers did not intimidate the ambitious Roosevelt.

The First One Hundred Days

During his first one hundred days in office, all of Roosevelt's proposals were passed by Congress. One of them was Roosevelt's most well-known reform, the New Deal, passed by a special session in Congress in 1933. This new plan for the American economy impacted every aspect of American life, from buying a home, to getting a job, to trading with countries overseas. The New Deal included two acts—the Emergency Banking Act and the Economy Act— as well as Roosevelt's three "R's": relief, recovery, and reform.

BTW: When it was first established, the minimum wage was twenty-five cents an hour.

Unlike his predecessor, Roosevelt befriended the concept of initiating government-funded works projects to slow the growing number of the unemployed in poverty. Roosevelt opened large-scale construction projects, focusing on conservation and cleanup—hiring hundreds of individuals while at the same time improving sanitation and hygiene in cities. Roosevelt also installed various government agencies to reform banking policy, to guide negotiations between businesses and their workers, to regulate laborers' working hours, and to establish the minimum wage.

In 1935, Roosevelt was still extending reforms to attempt to fix the never-ending Great Depression. Roosevelt raised income taxes for the wealthiest of Americans and instructed the Federal Reserve to tighten their regulation of private businesses to increase the government's control on the economy. Yet

BTW: At age thirty-nine, Roosevelt was stricken with polio, a disease that was common at this time, that left his lower body paralyzed. After spending three years in rehabilitation, Roosevelt still could not use his legs. He could only walk with the aid of heavy leg braces and canes, often resorting to a wheelchair.

LIBERTY Language

Embargo: An official ban on trade with a certain country, intended to punish the country.

Roosevelt did not see the drastic or miraculous turn-around he'd hoped to see. To kick off a long spell of bad luck, in 1935 and 1936, the Supreme Court declared two of the main pillars of Roosevelt's New Deal programs unconstitutional: the National Industrial Recovery Act and the Agricultural Adjustment Act. Despite his extensive attempts to boost the economy and reverse the Depression, Roosevelt had made only modest gains by 1937. Unemployment still stood at 14 percent, and in October the stock market suffered its largest drop since Black Tuesday. Industrial activity and manufacturing still remained sluggish and unresponsive, undergoing its largest decline in history. Between Labor Day and Christmas Day in 1937, more than two million Americans lost their jobs, and the same number lost their jobs in the first three months of 1938. Roosevelt ordered $3.4 billion added to the U.S. economy, but the stimulus money only moderately helped.

Reelection

Roosevelt won reelection, which was surprising in light of his lack of success. He attempted to boost national morale through his great speaking skills, claiming it was time for Americans to experience a "rendezvous with destiny." Despite his efforts, however, the Republicans gained many seats in the 1938 congressional elections, and many of Roosevelt's reforms were blocked.

World Problems

In the beginning years of his four terms in office, Roosevelt had little to worry about in regard to foreign affairs. During this time, he worked to improve American relations with Russia. He also initiated his "Good Neighbor" policy with Latin America, which strengthened trade agreements while ending American intervention in Latin-American domestic affairs. However, the rise of fascism in Germany and Italy soon emerged on the international stage, and military dictatorships gained power in Spain, Italy, Japan, and Germany.

CONGRESSIONAL CORNER

1. **Emergency Banking Act of 1933:** This act allowed the Federal Reserve Board to oversee various activities of American banks in an attempt to slow down the nation's banking crisis.

2. **Civilian Conservation Corps Act:** This act employed 250,000 unemployed American men to work on land improvement projects in exchange for food and shelter.*

3. **Agricultural Adjustment Act^:** This act passed on May 12, 1933, and formed the Agricultural Adjustment Administration. This agency purchased surpluses from farmers, and was deemed unconstitutional by the Supreme Court in 1936.*

4. **Securities Act of 1933:** This act formed the Securities and Exchange Commission, which monitored stocks and bonds, ensuring the legality of stock exchanges.*

5. **Homeowners Refinancing Act:** This act formed the Home Owners' Loan Corporation. This corporation assisted in refinancing homes to prevent individuals from defaulting on their home payments.*

6. **National Labor Relations Act:** This act guaranteed workers the right to organize and bargain with business owners. It also established the National Labor Relations Board, which helped form many labor unions.*

7. **Social Security Act:** This act established the Social Security System.*

8. **Banking Act of 1933:** This act established the Federal Deposit Insurance Corporation, which ensures the money placed in banks by individuals will be there for them in the future, up to 100,000 per person.*

9. **Neutrality Acts of 1935, 1936, and 1937:** These acts declared the U.S. would not become involved in foreign conflicts.

10. **Fair Labor Standards Act:** This act established the minimum wage and the maximum working hours for hourly workers (a forty-four-hour, seven-day work week).

11. **Public Health Service Act:** This act helped reform health services, disease treatment, and children's health care.

^ *Supreme Court deemed unconstitutional*

* *New Deal Reforms*

> The United States Constitution has proved itself the most marvelously elastic compilation of rules of government ever written.

In 1934, with the outbreak of World War II, America declared neutrality by prohibiting any shipment of weaponry to any country engaged in the fighting. Five years later in 1939, however, the embargo was repealed and shipment was allowed to any country that could pay cash for the American-manufactured weapons and could provide their own transportation. Congress initiated the Lend-Lease Program on March 11, 1941, which lent weapons and machinery to Great Britain on the basis that the machinery would be returned to America after the war. This program eventually cost America seven billion dollars. America's neutrality crumbled further when the U.S. sent fifty destroyer ships to Great Britain's Pacific military bases after the rest of Europe fell under Nazi domination. Many considered this action the first step toward American intervention in the war.

Although the prospects of war cast gloom and worry over the American people, the war efforts actually resulted in a lift from the Great Depression, causing aircraft production to double from 60,000 to 125,000 and tank production to triple from 25,000 to 75,000. This resulted in an industrial boom and the creation of three million jobs for working-age men and three and a half million jobs for women as well.

World War II Begins

In 1940, Roosevelt won reelection, becoming the first president to take a third oath of office. Yet Roosevelt had little time to celebrate, for tensions were rising in American-German relations. In September 1941, German torpedo boats fired at an American destroyer. The ship received orders to return fire, resulting in the first American-German cross fire in the war, though war was still not formally declared by the United States. However, it was the Asian front that proved more strenuous. As Japan advanced on China, America sided with the Chinese by banning shipments of iron and steel to Japan. This embargo resulted in one of the biggest surprise attacks America had suffered up to that time: the Japanese attack on the U.S. naval base in Pearl Harbor.

With the devastation at Pearl Harbor, Roosevelt and the rest of the American government had no choice but to declare war on Japan. Roosevelt delivered his declaration of war to Congress on December 8, 1941. His speech was broadcast over the radio, garnering an audience of 81 percent of America's

> During his presidency, most people did not know that Roosevelt used a wheelchair. The Roosevelt administration worked hard to hide the president's dependence on the chair, only allowing him to appear publicly in the wheelchair once. Not until after his death did the American people as a whole learn that their president had to be carried up and down stairs and lifted into bed at night.

BTW: On February 5, 1937 (after the Supreme Court ruled against seven of Roosevelt's nine New Deal programs) Roosevelt proposed a plan to "stack" the Supreme Court by adding six more seats to the bench and proposed that any justice seventy years of age or older should be replaced. Roosevelt claimed his plan would expedite the case-hearing process and that some of the judges were "old and senile." Needless to say, the plan was rejected.

population. During his speech, Roosevelt communicated the urgency of the situation, leading to the extreme jump in national support for the war. Roosevelt balanced the urgency with composure and calm, which prevented chaos from wrecking the nation.

Pros and Cons of War

The Second World War continued past Roosevelt's death and into the term of his successor, Harry Truman. Throughout the course of the war, fifteen million Americans served in the U.S. Army, and a great percentage did not return. Yet during the war, unemployment rates dropped from 17 percent in 1939 to 1 percent in 1944, and personal income for Americans doubled as a result of the wartime industrial boom.

Right before Roosevelt's death, he attended the Yalta Conference with British prime minister Winston Churchill, and Soviet leader Joseph Stalin. The three leaders negotiated an agreement for the three powerful nations to work in unison to defeat the Axis powers.

Death

Roosevelt's health began to deteriorate during the election of 1944, but he refused to let this stop his campaign. Ten months before the Yalta Conference, doctors had all but declared Roosevelt dead, diagnosing him with hypertension, heart disease, and failure of the left ventricle chamber of his heart. After attending the Yalta Conference, Roosevelt attempted to recover in his quiet home in Warm Springs—dubbed "the Little White House" because of the amount of time he spent there—but his health failed to rebound. He died from a cerebral hemorrhage in 1945 at the age of sixty-three. His funeral took place less than a month before Germany surrendered to the Allies.

BTW: FDR's last words were: "I have a terrific headache."

What Has He Done for Me Lately?

Speculation is always interesting, especially in regard to history. What would have happened if Roosevelt had not been president during the outbreak of World War II? It is very possible that without FDR's leadership, America would not have become involved in the war—after all, Americans were war-weary after the too-recent World War I. Imagine how the war would have ended without America's involvement.

PLATFORM SPEECH

[T]he only thing we have to fear is fear itself—nameless, unreasoning, unjustified terror which paralyzes needed efforts to convert retreat into advance. In every dark hour of our national life a leadership of frankness and of vigor has met with that understanding and support of the people themselves which is essential to victory.

FRANKLIN DELANO ROOSEVELT

In arguably one of the most quoted presidential quotes, Roosevelt warned the people in his 1933 State of the Union address that fear of the future would result in America's further decline. Only through hope could she survive.

BTW: The twenty-second amendment to the Constitution, sometimes called the FDR Amendment, was passed after Roosevelt's presidency, setting a term limit of two terms (eight years). However, a president can serve a total of 10 years if they become president for less than two years from the vice presidency.

Presidential Times

Written by Juliette Turner

ASSASSINATION ATTEMPT!

February 15, 1933—Earlier today, while president-elect Roosevelt was giving a speech in Miami, Florida, a man named Giuseppe Zangara fired five shots at President Roosevelt. All five shots missed the president, but one hit Chicago mayor Anton J. Cermak, who has now died from the gunshot wound. After he was laid off from his bricklaying job, Zangara became one of the millions of unemployed in the country. He blames Roosevelt for the rich capitalists he holds responsible for the Depression.

THE FIRST INAUGURAL ADDRESS OF FRANKLIN ROOSEVELT

March 4, 1933—Today, in the course of fifteen minutes and with only two thousand words in his inaugural address, Franklin Roosevelt was able to deliver what will surely be some of America's most recited and memorized mottos. Although most of the words were written by a team of a dozen speechwriters, Roosevelt nevertheless had great say over the words he would deliver. "There is nothing to fear but fear itself" reportedly came from Roosevelt's own hand. In the days before his inauguration, Eleanor Roosevelt found a book by Henry Thoreau on her husband's bedside open to a page reading, "Nothing is so much to be feared as fear."

ROOSEVELT USES RADIO TO ADDRESS PUBLIC

March 14, 1933—President Roosevelt took to the radio to chat more intimately with the American public, hoping these addresses will facilitate more direct communication.

His first chat, on March 12, discussed the bank crisis. He began by saying, "I know that when you understand what we in Washington have been about, I shall continue to have your cooperation as fully as I have had your sympathy and help during the past week."

His cheery voice and demeanor has already seemed to calm people's fears and instill confidence in their government. He explained, "First of all, let me state the simple fact that when you deposit money in a bank, the bank does not put the money into a safe deposit vault. It invests your money in many different forms of credit-bonds, commercial paper, mortgages, and many other kinds of loans. In other words, the bank puts your money to work to keep the wheels of industry and of agriculture turning around."

If you missed his first talk, you will have other opportunities to listen to the president. He plans a few more talks in the coming future.

JAPAN ATTACKS AMERICA AT PEARL HARBOR

December 7, 1941—Early this morning, Japanese fighter planes fired on the U.S. naval base at Pearl Harbor, Hawaii. It is already estimated that approximately three thousand military personnel were killed or wounded, two hundred aircrafts were destroyed, and eight battleships—along with ten other vessels—were either badly damaged or destroyed. Miraculously, none of America's four aircraft carriers were destroyed, because the ships had been sent out to sea for training the night before and were then alerted to not return until the attack ceased.

HOLOCAUST HORRORS REVEALED

November 24, 1944--Two years ago today, many Americans will remember Rabbi Stephen S. Wise's press conference revealing Germany's mass extermination of the Jews inside Europe. Hitler's and the Nazi's "Final Plan," or their plan for the systematic and deliberate extermination of the Jews, began after the Nazi leaders met at the Wannsee Conference on January 20, 1942. This plan resulted in the death of two out of every three of the nine million Jews in Europe. News of this plan was not discovered until August of 1942. Throughout the course of the war, millions of Jews residing in the Nazi occupied zones of Europe were shipped to concentration camps, most notably Dachau, Sachsenhausen, and Treblinka, where they were killed, commonly in gas chambers.

ROOSEVELT ASKS FOR WAR DECLARATION FROM CONGRESS

December 8, 1941—President Roosevelt appeared before Congress today and requested their approval for a measure to declare war on Japan. He called December 7 "a day which will live in infamy." In his address, the president stated, "No matter how long it may take us to overcome this premeditated invasion, the American people in their righteous might will win through to absolute victory." The Congress voted immediately in favor of the war declaration, with only one dissenting vote.

EXECUTIVE ORDER 9066

February 19, 1942—President Roosevelt signed into law Executive Order 9066, allowing for the detention and near-imprisonment of all Japanese-Americans. This comes after the Roberts Commission (a committee initiated by FDR to investigate the causes of Pearl Harbor) concluded that the Japanese attack involved all Japanese-Americans—though no conclusive evidence supports that claim. An estimated 110,000 Japanese, two-thirds of whom are American citizens, will be shipped to relocation camps located in isolated sections of the American West.

WORLD WAR II CONTINUES

November 7, 1944—Franklin Roosevelt won an unprecedented fourth term, but his victory is overshadowed by the continuation of World War II. Over sixty million individuals have died to date, and cities all across Europe have been destroyed by aerial bombings. Adolf Hitler of Germany remains the culprit behind the start of the war in Europe, as well as his ally, Benito Mussolini of Italy. Currently, all of Europe except for Great Britain is under the control of Adolf Hitler and the Axis powers.

STATE OF THE UNION

48 STATES

POPULATION IN 1933
126,712,719

$1 WORTH IN 1933
NOW WORTH
$17.86

$1 WORTH IN 1945
NOW WORTH
$12.99

UNITED STATES DEBT

Jan. 1 1933	$24,795,906,987
Jan. 1 1945	$264,052,143,292

HARRY S. TRUMAN

Thirty-Third President of the United States
Nickname: The High-Tax Harry
Terms in Office: 1945–1949; 1949–1953

The Bottom Line

Harry Truman assumed the presidency in 1945 after the death of Franklin Roosevelt. As president, he oversaw the conclusion of both the European and the Pacific front in World War II. Truman won a surprise second term, during which time he worked to stabilize the American economy to prevent a second depression and organized the American invasion of Korea during the Korean War.

FAST STATS

★ Born May 8, 1884, in Lamar, Missouri
★ Parents: John Anderson and Martha Ellen Young Truman
★ Died December 26, 1972, in Kansas City, Missouri; age 88
★ Age upon Start of First Term: 60; Age upon Conclusion of First Term: 64
★ Age upon Start of Second Term: 64; Age upon Conclusion of Second Term: 68
★ Religious Affiliation: Baptist
★ Political Party: Democrat
★ Height: 5 feet 9 inches
★ Vice President: none (1945–1949) and Alben W. Barkley (1949–1953)

What Was He Thinking?

Harry Truman was an honest politician who believed favors should not exist in the world of politics. He followed his predecessor—Franklin Roosevelt—in regard to his progressive attitude, endeavoring to protect labor unions, improve working conditions, and stabilize the American economy through government regulation and higher income taxes. An avid opponent of communism, Truman believed communist beliefs were a huge danger to democracies worldwide.

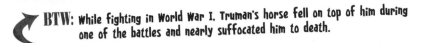 **BTW:** While fighting in World War I, Truman's horse fell on top of him during one of the battles and nearly suffocated him to death.

Why Should I Care?

One of Truman's most significant legacies is the Truman Doctrine. It was responsible for branding the United States as the nation charged with protecting new democracies across the globe from impending communist invasion. As a result, America took a lead role in the Cold War, the Korean War, the Vietnam War, and the Persian Gulf War. Since the adoption of the Truman Doctrine, trillions of dollars have been sent overseas to countries requesting American aid in their fight against communist regimes and dictatorships.

> If we falter in our leadership, we may endanger the peace of the world, and we shall surely endanger the welfare of this nation.

Breakin' It Down
Early Life

BTW: Harry and Elizabeth Truman received the first two Medicare registration cards.

Harry was the first of three children born to John and Martha Truman. A sickly child, Harry had bad eyesight and battled long bouts of diphtheria. His illness often kept him from participating in activities with kids his age. It did not stop him, however, from going to school. He quickly became an avid reader, reading everything from biographies and histories to accounts of military battles.

Harry also loved playing the piano, practicing for two hours before school every morning. After grade school, Harry wanted to attend the United States Military Academy at West Point, but his nearsighted vision and thick glasses prohibited him from doing so. At this time, he took on a series of odd jobs to provide for himself and his family. He worked as a timekeeper at the local Santa Fe railway line and then as a mail clerk at the *Kansas City Star* newspaper. He also worked for a construction company and then as a clerk at a bank, where he earned one hundred dollars a month. On top of his paying jobs, Harry worked the family farm, rising at five in the morning every day to care for the livestock and do chores. By saving his hard-earned money, Harry was later able to invest thousands of dollars in a zinc mine and an oil company.

In 1905, Harry was determined to join the army. Although his eyesight had not improved, Harry memorized the eye chart to pass the vision test. He joined the National Guard, eventually becoming first lieutenant of the Missouri Second Field Artillery. During the First World War, Harry served in the 129th Field Artillery, reaching the rank of major. Near the end of the war, in March 1918, Harry was promoted to captain for his bravery in battle.

After his service in the army, Harry returned home and became a co-owner of a local clothing store—but the store failed three years later. After his lack of success in the business realm, Harry decided to enter the world of politics.

First Couple

Harry Truman and Elizabeth "Bess" Wallace met for the first time in Sunday school at the local Presbyterian Church in 1890, when Harry was six and Bess was five. They would later attend fifth grade together. Although they were childhood

ELIZABETH TRUMAN

Truman referred to his wife, Bess, as "The Boss" and his daughter, Margaret, as "The Boss's Boss."

friends, it took a seven-year courtship (and three proposals) for Bess to agree to marriage. Harry, however, had loved Bess from the moment he saw her in Sunday school, saying, "She had tanned skin, blond hair, golden as sunshine; and the most beautiful blue eyes I've ever seen, or will see." They were married in 1919. Together they had one daughter. During the war, Harry carried a photo of Bess in his pocket, praying he would return to her. He did, and they eventually occupied the White House a to serve their country as president and first lady.

THE SAYINGS of Harry Truman

If you have ever said, "The buck stops here," then you have said the words of Harry Truman. Truman also created the idiom, "If you can't take the heat, get out of the kitchen."

Previous Political Career

- Appointed a supervisor of roads and buildings for Missouri's Jackson County. He worked to improve the local construction system and fired certain government officials to decrease corruption.
- 1922: Elected as a judge on the Jackson County Court. He lost reelection in 1924 but won again in 1926 and 1930.
- 1934: Elected to the U.S. Senate. He fervently supported Roosevelt's New Deal programs and quickly became active in the Senate. He was reelected in 1940. He was appointed to the Appropriations Committee and the Interstate Commerce Committee, and he created the Civil Aeronautics Board to regulate the airplane industry. He formed the "Truman Committee," which worked to eliminate government waste. Fraud and corruption had cost taxpayers $400,000 over just three years, and this committee saved the country $15 billion.
- 1945: Vice president under Franklin Delano Roosevelt.

Presidency

Truman served as vice president for a brief eighty-two days, meeting with the president only twice before FDR's death. With the president's death on April 12, Truman was sworn into office as the nation's seventh "accidental president."

FDR had told Truman little about what was happening in the administration; in fact, it wasn't until his first meeting with Sec-

Boys, if you ever pray, pray for me now. I don't know if any of you fellows ever had a load of hay fall on you, but when they told me what had happened, I felt like the moon, the stars, and all the planets had fallen on me.

HARRY S. TRUMAN

Percy Spencer patents the microwave oven, 1945
The first electronic computer is built, 1945
The charter for the United Nations is signed, 1945
Adolf Hilter commits suicide, April 30, 1945

The first U.N. meeting is held in London, 1946

The League of Nations dissolves, 1946

The twenty-second amendment to the Constitution is passed, 1947
The Diary of a Young Girl, from the diary of Anne Frank, is published, 1947
The Dead Sea Scrolls are discovered, 1947

The Berlin Blockade and Berlin Airlift take place, 1948
The nation of Israel is established, 1948
Mahatma Gandhi is assassinated in New Delhi, 1948

First Term in Office

| 1944 | 1945 | 1946 | 1947 | 1948 |

ELECTION RESULTS!

Election of 1948

		Electoral Votes
1st	Harry S. Truman	303
2nd	Thomas E. Dewey	189
3rd	J. Strom Thurmond	39

Truman campaigned tirelessly, traveling by train thirty thousand miles across the country with his "whistle-stop" campaign tour. He gave approximately three hundred speeches to a cumulative twenty million people, but no one thought he would pull it off. The *Chicago Tribune* even published an early edition newspaper with the headline "Dewey Defeats Truman." However, when the votes were counted, Truman came out on top.

- ■ Harry S. Truman — Democrat Won
- Thomas E. Dewey — Republican Won
- ■ J. Strom Thurmond — States Rights Democrat Won

retary of War Henry Stimson that Truman learned about America's atomic nuclear capabilities. To ease the transition, Truman requested Roosevelt's cabinet stay intact for the time being.

Atomic Bomb

On May 8, 1945, Truman experienced the day Roosevelt would have given anything to have experienced: the Allies' victory on the European front, known as V-E Day (Victory in Europe Day). However, the war with Japan still continued. Because of this, the possibility of America using the atomic bomb on Japan became greater and greater. America decided to drop the atomic bombs. After two bombings of Japan on August 7 and 10, Japan surrendered on September 2.

Beginnings of the Cold War

As soon as the war on the Pacific front ended, the Cold War began. Problems arose with Soviet Russia as soon as Japan surrendered. After the Yalta Conference, it was agreed that Germany would be divided between the Allied powers: the United States, Great Britain, France, and the Soviet Union. However, the Soviet Union refused to hold democratic and uncorrupted elections and slowly began cutting East Germany off from the rest of the world by stationing soldiers along the border to refuse access or exit. The Soviet Union also began supporting communist rebels in

> ### PRESIDENTIAL Personality
>
> ★ Harry Truman was known to his family, friends, and even enemies to be humble and courteous, but at the same time outspoken and blunt. Truman was confident in his judgments, and once he made a decision, he stuck to it. His temper often overtook his composure, oftentimes showing through in his impassioned speeches. Although he loved the world of politics, he remained honest and incorruptible.

Communists take over China, 1949

The first successful Soviet atomic test takes place, 1949

The North Atlantic Treaty Organization (NATO) is formed, 1949

McCarthyism begins, 1950

The Korean War begins, 1950

Color television is introduced, 1951

An airplane lands on the North Pole for the first time, 1952

Elizabeth II is crowned Queen of England, 1953

Joseph Stalin dies, 1953

Second Term in Office

1949 1950 1951 1952 1953

BERLIN

French sector

West

British sector

Soviet sector

East

American sector

━━━ Berlin Wall
------- sector border

Turkey and Greece. These actions resulted in the "Truman Doctrine," which sent U.S. dollars ($150 million to Turkey and $250 million to Greece) to help suppress the communist rebels.

The Marshall Plan

Truman's secretary of state, George Marshall, formed the Marshall Plan, which sent $12.5 billion to foreign nations over the next four years. This money was used to strengthen anti-communist countries, to prevent communist takeovers, and to fund projects to battle the postwar famines quickly spreading through most of Europe. It was based on the "domino theory," which theorized that if communism were allowed to spread to one country and take over the government there, then other countries would quickly fall to the same fate. The Marshall Plan could only go so far, however, and Eastern Europe—the countries between East Germany and the Soviet Union—fell under Soviet communist rule. Soon, contact with East Germany was shut off completely and roads leading into Berlin were blocked, preventing any resources from reaching the East Berliners and Germans. When conditions began to deteriorate, Truman issued the "Berlin Airlift," otherwise known as Operation Vittles, which delivered supplies to East Germany by air for almost a year.

Fair Deal and Civil Rights Reform

Although the war and the resulting industrial boom lifted America from the Great Depression, Truman was careful to prevent history from repeating itself, so he proposed his "Fair Deal" legislation: a series of price and wage controls, an expansion of public housing, extension of old-age benefits, and the formation of national health insurance. After the Republicans secured both houses of Congress in 1946, all of Truman's proposals were stalled.

Truman issued Executive Order 9981 on July 26, 1948, ordering the desegregation of the military—meaning the military could no longer separate and discriminate against soldiers based on race. This executive order created havoc inside the

Use of the Atomic Bomb

★★★★★★★★★★★★★★★★★★★★★★★★★★★★

The atomic bomb had the strength of two thousand British "Grand Slam" bombs—the largest bomb ever to be used up to that time—and could kill tens of thousands. In comparison to how many individuals would have died as a result of land invasion—up to five hundred thousand—the magnitude of the atomic bombings can be put in perspective. Land battles between the U.S. and Japanese were especially brutal because of the Japanese's dedication to their historic Bushido code, a code that required them to die before ever surrendering.

For instance, at the battle of Iwo Jima in Japan, approximately 27,000 American and Japanese soldiers were killed and nearly 20,000 more were wounded. At the battle of Okinawa, over 115,000 Japanese and American soldiers died and approximately 40,000 were wounded. The atomic bombing of Hiroshima resulted in 130,000 Japanese casualties (deaths or injuries) and the bombing of Nagasaki resulted in 70,000 casualties.

BTW: On April 12th, Eleanor Roosevelt called Harry Truman personally, asking for him to come and see her immediately—a call which reportedly drained the color from Truman's face. The moment Truman arrived in Eleanor's office, she said, "Harry, the president is dead." After a brief moment of silence, Truman asked if there was anything he could do for her. She replied, "Is there anything we can do for you? For you are the one in trouble now."

Pop Quiz! Do you remember how many times Grover Cleveland used his veto power? He vetoed 584 times! What about FDR? He vetoed 635 times! Harry Truman comes in third with 250 vetoes!

POLITICAL PARTIES

★★★★★★★★★★★★★★★★★★★★★★★★★★

> *The Dixiecrats:* **The Dixiecrats were former members of the Democrat Party who branched off after Truman desegregated the military. These southern Democrats favored the strong segregation rules in the south.**

Democrat Party, leading to the split of the Democrat Party and the southern Democrats during the presidential election of 1948.

Reelection

Because of the partisan divide and the constant debate in Washington, D.C., Truman's popularity sank to an all-time low. Labor unions were angry over the recently passed Taft-Hartley Act, which allowed the government to regulate and interfere in worker strikes. Business managers resented the continuation of the strict wartime government regulations, and Truman lost support over his anti-segregation policies. Everyone considered it impossible for Truman to be reelected, but in 1948 he won 49.5 percent of the popular vote, with two million more votes than his opponent, and won 57 percent of the electoral vote.

Success in the Midterm Election

Things turned around after the election of 1948 when the Democrats won the majority in both chambers of Congress. With Congress on his side, Truman was able to pass his "Fair Deal" legislation. However, Truman and the rest of the U.S. government struggled to combat communism inside America. The Red Scare (the anticommunist movement in the 1950s) led to a dramatic increase in suspicion among United States citizens: who might be secretly communist or leading a double life as a Soviet spy? At the height of the Red Scare, U.S. Senator Joseph McCarthy held his historic McCarthy Hearings—a practice called McCarthyism. Hundreds of people were brought before the Senate and the "House Committee on Un-American Activities" on the basis or suspicion of showing communist beliefs. As a result, hundreds of people lost their jobs and their reputations,

CONGRESSIONAL CORNER

★★★★★★★★★★★★★★★★★★★★★★★★★★

1. **Taft-Hartley Act of 1947: This act outlawed union-only workplaces and prohibited union activities. It also prevented unions from contributing to campaigns and allowed courts to stop strikes that could harm the public good. Truman vetoed the legislation, but Congress overrode the veto. This act was repealed with the change of political majority in the Congress.**

2. **Truman's Fair Deal Legislation: This piece of legislation increased federal funding for housing, increased the minimum wage, improved civil rights for African-Americans, and increased Social Security benefits.**

3. **Presidential Succession Act: Passed in 1947, this act established the process of presidential succession if the president and the vice president were to both die while serving. The succession would be Speaker of the House, president pro tempore of the Senate, secretary of state, secretary of the treasury, secretary of defense, and then attorney general.**

4. **National Security Act: This act, passed in 1947, established the Central Intelligence Agency (the CIA), the National Security Council, the Department of Defense, and the Department of the Air Force.**

5. **Internal Security Act: Also known as the McCarran Act of 1950, this act required all communist organizations to register with the government. It also legalized the arrest of all communist officials during a "national emergency," and it prohibited communists from working in national defense positions. The act also prohibited any individual who was a part of a totalitarian organization from immigrating to the United States.**

★★★★★★★★★★★★★★★★★★★★★★★★★★

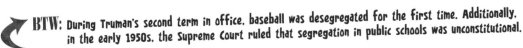

BTW: During Truman's second term in office, baseball was desegregated for the first time. Additionally, in the early 1950s, the Supreme Court ruled that segregation in public schools was unconstitutional.

The Federal Government has a clear duty to see the Constitutional guarantees of individual liberties and of equal protection under the laws are not denied or abridged anywhere in the Union.

and many were stripped of their constitutional rights with national security as the excuse.

Beginning of the Korean War

Although communist expansion in America was curbed, the communism scare at home was heightened when the international stage once again erupted with turmoil and warfare. This time, instead of Europe, the focus landed on the small country of Korea, which was now divided into the communist north and anticommunist south. An alliance was formed with the United Nations, fifteen other nations allied with the United States to support South Korea. North Korea received support from the People's Republic of China and the USSR. Within a matter of months, South Korea and her allies regained the "38th Parallel"—the previous border between the two countries. General Douglas MacArthur proposed a plan to push past the 38th parallel and into mainland China, but Truman rejected the plan, believing that the Marshall Plan only called for keeping existing countries safe. Nevertheless, MacArthur pushed his soldiers northward into North Korea in an attempt to destroy the communist forces there. In retaliation, the People's Republic of China deployed thousands of their own troops. As a result, the war continued months longer than it should have and many more lives were lost. The three-year-long Korean War between the United States and North Korea extended past Truman's leave from office, leaving 128,000 Americans dead, missing, or wounded.

PLATFORM SPEECH

No government is perfect. One of the chief virtues of a democracy, however, is that its defects are always visible and under democratic process can be pointed out and corrected.

Truman said this in his 1947 speech to the joint session of Congress. He explained that America's democratic government, although it is not perfect, is amendable and correctable.

HARRY S. TRUMAN

Post-Presidency

After leaving the presidency, Truman retired to his home state of Missouri, living in the city of Independence for the rest of his life. During his retirement, Truman wrote three books: *Year of Decisions* (1955), *Years of Trial and Hope* (1956), and *Mr. Citizen* (1960). Truman also oversaw the construction of his presidential library in Missouri. On the day after Christmas in 1972, Truman passed away in his own home.

What Has He Done for Me Lately?

The decision to drop the atomic bomb on Hiroshima and Nagasaki was one of the most significant decisions ever made by a U.S. president. However, had the bombs not been dropped, the fighting would have continued for many more months and the death toll would have risen considerably during that time—especially if a land-invasion tactic had been used instead. Either way, the options were bleak, for war will always result in tragic death.

Written by Juliette Turner

THE POTSDAM CONFERENCE

July 24, 1945—Victory has been declared in Europe, but the war in the Pacific continues. Japan is proving to be a difficult enemy to defeat as battles continue and result in massive casualties. To defeat Japan, President Truman believes the U.S. Army will need the help of the U.S.S.R. Last week on July 17, Truman traveled to Potsdam, Germany, to attend the Potsdam Conference with Winston Churchill and Joseph Stalin. The conference resulted in a pact with Joseph Stalin that guaranteed his assistance on the Japanese front. Also at this conference, an international council was proposed to conduct war-crime trials, named the Nuremberg Trials, against high-ranking Nazi officials.

"FAT MAN" AND "LITTLE BOY": THE ATOMIC BOMBS DROPPED ON JAPAN

August 7, 1945—Yesterday, Truman authorized the use of the atomic bomb on Hiroshima, Japan. The bomb was dropped at 9:15 a.m. Tokyo time. The bombing came after America gave Japan an opportunity to surrender earlier this week. However, Japan gave no sign of surrender. It is estimated that the bombing resulted in 130,000 casualties and 175,000 Japanese losing their homes. The Soviets are also now invading Manchuria and Korea.

***

August 10, 1945—After Sunday's bombings, Japan has still refused to surrender. Yesterday, President Truman authorized the second atomic bomb to be dropped on Nagasaki, Japan. The devastation at Nagasaki was just as horrendous: it appears that one-third of the entire city was destroyed and 70,000 Japanese were killed or injured.

***

September 2, 1945—Today, aboard the USS *Missouri*, Japan signed the terms of surrender, officially ending the Second World War. This comes after their verbal surrender on August 15, after several days of behind-the-scenes negotiations and a failed coup d'etat by Emperor Hirohito and the Japanese.

ASSASSINATION ATTEMPT

November 1, 1950—Two men attempted to force their way past guards to enter Blair House with the intention of assassinating President Truman. Shots were fired when the two men drew their guns, resulting in the death of one of the gunmen and the death of a secret service agent. The remaining gunman is now imprisoned. Truman has been staying in Blair House during the White House renovations, and security has been relatively relaxed. The extent of security comprises three secret service men guarding the main entrance to the house and a small guard shack on the road front. Security is likely to now be increased.

STATE OF THE UNION

48 STATES

POPULATION IN 1945
143,501,630

$1 WORTH IN 1945
NOW WORTH
$12.99

$1 WORTH IN 1953
NOW WORTH
$8.77

UNITED STATES DEBT

Jan. 1 1945	*$264,052,143,292*
Jan. 1 1953	*$268,665,330,374*

233

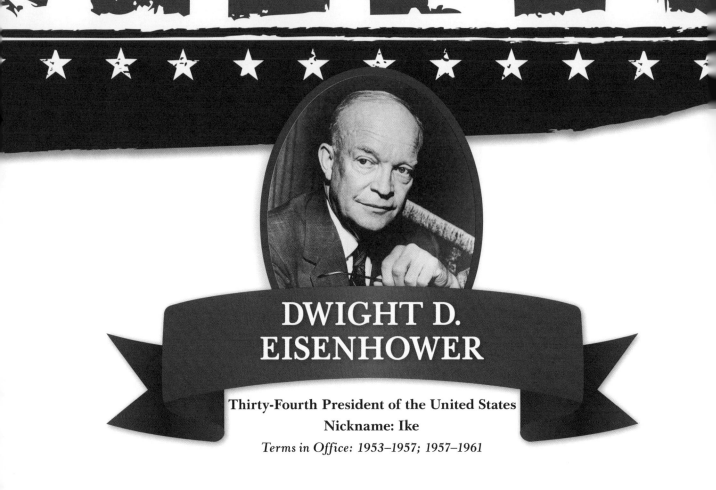

DWIGHT D. EISENHOWER

Thirty-Fourth President of the United States
Nickname: Ike
Terms in Office: 1953–1957; 1957–1961

The Bottom Line

Dwight D. Eisenhower ended American involvement in the Korean War during his first term and worked to keep relations with Russia as stable as possible during the Cold War. In his second term, he nearly balanced the national budget by reducing military spending but was cautious not to let Russia take the lead in the arms race.

FAST STATS

★ Born October 14, 1890, in Denison, Texas
★ Parents: David Jacob and Ida Elizabeth Stover Eisenhower
★ Died March 28, 1969, in Washington, D.C.; age 78
★ Age upon Start of First Term: 62; Age upon Conclusion of First Term: 66
★ Age upon Start of Second Term: 66; Age upon Conclusion of Second Term: 70
★ Religious Affiliation: Presbyterian
★ Political Party: Republican
★ Height: 5 feet 10.5 inches
★ Vice President: Richard Nixon

What Was He Thinking?

Dwight D. Eisenhower believed in living within one's means. He believed that the current generation should live modestly and wisely so that future generations could enjoy better lives without the burden of a large debt. Eisenhower also warned against the danger of a growing military, but ultimately believed that a strong military could be used to bring peace throughout the world.

Why Should I Care?

Throughout his presidency, Eisenhower reduced military spending, realizing the virtues of a

BTW: When he was in high school and college, Ike was "one of the most promising backs in eastern football."

limited military. Today America's defense spending currently stands at approximately $700 billion, over half of the world's military spending. Eisenhower also warned against government domination of the science and technological fields, but today the government funds 90 percent of all science and technological research in the country.

> [W]e—you and I, and our government—must avoid the impulse to live only for today, plundering for our own ease and convenience the precious resources of tomorrow. We cannot mortgage the material assets of our grandchildren without asking the loss also of their political and spiritual heritage.

Breakin' It Down
Early Life

If you said the name "Ike" in the Eisenhower household in the early 1900s, five young boys would have responded all at once—all the boys went by the nickname Ike. David Dwight Eisenhower (later changed to Dwight David) was born in a small Texas town among modest means; his parents' little house was less than adequate for their many boys. A couple of years later his family moved to Abilene, Kansas, where he grew up. Starting at a young age, Dwight worked small jobs—including some that people considered "women's jobs," such as washing dishes—to help support his large family. In school, young Ike was an above-average student who loved to play sports, especially football and baseball. Later, he received a football scholarship to the U.S. Military Academy at West Point. Ike graduated from West Point in 1915 in the middle of his class academically and in the bottom of his class in discipline.

Courtesy Dwight D. Eisenhower Library

> Because of his time spent in a kitchen making money for his family, Dwight became a pretty good cook—a skill he used during his presidency.

First Couple

In 1916, Dwight Eisenhower married Marie "Mamie" Doud. They were married when she was only nineteen and he was twenty-one. Together they had two children, but only their second son lived to adulthood. Because of Dwight's commitment to the military, the family moved constantly, relocating twenty-seven times in thirty-seven years. When Eisenhower became the Supreme Commander of the Allied Forces, he was only able to see his wife for a total of twelve days over the three-year course of the war. Mamie remained active during this time, volunteering for the USO and the Red Cross. In 1966, the couple celebrated their fiftieth anniversary—the first "first couple" to do so since John Quincy and Louisa Catherine Adams.

MARIE EISENHOWER

BTW: In college, Eisenhower was rebellious, often playing poker and smoking on occasion. This caused him to receive multiple demerits from his strict military school.

BTW: Eisenhower once visited France and wrote a guidebook on all the major battle sites of World War I.

After Eisenhower graduated from the U.S. Academy at West Point, he entered the fight in World War I. Eisenhower was commissioned to supervise the training of the Tank Corps in Fort Meade, Maryland. As part of his job, he helped transport the American tank fleet from Maryland to San Francisco, but because of the terrible road conditions, the trip took him sixty-one days. During this time he also served as a training instructor at Fort Oglethorpe, Georgia.

After the conclusion of World War I, Eisenhower enrolled in the Army Command and General Staff School, graduating first in his class of 245. In 1929, Eisenhower became the executive officer to Assistant Secretary of War George Mosley.

At the time of the Pearl Harbor attack and the U.S. entry into World War II, he had become Colonel Eisenhower and the newly appointed chief of staff for the U.S. Third Army. Secretary of Defense George C. Marshall employed Eisenhower to devise a strategy for the U.S. Army in the war. Since it was difficult for the United States to wage an effective fight on both the European and Pacific fronts simultaneously, Eisenhower proposed a defensive strategy on the Pacific front until the war in Europe was won. During the course of the war, Eisenhower was named Supreme Commander of the Allied Forces, controlling the whole of the Allied forces. Eisenhower recommended the "broad front" strategy, which prohibited any individual nation from the Allied forces from taking credit for victories at the expense of any other Allied country. He planned the invasion of Germany and German strongholds by landing in North Africa and invading through Italy. He was the chief planner at D-Day and commanded the army at the Battle of the Bulge.

At the conclusion of the war, and with the victory of the Allies, Eisenhower was received at home with a hero's welcome. During the festivities, however, Eisenhower remembered those who had lost their lives in the tragic and bloody war and was careful not to celebrate too joyfully after the death of so many millions. Two years later, Eisenhower spent two years as the Army's Chief of Staff and then retired as a five-star general—the highest ranking in the U.S. Army.

Like many of our countries leaders, Eisenhower did not stay in retirement for long. With such an incorruptible record and with his reputation as a military hero and genius (and with a presidential election upcoming), both the Democrats and the Republicans wanted Eisenhower to side with their party. Since he never expressed his political views while serving in the army, it was the guess of the American people where Eisenhower stood on issues. When push came to shove, Eisenhower broke his nonpartisan attitude and sided with the Republicans.

BTW: By the end of the Second World War, 45,000,000 civilians had died worldwide and 15,000,000 died in battle including 416, 800 U.S. military deaths, 383,600 Great Britain military deaths, and 5,533,000 German military deaths.

BTW: Major battles during the Second World War include the Battle of France, the Battle of Stalingrad, Battle of Midway, Battle of Britain, and the Battle of the Bulge.

Jonas Salk announces the development of a polio vaccine, 1953

The U.S. and North Korea sign an armistice ending the Korean War, 1953

The District of Columbia is desegregated, 1953

The Supreme Court outlaws segregation in public schools in Brown v. BOE, 1954

Henri Matisse dies, 1954

The U.S. Air Force Academy is created, 1954

Rosa Parks refuses to give up her seat on a bus in Montgomery, Alabama, 1955

Disneyland opens in California, 1955

"Under God" is added to the Pledge of Allegiance, 1955

Elvis Presley first appears on *The Ed Sullivan Show*, 1956

"In God We Trust" becomes the official American national motto, 1956

First Term in Office

| 1952 | 1953 | 1954 | 1955 | 1956 |

ELECTION RESULTS!

America was war-weary. As a five-star general, this could have been a problem for Eisenhower during the presidential campaign of 1952, but his charisma and peaceful plan for the United States overcame any hesitancies the American people had in electing a former military general. As the Korean War continued, Eisenhower campaigned to end America's involvement in Korea in addition to cutting military costs to balance the federal budget. With his hopeful promises and his endearing Texas accent, Eisenhower won in a landslide.

During this presidential election, both candidates used television commercials to appeal to voters on a whole new "homey" level. Campaign issues included inflation, the abnormally high cost of living (housing, food, energy, and so on) for Americans, and ending the Korean War. "I Like Ike!" was a common slogan for his campaign.

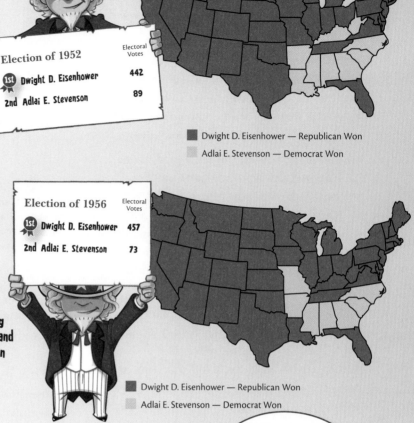

Election of 1952

		Electoral Votes
1st	Dwight D. Eisenhower	442
2nd	Adlai E. Stevenson	89

■ Dwight D. Eisenhower — Republican Won
■ Adlai E. Stevenson — Democrat Won

Election of 1956

		Electoral Votes
1st	Dwight D. Eisenhower	457
2nd	Adlai E. Stevenson	73

■ Dwight D. Eisenhower — Republican Won
■ Adlai E. Stevenson — Democrat Won

> Eisenhower didn't really want to run for the office of the presidency, but when his country called, he answered.

Presidency

The eight years of the Eisenhower administration are known as the Golden Age, an era of prosperity. On the international scale, Eisenhower achieved two major successes: ending the Korean War and controlling the U.S.S.R. during the Cold War. The space race with Russia also began during this time, causing American patriotism and support of her space programs to skyrocket. On the national scale, Eisenhower initiated America's highway system, expanded Social Security for more retired and older Americans, and approved goverment construction of low-income housing. Jobs were plentiful, racial equality in the army was promoted, and Americans were together and harmonious.

Alaska and Hawaii become states, 1959

The Guggenheim Museum opens in New York City, 1958

The development of NASA takes place, 1958

Fidel Castro takes over Cuba, 1959

Cuba confiscates $770 million worth of American property, 1960

East Germany begins construction of the Berlin Wall, 1961

The U.S.S.R. launches Sputnik; the space race begins, 1957

The U.S. launches *Explorer I* into orbit, 1958

Frank Lloyd Wright dies, 1959

Second Term in Office

| 1957 | 1958 | 1959 | 1960 | 1961 |

1. **Presidential Libraries Act:** This act, passed in 1955, specified that the construction for presidential libraries—libraries dedicated to information on the lives of past presidents—are to be funded by private donors but will be monitored and managed at federal expense after their opening.

2. **Federal Aid Highway Act:** This act, passed in 1956, standardized American interstates and ordered the construction of over forty thousand miles of four- and eight-lane highways all across America. Such an immense undertaking cost $25 billion dollars over the course of thirteen years and remains the largest public works project in American history.

3. **Civil Rights Act of 1957:** This act, passed on September 9, 1957, was the first civil rights act passed by Congress since the end of Reconstruction after the Civil War. This act helped protect African-Americans' right to vote and encouraged them to do so. It further banned discriminatory practices in public affairs.

4. **National Defense Education Act of 1958:** This act gave college scholarships to students interested in mathematics and sciences to increase the number of scientists and mathematicians who could work for the nation's defenses.

★★★★★★★★★★★★★★★★★★★★★★★★★

PRESIDENTIAL Personality

★ Throughout his life, Eisenhower tried to like people and make people like him, though he wasn't always successful. Eisenhower commanded and demanded respect and was known as a man who could quietly inspire confidence. Although he had a wide and bright smile, he could also sometimes explode in anger. As an odd habit, he carried in his pocket three lucky coins: a silver dollar, a five guinea gold piece, and a French franc.

Nuclear Nervousness

Although the U.S.S.R. was controlled for the time being, the possibility and the chance of a nuclear war still remained in the minds of many Americans. As a result, while Americans were busy rebuilding their lives, Eisenhower occupied himself with strengthening America's national security. He funded secret projects for the CIA to infiltrate governments in the Middle East and Central America. He also decided what to do with the nuclear weapons and facilities the U.S. had created during World War II. In attempts to use these advanced scientific chemical plants for peaceful purposes, Eisenhower began his "Atoms for Peace" campaign, through which he worked to educate the public on the positive uses of atomic energy. While keeping up America's defenses against a possible Soviet attack, Eisenhower managed to almost balance the national budget and reduce inflation to below 1 percent.

Post-Presidency

By the end of his presidency, Eisenhower had served his country either militarily or politically for forty-six years. Needless to say, retirement was well deserved. Eisenhower and his wife purchased a home near Gettysburg, Pennsylvania, the only actual permanent residence they had ever owned because of their constant travels with the military. Although Eisenhower remained in retirement, John F. Kennedy appointed him Army General, which was more of an honorary job than one requiring action. For the remainder of his

No treaty or international agreement can contravene the Constitution.

life, Eisenhower dedicated himself to golfing and writing. He published a two-volume memoir of his experiences in the White House: *Mandate for Change*, 1953–1956 and *Waging Peace*, 1956–1961. He also wrote *At Ease: Stories I Tell to Friends*, published in 1968.

What Has He Done for Me Lately?

Almost everyone has driven on a highway, and many people drive on one every day. Well, President Eisenhower secured congressional approval for his Federal Aid Highway Act, which added tens of thousands of miles of highways all across the United States. Before this act, one-fourth of all American roads were unfit for car or truck travel, and it could take up to two months to drive across the country. Today, without stopping, it takes approximately two days to drive from California to New York. Eisenhower and Congress not only made travel more expedient, they made American roadways a lot safer.

PLATFORM SPEECH

[We need] to maintain balance in and among national programs, balance between the private and the public economy, balance between the cost and hoped for advantages, balance between the clearly necessary and the comfortably desirable, balance between our essential requirements as a nation and the duties imposed by the nation upon the individual, balance between actions of the moment and the national welfare of the future.

Eisenhower spoke these words in his farewell address to the nation in 1961. He was always cautious to address how his decisions would impact the future of the country, not just the present. He urged Americans to do the same: balance their long-term actions with their short-term actions to prevent drastic and harmful change.

DWIGHT D. EISENHOWER

BTW: An avid but average golfer, Eisenhower admitted during his retirement that one of his happiest moments came when he shot a hole in one in February 1968.

Written by Juliette Turner

END OF THE MCCARTHY HEARINGS

December 2, 1954—Today Congress passed a motion in a 67 to 22 vote in the Senate to officially censure Senator Joseph McCarthy for his notorious McCarthy hearings. Early in his term, Eisenhower personally signed several laws passed by Congress suspending the fifth amendment to the Constitution during investigations regarding American security.

But after thousands of federal employees were fired over accusations of ties with the Soviet Union, Eisenhower pushed for congressional censure of Senator McCarthy.

PILOT FRANCIS GARY POWERS IS CAPTURED!

May 1, 1960—American pilot Francis Gary Powers has been taken captive by the Soviet Union after his plane was shot down over their land. Many are speculating that Powers is a part of the CIA program conducting secret surveillance of Soviet nuclear facilities. America has reportedly been using advanced aircraft technology to spy on Russia from the air. These High Altitude Surveillance Aircrafts, also known as U-2 aircrafts, were deployed over Russia to capture images of their nuclear production, and because of the aircrafts' high cruising altitude, they have rarely been seen, let alone shot down.

NEGOTIATIONS WITH KHRUSHCHEV ARE CANCELED

May 20, 1960—After the recent U-2 incident, all negotiations between Nikita Khrushchev of the U.S.S.R. and President Eisenhower have been called off. This comes as no surprise to the public after a long and confusing string of statements released by the Eisenhower administration about what really happened in the Soviet Union on May 1.

After initially saying the U.S. plane the Soviets found was monitoring weather patterns, Eisenhower altered his story and said that the plane was spying, but that he had not authorized the mission. Shortly after that statement, however, he came forward with the full truth: he had authorized the mission earlier in his term before negotiations were set to take place.

Eisenhower admitted, "I goofed."

As a result, the citizens of communist countries still have no direct communication with the free world, and the free world has no way to monitor what is happening inside those communist countries.

STATE OF THE UNION

50 STATES

POPULATION IN 1953
161,453,000

$1 WORTH IN 1953
NOW WORTH
$8.77

$1 WORTH IN 1961
NOW WORTH
$7.81

UNITED STATES DEBT

| Jan. 1 1953 | $268,665,330,374 |
| Jan. 1 1961 | $293,585,880,665 |

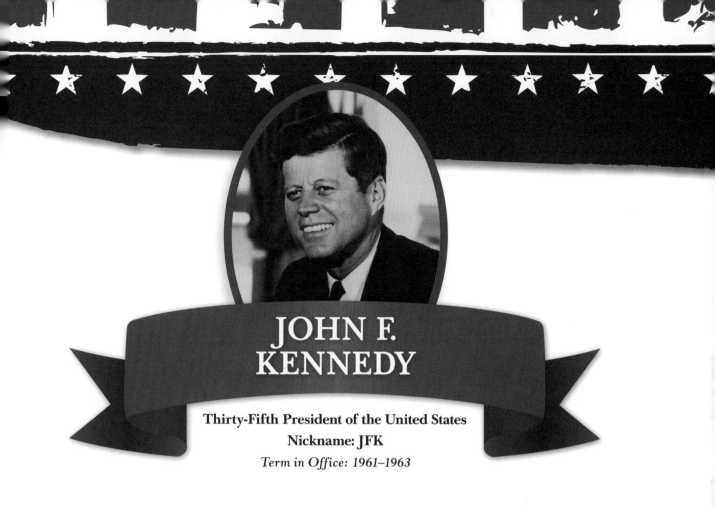

JOHN F. KENNEDY

Thirty-Fifth President of the United States

Nickname: JFK

Term in Office: 1961–1963

The Bottom Line

John F. Kennedy served three years in the office of the presidency before he was assassinated in 1963—the fourth president to be assassinated and the eighth president to die while in office. In office, Kennedy championed the civil rights movement in the south, supported NASA during the space race, effectively protected the United States during the Cuban Missile Crisis, and negotiated the first nuclear test ban treaty with the Soviet Union.

FAST STATS

★ Born May 29, 1917, in Brookline, Massachusetts
★ Parents: Joseph Patrick and Rose Elizabeth Fitzgerald Kennedy
★ Died November 22, 1963, in Dallas, Texas; age 46
★ Age upon Start of Term: 43; Age upon Assassination: 46
★ Religious Affiliation: Roman Catholic
★ Political Party: Democrat
★ Height: 6 feet
★ Vice President: Lyndon B. Johnson

What Was He Thinking?

Kennedy was a strong supporter of desegregation and racial equality. Economically, Kennedy believed in lowering taxes to promote economic growth. A self-proclaimed idealist, Kennedy wanted the best for his country, whether through securing the nation's safety, winning the race to the moon, increasing Social Security payments, or reforming education.

Why Should I Care?

One of the most dangerous and strenuous episodes of the Cold War occurred during Kennedy's presidency: the Cuban Missile Crisis. It was evident during this crisis that one small misstep could result in an all-out nuclear war. Given the missiles' immense power for destruction, such a catastrophe would have had long-lasting effects on the United States and probably the entire world. However, Kennedy revealed the strength of the United States when he refused to back down to the Soviet threat, remaining composed and collected throughout the crisis. As a result, the Soviets backed down and nuclear missiles were removed from Cuba. Although America did negotiate with the U.S.S.R. and agree to remove U.S. missiles from Italy and Turkey in exchange, America gained her first semivictory in the "war of laboratories."

Breakin' It Down
Early Life

John Fitzgerald Kennedy—known to his friends and family as Jack—was the first president to be born in the twentieth century. He was the second of nine children, with five brothers and three sisters.

Jack attended many different schools growing up, but was always a good student. In high school, though, he became rebellious while attending the Choate School in Wallingford, Connecticut, with his oldest brother, Joe Jr. Not wanting to live in Joe's shadow, he acted out, one time exploding a toilet seat with a powerful firecracker. While at Choate, Kennedy had several health problems, and in 1934, he was hospitalized and diagnosed with colitis.

John first attended college at the London School of Economics before transferring to Princeton and then to Harvard University, where he stayed for the remainder of his

ILL HEALTH

JFK was always sick. As a young boy, Kennedy was constantly sick with colitis and had serious back problems. He was also diagnosed with Addison's disease. From 1955 to 1957, he was hospitalized nine different times. His entire life, Kennedy's back gave him constant discomfort despite the many procaine injections, codeine, ethyl chloride spray, prednisone, exercise regimes, and hot compresses.

BTW: While he was president, Kennedy would sometimes wear a metal back brace, and once he was even lowered from an airplane in a wheelchair.

[T]hose who foolishly sought power by riding the back of the tiger ended up inside.

BTW: When he graduated from Choate High School in June 1935, he was voted the "most likely to succeed."

The Soviet spaceship *Vostok II* enters Earth's orbit, 1961

Alan Shepard becomes the first American to enter space, 1961

African-American James Meredith enrolls at the University of Mississippi, sparking violent race riots, 1961

The Bay of Pigs invasion is ordered, 1961

Nelson Mandela is jailed in South Africa, 1962

The Cuban Missile Crisis takes place, 1962

John Glenn becomes the first American to orbit the Earth, 1962

The twenty-fourth amendment is passed by Congress, ending the poll tax, 1962

Kennedy is assassinated and Lyndon B. Johnson becomes president, November 22, 1963

Martin Luther King Jr. delivers his "I have a dream" speech, 1963

The U.S. formally enters the Vietnam War, after the Gulf of Tonkin Resolution 1964

Term in Office

1960   1961   1962   1963   1964   1965

JACQUELINE KENNEDY

schooling. He majored in political science and graduated cum laude in 1940.

When John graduated from college, he attempted to volunteer for the army but was denied because of his chronic back pain. Refusing to take no as the final answer, John practiced strengthening exercises for his back and applied for the navy instead, where he was accepted a few months later. He served in the navy for four years, from 1941 to 1945, in the Pacific stage of World War II. He received a Purple Heart and a Marine Corps Medal for his heroism in the war.

First Couple

In 1953, John married Jacqueline Lee Bouvier. Together they had two children. During their courtship, Jacqueline—known as Jackie—worked as a photographer for the *Washington Times-Herald* newspaper. When Kennedy won the presidency, America viewed Jacqueline and John as the ideal American couple: young, beautiful and handsome, happy, and accompanied by two small children. Jacqueline, always into fashion, transformed the White House into a place of celebration, parties, and grandiosity, causing Americans to endearingly name the house "Camelot."

> I am not the Catholic candidate for the president. I am the Democratic Party's candidate for president, who happens also to be a Catholic.

Previous Political Career

- 1946: Elected to Congress as U.S. Representative from Massachusetts, holding the position until 1953.
- 1953: Elected to the U.S. Senate, serving until 1960.

ELECTION RESULTS!

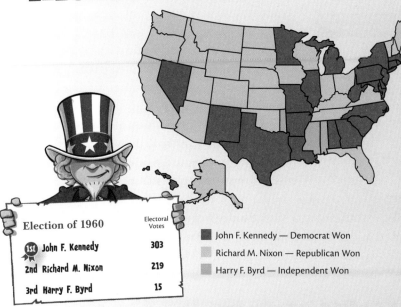

Election of 1960	Electoral Votes
1st John F. Kennedy	303
2nd Richard M. Nixon	219
3rd Harry F. Byrd	15

■ John F. Kennedy — Democrat Won
■ Richard M. Nixon — Republican Won
■ Harry F. Byrd — Independent Won

Kennedy was Roman Catholic, which was controversial at the time. Jacqueline Kennedy once commented, though, "After all, he's such a poor Catholic." No Roman Catholic had ever held the office of the presidency, and the only other Roman Catholic to run in a presidential race, Alfred Smith, had lost badly. So how did Kennedy win? Television. Television was Kennedy's best friend, especially when he debated the clammy and nervous Richard Nixon in the first-ever televised presidential debate. In a series of four debates, Nixon refused to wear makeup, making him appear pale and sweaty under the studio lights next to the young and cool John Kennedy. The debates marked a turning point in the campaign, and Kennedy slowly narrowed the large margin by which Nixon had been leading in the polls.

CONGRESSIONAL CORNER

★★★★★★★★★★★★★★★★★★★★★★★

1. **Foreign Assistance Act of 1961:** This act restructured America's plan for foreign assistance programs, separating military and nonmilitary aid programs. The act also established the United States Agency for International Development.

2. **Peace Corps Act of 1961:** This act established the United States Peace Corps, a volunteer organization intended to help Americans understand cultures of foreign countries, help foreign countries understand American culture, and help provide assistance to foreign countries.

3. **Arms Control and Disarmament Act of 1961:** This act was established to greatly reduce the amount of advance weaponry (such as nuclear missiles, bombs) in the world in an attempt to prevent nuclear war.

4. **Community Health Services and Facilities Act of 1961:** This act gave federal money to states to expand and improve medical facilities, such as nursing home and outpatient facilities.

5. **Equal Pay Act of 1963:** This act outlawed any wage discrimination based on gender.

★★★★★★★★★★★★★★★★★★★★★★★

> *The world is very different now ... yet the same revolutionary beliefs for which our forebears fought are still at issue around the globe—the belief that the rights of man come not from the generosity of the state, but from the hand of God.*

THOUGHTS ON THE CONSTITUTION

> *The Constitution makes us not rivals for power but partners for progress.*

- 1959: Won reelection for his seat in the Senate by the largest margin in Massachusetts history. He remained in the Senate for two more years before moving to the office of the presidency.

Presidency

Although Theodore Roosevelt remains the youngest president to assume the presidency (after McKinley's death in office), Kennedy holds the title of the youngest man to be elected to the presidency. During his time as president, Kennedy championed his "New Frontier Program," which included progressive social programs as well as plans to improve relations with foreign countries.

Foreign Affairs

On the international scene, Kennedy traveled overseas and gave successful speeches in France, West Germany, Ireland, and Mexico. Kennedy also worked to expand trade with Latin America and Europe. To reduce tension in the Cold War, the most significant international issue of the time, Kennedy negotiated the Nuclear Test Ban Treaty. The United States also agreed to open small amounts of trade between America and the Soviet Union to allow wheat into Russia, which was suffering from severe famine. On a less successful note, a military standoff nearly erupted in all-out war when Russia began organizing nuclear missiles along the coast of Cuba, aimed at the United States. Then Kennedy sent more Americans to Vietnam to help prevent communist expansion in the region, leading to an influx of American involvement in the Southeast Asian stage once again.

BTW: Kennedy's book *Profiles of Courage*, which contained minibiographies of eight U.S. senators who risked their political reputations to stand up for what they believed, won a Pulitzer Prize.

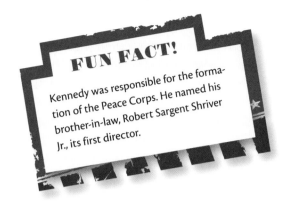

Civil Reforms and the Advance into Space

A staunch opponent of segregation, Kennedy worked hard to combat racism and promote the civil rights movement in America. Kennedy called the current situation for African-Americans a "moral crisis" and used federal troops to force several southern states to comply with desegregation measures and to protect African-Americans' endeavors for equal rights. He also appointed the first African-American to serve on a U.S. district court.

Additionally, Kennedy expanded NASA, the space institution founded by Eisenhower, by appropriating one billion dollars for space research. In an effort to win the space race, Kennedy urged NASA to have a man on the moon by 1970. As part of his "New Frontier Program," he worked to advance programs for developing natural resources, revising insufficient farming methods and increasing appropriation for education.

Some of Kennedy's plans faced opposition in Congress, including his tax cut proposals, a medical plan to assist senior citizens, his civil rights legislation, and his proposal to form a Department of Urban Affairs.

Assassination

It was almost election season again, and that meant it was time for the president to begin campaigning for reelection. In November 1963, Kennedy and his vice president, Lyndon B. Johnson, traveled to Dallas, Texas, for fund-raising and support building among the southern Democrats whose support had been affected by Kennedy's strong antisegregation beliefs. While Kennedy rode with his procession through downtown Dallas, he ordered his driver to remove the bulletproof dome from the car so they could enjoy the nice day. Nellie Connally and her husband, Texas governor John Connally, rode in the same car with the Kennedys. She turned to them and said, "You can't say that Dallas isn't friendly to you today." Right after she uttered those words, gunshots fired across the Dallas street. Two bullets hit Kennedy in the

BTW: Martin Luther King Jr. once commented on Kennedy's 1963 address on civil rights, noting, "[The speech was the] most eloquent, passionate, and unequivocal plea for civil rights ... ever made by any president."

THE KENNEDY
Curse

The Kennedy family has experienced more than their fair share of tragic death. Because of this, many have come to believe in the "Kennedy Curse." The curse begins with the death of President John F. Kennedy's brother, Joseph P. Kennedy Jr., who died during World War II. Most notably, John F. Kennedy was assassinated in Dallas, Texas, in 1963. In 1968, his brother Robert was also assassinated, during his presidential campaign in California. In July 1969, Kennedy's brother Ted Kennedy was involved in a car accident that killed his passenger. Most recently, in 1999, John F. Kennedy Jr., the son of President Kennedy, died in a plane crash over the Atlantic Ocean, also killing the junior Kennedy's wife and sister-in-law.

head, killing him almost immediately. He was rushed to Dallas's Parkland Hospital, but he was declared dead within the hour. The first lady and the vice president were rushed aboard Air Force One and taken back to Washington, D.C. Aboard the plane, Johnson was sworn into office. Kennedy's funeral was attended by representatives from ninety-two countries and nearly one million people.

What Has He Done for Me Lately?

Kennedy was intent on reversing and remedying the unfair treatment of African-Americans in the south. He not only deployed federal troops to protect the rights of African-Americans in several southern states, but he also devised a civil rights act that outlawed discrimination on the grounds of race, nationality, or gender for all Americans. Although this legislation was not passed before his assassination in 1963, it was later signed by Lyndon B. Johnson, his successor, largely due to Kennedy's efforts during his presidency.

FUN FACT!

President John F. Kennedy was a military hero. While monitoring the ocean for Japanese ships during World War II, Kennedy's boat, the PT–109, was rammed by a Japanese destroyer. Two of his crewmates were killed immediately and a third was badly burned. Kennedy decided with another crewman to swim to find land and help. However, Kennedy decided to take the injured man with them and he did so by dragging the man behind him by using his teeth to pull on the cord from the man's life preserver. Thankfully, the three men found land, and Kennedy inscribed a message on a coconut shell to relay to the natives to find help.

PLATFORM SPEECH

And so my fellow Americans: ask not what your country can do for you—ask what you can do for your country. My fellow citizens of the world: ask not what America will do for you, but what together we can do for the freedom of man.

In arguably his most famous statement, Kennedy urged the American people to sacrifice for their country for the betterment of society. Likewise, he encouraged the world to work together for the preservation of freedom and liberty.

JOHN F. KENNEDY

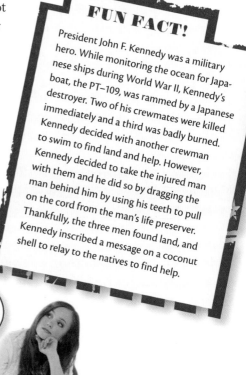

Written by Juliette Turner

BAY OF PIGS INVASION A FAILURE

April 19, 1961—Members of Brigade 2506, approximately 1,200 Cuban exiles sent into Cuba to overthrow Fidel Castro, were captured by the communist Cuban government officials today, and over one hundred Cuban exiles were killed. U.S. military leaders are calling it one of America's worst military disasters.

The invasion was planned by the CIA to make it look like an internal revolution to overthrow Castro, hoping anti-Castro rebels would unite in the region and successfully overthrow the dictator. No such movement occurred, and the invasion ended in failure.

For this attempt to overthrow the communist regime, the CIA trained over a thousand of the Cubans who had fled or were exiled from Cuba to America to prepare them to infiltrate Cuba and take the government from the communists. The results are reportedly due in part to Kennedy's failure to approve U.S. air support for the rebels. Kennedy refrained from doing so because he feared such an action would be considered an act of war, sparking a full-out war with Russia.

THE CUBAN MISSILE CRISIS

October 28, 1962—Soviet Premier Nikita Khrushchev has agreed to remove Soviet nuclear missiles from Cuba in exchange for the U.S. removing missiles from Turkey. This comes as a great relief to Americans, who for six days have lived in fear of a nuclear war outbreak.

The Kennedy administration had known of the missiles since October 14, when a U-2 plane dispatched by President Kennedy himself verified the presence of Soviet nuclear missiles on the Cuban island. Three days later another U-2 surveillance plane located intermediate range nuclear missiles on the island. On the 22nd, President Kennedy alerted the nation of the presence of the Soviet nuclear missiles in Cuba and on the 23rd, the U.S. Navy formed a quarantine line in an 800-mile radius around Cuba, but the quarantine line was moved to a 500-mile radius later that day.

Yesterday, Nikita Khrushchev "blinked" and agreed to remove the missiles, proposing an exchange: Russia will remove the missiles from Cuba if the U.S. removes her missiles from Turkey. Additionally, Khrushchev will allow the U.S. access to the missile sites in Cuba.

DID OSWALD ACT ALONE?

November 25, 1963—Lee Harvey Oswald, the man who killed President Kennedy, is now dead. He was shot and killed yesterday by Jack Ruby, for unknown reasons. Since President Kennedy's assassination in Dallas, Texas, last Friday, America has been reeling. The question for many: Did the gunman act alone? After the shots were fired across Dealey Plaza, Oswald was seen running from a nearby building and was later arrested inside a movie theater. The most officials knew of Oswald at that time was that he was a communist sympathizer. With Oswald's death, America might never learn his true motives or if he acted with an accomplice. Conspiracies are sure to run rampant.

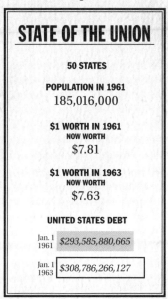

STATE OF THE UNION

50 STATES

POPULATION IN 1961
185,016,000

$1 WORTH IN 1961
NOW WORTH
$7.81

$1 WORTH IN 1963
NOW WORTH
$7.63

UNITED STATES DEBT

| Jan. 1 1961 | $293,585,880,665 |
| Jan. 1 1963 | $308,786,266,127 |

LYNDON B. JOHNSON

Thirty-Sixth President of the United States
Nickname: LBJ
Terms in Office: 1963–1965; 1965–1969

The Bottom Line

After John F. Kennedy's assassination, Johnson assumed the presidency and continued Kennedy's efforts to pass the nation's most significant civil rights bill since the time of Abraham Lincoln. During his only elected term, from 1965 to 1969, Johnson implemented his "Great Society" program and worked to combat rising tensions in Vietnam and an increase in violent race riots across the nation.

FAST STATS

★ Born August 27, 1908, in Johnson City, Texas
★ Parents: Samuel Ealy and Rebekah Baines Johnson
★ Died January 22, 1973, in Stonewall, Texas; age 64
★ Age upon Start of First Term: 55; Age upon Conclusion of First Term: 57
★ Age upon Start of Second Term: 57; Age upon Conclusion of Second Term: 61
★ Religious Affiliation: Disciples of Christ
★ Political Party: Democrat
★ Height: 6 feet 3 inches
★ Vice President: Hubert H. Humphrey

What Was He Thinking?

Johnson believed it was possible to create the greatest American society known to world history through use of government reform. He advocated escalating social welfare reforms, increasing government spending on the arts and humanities, and expanding government control over the private lives of American citizens. Johnson was also an avid supporter of racial equality.

Why Should I Care?

Johnson's good reputation among congressmen and senators helped increase the support of the

"I want to be the president who helped to end hatred among his fellow men and who promoted love among the people of all races and all regions and all parties."

LBJ Library photo by Yoichi Okamoto

"In this photo, President Johnson is "singing" with Yuki as the U.S. Ambassador to Great Britain, David K. E. Bruce, watches. Johnson owned many dogs while he was president and could often be seen walking or playing with them on the White House lawn."

Civil Rights Act. The act outlawed segregation in nearly all areas of life and greatly alleviated inequality for African-Americans, women, and all minorities, although it would still take decades for racial prejudices to subside in many southern states.

BTW: Lyndon grew up in a very small town—a very small town. His high school graduating class had six students!

Breakin' It Down
Early Life

Lyndon Baines Johnson was born on a small Texas farm to modest means. The eldest of five children, Lyndon had three sisters and a brother, and as a young child, he showed great potential in school. Lyndon's political aspirations began in high school, as was evident through his active involvement in his high school's debate program. As a teen, Lyndon worked as a shoeshiner and a cotton picker to help provide for his big family.

In the late 1920s, Lyndon enrolled in the Southwest Texas State Teachers College in San Marcos, Texas. While still a student himself, he began teaching in Cotulla, Texas. As a border town, Cotulla's schools were attended mostly by Mexican-American students from impoverished backgrounds. Seeing his students' many desperate needs, Lyndon helped establish free lunches for them. He also demanded all his students speak English to help them integrate better into American society. In 1930, he graduated from college and transferred to a teaching position at a Houston high school.

FUN FACT!

At age fifteen, Lyndon and a few of his friends took a long trip to California, where Lyndon was hired for a number of odd jobs, including as a dishwasher, grape picker, and auto mechanic.

First Couple

In 1935, Lyndon B. Johnson married Claudia Alta "Lady Bird" Taylor, and together they had two children. When her husband ran for president, Lady Bird delivered her own political speeches on subjects about which she felt impassioned, the first wife of a presidential candidate to do so. After becoming first lady, Lady Bird introduced "Lady Bird's Bill," asking for federal funding to plant trees and wildflowers along America's highway system. Lady Bird remains the longest-living presidential spouse, surviving to the age of ninety-five.

CLAUDIA JOHNSON

[The Great Society] is a place where men are more concerned with the quality of their goals than the quantity of their goods.

Previous Political Career

- 1931: Appointed secretary for U.S. House Representative Richard M. Kleberg.
- 1935: Became Texas director of Franklin D. Roosevelt's newly created National Youth Administration.
- 1937: Elected to U.S. House of Representatives. He held this position until 1949.
- 1940: Ran for a seat in the U.S. Senate, but lost.
- 1941: Deployed to Australia and New Guinea as a volunteer soldier in World War II. He received a silver star in the Pacific and always remained loyal to the navy, serving on the Committee of Naval Affairs.
- 1948: Elected to U.S. Senate.
- 1951: Nominated the majority whip in the Senate.
- 1955: Became the youngest Senate majority leader at the age of forty-six. He served as chairman of the Senate committee responsible for forming NASA.
- 1960: Elected vice president under John F. Kennedy.

LIBERTY Language

Majority Whip: A member of a political party who serves in the U.S. House of Representatives or the U.S. Senate and is elected by fellow members of his party to ensure party discipline and encourage fellow party members to vote certain ways on legislation.

Presidency

Always wanting to be in charge and running things, Vice President Johnson made sure he stayed well informed on the issues facing the Kennedy administration and was consulted before any decisions were made. On the day of Kennedy's assassination, Johnson and his wife were just two cars behind the Kennedys when the gunshots were

The twenty-fourth amendment to the Constitution is ratified by the states, 1964 •••

The Warren Commission Report concludes Lee Harvey Oswald acted alone, 1964 •••

Fifteen thousand U.S. military advisors reside in South Vietnam, 1963 •••

Nelson Mandela receives a life imprisonment sentence, 1964

Kenya becomes independent from Great Britain, 1963

The Gulf of Tonkin incident takes place, 1964

First Term in Office

| 1960 | 1961 | 1962 | 1963 | 1964 |

ELECTION RESULTS!

The major campaign issue of the year notably surrounded race relations and Johnson's Civil Rights Act. The Solid South had always belonged to the Democrat Party, but after Johnson's civil rights reform, most of the south went to Barry Goldwater. Regardless, Johnson won the election in one of the largest presidential landslides in history.

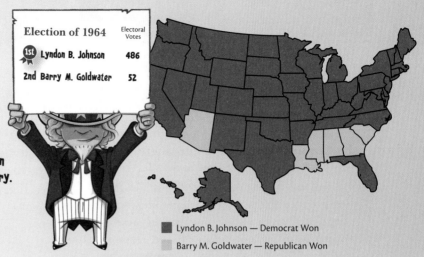

Election of 1964	Electoral Votes
1st Lyndon B. Johnson	486
2nd Barry M. Goldwater	52

■ Lyndon B. Johnson — Democrat Won

□ Barry M. Goldwater — Republican Won

fired. Just ninety minutes after Kennedy was declared dead, Johnson was sworn in as the thirty-sixth president of the United States—the nation's eighth "accidental president."

Johnson understood how important it was to reassure the nation after the assassination of their iconic president. As his first act as president, Johnson commissioned a committee to investigate Kennedy's assassination—the Warren Commission, led by Supreme Court Chief Justice Earl Warren.

We have the power to shape the civilization that we want. But we need your will, your labor, your hearts, if we are to build that kind of society.

Civil Rights Act

Johnson did his best to continue his predecessor's legacy by pushing for the completion of many of Kennedy's unfinished tasks. Most notably was Kennedy's civil rights legislation. Because Kennedy was viewed as a martyr and a man who died for his country,

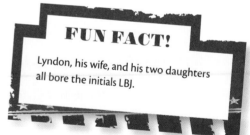

FUN FACT!

Lyndon, his wife, and his two daughters all bore the initials LBJ.

Martin Luther King Jr. and 2,600 protesters are arrested in Selma, Alabama, 1965

The first U.S. ground combat forces arrive in Vietnam, 1965

Tereshkova of the Soviet Union becomes the first woman in space, 1965

The U.S. Supreme Court establishes Miranda Rights in *Miranda v. Arizona*, 1966

Thurgood Marshall becomes the first African-American Supreme Court chief justice, 1967

Three Apollo astronauts are killed during a simulated launch, 1967

The twenty-fifth amendment to the Constitution is ratified by the states, 1967

Martin Luther King Jr. is assassinated, 1968

The Tet Offensive in Vietnam takes place, 1968

North Korea seizes the U.S. ship *Pueblo*, 1968

Peace negotiations begin between the United States and Vietnam in Paris, France, 1968

Second Term in Office

| 1965 | 1966 | 1967 | 1968 | 1969 |

CONGRESSIONAL CORNER

★★★★★★★★★★★★★★★★★★★★★★★★★

1. **Civil Rights Act:** Passed in 1964, this act originated with John F. Kennedy and outlawed all forms of racial, religious, or ethnic discrimination in any area of American life, including education, employment, housing, travel, lodging, restaurants, and transportation. In the House, 61% of Democrats and 80% of Republicans coted for the bill.

2. **Economic Opportunity Act:** Signed in 1964, this act established local Community Action Agencies, which sought to eliminate poverty, expand education opportunities, increase support for the poor and unemployed, and improve health care for the elderly.

3. **Elementary and Secondary Education Act:** This act was passed in 1965 and sent funds to state and local governments hoping to equalize education opportunities for America's youth.

4. **Social Security Act:** Passed in 1965, this act established Medicare and Medicaid.

5. **Voting Rights Act:** This act, passed in 1965, outlawed the poll tax and literacy tests required in some states for voting. All other barriers that kept African-Americans from voting were outlawed.

6. **Immigration and Neutrality Act:** Passed in 1965, this act abolished the "national origin quota," a quota for how many individuals from certain countries could immigrate to America.

7. **Freedom of Information Act:** Passed in 1966, this act allows for full or partial disclosure of previously unreleased information and documents controlled by the U.S. government.

8. **Public Broadcasting Act of 1967:** This act established the Corporation for Public Broadcasting, the Public Broadcasting Service, and National Public Radio.

9. **Air Quality Act:** This act, passed in 1967, set standards for air quality.

10. **Civil Rights Act (Fair Housing Act) of 1968:** This act ensured fair housing opportunities to all Americans, regardless of race or national origin.

★★★★★★★★★★★★★★★★★★★★★★★★★

the civil rights legislation was seen in a new light and passed easily in Congress.

Another Term

In 1964, Johnson easily won a second term over Republican opponent Barry Goldwater. Additionally, the Democrats gained a two-to-one majority in both the House of Representatives and the Senate. After winning the presidential election in his own right, Johnson proposed his new legislation, the "Great Society" program. This program reflected many aspects of Roosevelt's New Deal program in regard to its scope and magnitude. Johnson explained it as a plan that "rests on an abundance and liberty for all. It demands an end to poverty, and racial injustice, to which we are totally committed in our time."

A War in the Jungle

On the international front, things were complicated. As the Cold War marched on and U.S. involvement in an increasingly unstable Vietnam continued, relations abroad grew shakier. After the Gulf of Tonkin incident, where Vietnamese torpedo boats fired on the American destroyer USS *Maddox*, Johnson asked Congress for an increase in American troops in the region—though he didn't ask for a formal declaration of war. Both houses of Congress overwhelmingly approved the measure.

In February 1965, the communist Vietnamese army (Viet Cong Army) attacked an American military base in the region. Johnson called for air strikes in retaliation. Soon, more than 165,000 American soldiers occupied South Vietnam to help fight the Vietcong army. This escalation of U.S. involvement resulted in no obvious or immediate positive results. By the end of 1973, fifty-seven thousand American troops had died. On January 30, 1968, the Vietcong army launched their "Tet

BTW: During Johnson's time in office, the Supreme Court established that those arrested must be read their "Miranda Rights" before their statements can be recorded as evidence. This was established in *Miranda v. Arizona* in 1966.

THE JOHNSON
"Treatment"

Lyndon Johnson was famous for his "treatment," a method by which he persuaded most of his friends—and enemies—to do what he wanted them to do. The treatment included "supplication, accusation, cajolery, exuberance, scorn, tears, complaint, the hint of threats," according to journalists Rowland Evans and Robert Novak.

PRESIDENTIAL Personality

★ *Everyone who knew Lyndon Johnson considered him competitive, powerful, and manipulative. To achieve his desired results, Johnson often used his infamous "treatment" and deceptive means, even on his closest companions. However, as revealed by his wife, Johnson had a hidden soft side. Lady Bird described her husband as "warm and mellow ... gentle, extremely loving."*

Offensive" invasion into South Vietnam, revealing the unexpected and powerful force of their army. U.S. presence in the region failed to stop the communist offensive, and Johnson's approval ratings dropped from 40 to 28 percent in the course of six weeks.

FUN FACT!

Lyndon Johnson remains the only president to be sworn in by a woman. Texas federal judge Sarah T. Hughes gave Johnson the oath on Air Force One shortly after Kennedy's assassination.

The Fight for Civil Rights

Johnson also struggled to deter violence on the national stage. Although the civil rights legislation increased the legal rights of minorities, a substantial backlash occurred throughout the nation. In response to this, many African-Americans took to the streets in protest. In 1965, rioting occurred in Los Angeles, California, resulting in the death of thirty-five individuals and the destruction of thirty-five million dollars' worth of property. Unfortunately, these race riots hurt the progression of African-Americans' civil rights.

In 1965, George Wallace, the governor of Alabama, sent police to arrest a group of peaceful African-American protesters in his state. The arrest process turned to violence and, as the nation watched on television, the police clubbed protesters, leaving many seriously injured. In response, Johnson traveled to Alabama to speak privately with Governor Wallace. After the meeting, Wallace declared he had had a "change of heart." It was obvious that Wallace had received Johnson's notorious "treatment." Wallace himself noted, "If I hadn't left when I did, he'd have had me coming out *for* civil rights."

Rioting continued all across America. In 1967, rioting broke out in Detroit, Michigan, killing over forty people. The civil rights movement suffered its biggest blow in 1968, however, when Martin Luther King Jr. was assassinated in Memphis, Tennessee.

THOUGHTS ON THE CONSTITUTION

It is the genius of our Constitution that under its shelter of enduring institutions and rooted principles there is ample room for the rich fertility of American political invention.

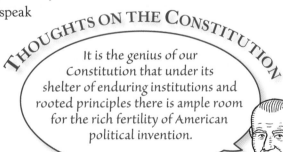

Declined to Run for Reelection

At the beginning of the election season in 1968, everyone assumed Johnson would run again. Between Vietnam and the race riots, however, things looked bleak for the incumbent president, and Johnson knew it. Johnson announced his resignation from the race on March 31, 1968.

Post-Presidency

After resigning from the 1968 presidential race, Johnson retired to his ranch in Texas near the Pedernales River. During his retirement, Johnson wrote *The Vantage Point: Perspectives of the Presidency, 1963–1969* in 1971. Two years later, Johnson suffered his third heart attack and died on January 22, nine days after the cease-fire was announced in Vietnam.

What Has He Done for Me Lately?

Many Americans listen to National Public Radio (NPR) on the radio or watch television channels sponsored by the Corporation for Public Broadcasting (such as PBS). By listening to or watching these stations, you are enjoying the benefits of legislation passed by Lyndon Johnson. He worked to promote the arts and humanities in American culture by creating the National Endowment for the Arts and the National Foundation of Arts and Humanities.

PLATFORM SPEECH

There is no Negro problem. There is no Southern problem. There is no Northern problem. There is only an American problem. And we are met here tonight as Americans—not as Democrats or Republicans—we are met here as Americans to solve that problem.

Johnson believed that, to solve America's problems, the country must unite together with the common goal of creating solutions, and communicated that to Congress in their joint session in 1965.

LYNDON B. JOHNSON

Written by Juliette Turner

VIETNAM WAR PROTESTS IN WASHINGTON, D.C.

October 21, 1967—Over one hundred thousand anti-Vietnam War protestors gathered at the Lincoln Memorial today in Washington, D.C. This demonstration was organized by the National Mobilization Committee to End the War in Vietnam. The protest comes as just one of the many antiwar protests that have occurred across the nation since May 12, 1964, when twelve men in New York burned their draft cards. While young American men are risking their lives in Vietnam in the fight against communism, a minority of young American citizens are taking to the streets in protest of the war. Other young men have also openly displayed their views on the war by burning their draft cards in public. When federal troops were deployed to hold back the protesters, the protesters stuck flowers inside the gun barrels of the soldiers in a demonstration of peace.

JOHNSON DECIDES AGAINST A SECOND TERM BUT LEAVES A LEGACY OF REFORM

March 31, 1968—In his radio address today, President Johnson shocked the nation by declaring he will not be seeking a second term in office. Johnson is, however, certainly leaving a legacy. His Great Society program has impacted the lives of thousands.

In regard to poverty, Johnson passed the Economic Opportunity Act of 1964, which created the Office of Economic Opportunity. In regard to education, Johnson proposed the Elementary and Secondary Education Act, which reformed public schooling by strengthening urban and rural schools and creating programs for students with special needs. The education reform also included the Higher Education Act, a student loan program, and the Head Start Program. In regard to welfare, Johnson created the Jobs Corps, signed the Fair Labor Standards Act, and also worked to increase health care coverage for America's senior citizens.

Johnson also oversaw the creation of Medicaid, which supplies medical benefits for low-income Americans who would otherwise not receive health care. In regard to housing, Johnson signed the Fair Housing Act of 1968, the Model Cities Act, and oversaw the creation of the Department of Housing and Urban Development in 1965.

WE BEAT THE SOVIETS

July 20, 1969--Today, American Neil Armstrong became the first man to walk on the moon, officially making America the winner of the Space Race between the Soviet Union and the United States. Armstrong, member of the Apollo 11 crew, took his first step at 10:56pm EST, leaving an American Flag in the moon before he left.

MARTIN LUTHER KING, JR. ASSASSINATED

April 4, 1968--Today, Civil Rights Activist Martin Luther King, Jr. was assassinated in Memphis, Tennessee. King was known for his promotion for peaceful activism as the most powerful way to protest against the injustices facing African Americans today. In his "I Have a Dream" speech on August 28 of last year, King spoke, "When the architects of our republic wrote the magnificent words of the Constitution and the Declaration of Independence, they were signing a promissory note to which every American was to fall heir. This note was a promise that all men, yes, black men as well as white men, would be guaranteed the "unalienable Rights" of "Life, Liberty and the pursuit of Happiness.[...] I have a dream that one day on the red hills of Georgia, the sons of former slaves and the sons of former slave owners will be able to sit down together at the table of brotherhood."

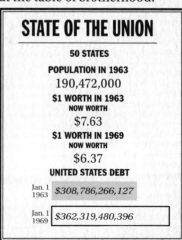

STATE OF THE UNION

50 STATES

POPULATION IN 1963
190,472,000

$1 WORTH IN 1963
NOW WORTH
$7.63

$1 WORTH IN 1969
NOW WORTH
$6.37

UNITED STATES DEBT

Jan. 1 1963	$308,786,266,127
Jan. 1 1969	$362,319,480,396

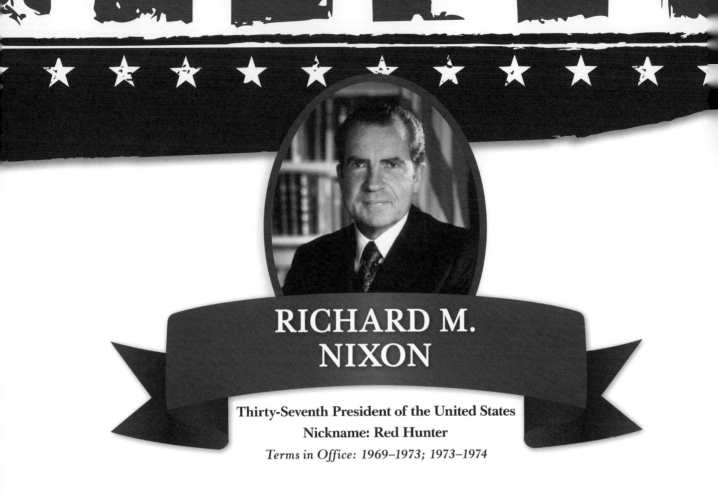

RICHARD M. NIXON

Thirty-Seventh President of the United States
Nickname: Red Hunter
Terms in Office: 1969–1973; 1973–1974

The Bottom Line

Most of Nixon's successes came from international policy: his treaty with the Soviet Union, his negotiation to open trade with the People's Republic of China, and his attempts to conclude the Vietnam War. In 1974, a year into his second term, Nixon resigned to avoid the humiliation of impeachment after the infamous Watergate Scandal.

FAST STATS

★ Born January 9, 1913, in Yorba Linda, California
★ Parents: Francis Antony and Hannah Milhous Nixon
★ Died April 22, 1994, in New York, New York; age 81
★ Age upon Start of First Term: 56; Age upon Conclusion of First Term: 60
★ Age upon Start of Second Term: 60; Age upon Conclusion of Second Term: 61
★ Religious Affiliation: Quaker
★ Political Party: Republican
★ Height: 5 feet 11.5 inches
★ Vice President: Spiro T. Agnew (1969–1973) and Gerald R. Ford (1973–1974)

What Was He Thinking?

Richard Nixon was anticommunist his entire life, but as president he learned to negotiate with communist countries to benefit the U.S. In the realm of economics, Nixon signed the Tax Reform Act during his time as president, which helped reduce tax loopholes and deductions. Nixon was also opposed to labor unions and frequent labor strikes, as evident through his support and contribution to the Taft-Hartley Act during his time in Congress.

 BTW: Nixon was sometimes known as "Gloomy Gus" during his childhood.

Why Should I Care?

During his five years in office, Nixon either ended or eased two wars. Although the Vietnam War escalated after he was first elected, Nixon eventually oversaw its end by negotiating and signing the Paris Peace Accords in 1973. Nixon also eased tension in the Cold War by signing the Nuclear Weapons Non-Proliferation Treaty, which decreased the number of nuclear weapons produced by both the United States and Russia.

Breakin' It Down
Early Life

Richard Milhous Nixon was the second of five sons born to Francis and Hannah Nixon. He enjoyed a religious and intellectual upbringing. His father ran a gas station and a general store, where Richard worked in his free time. In high school, he excelled in debate.

> A nation cannot remain great if it betrays its allies and lets down its friends.

Richard earned a scholarship to Harvard University, but his family did not have the funds to send him across the country, so he attended Whittier College instead, graduating in 1934 with a BA in history. After Whittier, Richard won another scholarship, this time to Duke University Law School. He graduated in 1937 with a law degree. In 1941, he took a job at the Office of Price Administration and the Office of Emergency Management, but a year later, at the age of twenty-nine, Nixon joined the navy to fight in World War II. Upon his return from the war, Nixon decided to run for political office.

First Couple

In June 1940, Richard Nixon married Thelma "Pat" Ryan. Together the couple had two daughters. During World War II, while Nixon worked at the Office of Emergency Management, Pat worked as a clerk for the Red Cross. Before Nixon entered politics, Pat had not affiliated with any political party, even voting for

> Richard Nixon graduated first in his high school class, second in his college class of eighty-five students, and third in his class at Duke University Law School.

Nixon's secretary of state, Henry Kissinger, wins the Nobel Peace Prize for his work in the Paris Peace Accords negotiations, 1973

Five men are caught breaking into the Democratic National Committee headquarters, leading to the Watergate Scandal, 1972

Richard Nixon resigns from the presidency, 1974

The Nuclear Weapons Non-Proliferation Treaty is signed between the United States and the Soviet Union, 1969

The Kent State University shootings occur, 1970

Columbus Day becomes a federal holiday, 1971

The twenty-one-year U.S. trade embargo with China ends, 1972

The Paris Peace Accords end U.S. involvement in the Vietnam War, 1973

First Term in Office — **Second Term**

| 1969 | 1970 | 1971 | 1972 | 1973 |

Democratic and Independent candidates. However, when Nixon entered politics as a Republican, Pat immediately registered as a Republican as well. Pat wasn't afraid to express her own views on issues, and openly disclosed her pro-choice views on abortion, her support of the Equal Rights Amendment, and her strong support of women's equality—even pushing for her husband to nominate a woman to the Supreme Court.

THELMA "PAT" NIXON

Previous Political Career

- 1946: Elected to U.S. House of Representatives. He was a member of the special committee that formed the Marshall Plan under President Harry Truman, a member of the Un-American Activities Committee, and a member of the House Education and Labor Committee.
- 1950: Elected to U.S. Senate. He served on the Government Operations Committee.
- 1953: Elected as vice president under Dwight Eisenhower.
- 1960: Ran for president against John F. Kennedy and lost.
- 1962: Ran for California governor and lost.

BTW: Throughout Nixon's political career, Nixon focused his campaigns on the one issue he knew was close to the people's hearts: anti-communism. Nixon somehow always found some way to peg his opponent as a communist sympathizer.

ELECTION RESULTS!

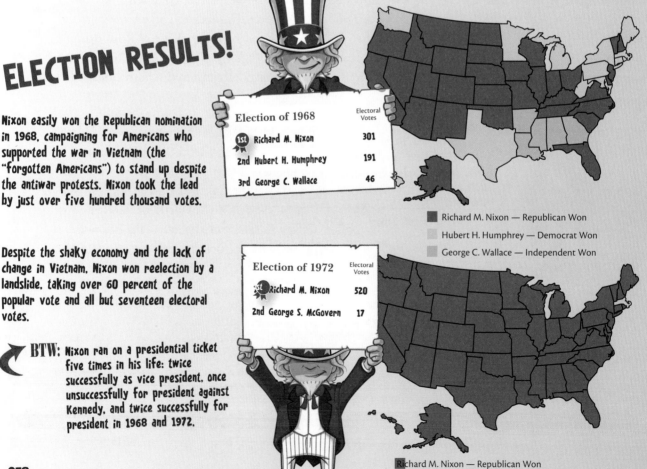

Nixon easily won the Republican nomination in 1968, campaigning for Americans who supported the war in Vietnam (the "forgotten Americans") to stand up despite the antiwar protests. Nixon took the lead by just over five hundred thousand votes.

Election of 1968	Electoral Votes
1st Richard M. Nixon	301
2nd Hubert H. Humphrey	191
3rd George C. Wallace	46

Richard M. Nixon — Republican Won
Hubert H. Humphrey — Democrat Won
George C. Wallace — Independent Won

Despite the shaky economy and the lack of change in Vietnam, Nixon won reelection by a landslide, taking over 60 percent of the popular vote and all but seventeen electoral votes.

Election of 1972	Electoral Votes
1st Richard M. Nixon	520
2nd George S. McGovern	17

BTW: Nixon ran on a presidential ticket five times in his life: twice successfully as vice president, once unsuccessfully for president against Kennedy, and twice successfully for president in 1968 and 1972.

Richard M. Nixon — Republican Won
George S. McGovern — Democrat Won

Presidency

When Nixon assumed the presidency in 1969, he had his work cut out for him. Domestic unrest regarding the Vietnam War was escalating, and all civil rights legislation was stalled due to violent race riots across the country. In addition, inflation from war spending was weakening the U.S. economy. To help remedy the economic crisis, Nixon established wage and price controls as a means to control spiraling costs for American households. Nixon lowered the number of goods imported to the United States to decrease spending and promote American businesses, and he increased the number of exported American products. By 1972, inflation began to slow down, but it reversed again in 1973 and continued to climb throughout the remainder of his term.

Vietnam and Foreign Policy

Events in Vietnam escalated as the U.S. Air Force dropped literally "tons" of bombs on Cambodia, Laos, and Vietnam. While Nixon was in office, the civilian death toll in Southeast Asia reached nearly one million and the U.S. death toll reached 20,533. However, Nixon did obtain foreign policy achievements in other areas. In February 1972, he became the first president to travel to and negotiate with a communist country (ironic because of his communism-bashing history). For the first time in twenty years, the People's Republic of China opened its doors to the U.S. and signed its first trade agreement since becoming a communist country. In May 1972, Nixon also visited the Soviet Union and negotiated a treaty that eased tension between the two countries by increasing diplomatic, commercial, and cultural contact. Additionally, the two countries signed SALT, the Strategic Arms Limitation Treaty, which reduced each country's missile development program.

National Archives and Records Administration

FUN FACT!

Shortly after Nixon assumed the presidency in 1969, he had a single-lane bowling alley built below the driveway leading to the White House North Portico. Nixon was crazy about bowling.

Watergate

Despite his great international victories in 1972, the year proved fateful. On June 17, five men were caught breaking into the headquarters of the Democratic National Committee, located in a complex of buildings called Watergate. The apparently inconsequential event turned into a nightmare for Nixon when reporters from the *Washington Post* discovered ties between the burglars and his administration. After nearly a month of questionings and arguments,

THOUGHTS ON THE CONSTITUTION

The Constitution supposes what the history of all governments demonstrates, that the executive is the branch of power most interested in war and most prone to it. It has accordingly with studied care, vested the question of war in the legislature. [If a president is successful in bypassing the Congress] it is evident that the people are cheated out of the best ingredients in the government, the safeguards of peace, which is the greatest of their blessings.

RICHARD NIXON

impeachment seemed inevitable. Instead of facing a humiliating trial, Nixon resigned, becoming the first and only president to do so.

Post-Presidency

After resigning from the presidency, Nixon moved to New York City and retired. During his retirement, Nixon wrote four books: *The Memoirs of Richard Nixon* in 1978, *The Real War* in 1980, *Real Peace: Strategy for the West* in 1985, and *Victory without War* in 1988. In April 1994, at the age of 81, Nixon died of a stroke at a Manhattan hospital.

What Has He Done for Me Lately?

Nixon was responsible for ending the twenty-one-year stalemate between the United States and the People's Republic of China. Because of his gutsy attempt to reach out to the communist country, Nixon succeeded in opening trade between the two countries, which slowly opened China to the rest of the world. Nixon also supported the 26th amendment which lowered the voting age from 21 to 18.

PLATFORM SPEECH

We have faced other crises in our history and have become stronger by rejecting the easy way out and taking the right way in meeting our challenges. Our greatness as a nation has been our capacity to do what had to be done when we knew our course was right.

In his "Silent Majority" speech, Nixon was asking Americans for support of the Vietnam War and an end to the antiwar protests. He urged Americans to remember that America was great because she had chosen to do the right thing and meet her challenges, not shrink from them.

RICHARD M. NIXON

Written by Juliette Turner

INVESTIGATION INTO KENT STATE UNIVERSITY SHOOTINGS CONTINUES

May 4, 1970—Three days ago, a group of student antiwar protesters at Ohio's Kent State University gathered to protest the war in Vietnam. After some of the students began throwing beer bottles at policemen, the local mayor declared a state of emergency. The next day, the Ohio National Guard arrived on the campus, using tear gas to control the protesters who had recently set fire to the abandoned ROTC building on campus. A member of the National Guard fired on the crowd of antiwar protesters and further gunfire ensued, leaving four students dead and nine others wounded. The reason for the shooting is still being investigated.

NIXON VISITS THE PEOPLE'S REPUBLIC OF CHINA

February 21, 1972—Richard Nixon landed today in the People's Republic of China, where he hopes to negotiate the first high-level engagement treaty between the two countries in twenty years.

Plans for the trip were long kept secret from the public, for fear of backlash from anticommunist Americans and international attention. Nixon kept his quest for negotiations top secret, even hiding the developments from his State Department. He only confided in his secretary of state, Henry Kissinger.

The meeting was negotiated through a mediator, Pakistani dictator Yahya Khan, who acted as the go-between for Chinese Premier

Chou En-Lai and Henry Kissinger. When the negotiations seemed positive, Kissinger traveled to Pakistan, where he "fell ill" and secretly traveled to China. In China, Kissinger met with officials and secured the formal invitation for Nixon to travel to the communist country. Only with the invitation in hand did Nixon release the news.

VIETNAM WAR ENDS!

March 29, 1973—The U.S. officially ended its involvement in the Vietnam region today, and the Nixon administration has proposed a plan that will have all American army personnel out of the region by next year. This comes as a great relief to the American public, which is weary of a war that seemed to have no end.

Since 1970, the war in Vietnam has been escalating, despite Nixon's promises to end it. Nixon ordered more ground troops into the region in 1970 and bombings of Laos in 1971. In addition to having

cont.

American troops in North and South Vietnam, Nixon ordered the U.S. invasion of Cambodia and Laos. In 1972, Nixon ordered bombings of North Vietnam, despite the protests of many U.S. citizens.

The number of bombs dropped on the region during the war is double the number dropped during World War II. However, a peace treaty has now been signed between the warring nations following peace talks that occurred between the two nations earlier this month.

VICE PRESIDENT SPIRO AGNEW RESIGNS

October 10, 1973—Agnew has been charged with having accepted bribes totaling more than $100,000 while holding office as Baltimore County Executive, Governor of Maryland, and Vice President of the United States.

Over the past few months, he has been charged with extortion, tax fraud, bribery, and conspiracy. He was allowed to plead no contest to a single charge that he had failed to report $29,500 of income received in 1967 on the condition that he resign from the vice presidency.

NIXON RESIGNS!

August 9, 1974—Richard Nixon is the first U.S. president to resign, and will hand over the presidency to Vice President Gerald Ford today at noon.

In yesterday's speech, Nixon acknowledged his faltering political support in Congress and his sadness over the decisions that were made concerning Watergate.

"I have never been a quitter," Nixon said. "To leave office before my term is completed is abhorrent to every instinct in my body. But as president, I must put the interest of America first.... Therefore, I shall resign the Presidency.... Vice President Ford will be sworn in as president at that hour in this office."

His resignation comes after a scandal that shook the White House. It was found earlier this year that Nixon was potentially connected to a group of politicians who set up secret surveillance of the Democrat Party and Nixon's future political rivals.

At first, Nixon denied he had any involvement in the Watergate break-in, but it was revealed that audio recorders installed in the Oval Office and other rooms in the White House by Nixon held conversations of Watergate and the intent behind it.

Nixon initially refused to release the audiotapes, saying it would endanger American national security, but the Supreme Court ruled that they must be released.

After listening to the tapes, the Judiciary Committee issued articles of impeachment. But hoping to save face, Nixon is choosing to resign.

NEW VICE PRESIDENT SWORN IN

December 6, 1973—House Minority Leader Gerald Ford has taken the oath of office as Vice President of the United States, replacing Spiro Agnew, who resigned in October.

Ford was nominated to take Agnew's position on October 12. The U.S. Senate voted 92 to 3 to confirm him on November 27, and earlier today the House confirmed Ford by a vote of 387 to 35.

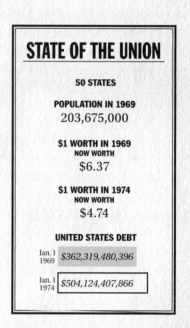

STATE OF THE UNION

50 STATES

POPULATION IN 1969
203,675,000

$1 WORTH IN 1969
NOW WORTH
$6.37

$1 WORTH IN 1974
NOW WORTH
$4.74

UNITED STATES DEBT

Jan. 1 1969	$362,319,480,396
Jan. 1 1974	$504,124,407,866

GERALD R. FORD

Thirty-Eighth President of the United States

Nickname: Mr. Nice Guy

Term in Office: 1974–1977

The Bottom Line

Gerald R. Ford became president after the resignation of President Richard Nixon, serving the remainder of Nixon's term. Ford struggled to combat inflation and economic instability while at the same time helping to support anticommunist regimes across the world.

FAST STATS

★ Born July 14, 1913, in Omaha, Nebraska
★ Parents: Leslie Lynch King and Dorothy Gardner King Ford; Stepfather: Gerald Rudolph Ford
★ Died December 26, 2006, in Rancho Mirage, California; age 93
★ Age upon Start of Term: 61; Age upon Conclusion of Term: 64
★ Religious Affiliation: Episcopalian
★ Political Party: Republican
★ Height: 6 feet
★ Vice President: Nelson Rockefeller

What Was He Thinking?

Gerald Ford believed a limited government was the best form of government. However, he also believed the government could pioneer useful reforms. Ford originally supported tax cuts for all Americans, but ended up increasing taxes on oil during the extreme spike in oil prices to try to cut consumption. Ford supported reforming America's education system, increasing federal spending in several areas of public education. He also believed having a balanced national budget was key to a strong and stable government.

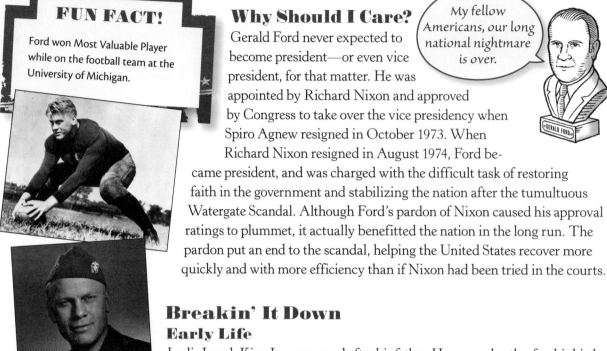

Why Should I Care?

> My fellow Americans, our long national nightmare is over.

Gerald Ford never expected to become president—or even vice president, for that matter. He was appointed by Richard Nixon and approved by Congress to take over the vice presidency when Spiro Agnew resigned in October 1973. When Richard Nixon resigned in August 1974, Ford became president, and was charged with the difficult task of restoring faith in the government and stabilizing the nation after the tumultuous Watergate Scandal. Although Ford's pardon of Nixon caused his approval ratings to plummet, it actually benefitted the nation in the long run. The pardon put an end to the scandal, helping the United States recover more quickly and with more efficiency than if Nixon had been tried in the courts.

Breakin' It Down
Early Life

Leslie Lynch King Jr. was named after his father. However, shortly after his birth, his parents divorced and his mother married a man named Gerald Rudolph Ford. Because young Leslie was too young to remember his father, his mother changed his name to mirror that of his stepfather's. Thus, Gerald R. Ford Jr. was born. Although he had no biological siblings, Gerald had three younger stepbrothers.

Gerald did not know his stepfather was not his biological father until he was seventeen years old. A short time later, Gerald met his biological father for the first time, an experience that left him shaken and near tears.

Gerald was always active in sports—especially football—and he also participated in Boy Scouts, becoming an Eagle Scout in his teens. He attended the University of Michigan, majoring in political science and economics, and graduating in 1935. Although he could have been a professional football player, Ford decided to attend Yale University Law School. While he was there he paid for his education by coaching Yale's football team. Ford graduated from Yale in 1941.

Four months after the attack at Pearl Harbor, Ford enlisted in the United States Navy. He served as gunnery officer aboard the aircraft carrier USS *Monterey* in the Pacific. Rising to lieutenant colonel, Ford accumulated ten battle stars during his almost four years of service, serving in nearly all of the Pacific

The Helsinki Accords, a human rights agreement, is signed by the U.S. and other foreign nations, August 1, 1975

The last group of Americans is evacuated from Saigon, South Vietnam, 1975

Ford escapes two assassination attempts in Sacramento and San Francisco, California, 1975

U.S. and Soviet spaceships dock in space, 1975

Viking 2 lands on Mars, becoming the second automaton to land successfully, 1976

The Supreme Court rules that the death penalty is constitutional, 1976

America begins her bicentennial celebration, July 4, 1976

Term in Office

| 1973 | 1974 | 1975 | 1976 | 1977 |

BTW: Ford's vice presidential appointment was approved in a 387 to 35 vote in the House and a 92 to 3 vote in the Senate.

naval battles, including at Wake Island, Okinawa, and the Philippines. Upon returning to the U.S. after the conclusion of the war, Ford moved to Grand Rapids, Michigan, and joined a local law firm.

First Couple

In 1948, Gerald Ford married Elizabeth "Betty" Ann Bloomer Warren. Together they had four children. Their courtship was short, only lasting a few months before Ford proposed. Betty was an outspoken advocate for women's health, openly discussing her battle with breast cancer and substance abuse, one of the first influential women to do so. She was very important in the formation of many rehabilitation and health care centers, one of which is the Betty Ford Center in Palm Springs, California.

BETTY FORD

In the 1940s, Betty briefly worked as a fashion model for *Cosmopolitan* and *Look* magazines.

Previous Political Career

- 1948: Elected to the U.S. House of Representatives to represent the state of Michigan. He served twelve consecutive terms.
- 1964: Served on the Warren Commission in charge of investigating John F. Kennedy's assassination.
- 1965: Became House Minority Leader. He held this position for eight years.
- 1973: Nominated as Richard Nixon's vice president, after the resignation of Spiro Agnew.

Presidency

Gerald Ford realized that after the Watergate Scandal, the American people needed to regain their faith in the office of the president. Ford attempted to help them do that by "personalizing" the presidency. For instance, he picked up the newspaper from the White House mailbox every morning and ordered the University of Michigan fight song to be played at presidential gatherings in place of "Hail to the Chief."

Pardoning Nixon

Just as both Ford's approval ratings and Americans' trust in their government increased, Ford issued Proclamation 4311, pardoning Richard Nixon. Americans—who still resented Nixon—responded vehemently to Ford's pardon, and his approval numbers dropped from 71 to 49 percent. To help Ford, Nixon offered to refuse the pardon. Ford realized, however, that the damage had already occurred and demanded that Nixon accept the pardon.

Despite his plummeting approval ratings, Ford continued serving the American people as best he could. As if one pardon was not sufficient, Ford put into effect the Vietnam Era Reconciliation Program, which offered amnesty to the young men who had avoided the draft with the condition that they affirm allegiance to the U.S. and serve two years working in a public service job. However, only 20 percent of those who avoided the draft applied for the conditional amnesty.

Gerald R. Ford was appointed to the vice presidency under the terms of the twenty-fifth amendment to the Constitution, which says, "Whenever there is a vacancy in the office of the vice president, the president shall nominate a vice president who shall take office upon a confirmation by a majority vote of both Houses of Congress." You can read more about that in *Our Constitution Rocks!*

I want to be remembered as a ... nice person, who worked at the job, and who left the White House in better shape than when I took over.

THOUGHTS ON THE CONSTITUTION

The Constitution is the supreme law of our land and it governs our actions as citizens. Only the laws of God, which govern our consciences, are superior to it.

Economic Problems

Additionally, America's economy was slowly collapsing. The cost of imported oil skyrocketed, causing the price of gasoline to increase as well. Attempting to cut oil and gas consumption, and therefore lower prices, Ford issued higher taxes on oil and gas. Ford also signed a $16 billion tax refund of personal and business income tax in an attempt to decrease unemployment.

To make matters worse, energy production in America (such as oil and natural gas drilling) dropped dramatically, causing a greater dependence on imports. Ford then initiated his WIN program, standing for Whip Inflation Now. He vetoed dozens of appropriations bills in an attempt to limit unnecessary government spending. He also called on Congress to reduce spending wherever possible.

Foreign Policy

Cambodia and Laos fell to communist invaders, reversing much of the work done by American soldiers during the Vietnam War. As a result, thousands of Americans and anticommunist Vietnamese were trapped in the region. Ford funded programs to help transport them to safety. Due to his decisive actions, fourteen thousand Americans and fifty-six hundred Vietnamese were safely removed from the two countries before the communists were able to completely conquer them.

In further attempts to combat communism, Ford sent several million dollars to aid Angola, a country in Africa where Cuban forces were attempting to infiltrate the government in favor of communist forces. Ford also sent money to Israel and Egypt in attempts to spark peace negotiations between the two countries.

Failure at Election Time

Despite his foreign policy successes, Ford struggled to keep the support of the American people. Although he succeeded in holding the country together after one of America's most confusing and disappointing times, his approval ratings still remained low. Ford tried running for president in 1976 and barely won the

Republican nomination, winning by roughly one hundred votes. In the national polls, however, he trailed his Democratic opponent by 30 percent. Although Ford actually won more states in the presidential election—twenty-seven to his opponent's twenty-three—Ford failed to win New York, Texas, and Ohio, giving the election to Democratic candidate Jimmy Carter.

Post-Presidency

Upon retiring from politics, Ford wrote an autobiography, *A Time to Heal: An Autobiography of Gerald Ford*, published in 1979. In 1980, Ford considered running again for president, fearing that the ultraconservative Ronald Reagan would not be able to defeat Jimmy Carter. However, Ford decided to remain in retirement.

In 1999, Ford was awarded the Presidential Medal of Freedom by President Bill Clinton for his great contribution to the national interests of the United States and for his efforts to heal a government that was hurt after Nixon's resignation. In 2001, Ford allied with his former opponent, Jimmy Carter, and cochaired the National Commission on Federal Election Reform, whose goal is to help reform election processes to prevent corrupted voting and also provide bipartisan voting results to Congress. Also in 2001, Ford received the Kennedy Profiles in Courage Award for his efforts to heal the nation and for his controversial pardoning of Nixon. After a successful post-presidential career, Ford died at the age of ninety-three, the oldest age of any former president up to that time.

What Has He Done for Me Lately?

During Ford's presidency, several questionable CIA activities were revealed to the public, including the Watergate cover-up attempts, illegal activities in foreign governments and foreign espionage, and spying activities against anti-Vietnam War protesters. To fix the situation without abolishing America's most treasured spy agency, Ford issued executive order 11905 to reform the CIA. First, it declared that the CIA's goals should originate from the National Security Council. Second, it established several boards and committees designated for surveillance of the CIA and their operations. Third, it prohibited some of the surveillance abilities of the CIA. Fourth, it reinforced that any political assassination of foreign leaders was strictly prohibited. Thanks to Ford, the CIA didn't become Big Brother, watching our every move.

PLATFORM SPEECH

I have promised to uphold the Constitution, to do what is right as God gives me to see the right, and to do the very best I can for America.

Ford understood how important it was to restore the American people's faith in their government. In his speech regarding his pardon of Nixon in 1974, he said he would do this by upholding the Constitution and doing what he believed was right for the country.

GERALD R. FORD

Written by Juliette Turner

PRESIDENT FORD ESCAPES A SECOND ASSASSINATION ATTEMPT IN CALIFORNIA!

September 22, 1975—Today a second woman, Sara Jane Moore, attempted to shoot the president in California. This attempt in San Francisco is the second made against Ford in only one month. Moore, a left-wing sympathizer and former FBI informant, was thwarted by a bystander, who grabbed her arm and caused her to miss the president. On September 5, Lynette "Squeaky" Fromme also attempted to shoot the president in Sacramento. Both women missed their target, and no one was hurt either time.

FORD READY TO SEND FUNDS TO AVOID NEW YORK'S BANKRUPTCY

November 26, 1975—In a question and answer session with the press today, President Ford said he has finally agreed to consider sending funds to New York City. He has decided "to ask the Congress when it returns from recess for authority to provide a temporary line of credit to the State of New York to enable it to supply seasonal financing of essential services for the people of New York City."

As the streets of New York and upkeep of the city slowly fall apart, the mayor has been planning to declare bankruptcy. However, before the mayor could act, President Ford issued a statement ordering the mayor to first clean up the city before any appropriations are sent. Ford also said today, "There will be stringent conditions. Funds would be loaned to the State on a seasonal basis, normally from July through March, to be repaid with interest in April, May, and June, when the bulk of the city's revenues comes in. All Federal loans will be repaid in full at the end of each year."

AMERICA'S BICENTENNIAL CELEBRATION COMES TO AN END

July 9, 1976—After five days of celebration, America's two-hundredth birthday celebration is finally over. The bicentennial celebration had many parades, performances, and tons of fireworks. The parade in New York City included boats sent by thirty different countries to celebrate the birth of America. President Ford, who always enjoyed the Fourth of July as a boy, recently said, "Never in my wildest dreams had I imagined that I would be President of the United States on its two-hundredth birthday."

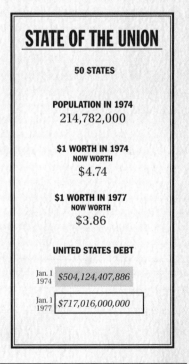

STATE OF THE UNION

50 STATES

POPULATION IN 1974
214,782,000

$1 WORTH IN 1974
NOW WORTH
$4.74

$1 WORTH IN 1977
NOW WORTH
$3.86

UNITED STATES DEBT

Jan. 1 1974	*$504,124,407,886*
Jan. 1 1977	*$717,016,000,000*

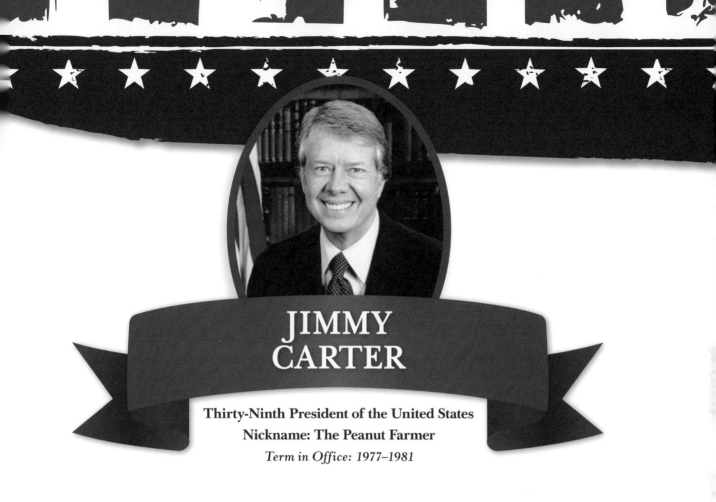

JIMMY CARTER

Thirty-Ninth President of the United States

Nickname: The Peanut Farmer

Term in Office: 1977–1981

The Bottom Line

Jimmy Carter tried to fix a struggling U.S. economy while simultaneously working to promote international peace and stability, winning a Nobel prize in 2002.

What Was He Thinking?

Jimmy Carter believed the government should be used to help reform the lives of individuals for the better. He also believed taxes should be reduced for the lower- and middle-income earners and that the American tax system should be reformed. Although he believed in eliminating excess government regulation, during his term in Congress he created the Department of Energy and the Department of Education. Carter was an avid support of clean and renewable energy and education reform. He moved to increase federal funding for public schools while leaving private schools to act as they see fit. Carter also supported the promotion of equal rights for African-Americans, appointing several African-American men and women to his cabinet.

FAST STATS

★ Born October 1, 1924, in Plains, Georgia
★ Parents: James Earl and Lillian Gordy Carter
★ Jimmy Carter is still living
★ Age upon Start of Term: 52; Age upon Conclusion of Term: 56
★ Religious Affiliation: Southern Baptist
★ Political Party: Democrat
★ Height: 5 feet 9.5 inches
★ Vice President: Walter Mondale

Why Should I Care?

The greatest levels of success during Jimmy Carter's time in office occurred in the international field. In addition to formally opening diplomatic relations with China, Carter also worked to promote peace in the Middle East through his Camp David Accords. Although the peace treaty was short-lived (Egyptian leader Anwar al-Sadat was assassinated two years after he signed the Accords), the peace negotiations helped stabilize relations between Egypt and Israel, which had previously been hostile and deadly.

SIBLING Problem

Jimmy Carter was born thirteen years before his youngest brother, Billy. Billy was a character, to say the least. During Jimmy's political campaign, Jimmy's opponents often used Billy as a controversial figure in the Carter family. Billy was often found drinking to excess during his youth and would later serve as a political lobbyist in Washington, D.C., for the Libyan government.

Breakin' It Down
Early Life

James Earl Carter Jr. was the eldest of four children born to the Carter family. As a young kid, James would help "mop" the cotton and peanut crops on the farm by picking the cotton and peanuts from the small bushes. James earned a dollar for every day he worked.

Growing up in the Deep South before segregation was declared unconstitutional, Jimmy attended segregated public schools. Starting in elementary school, he aspired to attend the Annapolis Naval Academy, writing to the school as a young boy for information. Although he graduated from his high school as class valedictorian, he feared he wasn't ready to apply to the naval school. He attended Southwestern Junior College for a year and Georgia Tech University for math and physics to further prepare.

In 1943, he entered the Naval Academy, graduating in 1946 in the top 10 percent of his class. After graduation, he was assigned to the USS *Wyoming*, and then to the USS *Mississippi* before being transferred to the navy's submarine branch. In 1948, Carter was assigned to the USS *Pomfret*, based in Pearl Harbor, Hawaii. During his time there, he almost lost his life when a storm surge caused him to fall overboard.

He also served in the Korean War, starting in 1951 on the USS *K-1*. Carter was chosen by Admiral Hyman Rickover to help develop the first nuclear submarine. Before doing so, Carter returned to New

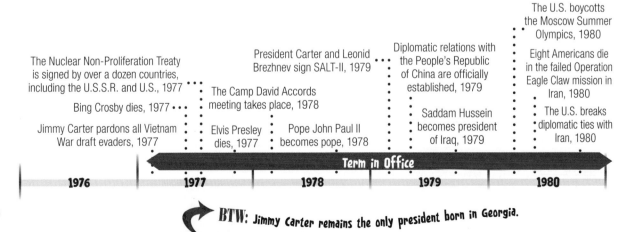

The Nuclear Non-Proliferation Treaty is signed by over a dozen countries, including the U.S.S.R. and U.S., 1977

Bing Crosby dies, 1977

Jimmy Carter pardons all Vietnam War draft evaders, 1977

The Camp David Accords meeting takes place, 1978

Elvis Presley dies, 1977

Pope John Paul II becomes pope, 1978

President Carter and Leonid Brezhnev sign SALT-II, 1979

Diplomatic relations with the People's Republic of China are officially established, 1979

Saddam Hussein becomes president of Iraq, 1979

The U.S. boycotts the Moscow Summer Olympics, 1980

Eight Americans die in the failed Operation Eagle Claw mission in Iran, 1980

The U.S. breaks diplomatic ties with Iran, 1980

Term in Office

1976   1977   1978   1979   1980

York and attended Union College to gain a graduate degree in nuclear physics. Although he showed exceptional promise in the navy, Carter retired after the news of his father's death to return home and help his mother with the family business.

First Couple

In 1946, Jimmy Carter married Eleanor Rosalynn Smith when she was just eighteen years old. Rosalynn, as she is called, actually rejected Carter's first marriage proposal because they had just begun dating and she considered it too soon. Two months later, however, Rosalynn accepted. Together, Jimmy and Rosalynn had four children, all of whom are still living today. During the presidency, Jimmy constantly consulted Rosalynn on the issues he faced as president—from international affairs to appointment dates and writing speeches.

ROSALYNN CARTER

Unlike any first lady before her, Rosalynn attended cabinet meetings with her husband and took detailed notes in a notebook she carried around with her. Today Rosalynn works alongside her husband to promote human rights and many social issues facing the world.

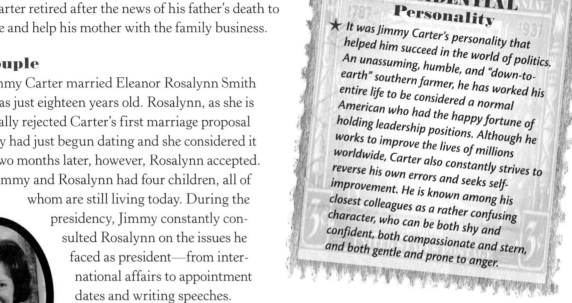

PRESIDENTIAL Personality

★ It was Jimmy Carter's personality that helped him succeed in the world of politics. An unassuming, humble, and "down-to-earth" southern farmer, he has worked his entire life to be considered a normal American who had the happy fortune of holding leadership positions. Although he works to improve the lives of millions worldwide, Carter also constantly strives to reverse his own errors and seeks self-improvement. He is known among his closest colleagues as a rather confusing character, who can be both shy and confident, both compassionate and stern, and both gentle and prone to anger.

ELECTION RESULTS!

Carter's brief career in politics and his detachment from Capitol Hill worked in his favor in the election of 1976. He campaigned as a soft-spoken peanut farmer from the Deep South, who provided a break from the Washington-as-usual scandals, lies, cover-ups, and party politics. Almost no one in America outside of Georgia knew a man by the name of "Jimmy Carter," but Carter overcame this. When he met people for the first time, he would shake their hand, saying, "Hello, I'm Jimmy Carter, and I'm going to be your next president." It also helped that he had very little "baggage" for his opponents to bring forth. By emphasizing the need for a people-oriented and virtuous government, Carter became the first man to win the presidency from the Deep South since Zachary Taylor in 1848.

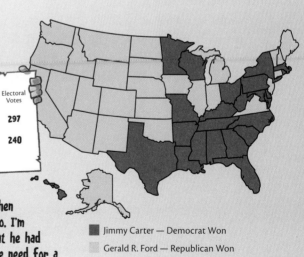

Election of 1976	Electoral Votes
1st Jimmy Carter	297
2nd Gerald R. Ford	240

■ Jimmy Carter — Democrat Won
Gerald R. Ford — Republican Won

> The confidence that we have always had as a people is not simply some romantic dream or a proverb in a dusty book that we read just on the Fourth of July. It is the idea which founded our Nation and has guided our development as a people. Confidence in the future has supported everything else — public institutions and private enterprise, our own families, and the very Constitution of the United States.

JIMMY CARTER

CONGRESSIONAL CORNER

★★★★★★★★★★★★★★★★★★★★★★★★★

1. **International Emergency Economic Powers Act:** This act was passed in 1977 and gave the president the authority to regulate the U.S. economy and commerce after declaring a national emergency in response to a foreign attack or threat.

2. **Foreign Intelligence Surveillance Act:** This act, passed in 1978, established the guidelines for the physical or electronic surveillance of foreign nations and the collection of foreign intelligence information.

3. **Presidential Records Act:** This act, passed in 1978, declared all presidential papers as public property available for public viewing.

4. **Panama Canal Act of 1979:** This act implemented the Panama Canal Treaty, which gave the Panamanian government control of the Panama Canal.

★★★★★★★★★★★★★★★★★★★★★★★★★

Previous Political Career

- 1962: Elected to the Georgia state senate after proving his opponent was guilty of voter fraud, and served two terms.
- 1966: Ran for Georgia governor, but lost.
- 1970: Elected Georgia governor, and became a leader of the New South movement, which called for an end to racial segregation in the south.

Presidency

Domestic Issues

Almost immediately upon becoming president, Carter was faced with a slew of domestic problems. Inflation was still increasing and unemployment numbers were rising. The real estate market was also floundering due to the high interest rates resulting from inflation. America also encountered an energy problem: oil imports from the Middle East were priced at all-time highs and were entering America more and more sporadically. Television channels displayed long lines of cars waiting for gasoline. Carter first appealed to the American people, asking them to cut back on consumption of oil in addition to tolerating the higher taxes and prices.

Energy Problems

Carter then proposed an alternative energy plan, outlining the benefits of new energy sources, such as solar panels and nuclear energy, promoting it to the American people as the future of energy creation and consumption. The appeal for alternative energy sources failed, largely due to the unreceptive American

BTW: During the energy crisis. Carter described America as the "most wasteful nation on earth." Not exactly consoling words for the millions of Americans who were struggling to fill up their gas tanks to get to work.

public; they were more concerned with when they would once again be able to afford a tank of gas. Additionally, Carter's proposal was dampened by coal miner strikes (which also increased the cost of energy) and the nuclear power plant accident — a nuclear melt-down that occurred on Three Mile Island in Pennsylvania in 1979, resulting in radioactive gases being released into the environment. To make matters worse, the increasing dependence on foreign oil lessened the value of the U.S. dollar, worsening inflation. Carter's approval ratings plummeted within months.

International Affairs

Carter experienced more successes in regard to international affairs than he experienced on the domestic side. His first success was with the People's Republic of China, when he formally recognized the Chinese government as legal and legitimate. That action allowed for the opening of normal diplomatic relations between the two countries. Carter also negotiated a treaty with Panama, which turned the Panama Canal over to their government. Carter was close to negotiating SALT-II with the Soviet Union, but relations turned icy once again when the Soviets invaded Afghanistan in December 1979—an action the United States viewed as a dangerous expansion of communism. This led to Carter's issuance of the Carter Doctrine, which stated that the U.S. would not tolerate any attempt by the Soviet Union to control the Persian Gulf region. Because of the increase in tension between the two nations, America did not attend the 1980 Summer Olympics in Moscow. Russia likewise refused to attend the 1984 Summer Olympics in Los Angeles.

Putting the Soviet Union aside, Carter also cut all federal aid to foreign countries whose governments he viewed as human rights violators, including Argentina and Uruguay. Carter's biggest foreign policy victory perhaps occurred with his Camp David Accords. This meeting at Camp David, with Egyptian president Anwar al-Sadat, Israeli prime minister Menachem Begin, and Carter, resulted in a "Framework for Peace" between Israel and Egypt after years of hostile relations.

Despite accomplishments on the world stage, Carter's presidency was indelibly impacted by the Iranian hostage crisis in which 52 Americans diplomats were held captive in the U.S. Embassy in Iran for 444 days.

Reelection Failure

Perceived as weak and incapable of addressing the challenges facing the country economically and globally, Carter was not in the best position politically. Carter did seek reelection, but lost to Republican candidate Ronald Reagan.

Jimmy Carter had solar panels installed on the White House roof, but his successor, Ronald Reagan, had them removed.

Pop Quiz! Do you remember what SALT stands for? It stands for Strategic Arms Limitation Treaty. The first SALT negotiations took place under President Nixon.

273

Post-Presidency

During his retirement, Carter revealed his prolific writing skills, writing more than twenty books. They included *Keeping Faith: Memoirs of a President*, published in 1982 and again in 1995; *Talking Peace: A Vision for the Next Generation*, published in 1993; *Our Endangered Values: America's Moral Crisis*, published in 2005; *Beyond the White House: Waging Peace, Fighting Disease, Building Hope*, published in 2008; and *We Can Have Peace in the Holy Land: A Plan That Will Work*, published in 2009.

Most of Jimmy Carter's legacy occurred after his leave from office. In one of the most active post-presidential careers of any president, Carter has worked to promote civil rights in dozens of countries worldwide. He has served as a human rights spokesman under several presidents, and worked as the mediator between foreign countries during international disputes, supervised foreign elections to lower corruption and fraud, and formed various organizations dedicated to solving social problems. Carter is also an active member and spokesman for Habitat for Humanity and the founder of the Carter Center in Atlanta, Georgia. The Carter Center promotes freedom, democracy, health, and agriculture. For his unending service to America, Carter won the Hoover Medal in 1998 and the Nobel Peace Prize in 2002.

What Has He Done for Me Lately?

Constantly working to increase human rights awareness worldwide, Carter has often entered dangerous countries to help secure safety and liberty for the oppressed. One example is Carter's work in North Korea. Under President Bill Clinton, Carter negotiated with North Korea to try to limit their nuclear testing facilities and their nuclear weapons creation. In 2010, Carter traveled to North Korea a second time on his own accord and successfully negotiated the release of American Christian missionary Aijalon Mahli Gomes.

PLATFORM SPEECH

In ancestry, color, place of origin, and cultural background, we Americans are as diverse a nation as the world has ever seen. No common mystique of blood or soil unites us. What draws us together, perhaps more than anything else, is a belief in human freedom.

In a commencement speech given by Carter at Notre Dame University in 1977, he noted that America is not united by race or ancestry. Though America is often called the "melting pot of the world," citizens are united in our belief in the value of freedom and equality for all people.

JIMMY CARTER

Presidential Times

Written by Juliette Turner

THE CAMP DAVID ACCORDS

March 26, 1979—The Camp David Accords were officially signed today by Anwar al-Sadat of Egypt and Menachem Begin of Israel. The document was unofficially agreed upon by the two leaders under the supervision of President Carter on September 17, 1978. In a thirteen-day-long meeting at Camp David, Jimmy Carter organized negotiations between the leaders of the two opposing, belligerent Middle Eastern countries. Carter refused to let either of the leaders leave the Presidential Ranch before negotiations for peace were outlined. President Carter is hoping that this peace treaty will help restore stability in a region that has seen war for decades.

MOHAMMAD REZA PAHLAVI SEEKS REFUGE IN THE U.S.

November 4, 1979—President Jimmy Carter allowed exiled Iranian dictator Mohammad Reza Pahlavi to seek refuge in the United States today. Upon entering the country, he was admitted to a New York hospital, where he will receive treatment for cancer. The action has enraged Iranians in the Middle East, who recently ousted Pahlavi during their revolution. The Iranian Revolution is resulting in a drastic radicalization of the country as the Iranian people move to break away from foreign occupation or influence and return to their religious and cultural heritage.

THE IRANIAN HOSTAGE CRISIS

April 25, 1980—An attempt by the Carter Administration to rescue the American hostages in Iran has failed miserably. The operation, dubbed Operation Eagle Claw, began yesterday, but half of the helicopters sent into Iran to rescue the hostages experienced technical difficulty and another helicopter crashed into a transport plane, killing eight Americans. The hostage crisis began last year after Mohammad Reza Pahlavi was allowed to seek refuge in the United States. In November of last year, a group of Iranian radicals stormed the U.S. embassy, capturing fifty-two Americans. The hostages were held in the embassy for twenty days under the supervision of the Iranians before being transferred to makeshift holding cells. The prisoners were transported bound, blindfolded, and covered in blankets to conceal their identity from onlookers. While imprisoned, the Americans were forced to stand, blindfolded, as mock firing squads fired blank rounds at their heads. The prisoners were repeatedly beaten and humiliated by their jailers. President Carter has announced he will now be enforcing economic sanctions on Iran by limiting trade in an effort to coerce the Iranians to free the hostages.

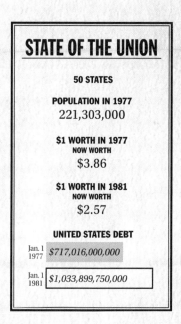

STATE OF THE UNION

50 STATES

POPULATION IN 1977
221,303,000

$1 WORTH IN 1977
NOW WORTH
$3.86

$1 WORTH IN 1981
NOW WORTH
$2.57

UNITED STATES DEBT

Jan. 1 1977	$717,016,000,000
Jan. 1 1981	$1,033,899,750,000

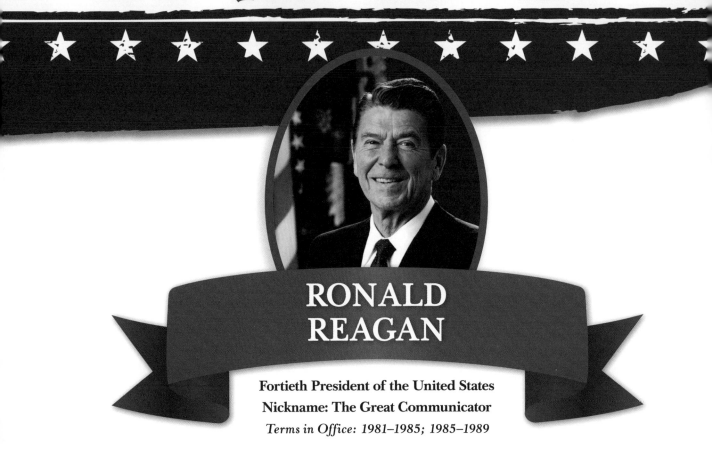

RONALD REAGAN

Fortieth President of the United States
Nickname: The Great Communicator
Terms in Office: 1981–1985; 1985–1989

The Bottom Line

Ronald Reagan helped to energize the American economy through tax reform and eliminating unnecessary government programs. He also expanded military spending during the Cold War, decreasing the power of the Soviet Union and his pro-democratic policies freed dozens of counries worldwide from the control of communism, leading to ultimate demise of the Soviet Union. A naturally gifted and charismatic leader, Ronald Reagan's vision of America as "City on a Hill" led to the revitalization of the nation impacting all aspects of American society. He focused on rebuilding America's economy at home and her strength and influence internationally and he was successful with both.

FAST STATS

★ Born February 6, 1911, in Tampico, Illinois
★ Parents: John Edward and Nelle Wilson Reagan
★ Died June 5, 2004, in Los Angeles, California; age 93
★ Age upon Start of First Term: 69; Age upon Conclusion of First Term: 73
★ Age upon Start of Second Term: 73; Age upon Conclusion of Second Term: 77
★ Religious Affiliation: Presbyterian
★ Political Party: Republican
★ Height: 6 feet 1 inch
★ Vice President: George H. W. Bush

BTW: Reagan received a star on the Hollywood Walk of Fame in 1952.

What Was He Thinking?

President Reagan was a strong advocate for small government, for reducing business regulations, and for reforming America's tax code and government programs. On the international stage (when dealing with the Cold War), Reagan believed Americans must "trust but verify," a Russian proverb which means to be willing to rely upon the assurances offered, but to continue to investigate in order to make sure the assurances are valid. Reagan ceaselessly promoted democracies and supported anti-communist regimes across the world.

Why Should I Care?

As the Great Communicator, Reagan instilled a greater sense of patriotism and a love of liberty in the hearts of Americans through his words as well as his actions. In light of the threat of communist expansion and oppression, Reagan realized the importance and value of democratic principles. During his lifetime—and even more so during his presidency—Reagan worked to preserve and protect the American principles of freedom and liberty, as well as to expand democracy to every corner of the globe.

Breakin' It Down
Early Life

Because he weighed ten pounds when he was born, Ronald Wilson Reagan earned the nickname "Little Fat Dutchman," or "Dutch" for short. Born into the Great Depression, Ronald understood hardships at a young age. He had one brother, named Neil.

> What I'd really like to do is go down in history as the president who made Americans believe in themselves again.

Reagan attended Eureka College in California and participated in many extracurricular activities there. He served as president of the student body and the captain of the swimming team, participated in theater productions and the debate team, and played on the football team. He graduated in 1932 with a degree in economics.

Despite his interest in economics, Reagan entered show business in 1937, when he signed a contract with Warner Bros. Studios in Hollywood. He appeared in roughly fifty movies during his acting career, though most of them were not very well known. Some of his more well-known movies, however, include *Love Is in the Air* (1937), *The Killers* (1964), *King's Row* (1942), *Bedtime for Bonzo* (1951), and *Knute Rockne—All American* (1940), where he played the iconic character "the Gipper." During his acting career, which spanned from 1937 to 1965, Reagan was known as a diligent and well-prepared actor who enjoyed his work.

Since the 1930s, Reagan had been a member of the U.S. Army Cavalry Reserve. Because of this, when the Japanese attacked Pearl Harbor, Reagan was called into active service, rising to second lieutenant—but he never saw any action because of his bad eyesight. Not allowing his visual impairment to hinder his ability to serve, Reagan joined the Army Air Corps First Motion Picture Unit, where he narrated and appeared in several training films for the army. After the conclusion of the war, Reagan was elected as president of the Screen Actors Guild, serving one six-year term from 1947 to 1952.

Reagan spoke all over the country, sometimes giving fourteen twenty-minute speeches a day, promoting General Electric and its products, while including elements about the greatness of America's social and political system.

Courtesy Ronald Reagan Library

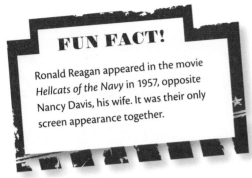
First Couple

Ronald Reagan remains the only president to have divorced his first wife and remarried before entering the White House. He married actress Jane Wyman in 1940 but they were divorced eight years later. In 1952, he married actress Nancy Davis. Reagan had four children, two with Jane, including one adopted son, and two with Nancy. Nancy and Ronald Reagan were well known for their supportive and loving relationship during their days in the White House. During her time as first lady, Nancy was an avid supporter of the Foster Grandparents program and the founder of the Just Say No anti-drug-use campaign.

JANE REAGAN

NANCY REAGAN

Previous Political Career

- 1964: Supported Republican presidential candidate Barry Goldwater by giving several speeches, including his "A Time for Choosing Speech," which led to a $1 million leap in campaign donations and also a dramatic increase of recognition and support for Reagan as a political figure.
- 1966: Elected governor of California. He balanced California's state budget, slowed the growth of the state's government, eliminated unnecessary government programs, and lowered property taxes. Arguably his most notable feat was reforming welfare programs, including improving welfare eligibility — hoping to better identify those with true need — and increasing financial assistance for a set amount of time for qualified people. He was re-elected, holding this position for eight years.
- 1972: Lost the Republican presidential nomination.

Presidency

When Reagan became president in 1980, inflation was in the double digits and the deficit was steadily increasing. Alongside Congress, Reagan initiated tax cuts to stimulate the economy, eliminated many business regulations, and decreased the size of government by ending several social welfare programs.

Reaganomics

To revitalize the stagnant economy he inherited from his predecessor, Reagan pushed a bold economic plan which cut taxes and limited regulation. Reagan claimed his plan would help begin "an era of national renewal" and mirrored the successful economic policies of Harding and Coolidge that had helped lead

An assassination attempt is made against President Reagan, 1981

First woman is appointed to the Supreme Court, Sandra Day O'Connor, 1981

National air traffic controller strike takes place, 1981

Israel invades Lebanon, 1982

Sally Ride becomes the first U.S. woman to enter space, 1983

Martin Luther King's birthday becomes a national holiday, 1983

Apple Macintosh releases its first personal computer, 1984

The Soviet Union withdraws from the Summer Olympic Games, 1984

First Term in Office

| 1980 | 1981 | 1982 | 1983 | 1984 |

ELECTION RESULTS!

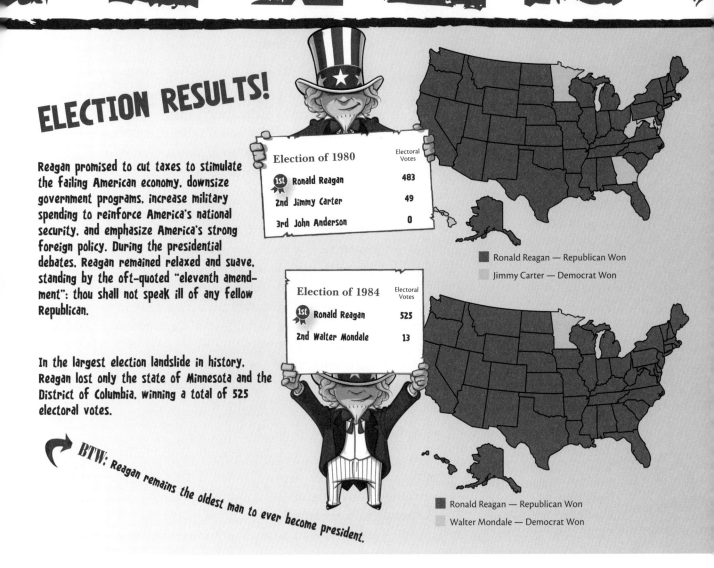

Reagan promised to cut taxes to stimulate the failing American economy, downsize government programs, increase military spending to reinforce America's national security, and emphasize America's strong foreign policy. During the presidential debates, Reagan remained relaxed and suave, standing by the oft-quoted "eleventh amendment": thou shall not speak ill of any fellow Republican.

In the largest election landslide in history, Reagan lost only the state of Minnesota and the District of Columbia, winning a total of 525 electoral votes.

Election of 1980

		Electoral Votes
1st	Ronald Reagan	483
2nd	Jimmy Carter	49
3rd	John Anderson	0

■ Ronald Reagan — Republican Won
■ Jimmy Carter — Democrat Won

Election of 1984

		Electoral Votes
1st	Ronald Reagan	525
2nd	Walter Mondale	13

■ Ronald Reagan — Republican Won
■ Walter Mondale — Democrat Won

BTW: Reagan remains the oldest man to ever become president.

to the "Roaring Twenties". Derided by oppponents as Reaganomics, his plan would ultimately astound his critics. It included more tax cuts for businesses and for the wealthy, focused on reduction of America's debt and deficit, and balanced the budget. Reagan followed Mellon's strategy as well as the "trickle-down theory," which hypothesized that when taxes and regulations were lessened for big businesses, the effects would gradually benefit every working American. With fewer regulations on businesses, the stock market surged and helped stimulate the economy and ease economic tensions for many Americans.

BTW: Jelly Belly jelly beans had no bigger fan than President Ronald Reagan. To honor their loyal customer, Jelly Belly created the blueberry flavor for his 1981 inauguration. In return, Reagan ordered three tons of the sweet treat for the occasion.

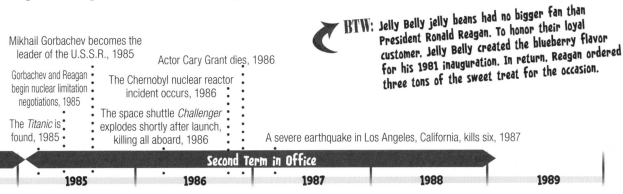

Mikhail Gorbachev becomes the leader of the U.S.S.R., 1985

Gorbachev and Reagan begin nuclear limitation negotiations, 1985

The *Titanic* is found, 1985

Actor Cary Grant dies, 1986

The Chernobyl nuclear reactor incident occurs, 1986

The space shuttle *Challenger* explodes shortly after launch, killing all aboard, 1986

A severe earthquake in Los Angeles, California, kills six, 1987

Second Term in Office

1985	1986	1987	1988	1989

Welfare programs: These are state or federal government programs that use taxpayer money to fund help for the poor, such as food stamps, government-funded housing, or medical care.

Deficit: The amount of money spent that exceeds the amount of income.

Cold War

On the international stage, Reagan greatly expanded military spending to enable Americans to capably handle any threats tha she might face and also force the Soviet Union to negotiate over the number of nuclear missiles each country possessed. Military spending jumped 50 percent during Reagan's eight years in office.

Reelection and the Reykjavik Conference

After Reagan's reelection, the country's economic rebound continued and he persisted in promoting American strength abroad. In October 1986, President Reagan and Soviet premier Mikhail Gorbachev met in Reykjavik, Iceland, to negotiate a treaty that would begin to eliminate both countries' nuclear arsenals. However, Reagan refused to abandon his "Star Wars" program, walking out of the negotiation, and Gorbachev feared the existence of this program would tilt the power balance in favor of America. As a result, it appeared that the negotiations were a failure. Fourteen months later, however, the two countries negotiated a smaller, but just as significant, treaty that resulted in the elimination of all SS-20 and Pershing missiles belonging to the two countries.

> The SDI program followed Reagan's mantra of "peace through strength." This showcase of American military strength deterred any nuclear attacks, thus bringing peace.

Economic Recovery

During his second term there was a dramatic drop in the stock market near the end of 1987. However, 1988 brought a successful economic turnaround, and the economy recovered and continued to grow. Despite the infamous Iran-Contra Affair that began in 1985, Reagan continued to de-emphasize the role of federal government and worked to improve the economy, leaving office with the highest approval ratings for any retiring chief executive.

FUN FACT!

In June 1989, President Reagan received an honorary knighthood from Queen Elizabeth II of Great Britain. The knighthood was officially entitled "Knight Grand Cross of the Order of Bath," or GCB for short. However, Reagan could not be called "Sir Ronald Reagan"; that would have been in conflict with the U.S. Constitution, which prohibits any government member from taking a title of nobility.

> If we ever forget that we're one nation under God, then we will be a nation gone under.

➤ BTW: Did you know that Ronald Reagan was claustrophobic?

PRESIDENTIAL
Personality

★ Reagan was known not only for his great sense of humor, but for his ability to connect with the American people through his personal and heartfelt addresses, whether over the television, radio, or in person to a crowd of people. This skill is often accredited to his days in Hollywood. He was loved by many Americans for his sincerity and optimism. Although he was known to his close friends as a private man reluctant to share much about his personal life, Reagan strove to make those around him feel comfortable and at ease. he was always a great host.

★ BREAKING
The Prophet's Curse

Since William Henry Harrison, every president elected in a year ending in a zero either died in office or was assassinated as predicted during the battle of Tippecanoe by the Shaunee Indian prophet: Harrison in 1840; Lincoln in 1860; Garfield in 1880; McKinley in 1900; Harding in 1920; Franklin Roosevelt in 1940; and Kennedy in 1960. Ronald Reagan was the next president to fall into the fated pattern, elected in 1980. Two months and ten days into his presidency, it seemed Reagan would fall victim to the curse when John Hinckley Jr.—a mentally ill man claiming he just wanted to impress actress Jodie Foster—attempted to assassinate the president. The bullet Hinckley fired ricocheted off the presidential limousine, punctured Reagan's left side, deflected off his rib, punctured his lung, and stopped an inch from his heart. In the process, police officer Thomas Delehanty was wounded, along with secret service agent Timothy McCarthy and Press Secretary James Brady, who was partially paralyzed. Reagan was pushed into the presidential limousine and driven to safety, yet no one knew he was shot until he began coughing up blood. By the time Reagan entered the hospital, he had lost three pints of blood—nearly one-third of his blood supply. Doctors immediately rushed him into surgery, claiming that if Reagan had arrived five minutes later, he would have died in surgery because of loss of blood.

On the way into surgery, the ever-witty Ronald Reagan looked at a surgeon and said, "I hope you're a Republican." One surgeon replied, "Today, Mr. President, we're all Republicans." When Reagan first saw his wife after the assassination attempt, Reagan said, "Honey, I forgot to duck." Regardless, Reagan lived and recovered in less than two weeks. He broke the curse. After this national scare, Reagan's approval ratings approached 70 percent.

CONGRESSIONAL CORNER
★★★★★★★★★★★★★★★★★★★★★★★★★

1. **Economic Recovery Act of 1981:** Signed by Reagan on April 13, 1981, this tax cut bill led to a 20 percent decrease in federal taxes over a three-year time span.

2. **Tax Equity and Fiscal Responsibility Act of 1982:** This act attempted to increase government revenue by closing tax loopholes and enforcing more stringent tax rules instead of increasing taxes.

3. **Nuclear Waste Policy Act of 1983:** This act created a standard procedure for nuclear waste disposal. It created an underground receptacle for high-level radioactive waste, which was to be built by the mid-1990s.

4. **Firearm Owners Protection Act:** This act, passed in 1986, loosened gun ownership regulations, and legalized ammunition shipments through the U.S. postal service.

5. **Immigration Reform and Control Act of 1986:** This act required employers to record their employees' immigration statuses, prohibited the hiring of illegal immigrations and legalized all illegal immigrants in the U.S. who had arrived before January 1, 1982.

6. **Tax Reform Act of 1986:** This bill was the second of the "Reagan tax cuts" and further reformed taxes to grant tax exemption for millions of low-income families.

7. **Civil Rights Restoration Act of 1987:** This act established that all businesses and recipients of federal funds must comply with all civil rights laws in all areas, not just in the area receiving federal funding.

8. **Civil Liberties Act of 1988:** This act gave money to the Japanese-American families who had been sent to isolation camps during World War II.

9. **Intermediate-Range Nuclear Forces Treaty:** This treaty, signed by President Reagan in 1987, was ratified by the Senate on May 27, 1988.

★★★★★★★★★★★★★★★★★★★★★★★★★

THOUGHTS ON THE CONSTITUTION

> Ours was the first revolution in the history of mankind that truly reversed the course of government, and with three little words: "We the people." ... Our Constitution is a document in which "We the people" tell the government what it is allowed to do. "We the people" are free. This belief has been the underlying basis for everything I've tried to do these past eight years.

Post-Presidency

Five years after his retirement, Ronald Reagan was diagnosed with Alzheimer's disease. To raise awareness of the disease, he founded the Ronald and Nancy Reagan Research Institute branch of the National Alz-heimer's Association. His last public appearance was in 1994 at the funeral of Richard Nixon. In 2000, the U.S. House of Representatives awarded Ronald and Nancy the Congressional Gold Medal. Four years later, Reagan died at the age of ninety-three, becoming the longest-living president.

What Has He Done for Me Lately?

Domestically President Reagan achieved robust and enduring growth policies in America that would last over two decades. Internationally, he made America the world's greatest foe of communism. With his refusal to shy away from the threat and power of the Soviet Union, the strength of communism began to falter. One example of this is the tearing down of the Berlin Wall and the liberation of East Germany. Although the Soviet Union did not collapse during Reagan's terms in office, it would fall apart during his successor's term. Thanks to Reagan's prodemocratic policies, dozens of countries were liberated with the fall of the communist regimes.

Pop Quiz! Do you remember what the word inflation means? Inflation is the rise of the price of goods and services as a result of a decreasing value of the dollar. This usually happens when the federal government prints a substantial amount of money at one time and gives it to banks.

PLATFORM SPEECH

> It is my intention to curb the size and influence of the Federal establishment and to demand recognition of the distinction between the powers granted to the Federal Government and those reserved to the States or to the people. All of us need to be reminded that the Federal Government did not create the States, the States created the Federal Government.

> In his 1981 State of the Union address, Reagan communicated his belief that progress could only be achieved after reducing the size of the federal government. Reagan also believed that state sovereignty was very important—the states created the federal government and not the other way around.

RONALD REAGAN

BTW: Reagan and Speaker of the House Tip O'Neill frequently played golf together, despite their strong political differences – one example of Reagan's special talent and effectiveness as a leader

Presidential Times

Written by Juliette Turner

TEAR DOWN THIS WALL!

June 12, 1987--Today, President Reagan spoke in Berlin, Germany in front of the Brandenburg Gate, urging for Soviet Premier Gorbachev to tear down the Berlin Wall and end the communist regime in the Soviet Union. Reagan stated earlier in his speech, "General Secretary Gorbachev, if you seek peace, if you seek prosperity for the Soviet Union and Eastern Europe, if you seek liberalization: Come here to this gate! Mr. Gorbachev, open this gate! Mr. Gorbachev, tear down this wall! [...This wall] cannot withstand faith; it cannot withstand truth. The wall cannot withstand freedom."

WAR ON DRUGS OFFICIALLY DECLARED

September 14, 1986—In a radio address to the nation today, first lady Nancy Reagan launched her own Just Say No campaign to encourage children to refuse drugs despite pressure from their peers. Her campaign comes after the recent statistics showing a growing crack epidemic that is crippling America's youngest generation. To raise awareness of the epidemic and to help remedy the problem, both Nancy and Ronald Reagan are also pushing to enforce harsher and longer sentences for drug traffickers.

IRAN-CONTRA AFFAIR

August 5, 1993—The verdict over the Iran-Contras Affair Trial has finally been reached today. The federal court has resolved evidence points toward Reagan's innocence in the matter; there is no credible evidence proving he was involved in the affair. Hearings began on May 5, 1987 in Congress.
The Iran-Contra Scandal arose during the second half of Reagan's second term. The scandal stemmed from a covert arms sale to Iran. Congress outlawed the sale, but the sales continued and the funds were used to help the rebel group known as the Contras in their protest against the communist Nicaraguan government. There was speculation that President Reagan was alerted of these events prior to their occurrence, but now that speculation has been disproven.

RONNIE AND MAGGIE

June 20, 1984--Many are accrediting the weakening of communism and the Soviet Union not only to President Reagan, but to his political ally, British Prime Minister Margaret Thatcher. Thatcher, known by many as the Iron Lady, has proved during her time in the British government to be a potent and powerful opponent to communism. The gradual fall of the Soviet Union and the promotion of democracy lies safely in the hands of this powerful pair.

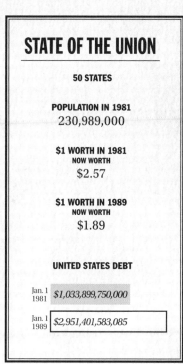

STATE OF THE UNION

50 STATES

POPULATION IN 1981
230,989,000

$1 WORTH IN 1981
NOW WORTH
$2.57

$1 WORTH IN 1989
NOW WORTH
$1.89

UNITED STATES DEBT

Jan. 1 1981	*$1,033,899,750,000*
Jan. 1 1989	*$2,951,401,583,085*

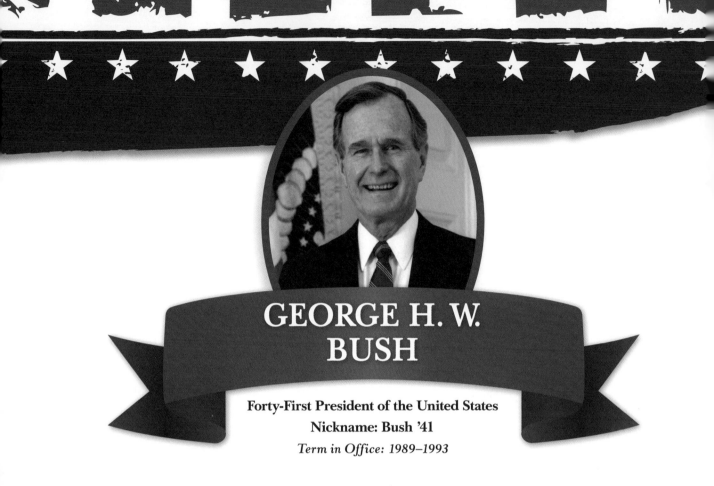

GEORGE H. W. BUSH

Forty-First President of the United States
Nickname: Bush '41
Term in Office: 1989–1993

The Bottom Line

George Herbert Walker Bush succeeded in supporting America's international policy and providing aid for various countries across the globe struggling through humanitarian or political crises. On the global scale, Bush used American influence and power to promote freedom and equality around the world, from the fall of the Soviet Union and ending communism in many countries, to South Africa and promoting the end of apartheid, to the Middle East and his success in the Persian Gulf War. He also witnessed the fall of the Soviet Union during his presidency. In 1990, Bush displayed outstanding leadership abilities in the Gulf War, beginning and ending an invasion of Iraq with few American casualties.

FAST STATS

★ Born June 12, 1924, in Milton, Massachusetts
★ Parents: Prescott Sheldon and Dorothy Walker Bush
★ George Herbert Walker Bush is still living
★ Age upon Start of Term: 64; Age upon Conclusion of Term: 68
★ Religious Affiliation: Episcopalian
★ Political Party: Republican
★ Height: 6 feet 2 inches
★ Vice President: Dan Quayle

What Was He Thinking?

George H. W. Bush was more moderate than his predecessor in regard to government programs and federal spending. Bush believed in small government and the necessity of a balanced budget, but he also believed in enforcing and expanding various regulations to ensure the well-being of the nation. He wanted to lower taxes, but the economic instability at the time did not allow for that luxury.

Why Should I Care?

One of Bush's greatest and most lasting successes as president remains the signing of the Strategic Arms Reduction Treaty (known as START I). This treaty, signed by Russian leader Mikhail Gorbachev and President Bush on July 31, 1991, resulted in the gradual but dramatic reduction in armament in both countries. START I was the ultimate conclusion of the Cold War and the beginning of the denuclearization of two of the world's greatest powers. By 2001, 80 percent of all strategic nuclear weapons previously in existence had been removed.

[W]e must ensure that America stands before the world united, strong, at peace, and fiscally sound.... We need to compromise; we've had dissensions. We need harmony; we've had a chorus of discordant voices.

GEORGE H.W. BUSH

Breakin' It Down
Early Life

George grew up in Greenwich, Connecticut, with his three brothers and one sister. As a young boy, he attended prestigious private schools. At the age of eighteen, just after graduating high school, George entered the navy as its youngest pilot to serve in World War II. During his service, he was deployed on fifty-eight combat missions in the Pacific against Japan. While executing one of his missions, George's plane was shot down. They crashed into the ocean, and the impact killed his two fellow crew members. Fortunately, he was rescued by a submarine and later decorated with a Distinguished Flying Cross, along with several other medals, for his bravery.

This photo of the Bush family—with George H. W. Bush and his wife, Barbara; George W. and his wife, Laura; Jeb and his wife, Columba; Neil and his ex-wife, Sharon; Marvin and his wife, Margaret; Dorothy; and the Bush grandchildren—was taken in the 1980s. Notice President Bush's cowboy boots adorned with the Texas flag.

George Bush Presidential Library and Museum

With the conclusion of the war, Bush enrolled in Yale University. Graduating in two and a half years through an accelerated program, Bush majored in economics and was captain of the university's baseball team. After graduating, he and his family moved to Texas, where he accepted a job as an administrator for an oil field supply company. Within a few years, Bush created his own company,

The solidarity movement defeats the communists in Poland's first free elections, 1989

The Berlin Wall falls, 1989

Colin Powell becomes the first African-American chairman of the Joint Chiefs of Staff, 1989

The Hubble Space Telescope is launched, 1990

The Bush administration bans the importation of semiautomatic rifles, 1989

Nelson Mandela is released from prison in South Africa, 1990

Iraq invades Kuwait, 1990

The twenty-seventh amendment to the Constitution is passed, 1992

Mikhail Gorbachev resigns, and the U.S.S.R. dissolves, 1991

The Persian Gulf War begins, 1991

The U.S. leaves the Philippines after nearly a century, 1992

U.S. trade sanctions are removed from China, 1992

The official end of the Cold War, 1992

Term in Office

| 1988 | 1989 | 1990 | 1991 | 1992 |

BTW: Bush was very close to President Reagan, meeting with him once a week for lunch.

BARBARA BUSH

the Bush-Overby Oil Development Company, in Midland, Texas. His company prospered, and by the age of forty-one, Bush was a self-made millionaire.

First Couple

George proposed to Barbara Pierce when she was just seventeen years old. Their marriage was delayed by World War II, but the couple married the year the war concluded. Together the couple had six children, five of whom lived to adulthood—their daughter, Robin, died of leukemia at age four in 1953. Their eldest son, also named George, later became the forty-third president of the United States, making Barbara Bush the second woman in history whose husband and son both served as president. During and after their time in the White House, the Bushes have continued to serve their country, through humanitarian work and most especially through Barbara's Foundation for Family Literacy to help increase literacy rates across America.

Previous Political Career

- 1964: Ran for U.S. Senate, but lost.
- 1966: Elected to U.S. House of Representatives. He served in the position for two terms, until 1971, becoming the first Republican to represent the seventh district of Texas.
- 1970: Ran for U.S. Senate, but lost again.
- 1971: Appointed U.S. ambassador to the United Nations by President Nixon. As ambassador, Bush helped to

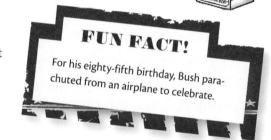

[O]ur problems are large, but our heart is larger. Our challenges are great, but our will is greater. And if our flaws are endless, God's love is truly boundless.

GEORGE H. W. BUSH

FUN FACT!

For his eighty-fifth birthday, Bush parachuted from an airplane to celebrate.

ELECTION RESULTS!

Bush realized that the priority of his presidency would be to lower the growing federal deficit. Yet, at the same time, Bush realized that no one wanted higher taxes or an extreme abolition of government programs. Campaigning as a more moderate Reagan, Bush realized that some government programs cut by the Reagan administration would need to be reinstated. Bush also made a campaign promise he would live to regret: "Read my lips—no new taxes."

Election of 1988	Electoral Votes
1st George H. W. Bush	426
2nd Michael Dukakis	111

■ George H. W. Bush — Republican Won

□ Michael Dukakis — Democrat Won

BTW: George H. W. Bush was the first vice president to be elected president since Martin Van Buren one hundred and fifty years earlier (excluding "the accidental president").

establish a peacekeeping corps in the Middle East and also reduced U.S. financial support to the United Nations.

- 1973: Appointed chairman of the Republican National Committee. He served as chairman during the Watergate Scandal and was charged with the responsibility of holding the Republican Party together. Bush continued to support Nixon until his impeachment seemed inevitable, at which time Bush mailed a letter kindly suggesting Nixon resign before he was officially impeached.
- 1974: Appointed chief of the U.S. Liaison Office in the People's Republic of China.
- 1976: Appointed director of the Central Intelligence Agency by President Ford. He served for one year.
- 1980: Made a bid for Republican presidential nomination but lost to Ronald Reagan. He then became vice president under Ronald Reagan.

Presidency

Upon becoming president, Bush established three goals: reduce the national budget deficit, initiate business reform, and restore various education and environmental government programs. His moderate approach to reforms alienated many of his fellow Republicans, causing problems with Congress later in his presidency. Shortly into his presidency, the economy declined. Fourteen percent of Americans still lived in poverty despite Reagan's economic reforms and the $2.7 trillion deficit was not becoming any smaller. As a result, Bush broke his campaign promise and increased taxes in an attempt to bring in more federal revenue, resulting in a dramatic loss of support for his presidency.

PRESIDENTIAL Personality

★ George H. W. Bush is known for developing personal relationships with his peers. Whereas other leaders kept cool and distant relationships with foreign leaders, Bush built friendships that he strove to maintain. To his friends, Bush is known as humble, polite, down-to-earth, and a hard worker. He was not afraid to open up to the public, and he preferred to hold impromptu press conferences rather than formal ones, addressing the American people as a fellow citizen. He was known for his loyalty during his vice presidency, and upon becoming president, no one doubted that he was a strong and capable leader.

FUN FACT!

George H. W. Bush was president for four years ... and eight hours. In the first temporary transfer of power, Vice President Bush served as president on July 13, 1985, from 11:30 a.m. to 7:30 p.m. while Reagan had cancer surgery.

International Success

Despite his domestic difficulties, Bush thrived in the international field. He helped to initiate worldwide humanitarian reforms, aiding countries on almost every continent. In South Africa, Bush helped promote the end of the oppressive apartheid. In 1989, he ordered Operation Just Cause to help overthrow corrupt Panamanian leader General Manuel Antonio Noriega, who openly supported the international drug trade and forged votes to win his national election as the nation's leader. This operation, one of the shortest military conflicts in American history (just over seventy-two hours), deposed Noriega, and a new pro-U.S. leader was sworn into office. Also, Bush saw the end of the forty-one-year Cold War during his term.

BTW: The success of the Gulf War caused President Bush's approval ratings to skyrocket close to 90 percent, the highest approval ratings recorded of any president in American history.

CONGRESSIONAL CORNER

1. **The Whistleblower Act:** This act, passed in 1989, protected the rights of workers to report fraud or abuse in federal programs without retribution.

2. **The Fair Labor Standards Amendment:** This act, passed in 1989, increased the minimum wage to $4.25 an hour.

3. **Americans with Disabilities Act:** This act was passed in 1990 to prevent discrimination based on disabilities. It also helped establish more protections for disabled workers.

4. **Clean Air Act:** This act, passed in 1990, established new antipollution standards for fuel burning.

5. **Immigration Act of 1990:** This act lifted immigration limits and expanded and revised the Visa Waiver Pilot Program. It also established the Diversity Immigrant Visa.

6. **Civil Rights Act of 1991:** This act provided compensation to individuals having experienced discrimination in the workplace.

7. **Strategic Arms Reduction Treaty:** The Senate ratified this treaty in 1992. The treaty was between Russia and the United States and greatly reduced the number of nuclear weapons possessed by both countries.

End of the Presidency

In spite of his international success, the economy was still failing and his fellow Republicans did not forget his broken tax promise. Bush might have managed to win reelection, if not for the presence of third-party candidate Ross Perot. The vote split between three candidates and Bush lost the election.

Post-Presidency

Bush continues to serve his country and the world even after his time as president. Partnering with former presidential rival Bill Clinton, Bush has worked to raise funds for worldwide humanitarian crises, such as the 2004 tsunami in Indonesia. Bush founded several foundations, such as his Points of Light foundation, dedicated to increasing awareness about the importance of volunteer service. *"[A] Thousand Points of light, of all the community organizations that are spread like stars throughout the Nation, doing good."*

What Has He Done for Me Lately?

Bush continues to promote freedom and equality across the globe, either through raising awareness of humanitarian needs in underprivileged countries or promoting volunteerism in America. He has spent his entire life in his country, beginning at the age of eighteen when he entered the navy, and he is committed to serving others for the betterment of not only the nation but the world.

PLATFORM SPEECH

For a new breeze is blowing, and a world refreshed by freedom seems reborn. For in man's heart, if not in fact, the day of the dictator is over. The totalitarian era is passing, its old ideas blown away like leaves from an ancient lifeless tree. A new breeze is blowing, and a nation refreshed by freedom stands ready to push on.

Bush said these words in his 1989 State of the Union address. He became president on the verge of the collapse of the Soviet Union, a time when many countries in Europe were finally being released from decades of communist oppression.

GEORGE HERBERT WALKER BUSH

Presidential Times

Written by Juliette Turner

THE PERSIAN GULF WAR—OPERATION DESERT STORM

February 28, 1991—Today President Bush declared a cease-fire just four days after the Operation Desert Sabre ground campaign began, ending the short-lived but successful Persian Gulf War.

The conflict began after Iraqi leader Saddam Hussein ordered an invasion of Kuwait in August of last year, sparking an international uproar. The neighboring nations of Saudi Arabia and Egypt appealed to the U.S. and the United Nations to reprimand Iraq for their actions. When Hussein refused the United Nation's demands to withdraw from Kuwait, President Bush and the U.S. military led

U.N. forces in mid-January in an air raid named Operation Desert Storm. For thirty-eight days, the allies bombed and fired upon Iraqi cities.

The raid then moved to the ground four days ago when U.S. and allied soldiers landed on Kuwait soil.

FALL OF THE SOVIET UNION

December 25, 1991—Mikhail Gorbachev resigned as head of state in the U.S.S.R. today, marking the end of Communist Russia. Also today, the Soviet flag flew over the U.S.S.R. for the last time. This comes after eleven nations who were previously under the control of the Soviet Union announced earlier this week that they would no longer be a part of Communist Russia. After this announcement was made, only one state remained a part of the Soviet Union: Georgia. This resulted in the end of communist control over the world's largest nation.

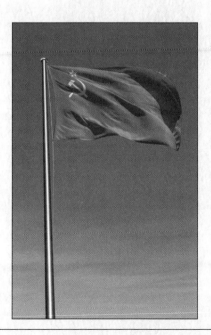

STATE OF THE UNION

50 STATES

POPULATION IN 1989
248,479,000

$1 WORTH IN 1989
NOW WORTH
$1.89

$1 WORTH IN 1993
NOW WORTH
$1.62

UNITED STATES DEBT

Jan. 1 1989	$2,951,401,583,085
Jan. 1 1993	$4,535,687,054,406

BILL CLINTON

Forty-Second President of the United States
Nickname: The Comeback Kid
Terms in Office: 1993–1997; 1997–2001

The Bottom Line

Bill Clinton dealt with two government shutdowns during his presidency: one from November 14 to November 19, 1995, and another from December 16, 1995, to January 6, 1996. He still managed to stabilize the American economy and balance the national budget. Clinton also experienced several international successes and continued national prosperity, but he was forced to fight to overcome three scandals.

FAST STATS

★ Born August 19, 1946, in Hope, Arkansas
★ Parents: William Jefferson Blythe III and Virginia Dell Cassidy; Stepfather: Roger Clinton
★ Bill Clinton is still living
★ Age upon Start of First Term: 46; Age upon Conclusion of First Term: 50
★ Age upon Start of Second Term: 50; Age upon Conclusion of Second Term: 54
★ Religious Affiliation: Baptist
★ Political Party: Democrat
★ Height: 6 feet 2.5 inches
★ Vice President: Al Gore

What Was He Thinking?

Bill Clinton believed the government should provide programs to protect and enhance the well-being of United States citizens. At the same time, however, Clinton realized that government could get out of hand with too many regulations and too much spending, and agreed with Republicans that reforms were necessary. Clinton also believed that a balanced budget was crucial to economic stability. Throughout his political career, Clinton's political stances evolved to fit the needs and desires of his constituents.

Why Should I Care?

One of Clinton's greatest achievements while in office was his success in recovering the American economy.

Clinton paid off $360 billion of the national debt and converted the largest budget deficit in American history to the largest surplus, $237 billion. Additionally, Clinton decreased government spending to the lowest level in three decades while simultaneously decreasing federal income tax levels to the lowest in thirty-five years. During Clinton's presidency, America experienced her longest period of economic expansion: 115 months of economic growth—4 percent economic growth per year after he assumed office.

Nationalized health care: When a government strictly regulates private health care providers to ensure coverage for all citizens and is paid for with government subsidies (coming from taxpayer money).

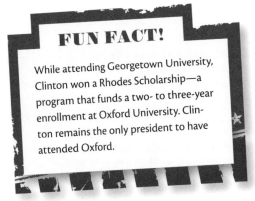

FUN FACT!

While attending Georgetown University, Clinton won a Rhodes Scholarship—a program that funds a two- to three-year enrollment at Oxford University. Clinton remains the only president to have attended Oxford.

Breakin' It Down

Early Life

Three months before Bill Clinton was born, his biological father died in a car accident. His mother, Virginia, named her son William Jefferson Blythe IV after his late father.

When Bill was four years old, his mother married Roger Clinton. Although he has no biological siblings, Bill has one half brother. He was officially adopted by his stepfather in 1962, and his name was changed to William Jefferson Clinton. In school, Bill enjoyed government classes, but he found the most enjoyment in music and playing his saxophone. He even considered a career in music at one point in his childhood!

In 1964, Clinton began college at Georgetown University. During his years at the college, he worked as an intern for a U.S. senator from Arkansas, wanting to become more engaged in politics. He also signed a letter of intent to join the Reserve Army Training Corps in Arkansas, but he never followed through.

Clinton then pursued a law career by entering Yale University Law School. He graduated in 1973 and took a job at the University of Arkansas Law School. Less than a year later, he ran for his first government position.

First Couple

Bill Clinton married Hillary Rodham in 1975. They are considered the powerhouse couple of politics, because they both can withstand the rough-and-tumble world of politics. The lifelong politicians have one daughter.

Hillary Clinton became the first first lady to run for her own political position when she ran for the U.S. Senate in 2000. Hillary won the election and so became the first female senator from New York. Additionally, in 2008, Hillary ran for president, but lost the Democrat Party nomination to Barack Obama. She later became secretary of state under President Barack Obama.

Previous Political Career

- 1974: Ran for a position in the U.S. House of Representatives, but lost.
- 1976: Elected Arkansas attorney general.
- 1978: Elected governor of Arkansas.
- 1980: Ran for reelection as governor, but lost.
- 1982: Elected governor of Arkansas once again. He served four two-year terms.
- 1990: Became chairman of the Democratic Leadership Council.

HILLARY CLINTON

BTW: Bill Clinton was the first president born during the Baby Boom, the post-World War II time period when the U.S. population increased dramatically.

ELECTION RESULTS!

Together, Bill Clinton (age 46) and Al Gore (age 44) made the youngest presidential ballot in American history. Clinton campaigned on plans to improve the floundering economy by decreasing the federal deficit, creating new jobs for the thousands out of work, and establishing national health care insurance. He used slogans such as "It's the economy, stupid" and targeted the "forgotten middle class." In doing this, Clinton received 43 percent of the popular vote. Clinton's success in the election, however, was partly because of the presence of third-party candidate Ross Perot, who took nearly 19 percent of the popular vote from George H. W. Bush.

When the Republican Party gained the majority in Congress with the election of 1994, many speculated that Clinton would lose reelection. However, since many Americans blamed Republicans for the government shutdown of 1995, Clinton's popularity in the polls skyrocketed. Ross Perot once again ran as a third-party candidate, taking much-needed support from Clinton's opponent, Robert Dole.

Election of 1992

		Electoral Votes
1st	Bill Clinton	370
2nd	George H. W. Bush	168
3rd	H. Ross Perot	0

■ Bill Clinton — Democrat Won
George H. W. Bush — Republican Won

Election of 1996

		Electoral Votes
1st	Bill Clinton	379
2nd	Robert Dole	159
3rd	H. Ross Perot	0

■ Bill Clinton — Democrat Won
Robert Dole — Republican Won

Presidency

Upon assuming the presidency, Clinton appointed a record number of women and minorities to executive positions. He began his term by fulfilling his campaign promise, passing a new medical care reform. In 1993 he signed the Family and Medical Leave Act. However, Clinton's more radical health care reform bill was voted down by Congress. Clinton then ignored party lines and signed a welfare reform package that reduced government involvement in and funding for major social programs.

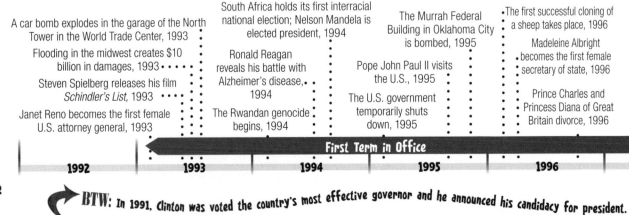

A car bomb explodes in the garage of the North Tower in the World Trade Center, 1993

Flooding in the midwest creates $10 billion in damages, 1993

Steven Spielberg releases his film *Schindler's List,* 1993

Janet Reno becomes the first female U.S. attorney general, 1993

South Africa holds its first interracial national election; Nelson Mandela is elected president, 1994

Ronald Reagan reveals his battle with Alzheimer's disease, 1994

The Rwandan genocide begins, 1994

The Murrah Federal Building in Oklahoma City is bombed, 1995

Pope John Paul II visits the U.S., 1995

The U.S. government temporarily shuts down, 1995

The first successful cloning of a sheep takes place, 1996

Madeleine Albright becomes the first female secretary of state, 1996

Prince Charles and Princess Diana of Great Britain divorce, 1996

First Term in Office

1992   1993   1994   1995   1996

BTW: In 1991, Clinton was voted the country's most effective governor and he announced his candidacy for president.

Government Shutdown

In the midterm election of 1994, the Republicans took the majority in both the House and Senate. With this drastic change, Washington, D.C., became a place of stalemate, especially concerning Clinton's budget. In May 1995, Clinton proposed a plan that would balance the federal budget in ten years. The Republicans also had a plan to balance the budget, which would take seven years. The Republicans passed their bill through Congress but Clinton vetoed it. Due to the lack of compromise and failure to agree on any budget, the government shut down. When it finally reopened, the polls showed that America blamed the Republicans for the shutdown, and as a result, Clinton garnered more support for his Social Security and Medicare reforms.

Reelection

With the government up and running again, the economy was booming. which helped Clinton win reelection in 1996. Whereas Clinton's first term focused mainly on domestic affairs, his second term focused largely on international affairs. In 2000, he sent his secretary of state, Madeleine Albright, to North Korea to negotiate with the communist leaders to shut down factories the U.S. suspected were used for production of nuclear weapons. Also in 2000, Clinton signed a trade bill with China that established permanent, normal trade status to the communist country. Clinton believed that the open trade would encourage a more democratic government in China.

Scandal!

Clinton's second term began with international success and domestic prosperity. Three scandals, however, halted all progress in the Clinton administration. The first scandal was the Whitewater Controversy. Although the scandal was unearthed during his

> I like the job of the president... The bad days are part of it. I didn't run to have a pleasant time. I ran to have a chance to change the country and if the bad days come with it, that's part of life, and it's humbling and educational. It keeps you in your place.

LIBERTY Language

Government shutdown: A government shutdown occurs when Congress fails to pass a spending bill and the government discontinues providing services that are not considered "essential." Typically, essential services include police, firefighting, armed forces, utilities, and correctional facilities.

PRESIDENTIAL Personality

★ Bill Clinton is known as an outgoing and amiable man who sincerely enjoys the life of politics. Extremely persuasive and talented at maneuvering his opponents to stand on his side of issues, Clinton is able to personally appeal to almost anyone, regardless of political affiliation. One nickname, Slick Willie, came not only from his tendency to reshape his political views to best suit his constituents but also his ability to bend his opponents' views and strategically avoid political attack.

The *Mars Pathfinder* lands on Mars, 1997

Mother Teresa dies, 1997

Princess Diana dies in a Paris car crash, 1997

The House of Representatives moves to impeaches Clinton, 1998

Frank Sinatra dies, 1998

Vladimir Putin becomes president of Russia, 1999

Mad cow disease breaks out in Europe, 2000

The USS *Cole* is attacked in Aden, 2000

Israel; military forces withdraw from Lebanon, 2000

Second Term in Office

| 1997 | 1998 | 1999 | 2000 | 2001 |

1. **Family and Medical Leave Act:** This act initiated a required three-month, job-protected leave of absence for employees with a serious family or medical need.

2. **National Voter Registration Act:** This act was passed in 1993 and required states to allow citizens to receive or update their voter registration cards when they renew their driver's licenses or apply for Social Security benefits.

3. **Brady Handgun Violence Prevention Act:** This bill, passed in 1993, created a five-day waiting period and background checks for handgun purchases.

4. **North American Free Trade Agreement Implementation:** This treaty was approved by the Senate in 1993 and called for a gradual elimination of all tariffs and taxes placed on goods and produce shipped between the U.S., Mexico, and Canada.

5. **Line Item Veto Bill:** This bill, signed in 1996, allowed the president to only execute certain aspects of congressionally approved bills. This bill was deemed unconstitutional by the Supreme Court in 1998 in a 6–3 vote.

6. **Defense of Marriage Act:** This act was passed in 1996 and allowed states to refuse to recognize same-sex marriage.

7. **Balanced Budget Act of 1997:** This act would reduce spending by $160 billion over four years. The increase in spending for welfare and children's health care, however, resulted in only $127 billion being saved.

8. **Children's Heath Act:** This act was passed in 2000 and formed federal child health funding programs initiated for pediatric health research.

★★★★★★★★★★★★★★★★★★★★★★★★★

THOUGHTS ON THE CONSTITUTION

When we got organized as a country and we wrote a fairly radical Constitution with a radical Bill of Rights, giving a radical amount of individual freedom to Americans, it was assumed that the American who had that freedom would use it responsibly.

—BILL CLINTON

first presidential bid, it was not highlighted until Clinton had secured his second term in office. The controversy was linked to Clinton's Arkansas governorship in 1978. He was accused of illegal real estate purchases paid for by siphoning off money given to the state of Arkansas for state projects. In January 1996, Hilary Clinton became the first first lady to receive a subpoena from a judge when she was asked to testify on behalf of her husband regarding the scandal. She denied any claims of misdemeanor.

The second scandal was named Trooper-Gate, and was also linked to Clinton's time as Arkansas governor. The scandal alleged that Clinton ordered two Arkansas state troopers to arrange a secret meeting for him with two women for inappropriate activities.

This scandal was soon overshadowed by the Monica Lewinsky Scandal, which nearly cost Clinton his presidency. This third scandal began when a former Arkansas state employee sued Clinton for harassment. The court subpoenaed Clinton, and the Supreme Court ruled that, even though he was the president, he must answer the subpoena.

During the scandal, former White House intern Monica Lewinsky was asked to testify whether or not she had engaged in any improper relations with the president or had ever been harassed by him. Both Lewinsky and Clinton denied any accusations. It was found later through a taped conversation between Lewinsky and her friend that Lewinsky and Clinton had indeed engaged in improper relations during the winter of 1995 and 1996. The House of Representatives composed four articles of impeachment against Clinton (reasons why he should be impeached), including obstruction of justice and perjury. On two of the four articles, Clinton was impeached by the House, sending to the Senate for

 Pop Quiz! Do you remember the definition of a midterm election? A midterm election is the congressional election that takes place two years into the president's term of office—the halfway point.

trial, where Chief Supreme Court Justice Willaim Renquist presided as judge. However, 62 percent of Americans opposed Clinton's impeachment. The Senate voted two times. The first vote ended in a 50–50 tie and the second ended in a 45–55 result, both times without the two-thirds majority necessary for the Senate impeachment.

Post-Presidency

Clinton remains active in the political field, supporting many Democratic candidates in various political races across the country. He has authored several books, including *My Life*, in 2004; *Giving: How Each of Us Can Change the World*, in 2007; and *Back to Work: Why We Need Smart Government for a Strong Economy*, in 2011. In 2009, Clinton became a U.S. Special Envoy to Haiti. He has also partnered with former political opponent and former president George H. W. Bush to raise awareness about various humanitarian crises around the world.

During Clinton's presidency, economic growth was only one of the improvements Americans enjoyed. More than twenty-two million jobs were created, unemployment was the lowest in thirty years, education standards were increased, 95 percent of schools were connected to the Internet (a novelty in Clinton's time), and one hundred thousand new police officers and new gun laws led to the lowest U.S. crime rates in twenty-six years.

LIBERTY Language

Subpoena: An official order requiring an individual to come before a court or a congressional committee.

What Has He Done for Me Lately?

Today, welfare programs still exist and many disadvantaged Americans rely on the system. Before Clinton, many Americans were "riding the system," never looking for work or ways to improve their situation. In a risky political move, Clinton sided with many Republicans in signing the Personal Responsibility and Work Opportunity Reconciliation Act. This act, opposed by many Democrats, ended the "open-ended" guarantee to federal aid, and imposed a five-year limit to benefits and required able individuals to look for work after two years of receiving federal aid. It also supplied states with incentives, such as extra funds, to provide jobs for dependent individuals. Thanks to Clinton's welfare reform, the percentage of Americans on welfare shrank to its lowest number in thirty-two years.

PLATFORM SPEECH

Our democracy must be not only the envy of the world but the engine of our own renewal. There is nothing wrong with America that cannot be cured by what is right with America.

Clinton said this in his 1993 inaugural address. He believed that every problem facing America at the time could be overcome because of America's previous successes and her democratic form of government.

BILL CLINTON

Presidential Times

Written by Juliette Turner

CONGRESS APPROVES NAFTA

November 14, 1993—Congress approved the North American Free Trade Agreement (NAFTA) yesterday. Clinton signed NAFTA with Canada and Mexico earlier in his term. This agreement created the largest free-trade zone in the world by eliminating any tariffs or import/export taxes on goods and produce shipped between the U.S., Mexico, and Canada. Clinton's presidential opponent Ross Perot is claiming this agreement will cause American businesses to move their production facilities to either Mexico or Canada, where they will be able to hire cheaper labor and face less business taxation. As a result, Perot argues, America's industrial economy will sag and many American jobs will be lost.

CLINTON'S QUEST FOR HEALTH CARE REFORM FAILS

November 8, 1994—The Republicans took the majority in Congress today, officially ending President Clinton's hopes for health care reform. During his first two years as president, Clinton has avidly supported health care reform. In 1993, thirty-seven million Americans had no health care coverage. To help reform the system, Clinton asked over five hundred experts, White House officials, cabinet members, and even his wife, Hillary Rodham Clinton, to begin composing a bill. The bill quickly became known as Hillary Clinton's bill. The bill garnered many opponents, including politicians who opposed nationalized health care, drug companies, and insurance companies, all of whom accused the bill of camouflaging a government takeover of health care. Opposition became so intense that White House officials feared for Hillary Clinton's life and ordered her to wear a bulletproof vest to rallies. Various problems have surrounded the health care bill, including the lack of public support and the delayed formation of grassroots support systems.

GOVERNMENT SHUTDOWN ENDS

January 6, 1996—The government reopened today as Republicans finally agreed to Clinton's budget, which will reopen the government and is expected to create twenty million new jobs and transform the national deficit of $29 billion to a national surplus of $106 billion.

The government shutdown on December 16, 1995 was a result of a lack of compromise between the Republican Congress members (deemed the Gingrich Revolutionaries after Speaker of the House Newt Gingrich) and President Clinton. The Gingrich Revolution- aries wanted to balance the budget in seven years by cutting $270 billion from Medicare in addition to providing a $240 billion tax cut. Clinton disagreed with the tax cuts and vetoed the bill. On November 14, 1995, 800,000 government employees (40 percent of the nation's workforce) were furloughed—temporarily laid off. This temporary and partial November shutdown ended after six days. In December, the government shut down again due to a continuing lack of compromise.

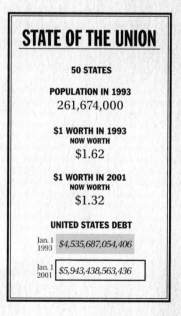

STATE OF THE UNION

50 STATES

POPULATION IN 1993
261,674,000

$1 WORTH IN 1993
NOW WORTH
$1.62

$1 WORTH IN 2001
NOW WORTH
$1.32

UNITED STATES DEBT

Jan. 1 1993	$4,535,687,054,406
Jan. 1 2001	$5,943,438,563,436

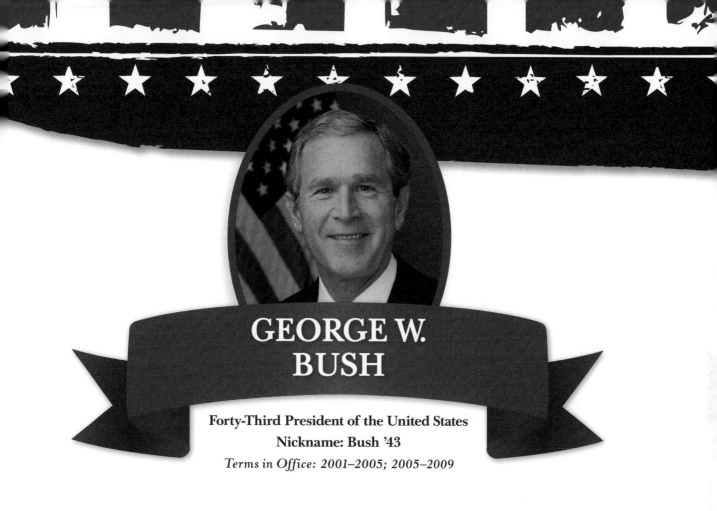

GEORGE W. BUSH

Forty-Third President of the United States
Nickname: Bush '43
Terms in Office: 2001–2005; 2005–2009

The Bottom Line

George W. Bush helped guide America through the aftermath of the September 11, 2001, terrorist attacks on U.S. soil and initiated the wars in Iraq and Afghanistan. For the rest of his term he ensured that America was kept safe by warding off other terrorist attacks on the U.S. His strong leadership protected Americans. In his second term, he confronted a floundering economy and housing market.

FAST STATS

★ Born July 6, 1946, in New Haven, Connecticut
★ Parents: George Herbert Walker Bush and Barbara Pierce Bush
★ George W. Bush is still living
★ Age upon Start of First Term: 54; Age upon Conclusion of First Term: 58
★ Age upon Start of Second Term: 58; Age upon Conclusion of Second Term: 62
★ Religious Affiliation: Methodist
★ Political Party: Republican
★ Height: 6 feet
★ Vice President: Richard B. Cheney

What Was He Thinking?

Bush believed in low taxes and small government. Like his father, Bush believed that government programs, when managed correctly, could help the American people. Bush was a strong supporter of state sovereignty and a big advocator for education reform, believing that educating America's youth was vital to the health of the nation. Strengthening U.S. national security was also a major issue for Bush, and he sometimes took risky moves to keep the United States and her people safe from danger.

Why Should I Care?

The September 11 terrorist attacks will remain forever in the minds of all who witnessed the event, either in person or on television. The tragedy required a president who could remain calm in the face of chaos and project an image of stability and strength to the rest of the world as they watched to see how the United States would respond. Bush helped keep the U.S. unified and strong during one of her most tragic times and also moved to protect her from future attacks.

> Republicans want the best for our nation—and so do Democrats. Our votes may differ but not our hopes.

Breakin' It Down
Early Life

Born in New Haven, Connecticut, two days after the Fourth of July, George Walker Bush was the first of six children born to the future forty-first president, George H. W. Bush. Although the Bush family was blessed with a prosperous business, they encountered their fair share of trials. One of them was when George W. was seven years old. His four-year-old sister, Robin, died of leukemia.

At school, George was an average student, a talented and versatile athlete, and a slight troublemaker. Like his father, he was sent to the Phillips Academy in Andover, Massachusetts. Once again following in his father's footsteps, George attended Yale University, where he studied history. George became the president of his fraternity before graduating with a bachelor's degree in 1968.

> In the seventh grade, George won the school election for class president. Foreshadowing?

After college, Bush joined the Texas Air National Guard and completed a fifty-three-week program, during which time he commanded and piloted fighter planes, rising to the rank of lieutenant. He then transferred to the Air Force Reserve for inactive duty. Although the Vietnam War continued during his time in the Reserve, Bush's unit was not called to fight, and he received his honorable discharge in 1974. After working several jobs simultaneously, Bush entered Harvard Business School, graduating with an MBA in 1975. Bush then moved back to Texas and invested in the Texas Rangers baseball team before entering

The U.S. invades Afghanistan, 2001

The Department of Homeland Security is established, 2001

Foreign terrorist attacks occur in New York and Washington, D.C., and a third hijacked plane crashes in Pennsylvania, September 11, 2001

The CIA kills six Al-Qaeda members in Yemen, 2002

The anthrax scare in the U.S. takes place, 2001

North Korea admits to having nuclear weapons, 2002

The U.S. invades Iraq, 2003

The space shuttle *Columbia* explodes over Texas, killing all seven aboard, 2003

Iraq leader Saddam Hussein is captured by U.S. troops, 2003

A tsunami hits Asia, killing 225,000, 2004

Yasir Arafat dies, 2004

Massachusetts becomes the first state to legalize same-sex marriage, 2004

First Term in Office

2000   2001   2002   2003   2004

ELECTION RESULTS!

The election of 2000 was the closest and most disputed election since the 1876 election between Rutherford B. Hayes and Samuel J. Tilden. In both elections, Florida was the center of dispute. On the night of the 2000 election, news organizations were calling the race too close to call, particularly in the states of Michigan, Pennsylvania, and Florida. Michigan and Pennsylvania eventually went to Gore, and Florida became the deciding state. Exit polls in Florida projected Gore to win, but actual results were proving otherwise. Bush edged out Gore by such a slim margin that Florida law required an immediate recount. Palm Beach County reported a total of nineteen thousand disqualified votes due to discrepancies in the butterfly ballots—the new form of ballot Florida used in the election. On November 26, the votes were confirmed. Bush had won.

U.S. senator from Massachusetts, John Kerry, was George Bush's opponent in the election of 2004. In light of the recent September 11 attacks, the campaign focused on the issues of terrorism and the Iraq War.

Election of 2000

		Electoral Votes
1st	George W. Bush	271
2nd	Albert Gore	266

George W. Bush — Republican Won

Albert Gore — Democrat Won

Election of 2004

		Electoral Votes
1st	George W. Bush	286
2nd	John Kerry	251

George W. Bush — Republican Won

John Kerry — Democrat Won

politics. He invested one million dollars, but when he sold his shares, he earned fifteen million dollars.

First Couple

George W. Bush and Laura Welch attended the same junior high school in Texas but never met. They also lived in the same Houston apartment complex, but their paths never crossed. The two finally met in 1977 at a Midland, Texas, barbecue. They were married in 1981, and they had twin girls. During her time as first lady, former librarian Laura Bush became a strong advocate for literacy in America. She continues to host the National Book Fair at the Library of Congress and works alongside many

LAURA BUSH

Hurricane Katrina hits the U.S. coastline on the Gulf of Mexico, 2005

Saddam Hussein is executed in Baghdad, 2006

Pluto is no longer considered a planet, 2006

Fidel Castro steps down from the Cuban presidency, 2008

Iran takes fifteen British sailors hostage, 2007

The U.S. housing market crash occurs, 2008

Second Term in Office

2005 — 2006 — 2007 — 2008 — 2009

BTW: George W. Bush was the fourth president to win the election without winning the majority of the popular vote.

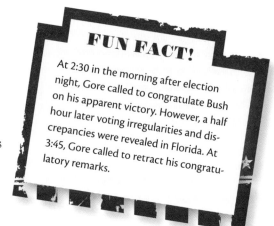

Terrorist attacks can shake the foundations of our biggest buildings, but they cannot touch the foundation of America. These acts shatter steel, but they cannot dent the steel of American resolve.

education-based foundations, including Helping America's Youth, Teach for America, New Teacher Project, and Troops to Teachers. During her time in the White House, Laura visited Afghanistan three times, as well as Africa and parts of Asia.

Previous Political Career

- 1978: Ran for a seat in the U.S. Congress, but lost.
- 1988: Managed his father's presidential campaign.
- 1994: Elected governor of Texas. After just one year as governor, Bush was named the most popular big-state governor, earning a national reputation as a "compassionate conservative," easily winning reelection, holding the position for six years, and leaving this position to become president.

Presidency

Bush entered office with several goals: reduce poverty and the need for social welfare programs, reduce taxes, reform education, and reform Social Security. Bush first tacked tax reform — signing into law a massive tax cut in June 2001. Unfortunately for President Bush, the Democrats in the Senate effectively blocked most of his first year agenda.

Terrorist Attacks

On the international stage, Bush improved relations between the U.S. and Mexico as well as promoting former President Reagan's missile defense idea. On September 11, 2001, however, the United States experienced the largest, deadliest, and most horrific foreign attacks on U.S. soil in its history. On 9/11, terrorists hijacked four airplanes, crashing two into New York City's north and south World Trade Center towers and one into the Pentagon. On one flight, speculated to have been heading for the White House, passengers overtook the hijackers and it crashed into a field in Pennsylvania. The 2001 attacks resulted in the death of nearly three thousand civilians: 246 victims from the four aircrafts, 2,606 in New York City, and 125 at the Pentagon. As a result, the U.S. invaded Afghanistan to uproot the terrorist organization cells in the region responsible for the attacks.

Bush appealed to Congress to approve a U.S. invasion of Iraq. Congress complied on October 2, 2002, and shortly thereafter Operation Iraqi Freedom began. U.S. and allied troops invaded the region and captured

BTW: During one of the presidential debates, Bush and his opponent, Al Gore, were both asked to name their favorite philosopher. Bush responded, "Jesus Christ."

THOUGHTS ON THE CONSTITUTION

[School children] should know about the nearly impossible victory of the Revolutionary War, and the debates of the Constitutional Convention.

GEORGE W. BUSH

vital strongholds by April of the following year. However, American troop presence in the region would continue beyond Bush's second term.

National Reforms

As the United States strove to recover from 9/11 and faced a new war in the Middle East, President Bush attempted to continue running the country as normal. In May 2002, he authorized the largest tax cut in U.S. history, cutting taxes by $350 billion. The following year, Bush signed the Jobs and Growth Tax Relief Reconciliation Act.

Reelection

In 2004, Bush won reelection and Republicans maintained control in both chambers of the House and the Senate. During this term, the United States experienced two major catastrophes: Hurricane Katrina in 2005 and the housing market collapse of 2008. Both events greatly hurt Bush's national approval, though neither were directly his fault. Emergency care after Katrina, which Americans thought Bush had handled poorly, was actually the responsibility of the states that were affected, not the national government. Likewise, the housing market collapse was partly the result of legislation passed by the Democratic Congress during Clinton's presidency, which allowed for unchecked housing loans, inflating and increasing prices of houses on the market. The collapse of the housing market produced a stark economic downturn, leading to a spike in unemployment numbers. In 2008, Bush signed a $170 billion Economic Stimulus Act, which pumped money into the failing economy to restart businesses and try to get people back to work.

Before leaving office, Bush also attempted to reform Social Security, but due to the effects of Hurricane Katrina and lingering effects of the wars in Iraq and Afghanistan, his party lost control of both houses of Congress and along with

CONGRESSIONAL CORNER

★★★★★★★★★★★★★★★★★★★★★★

1. **Economic Growth and Tax Relief Reconciliation Act of 2001:** Often referred to as the Bush Tax Cut, this act made significant reductions in regard to taxes and also simplified retirement plan rules.

2. **USA PATRIOT Act:** This act, the Uniting and Strengthening America by Providing Appropriate Tools Required to Intercept and Obstruct Terrorism Act, was passed in 2001 and allows for wiretapping American citizens' phones, searching business records, and conducting surveillance of individuals suspected of terrorist-related activities.

3. **No Child Left Behind Act:** This act was passed in 2001 to help aid disadvantaged students.

4. **Iraq Resolution:** This resolution authorized the U.S. to take military action against Iraq.

5. **Homeland Security Act:** This act, passed in 2002, established the Department of Homeland Security to help protect the nation from future terrorist attacks.

6. **Jobs and Growth Tax Relief Reconciliation Act:** This act was passed in 2003 and established lower rates for capital gains taxes, among other taxes. This was the second Bush tax cut.

7. **Intelligence Reform and Terrorism Prevention Act:** This act, passed in 2004, amended several federal terrorism laws.

8. **Energy Policy Act of 2005:** This act helped alleviate growing energy problems by providing tax incentives and loan guarantees for energy production business in the U.S.

9. **Economic Stimulus Act of 2008:** This act helped boost the U.S. economy and reverse the recession by providing tax rebates and increasing mortgage eligibility. It also approved the government purchase of mortgage and housing associations Fannie Mae and Freddie Mac. The bill cost $152 billion dollars.

10. **Housing and Economic Recovery Act of 2008:** This act addressed the mortgage crisis in the U.S. by allowing the Federal Housing Administration to guarantee $300 billion in fixed-rate mortgages for American home buyers.

★★★★★★★★★★★★★★★★★★★★★★

any chance to address the serious problems facing Social Security. When Bush left office, the economy was still struggling despite the stimulus bill, but more importantly, Americans were safer after experiencing the most tragic and horrific attacks known on American soil.

Post-Presidency

George W. Bush stepped back from the political scene after his time in office, claiming that President Obama "deserves my silence." Noted as a sign of courtesy by many, his absence from the political field has left Bush free to pursue his own interests: promoting various causes with his family, from literacy promotion to volunteerism to education reform In 2010, Bush published his book *Decision Points*. He has also become an accomplished painter.

What Has He Done for Me Lately?

In 2001, George W. Bush passed an education reform plan called the No Child Left Behind Act, which mandated that all American children have access to premium education. As a result of this act, more children, especially from underprivileged or minority backgrounds, received quality public education. He also enacted the President's Energy Plan for AIDS Relief (PEPFAR), which has helped save millions of lives across the globe.

PLATFORM SPEECH

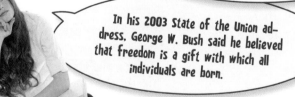

Americans are a free people, who know that freedom is the right of every person and the future of every nation. The liberty we prize is not America's gift to the world; it is God's gift to humanity.

In his 2003 State of the Union address, George W. Bush said he believed that freedom is a gift with which all individuals are born.

GEORGE W. BUSH

Written by Juliette Turner

ATTACKS BY TERRORISTS SHAKE THE NATION

September 12, 2001—The nation is shaken and nearly paralyzed after the horrendous attacks that took place in New York City and Washington, D.C., yesterday, as well as in Pennsylvania.

The remains of the twin World Trade Center towers now lay in ashes following their collapse in lower Manhattan, and the Pentagon is greatly damaged as well. The White House is thought to have been the terrorists' third target, but apparently the fourth plane's passengers heroically overthrew the hijackers, which resulted the plane's detour to Pennsylvania. It is not yet known how many were killed in the crash.

Americans fear another attack may be imminent, and the Bush administration has placed the nation on high alert.

At the time of the attack, President Bush was reading to a second grade class at the Emma E. Booker Elementary School in Florida, an event that was televised live on several news stations. Bush ap-

Brad Rickerby/Reuters/Landov

peared calm, and then his chief of staff, Andrew Card, approached him and whispered that a plane had crashed into the South Tower of the World Trade Center following a plane crash in the North Tower minutes before. Card confirmed that the attack was indeed thought to be organized by foreign terrorists. Bush continued his meeting with the students before taking the microphone and addressing the public.

Bush said, "I ... have ordered that the full resources of the federal government go to help the victims and their families, and to conduct a full-scale investigation to hunt down and to find those folks who committed this act. Terrorism against our nation will not stand."

Bush then boarded Air Force One, which followed an emergency rerouting to Barksdale Air Force Base in Louisiana. Upon arriving at the base, President Bush said, "The resolve of this great nation is being tested, but make no mistake. We will show the world that we will pass this test ... We will not waver. We will not tire. We will not falter, and we will not fail."

9/11 COMMISSION IS ORGANIZED

November 27, 2002—Today President Bush organized the 9/11 Commission to gather information concerning the precursors to the 9/11 attacks on U.S. soil. The commission is also charged with designing plans to prevent future attacks. The 9/11 Commission hopes to design a plan that will uproot terrorist sanctuaries, strengthen diplomatic relations with Afghanistan and Pakistan, reverse America's dependence on Middle Eastern oil, increase America's defenses, and develop an emergency response plan.

OPERATION SHOCK AND AWE

October 2, 2002—The U.S. Congress has approved a measure to send troops into Iraq. Iraqi-American relations have been icy for years, and the recent 9/11 terrorist attacks set American intelligence agencies toward extreme surveillance. Iraq and the Iraqi dictatorship under the leadership of Saddam Hussein have long been charged with human rights violations. Addition-ally, during the Persian Gulf War under the previous Bush administration, Iraq fired on American war planes in the no-fly zone, violating sanctions. President Bush has publicly labeled Iraq as part of an "axis of evil" allied with terrorists. He believes they are a danger to U.S. interests through possession of "weapons of mass destruction."

PROBLEMS PAYING THE BILLS

January 2, 2009—Nothing can drain the federal treasury like war, national defense, and stimulus packages. Bush is leaving office with a $10 trillion U.S. debt, or thirty-five thousand dollars for every American man, woman, and child. The tax cuts approved by Bush led to a $1.35 trillion reduction in federal revenue over ten years. Additionally, the wars in Iraq and Afghanistan are estimated to cost anywhere from $1 to $3 trillion. The newest Medicare plan (Medicare Part D) will cost $60 billion per year. The stimulus and the bailout of airline and various production industries will cost an additonal and considerable sum of money.

OPERATION ENDURING FREEDOM

October 8, 2001—With less than a month's preparation, the U.S. and allied forces entered Afghanistan yesterday for Operation Enduring Freedom. Yesterday, the troops successfully overthrew the terrorist-led government, destroying the terrorist stronghold with fifteen U.S. and allied troops lost.

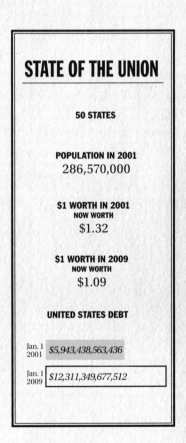

STATE OF THE UNION

50 STATES

POPULATION IN 2001
286,570,000

$1 WORTH IN 2001
NOW WORTH
$1.32

$1 WORTH IN 2009
NOW WORTH
$1.09

UNITED STATES DEBT

| Jan. 1 2001 | $5,943,438,563,436 |
| Jan. 1 2009 | $12,311,349,677,512 |

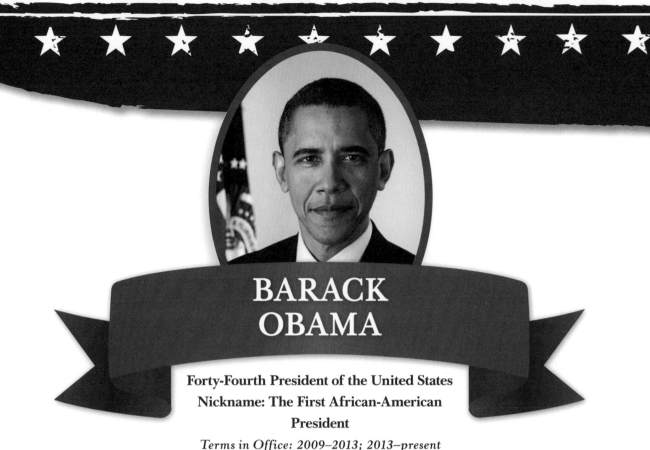

BARACK OBAMA

Forty-Fourth President of the United States

Nickname: The First African-American President

Terms in Office: 2009–2013; 2013–present

The Bottom Line

President Obama is the current president of the United States and is serving his second term in office. Obama passed his landmark legislation, the Affordable Care Act; oversaw the capture and death of terrorist mastermind Osama bin Laden; and enforced a multibillion dollar stimulus in an attempt to help the economy. He has struggled with a scandal regarding the surveillance of the American people by the federal government and an ever-growing debt and deficit.

FAST STATS

★ Born August 4, 1961, in Honolulu, Hawaii
★ Parents: Barack Obama Sr. and Stanley Ann Dunham Obama Soetoro
★ Barack Obama is still living and in office
★ Age upon Start of First Term: 47; Age upon Conclusion of First Term: 51
★ Age upon Start of Second Term: 51
★ Religious Affiliation: Congregationalist (Protestant)
★ Political Party: Democrat
★ Height: 6 feet 1 inch
★ Vice President: Joseph Biden

What Was He Thinking?

Barack Obama champions a large government that can care equally for all Americans. Not afraid to raise taxes for the wealthiest citizens or spend federal dollars, Obama has worked to increase various welfare and health care benefits, and he has successfully passed the first legislation that mandates nationalized health care for all Americans.

 BTW: Obama has made no efforts to curb and reduce the over 17 trillion-dollar U.S. debt—in fact, Obama's administration has spent more and increased the national debt by more than all past presidents combined.

Change will not come if we wait for some other person or some other time. We are the ones we've been waiting for. We are the change that we seek.

Why Should I Care?

Barack Obama is the first African-American to become president of the United States. He is also the first president who was raised by a single mother and his grandparents. During his presidency, Obama has worked to promote equality in America, most notably between genders, by passing legislation to promote women's equality in the workplace and appointing two women to the Supreme Court, more than any other president.

Breakin' It Down
Early Life

Barack Hussein Obama II is the only child of Barack, an African man from Kenya, and Stanley Ann, a white woman from Kansas. Barack and Stanley Ann's marriage in 1960 was extremely controversial; interracial marriage was still illegal in half of the U.S. at the time. The marriage, however, was short-lived: the couple divorced after just three years of marriage. It was revealed that Barack Sr. had another wife in Kenya to whom he returned after divorcing Stanley Ann. The following year, Barack's mother remarried, this time to Lolo Soetoro, an Indonesian native. Young Barack then moved with his mother to Jakarta, Indonesia. Within a few years, Stanley Ann sent Barack back to Hawaii to live with his maternal grandparents and to grow up in what she considered a safer environment. In Hawaii, Barack attended high school at the Punahou Academy, graduating in 1979 with academic honors.

After high school, Obama first enrolled at Occidental College in Los Angeles, California, but he transferred to New York's Columbia College in 1981, where he earned a bachelor's degree in political science. Obama then took a job at the Business International Corporation as a financial service officer. Within a year, he transferred to New York's Public Research Group and traveled to college campuses to encourage students to become active in politics and social justice. In 1984, Obama worked as a community organizer for the City University of New York at their Harlem campus. In 1988, he decided to return to school, and three years later he received his JD from Harvard Law School. During his time at Harvard Law School, Obama was involved in various student protests, often leading the protests and speaking to his fellow students. Obama also became the first African-American president of the Harvard Law Review. In 1992, after graduating, he returned to

Although Obama has no biological siblings, he has nine stepsiblings.

Bombings in Baghdad, Iraq, kill 155 people, 2009

Sonya Sotomayor is the first Latino to be appointed to the Supreme Court, 2009

A catastrophic earthquake hits Haiti, 2010

The BP oil spill occurs in the Gulf of Mexico off the coast of Louisiana, 2010

Prince William marries Catherine Middleton, 2011

Osama bin Laden is killed, 2011

Twenty-six lose their lives at the hand of a gunman inside Sandy Hook Elementary School in Connecticut, 2012

The Summer Olympics begin in London, England, 2012

The Supreme Court upholds the Affordable Care Act's individual mandate, 2012

First Term in Office

| 2008 | 2009 | 2010 | 2011 | 2012 |

BTW: In 1995, Obama published his first book, *Dreams from My Father: A Story of Race and Inheritance.*

Chicago to teach constitutional law at the University of Chicago. He continued teaching seminars at the college until 2004.

First Couple

MICHELLE OBAMA

Barack Obama and Michelle Robinson first met in 1989 at the Sidley & Austin law firm, where Michelle worked as an attorney. They married in 1992 and have two daughters, Malia and Sasha. During her husband's political campaigns, Michelle remained very active, traveling across the country on his behalf to gather support for his presidential campaigns. As first lady, Michelle is a strong advocate for health and dietary concerns.

Previous Political Career

- 1996: Elected state senator in Illinois. He served on the Joint Committee on Administrative Rules and as the head of the Health and Human Services Committee.
- 1998: Reelected to Illinois state senate.
- 2000: Ran for a position in U.S. House of Representatives but lost.
- 2002: Elected again to the Illinois state senate.
- 2004: Elected to the U.S. Senate, becoming only the third African-American U.S. Senator since the Reconstruction Era.

Presidency

Shortly before Obama entered the office of the president, the U.S. suffered its worst economic collapse since the Great Depression. To counter the severe recession and prevent the economy from further decline, Obama and the U.S. Congress implemented a $787 billion stimulus package that pumped federal funds into private businesses and the economic market in an attempt to help restart failing banks and businesses.

International Policy

Within his first one hundred days, Obama concentrated on international policy, improving relations with China and Russia and opening diplomatic dialogue with Iran, Venezuela, and Cuba. Although Obama had said as he campaigned

BTW: Michelle Obama is 5 feet 11 inches tall—the same height as previous first lady Eleanor Roosevelt, making them the tallest first ladies in U.S. history.

THOUGHTS ON THE CONSTITUTION

I have studied the Constitution as a student; I have taught it as a teacher; I have been bound by it as a lawyer and legislator. I took an oath to preserve, protect and defend the Constitution as Commander-in-Chief, and as a citizen, I know that we must never—ever—turn our back on its enduring principles for expedience sake.... We uphold our most cherished values not only because doing so is right, but because it strengthens our country and keeps us safe.

BARACK OBAMA

Prince William and Kate's first child, George, is born, 2013

Edward Snowden begins leaking NSA secrets, 2013

The government shuts down, between October 1 and October 16, 2013

The Boston Marathon bombings take place, 2013

Nelson Mandela, former president of South Africa, dies, 2013

Second Term in Office

| 2013 | 2014 | 2015 | 2016 | 2017 |

ELECTION RESULTS!

Obama not only made history as the first African-American Democratic presidential candidate, but he was also the first first-term U.S. Senator to go so far in a presidential election. On November 4, voter turnout was at its highest in four decades. The election was also historic because Obama's Republican opponent, John McCain, became the first Republican presidential candidate to choose a female running mate, Sarah Palin, governor of Alaska.

Barack Obama's opponent in the 2012 election was former governor of Massachusetts Mitt Romney, whose vice presidential candidate was Paul Ryan, a congressman from Wisconsin. Campaign issues spanned from Obama's Affordable Care Act to the growing debt and federal deficit. The recent scandals, including the suspected government cover-up regarding the terrorist attack in Benghazi, Libya, also made headlines during the election. It appeared Mitt Romney held the lead after the first televised presidential debate, but after the next two debates, Obama gained the lead and won the election.

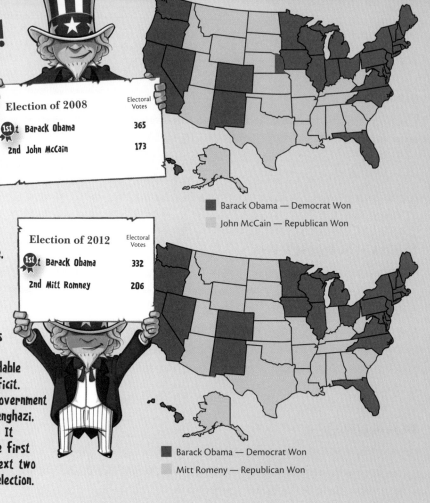

Election of 2008	Electoral Votes
1st Barack Obama	365
2nd John McCain	173

■ Barack Obama — Democrat Won
□ John McCain — Republican Won

Election of 2012	Electoral Votes
1st Barack Obama	332
2nd Mitt Romney	206

■ Barack Obama — Democrat Won
□ Mitt Romeny — Republican Won

PRESIDENTIAL Personality

★ Barack Obama's charisma and appeal has drawn millions of voters to him during his political career. Often categorized as a family man, the current president of the United States is a leader with a strong personality but a soft and respectful nature. He is known for his ability to deliver rousing speeches, a skill that has greatly helped him in the political arena.

that he would end the war in Afghanistan and Iraq, he sent 21,000 more troops to Afghanistan. He vowed to withdraw troops in Iraq by 2010, although it was not completed until the end of 2011. Obama also used military force to confront the Somalian pirates who had been terrorizing tourists and U.S. ships for years in the Gulf of Aden and Arabian Sea In 2009, America suffered from her first successful terrorist attack since the 9/11 terrorist attack with the Fort Hood Massacre on the Fort Hood military base in Texas. America then suffered a similar attack in 2012 but on foreign land—at the U.S. Consulate in Benghazi, Libya—where terrorists killed four americans, including U.S. ambassador Chris Stevens.

 BTW: Obama was the fourth president to win the Nobel Peace Prize. He was awarded the medal for his extraordinary efforts to strengthen international diplomacy and cooperation between peoples.

Successes

In 2010, Obama achieved one of his greatest successes, the passage of the Affordable Care Act, helping to make health insurance coverage more accessible to every American. Obama also advocated for the repeal of the Don't Ask, Don't Tell policy passed by the previous Democratic president, Bill Clinton. Although the U.S. economy still struggled to regain ground after the 2008 collapse, the Obama administration gained fresh momentum with the killing of Al-Qaeda leader and 9/11 mastermind Osama bin Laden.

Reelection

In 2012, the Supreme Court upheld the constitutionality of the Affordable Care Act, a major win for Obama's landmark achievement in the election year. After a record-setting amount of money was spent in the campaign by both candidates, Obama won a second term in office. However, his victory celebration was short-lived; in April 2013, less than four months after his second inauguration, two terrorists bombed the annual marathon in Boston, Massachusetts, killing three civilians and injuring many more.

NSA Scandal!

In 2013, former government employee Edward Snowden revealed that the National Security Agency had been monitoring American citizens through their web, cell phone, computer, and email communications. The Obama administration claimed that the security agency was doing this legally and that it was in the interest of national security. Soon it was also revealed that the surveillance extended outside American borders and affected other countries worldwide.

Problems in Syria

In late 2013, the international field erupted in debate over the Syrian civil war and Syria's possible use of chemical weapons. President Obama had previously claimed that the

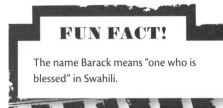

FUN FACT!

The name Barack means "one who is blessed" in Swahili.

There is not a liberal America and a conservative America—there is the United States of America. There is not a black America and a white America and Latino America and Asian America—there's the United States of America.

use of chemical weapons would cross a "red line," which would require U.S. intervention. Although U.S. involvement seemed inevitable and the danger of chemical weapons being spread to terrorist organizations sparked a high security alert in the Middle East, the U.S. decided not to invade Syria, and a war was averted.

Another Government Shutdown

October 2013 brought the third government shutdown in two decades. After over two weeks of inaction, Congress and the president finally negotiated legislation to reopen the government and prevent the U.S. from defaulting on her loan payments. The close of 2013 saw Obama's approval ratings plummet as a result of the NSA scandals, problems with enrollment for the Affordable Care Act, and gridlock in Washington, D.C., over America's economy.

FUN FACT!

In 2006, Obama was honored with a Grammy award for the Best Spoken Word Recording of his audio book of *Dreams from My Father*.

What Has He Done for Me Lately?

Though the Affordable Care Act has yet to be fully funded, and is still in its trial stage, it was passed to ensure that every American possesses some form of health insurance. To comply with the new laws and regulations, insurance companies were required to alter their existing policies and amend what kind of patients they covered. Because of this, regardless of what insurance company your parents have, you are allowed to stay on their health plan until you are twenty-six. Also, all individuals must be covered by insurance, regardless of preexisting medical conditions that previously prevented some individuals from finding medical coverage.

PLATFORM SPEECH

What the American people hope—what they deserve—is for all of us, Democrats and Republicans, to work through our differences; to overcome the numbing weight of our politics. For while the people who sent us here have different backgrounds, different stories, different beliefs, the anxieties they face are the same. The aspirations they hold are shared: a job that pays the bills; a chance to get ahead; most of all, the ability to give their children a better life.

In his 2010 State of the Union address, President Obama attempted to bring Washington, D.C., together despite their political differences to provide Americans and their children a better life.

BTW: Obama is left-handed.

BARACK OBAMA

Presidential Times

Written by Juliette Turner

ATTACKS ON THE BENGHAZI CONSULATE

September 12, 2012—On the eleventh anniversary of 9/11, the U.S. consulate in Benghazi, Libya, was attacked by a group of terrorists, killing the U.S. ambassador to Libya, Chris Stevens; Foreign Service Information officer Sean Smith; and two Navy SEALs, Tyrone Woods and Glen Doherty. The Obama administration originally claimed the attack occurred after the release of an anti-Muslim YouTube video created by an American. However, it was later revealed that the attack was orchestrated by terrorists in the region over an unrevealed cause.

Questions continue as to why no aid was sent to the consulate at the time of the attack. Though several military bases within a 60-mile radius were on alert, no aid was delivered, and four Americans died.

OSAMA BIN LADEN DEAD!

May 2, 2011—Terrorist mastermind Osama bin Laden has been killed in Pakistan in his secret compound. Obama gave the green light yesterday for U.S. Navy SEALs to invade the compound, where CIA and FBI operatives claimed bin Laden was living. The leads proved to be correct, and the Navy SEALs found and killed bin Laden.

BOSTON MARATHON BOMBING SUSPECT KILLED

April 19, 2013—One of the Boston Marathon bomb suspects, Tamerlan Tsarnev, was killed in a police shootout yesterday. His brother, Dzhokhar Tsarnev, is still at large. Earlier this week, at 2:49 EST on April 15, two amateur bombs exploded during the annual Boston Marathon, killing three people and injuring more than 260 runners and bystanders. The Tsarnev brothers, from Chechnya, have been living in a Boston suburb.

WHITE HOUSE...CLOSED?

March 9, 2013--If you are trying to book a White House tour, you may be running into some difficulties. Today, the Obama administration has decided to close the White House in attempt to cut costs in light of the recent budget cuts passed by Congress--although the cost of White House tours is almost negligible. The White House is predicted to be closed for months

GOVERNMENT SHUTDOWN OF 2013 TO END

October 16, 2013—The president and Congress have agreed on a plan to reopen the government after a sixteen-day shutdown, which began October 1. The shutdown resulted in 800,000 federal workers being laid off. Similar to the government shutdowns during President Clinton's administration, it resulted from a lack of negotiation for addressing America's growing debt. During the shutdown, Republicans and Democrats in Congress composed and disregarded several bills proposing economic plans, but it was not until tonight that a plan was agreed upon.

IRS SCANDAL

May 20, 2013—Earlier this month, the American public became aware of a scandal involving the country's Internal Revenue Service and its interference in political parties. It was released that several IRS officials had unjustly targeted Tea Party Activist groups, sparking concern of the partisan nature of the nation's economic bureau. This comes shortly after the release of the NSA scandal, causing many to fear the rapid overexpansion of the government.

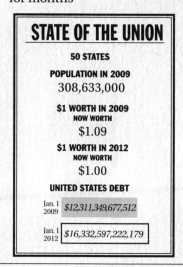

STATE OF THE UNION

50 STATES

POPULATION IN 2009
308,633,000

$1 WORTH IN 2009
NOW WORTH
$1.09

$1 WORTH IN 2012
NOW WORTH
$1.00

UNITED STATES DEBT

Jan. 1 2009	$12,311,349,677,512
Jan. 1 2012	$16,332,597,222,179

THE PRESIDENTIAL CABINET

Then and Now

No one can disagree that the government, let alone the presidential office, has grown substantially in size and power since the days of George Washington. One extreme example is the size of the President's "cabinet." One of George Washington's first acts as president was to form a select group of advisors. Congress agreed to create five positions: Secretary of State, Secretary of War, Secretary of the Treasury, Attorney General, and Postmaster General. This then became the "Presidential Cabinet," his appointed group of consultants. Today, however, Barack Obama's Presidential Cabinet contains twenty-two positions. This does not include the current thirty-two "czars," (a term that was coined under past presidents) or non-appointed and congressionally unapproved individuals who serve as the president's advisors and are not accountable to the people.

GEORGE WASHINGTON'S CABINET

CABINET POSITION	NAME OF OFFICER	YEARS IN OFFICE
Vice President	John Adams	1789-1797
Secretary of State	Thomas Jefferson	1790-1793
	Edmund Randolph	1794-1795
	Timothy Pickering	1795-1797
Secretary of War	Henry Knox	1789-1795
	Timothy Pickering	1795
	James McHenry	1796-1797
Secretary of the Treasury	Alexander Hamilton	1789-1795
	Timothy Pickering	1795-1797
Attorney General	Edmund Randolph	1789-1794
	William Bradford	1794-1795
	Charles Lee	1795-1797
Postmaster General	Samuel Osgood	1789-1791
	Timothy Pickering	1791-1795
	Joseph Habersham	1795-1797

BARACK OBAMA'S CABINET

CABINET POSITION	NAME OF OFFICER	YEARS IN OFFICE
Vice President	Joseph Biden	2009–present
Secretary of State	Hillary Clinton John Kerry	2009–2013 2013–present
Secretary of War	—	—
Secretary of the Treasury	Timothy Geithner Jack Lew	2009–2013 2013–present
Attorney General	Eric Holder, Jr.	2009–present
Postmaster General	—	—
Secretary of Defense	Robert Gates Leon Panetta Chuck Hagle	2009–2011 2001–2013 2013–present
Secretary of the Navy	—	—
Secretary of the Interior	Ken Salazar Sally Jewell	2009–2013 2013–present
Secretary of Agriculture	Thomas J. Vilsack	2009–present
Secretary of Labor	Hilda Solis Thomas Perez	2009–2013 2013–present
Secretary of Commerce	Gary Locke John Bryson Penny Pritzker	2009–2011 2011–2012 2013–present
Secretary of Health, Education, and Welfare	—	—
Secretary of Health and Human Services	Kathleen Sebelius	2009–present
Secretary of Housing and Urban Development	Shaun L.S. Donovan	2009–present
Secretary of Transportation	Ray LaHood Anthony Foxx	2009–2013 2013–present
Secretary of Energy	Steven Chu Ernest Moniz	2009–2013 2013–present
Secretary of Education	Arne Duncan	2009–2013
Secretary of Veterans Affairs	Eric Shinseki	2009–present
Secretary of Homeland Security	Janet Napolitano Jeh Johnson	2009–2013 2013–present

PRESIDENTIAL HEIGHT CHART

GEORGE WASHINGTON	JOHN ADAMS	THOMAS JEFFERSON	JAMES MADISON	JAMES MONROE	JOHN QUINCY ADAMS	ANDREW JACKSON	MARTIN VAN BUREN	WILLIAM HENRY HARRISON	JOHN TYLER
6'2"	5'7"	6'2"	5'4"	6'0"	5'7"	6'1"	5'6"	5'8"	6'0"

GROVER CLEVELAND	BENJAMIN HARRISON	WILLIAM McKINLEY	THEODORE ROOSEVELT	WILLIAM HOWARD TAFT	WOODROW WILSON	WARREN HARDING	CALVIN COOLIDGE	HERBERT HOOVER	FRANKLIN DELANO ROOSEVELT	HARRY S. TRUMAN
5'11"	5'6"	5'7"	5'10"	6'2"	5'11"	6'0"	5'10"	6'0"	6'2"	5'9"

JAMES POLK	ZACHARY TAYLOR	MILLARD FILLMORE	FRANKLIN PIERCE	JAMES BUCHANAN	ABRAHAM LINCOLN	ANDREW JOHNSON	ULYSSES S. GRANT	RUTHERFORD B. HAYES	JAMES GARFIELD	CHESTER A. ARTHUR
5'8"	5'8"	5'9"	5'10"	6'0"	6'5"	5'10"	5'8"	5'9"	6'0"	6'0"

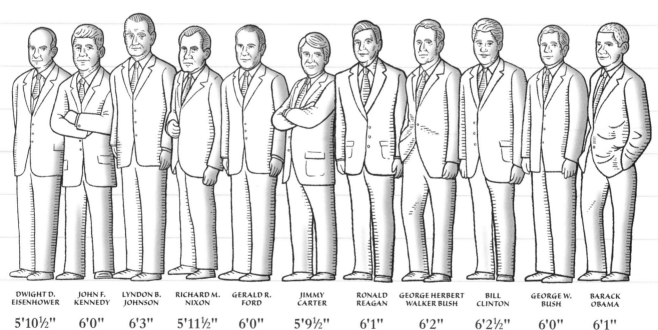

DWIGHT D. EISENHOWER	JOHN F. KENNEDY	LYNDON B. JOHNSON	RICHARD M. NIXON	GERALD R. FORD	JIMMY CARTER	RONALD REAGAN	GEORGE HERBERT WALKER BUSH	BILL CLINTON	GEORGE W. BUSH	BARACK OBAMA
5'10½"	6'0"	6'3"	5'11½"	6'0"	5'9½"	6'1"	6'2"	6'2½"	6'0"	6'1"

BIBLIOGRAPHY

Books

Eckman, Walter. *Meet the Presidents.* Schiffer Publishing Ltd. 2011

Flagel, Thomas R. *The History Buff's Guide to the Presidents.* Cumberland House Sourcebooks, Inc. 2007.

Gaffney, Peter and Dennis. *The Presidents.* Hyperion/Harper's Collins. 2012

Hudson, Jr., David L. *The Handy President's Answer Book.* Visible Ink. 2012

Matuz, Roger. *The Presidents Fact Book.* Black Dog & Leventhal Publishing. 2009

Moore, K. *The American President.* New York, NY: Fall Rivers Press. 2007

Vilade, C. Edwin. *The President's Speech.* Lyons Press BlueRed Press Ltd. 2012

Web Sites

Information on Supreme Court Justices: http://www.senate.gov/pagelayout/reference/nominations/Nominations.htm

Population statistics: http://www.thirty-thousand.org/documents/QHA–01.pdf http://www.census.gov/history/www/through_the_decades/fast_facts/1790_fast_facts.html

Debt statistics: http://metricmash.com/us-national-debt.aspx http://www.treasurydirect.gov/govt/reports/pd/histdebt/histdebt_histo1.htm

"State of the Union" section: http://www.shmoop.com/federalists/statistics.html

Value of the dollar: http://www.davemanuel.com/inflation-calculator.php?

List of Chief Justices: https://en.wikipedia.org/wiki/Chief_Justice_of_the_United_States#List_of_Chief_Justices

Information on the Monroe family: http://www.archives.com/genealogy/president-monroe.html

Voter Turnout facts: http://www.presidency.ucsb.edu/data/turnout.php

Military Hierarchy: http://www.hierarchystructure.com/wp-content/uploads/2012/07/Military-Unit-Hierarchy.jpg

List of Speakers of the House: http://history.house.gov/People/Office/Speakers/

Information on the Territories: http://www.u-s-history.com/pages/h1049.html

Birth/death organization of presidents: http://en.wikipedia.org/wiki/List_of_Presidents_of_the_United_States_by_date_of_birth

Civil War resources: http://americanhistory.about.com/od/civilwarmenu/a/secession_order.htm

White House Weddings: http://www.whitehousehistory.org/whha_history/history_faqs–06.html

Voter Turnout: http://www.presidency.ucsb.edu/data/turnout.php

Presidential Personalities: http://presidentialham.com/u-s-presidents/

Miller Center: http://millercenter.org/